UNIVERSITY OF OKLAHOMA PRESS : NORMAN

The Immigrant Upraised

ITALIAN ADVENTURERS
AND COLONISTS IN
AN EXPANDING AMERICA

Andrew F. Rolle

WITH A FOREWORD BY
RAY ALLEN BILLINGTON

BY ANDREW F. ROLLE

Riviera Path (Verona, Italy, 1948)
An American in California: The Biography of William Heath Davis
  (San Marino, 1956)
The Road to Virginia City: The Diary of James Knox Polk Miller
  (editor) (Norman, 1960)
Lincoln, a Contemporary Portrait (with Allan Nevins and
  Irving Stone) (New York, 1962)
Occidental College: The First Seventy-Five Years (Los Angeles, 1962)
California: A History (New York, 1963)
California: A Students' Guide to Localized History (New York, 1964)
A Century of Dishonor: The Early Crusade for Indian Reform
  (editor) By Helen Hunt Jackson (New York, 1965)
The Lost Cause: The Confederate Exodus to Mexico (Norman, 1965)
Los Angeles: A Students' Guide to Localized History (New York, 1965)
*The Immigrant Upraised: Italian Adventurers and Colonists in an
  Expanding America* (Norman, 1968)

LIBRARY OF CONGRESS CATALOG CARD NUMBER 68–10302

Ad familiam meum

Foreword

VERY OCCASIONALLY a historian enjoys the ability, perception, and good fortune to produce a book that significantly alters the interpretation of past events. Andrew F. Rolle has written such a volume. With its appearance students of immigration history must restudy their subject, abandoning some of the clichés that have distorted the image of the immigrant they have presented to their readers, and discarding a stereotype that has been commonly accepted for a generation. For Professor Rolle demonstrates that many of the newcomers to America—those with the ambition and means to press beyond the Atlantic seaboard—were able to compete with the native-born for positions at the very pinnacle of the economic and social pyramid. They were, he tells us, the "upraised."

This interpretation differs startlingly from the traditional one in American historiography. Historians and sociologists who first paid serious attention to the immigrants' contributions to the United States saw them as degrading influences, lowering living standards, depressing wages, and fostering the spread of disease and crime. Thus Prescott F. Hall in his book *Immigration* (1906) listed as the "Effects of Immigration" the sweating system, the padrone system, unemployment, illiteracy, crime, insanity and disease, pauperism, the burden of dependents and delinquents, and congestion in cities. Twenty years later Henry Pratt Fairchild, in his *Immigration: A World Movement and Its American*

Significance (1926), saw aliens as responsible for slums, poverty, pauperism, and lowered living standards, and ascribed not a single beneficial result to their coming. Gross misinterpretations such as these not only assaulted the truth, but stirred the nativistic prejudices that marred American behavior during the nineteenth and early twentieth centuries.

Fortunately, a later generation of scholars realized the error of their predecessors' ways and set out to correct the image that they had created. Newcomers from Europe, Asia and Africa, they proved, vastly benefited American society, diversifying and strengthening its culture, elevating its economy, and contributing to its emergence as a leading world power. But while improving the nation, these historians believed, the immigrants degraded themselves. Their intrusion aroused such resentment that they were doomed to a miserable existence in urban ghettos, where they were victimized by landlords and travel agents, abused by prejudiced natives, and exploited by flint-hearted employers. Scholars branded them as the "uprooted," deserving of sympathy for the suffering that they endured in their hazardous ascent of the social structure, and worthy of compassion for their failure to keep pace with the native-born in the struggle for self-improvement.

This picture of the immigrant, while a healthy corrective to the prejudiced distortions of the prior generation, still missed the mark, for historians focused on only one portion of the alien population. The foreign-born who lived in New York or Boston or other eastern cities *were* crowded into slums, rejected by Americans, and oppressed by factory owners. But what of the 15 or 20 per cent of the new arrivals who escaped from eastern cities to the newer lands beyond the Mississippi River? Were they the uprooted? Or did they find assimilation easier than their urban counterparts?

These are the questions that Professor Rolle asks so cogently and answers so convincingly in this book. His findings, based on careful research in both Italian and American sources, will prove startling to all who have accepted the traditional picture of the immigrant in America. For he shows that the portion of Italian foreign-born who did migrate suffered little discrimination, were readily assimilated, and rivaled the native-born in their rapid rise to wealth and power. They were, he concludes, the "upraised" rather than the "uprooted."

This was only natural, for upgrading was a normal function of the American West. During pioneer days especially, and for many years thereafter, the opportunity for individual self-betterment was greater there than in the thickly settled East. In the West a lower man-land ratio allowed the relatively propertyless individual, whether he was native- or foreign-born, to acquire a larger stake in society, whether he labored as farmer, merchant, small manu-facturer, or professional man. In the West the more fluid social order imposed fewer restraints on those aspiring to higher social or economic status; lineage and inherited wealth were less essential to progress there than in the tradition-governed eastern cities. Those who moved toward the frontier were able to capitalize on their own abilities to a greater degree than those who stayed be-hind. They could be upraised, as their fellows who remained could not.

On the pages that follow, Professor Rolle vividly illustrates the impact of this favorable environment on Italians who escaped the urban ghettos. In doing so he creates a whole series of new immi-grant images that bear little resemblance to the stereotypes that have been commonplace for generations. Italian explorers clad in leather leggings and moccasins, Italian miners unearthing fortunes on the rich Mesabi Range, Italian homesteaders unloading bags of bread and macaroni from an immigrant train at a water-tower stop on the Great Plains, Italian businessmen gathering for a social hour at Omaha's Dal Cenisio All'Etna Lodge, Italian cattle kings riding over a 100,000 acre ranch along the Río Grande, Italian nationalists meeting atop the Comstock Lode to celebrate the unification of Italy or in San Francisco to organize the Swiss-Italian Anti-Chinese Company of Dragoons, Italians such as Andrea Sbarboro and Amadeo Pietro Giannini amassing fortunes as vintners and bankers—these are the fascinating characters in Professor Rolle's drama, not slum dwellers or sweat-shop laborers.

He demonstrates for the first time that the western environment could escalate the foreign- no less than the native-born.

These are important findings, and because of them Professor Rolle has written an important book. Students who harken to his results must direct their attention to other immigrant groups, and determine whether the Irish, the Germans, the Swedes and Norwegians, who journeyed westward were similarly upraised. Only when those investigations have been completed will the true relationship of the foreign-born to the native-born in America as a whole be brought into focus. In posing this problem, and providing the answer for one ethnic group, Professor Rolle has prepared the way for a completely new interpretation of immigration history.

RAY ALLEN BILLINGTON

The Huntington Library
March 11, 1968

Acknowledgments

DURING THE YEARS since 1945, when I first began to write this book, I have become indebted to many individuals and institutions. As in the past, the Henry E. Huntington and Bancroft libraries have been major haunts of mine. I am grateful for the encouragement received there, especially from A. L. Rowse, Allan Nevins, and Ray Allen Billington. Professor Billington, who has written such a gracious foreword, began his career as an expert in American nativism. From the start of this project he, thus, was in a position to perceive the significance of the western immigrant story.

I have been the beneficiary of grants from the American Council of Learned Societies and from the John Randolph and Dora Haynes Foundation, as well as leaves of absence from Occidental College during the crucial years 1962–63 and 1967–68.

Various colleagues and friends rendered counsel or provided insights and aid. My thanks go to Judith Austin, who edited an early version of the manuscript, to Professors John Higham, Austin Fife, Leonard Arrington, John Schutz, Roger Daniels, Mary Elizabeth Massey, Wilbur Jacobs, Richard G. Lillard, Ernest J. Burrus, and Carleton Qualey. Professor Moses Rischin gave me the benefit of especially penetrating insights into the immigrant mentality.

I was American Vice Consul at Genoa, Italy, from 1945–48. During that period after the Second World War, immigration to the United States from northern Italy was reopened by my office. I have revisited Italy on five occasions since then.

The years spent in Europe widened the outlook inculcated in me by my parents. To their memory I dedicate this book, and acknowledge also the encouragement of Frances Rolle, of many foreign friends, and of all those acquaintances whose view of America is the opposite of narrow, brittle, and insular.

A. R.

Contents

Illustrations

Drawings

The Immigrant Upraised

Italian Adventurers and Colonists in an Expanding America

Who crossed the prairies, as of old
Their fathers crossed the sea,
To make the West, as they the East,
The homestead of the free.

—Egisto Rossi, xvi

Introduction

"THE MAN WHO ASPIRES to make his way in a new country should be hampered with no recollections or aspirations—no repining or hankering after the things he may have left behind in the old one. He must start with a stout determination to be a settler among settlers; he must be ready to do in America as the Americans do."[1] So wrote Antonio Gallenga, an Italian immigrant to the American West of the nineteenth century. His words conveyed the thoughts of thousands who came to the New World in quest of opportunity.

Those fateful years of searching have passed, those years of toil and of what men call history. A vital part of that history—the immigrant experience in America—is almost over. Ellis Island, the eastern portal through which foreigners tumbled into the United States by the millions, has long since closed down. And the immigrants who went on westward to devote a lifetime to their own uplifting in an adopted homeland are mostly a memory. Today, in another age, we can, however, look at their record with less emotion than was once possible. Now that most foreigners have melded into the American environment and are at home on the land, we can truly consider whether there have been distortions in the telling of their story.

The subject of my book is the foreign traveler, adventurer, and immigrant in the American West—one particular foreigner, the Italian. It traces his record in twenty-two states west of the Missis-

[1] Antonio Gallenga, *Episodes of My Second Life*, 110.

3

sippi. This is not another history of an immigrant minority in America; it is primarily the story of their western experience. Therefore the book ranges widely, examining both regional and national factors well before the major migration of Italians to the United States; it also treats some of their activities in the present. This book could have been written about almost any nationality—the Germans, the Scots, the Finns, the French. Part of its theme is the effect the American West had in shaping life and character.

Since 1893, when the historian Frederick Jackson Turner first stressed the importance of the frontier in history, many writers have reassessed the meaning of the West in the American experience. Turner's concept of that West as a fluid "form of society," rather than as a definable entity, carried with it a certain vagueness about the area. Historians have called attention to individualism as one of the West's accepted hallmarks. And nowadays, westerners are stamped by both literature and the cinema as rugged and Anglo-American. There is more than ample evidence that the West was not exclusively "Anglo" in character, nor was it composed only of native stock. The assumption that its population pattern was racially homogeneous and well-knit is by no means borne out by a close study of census statistics, travel accounts, corporation records, newspapers, and local annals. These reveal that a conspicuous cosmopolitan element helped to shape life on many a ranch, mine, logging town, or railroad camp. The farms and cities of the West once teemed with immigrants. In San Francisco in 1880, for example, out of a population of 233,959 persons, some 104,244 had been born abroad. By 1900, with a foreign-born population of close to 40 per cent, San Francisco, along with New York and Chicago, remained a major cosmopolitan center.[2]

The western immigrant, like the trapper and the cowboy, could be pictured as a new type of man. Sometimes he, too, dressed differently from the way his seaboard counterparts did. Yet dress was

[2] United States Industrial Commission, "Agricultural Distribution of Immigrants," *Reports of the Immigration Commission*, XV (Washington, 1901), xx; *Abstract of the Twelfth Census of the United States*, 1900 (Washington, 1904), 105.

Lithograph by an American artist depicting what an Italian is supposed to look like. About 1880.

From *Hutchings' Illustrated California Magazine* (1857)

not what distinguished him from the eastern resident immigrant. It was rather, that he developed new attitudes about his role and future in America. His ambitions transcended the cramped atmosphere of iron fire escapes and cold-water tenements. The historic stereotype of a mustachioed organ-grinding Italian with rings in his ears and a monkey on a leash simply does not correspond with the real western Italian immigrant. Whether in mountains or deserts, the West was generally tradition-free. It offered the immigrant opportunities not available in the mills and factories of the eastern city. Instead of becoming a bootblack, barber, or fish-peddler, the Italian who deserted his first American home on New York's crowded Mulberry Street might, thus, move toward more rewarding pursuits, although he formed but a small part of other national groups out west. Not always was his home in the West blessed by the absence of prejudice. But, as one interpreter notes, internal migration was "phenomenally successful" for most Americans: "The immigrants from abroad did find superior economic opportunities and, if they were fleeing oppression, they found freedom."[3]

Historians who have been able to see the immigrant only in an urban setting stress a different view. One of these, Oscar Handlin, characterizes the immigrant record as primarily "a history of alienation and of its consequences." For him the bulk of America's immigrants were of peasant origin, downtrodden, backward-looking, ghettoed and changeless. They seemed to be enslaved by an all-pervasive pessimism characteristic of eastern Europe. Such a negative approach to the immigrant experience clashes perceptibly with the admittedly oversimplified optimism that Turner ascribed to persons on the frontier, whether foreigners or natives of the country. Yet, it fails to take into account the probability that, even among the ghettoed eastern Europeans, a minority of persons entered America's cities directly from a farm background. Although they had been city dwellers, once they moved beyond

[3] Everett S. Lee, "The Turner Thesis Reexamined," *American Quarterly*, Vol. XIII (Spring, 1961), 83.

America's eastern seaboard, many a western immigrant was never inside a steel mill or a really big factory.[4]

No doubt, however, the conditions of immigrant life on the East Coast were different from those west of the Mississippi. Nathan Glazer and Daniel P. Moynihan's *Beyond the Melting Pot* (Cambridge, 1963) stresses that in New York City the principal ethnic groups maintained a distinct, if changing, identity from generation to generation, each different from the other in religious and cultural values. But material and spiritual growth did take place in America. Both by heritage and by choice, newcomers evolved deliberate new identities while perpetuating certain traditional beliefs and values.[5]

[4] See Oscar Handlin, *The Uprooted*, 4, an impressionistic work that has increasingly come under attack. James P. Shannon, one of the few historians to deal with the *western* foreigner writes: "In general, research done for the present study does not support Handlin in his description of the hopeless odds against which rural immigrants labored. . . . In spite of the admitted hazards of grasshopper plagues, winter blizzards, summer heat, and monotonous diets . . . their lot was by and large not a bad one." (See Shannon, *Catholic Colonization on the Western Frontier*, 204n.) Another critic, Rudolph J. Vecoli, adds: "The basic error of the Handlin approach, I suggest, is that it subordinates historical complexity to the symmetrical pattern of a sociological theory." (See Vecoli, "Contadini in Chicago: A Critique of the Uprooted," *Journal of American History*, Vol. LI (December, 1964), 417.) Handlin's view of immigration is geographically confining, as Merle Curti, in his preface to historian Paul Knaplund's autobiography, states: "Those who have accepted without reservation such books on immigration as Oscar Handlin's *The Uprooted* should especially appreciate *Moorings Old and New*. . . . it shows clearly and in a factually straight-forward way how one-sided any picture of immigrant experience is that neglects the rural Middle West." (See Knaplund, *Moorings Old and New* (Madison, 1963), vii.) Norman Pollack, "Handlin on Anti-Semitism: A Critique of American Views of the Jew," *Journal of American History*, Vol. LI (December, 1964), 391–403, criticizes Handlin's interpretation of American Jewry: "The logic is impeccable; the facts are not. Of 112 works Handlin cites in evidence, 106 are totally irrelevant to the discussion, five are barely relevant but do not support his thesis, and only one . . . has any bearing. Yet it too has been over-simplified and misinterpreted" (391). Pollack, in criticizing this particular research, considered that only 1 per cent of Handlin's evidence was germane; yet Handlin's writings, although lacking in "balanced perspective," had produced a "snow-ball effect," because failure to check his documentation led to widespread acceptance of his damaging conclusions about anti-Semitism and the Populist movement (391, 397).

[5] William Foote Whyte, *Street Corner Society, the Social Structure of an Italian Slum*, is a good sociological study of acculturative problems.

What the immigrant experienced in New York was not what many immigrants encountered who went westward to settle a new land (new to all of them, both native Americans and Europeans). Indeed some of these came to have more in common with fellow western pioneers than they did with former villagers left behind on the East Coast in an environment of sweated labor and industrial slums.

Histories of immigration which present a picture of the foreigner's total acculturative process are overdue. The field of western immigration clearly deserves some of the attention devoted to cowboys, Indians, outlaws, and vigilantes. One historian has asserted that the history of western America has, indeed, developed an "unfortunate tendency" to emphasize "the sensational, the transitory, the erratic, and the pathological."[6] As writers parade the gun-slingers, bartenders, cattle barons, bad men, naughty women, gamblers, English lords, white heroes, and swarthy villains across the stage of western history, we seldom remember that immigrants were there too.

Lack of research on foreign influences in the American West has allowed the distortion that the West was essentially Anglo-American in composition. As to origin, the Irish and English were, of course, "Anglos." Despite past rivalries, they were closer to each other in outlook than the Latins. The Irish, usually Catholics like the Italians, were very different from them in background, language, and outlook. The Irish, who sometimes competed fiercely with the Italians, were joined in loyalties to the English, Welsh, and Scots. These nationalities developed close sympathies with two other Nordic groups, the Scandinavians and Germans. The Italians—Mediterraneans closer to the French, Spanish, and Greeks in background—remained relatively unjoined in friendships or hatreds. As a result, the Italians were forced, so to speak, to join their new environment.

By way of definition, the term "Italian," when used in this book, concerns those persons whose origins were in the Italian peninsula,

[6] Paul F. Sharp, "The Northern Great Plains: A Study in Canadian-American Regionalism," *Mississippi Valley Historical Review*, Vol. XXXIX (June, 1952), 61.

from Sicily to Piedmont, and who journeyed beyond the Mississippi. Large numbers of these came from northern Italy. Although this affected their acculturation somewhat (differences between northern and southern Italians are discussed in Part III), it is impractical to deal with only one segment of a people who claim the same nationality.

The Italian who moved west, although a member of a minority, for once in his national history became an invader, part of the wave of migration that engulfed the West. There is a substantial difference between a minority on the defensive and one which becomes aggressive. Whereas the Spanish remnants ("Hispanos") in the Southwest lost their land to encroaching "Anglos," Italian immigrants had no such experience. They were neither Indians to be got rid of nor "Greasers" who stood in the way of America's "Manifest Destiny." Although they might be called "Wops" or "Dagos," they on occasion actually joined the "Anglos" in an assault on land that belonged to the Indian—as when they squatted upon a Paiute Indian reservation in Nevada. Whereas destruction of the economic base of the southwestern "Hispano" created a migratory body of agricultural workers, only for a time did Italians do such seasonal work. Eventually, indeed, they provided a "cultural bridge" between the Hispanic environment and the invading Anglo-Americans. But, like the latter, they coveted land, and achieved ownership of it as fast as they could.[7]

As with other nationalities in the West, the Italians (except in California and Louisiana) formed a relatively small percentage of the total population. Statistics, however, do not adequately tell the story. The Italians—like the French, Dutch, and Germans—helped to colonize America; yet they did not extensively pervade its society or politics, nor did they form lasting ethnic enclaves out west. Today, as ethnic differences fade, the roles of such minorities fall into better perspective.[8] One population study observes:

[7] Consult Morris E. Garnsey, *America's New Frontier, the Mountain West* (New York, 1950), 83.

[8] See John Higham, "From Immigrants to Minorities: Some Recent Literature," *American Quarterly*, Vol. X (Spring, 1958), 84.

A review of the proportion of the population reported as foreign-born at the successive censuses tells only part of the story of the foreign born in the settlement of the country. It ignores the substantial contributions that [such] groups and individuals made in the opening and development of the expanding area of the United States.[9]

The Italians in the West found there more of the outdoor rusticity of life familiar in rural Italy than did their compatriots who settled in the large cities of the East. Also, they encountered an acculturation usually based upon less friction than immigrants to the eastern cities or the midwestern urban centers of Chicago or Kansas City faced. As viniculturists, cotton-raisers, hostelers, miners, or restauranteurs, to name only a few occupations, they were accepted quite readily as members of the society in which they lived.

Eric Hoffer, who writes in a cheery and loosely idealistic way about immigrants, insists that a predictable by-product of their experience was accommodation to the environment: "They came here," he points out, "with the ardent desire to shed their old world identity and be reborn to a new life; and they were automatically equipped with an unbounded capacity to imitate and adopt the new. The strangeness of the new country," Hoffer believes, "attracted rather than repelled them. They craved a new identity and a new life—and the stranger the new world the more it suited their inclination. Perhaps, to the non–Anglo-Saxons, the strangeness of the language was an added attraction. To have to learn to speak enhanced the illusion of being born anew."[10]

Although fascinated by the new, the Italians were frequently conservative and cautious migrants. Compared to native pioneers, they were sometimes ill-prepared for farm life. They faced years of hard work in order to save enough money to buy improved land or a going business. As relative latecomers to the American scene, their ability to "make do" with little was most helpful. Because

[9] Conrad and Irene B. Taeuber, *The Changing Population of the United States*, 63.

[10] Hoffer, *The True Believer* (New York, Sixth Printing, 1964), 95–96.

Italian settlers had to rely upon whatever employment they could find, they chose the environments and occupations closest to those they had known. Settlers usually avoided dry, windswept prairies in favor of the greenery of river bottoms, forested valleys, and hilly vineyard country. Italians frequently followed those native Americans with specialized talents and money who had already established farms and villages in the wilderness.

In the Far West what proved to be more important than nationality were such more tangible matters as how well a man integrated himself into frontier life; how quickly he could put up a house or clear a field; how well he could break the sod. These qualities frequently determined acceptance. In this sense the frontier did not coerce; it emancipated.

It was not coincidental that America's most active period of immigration paralleled the nation's explosive urban and agricultural growth in the nineteenth and early twentieth centuries. Unadulterated by later subtleties, the original Turner frontier thesis, controversial but influential among historians, over-stated westward expansion as a factor in our national development. But another part of Turner's thinking concerned regional diversity and sectional differences. Immigrant manpower helped to people America's agrarian growth just as it did its industrial scene. Whether risk-taking, migratory, or conservative, many western immigrants stood outside the eastern ghetto acculteration pattern. To appraise their special role is to clarify further the history of the American West. Just as Americans moved westward, so did Europeans.

Historians have generally focused upon the immigrant's trip across the ocean, or his settlement along the eastern seaboard rather than in the interior. The Italians were but one of many foreign groups, but their western story forms one of the obscurest passages in America's history, whether in the California vineyards or deep in the copper pits of Arizona. As these immigrants reached the farthest west, California's land, above all, reminded them of the homeland from whence they came. True, most western Italians were not trail-blazing frontiersmen, although a few were. Except for adventurers among them who came to the New World just after the late eighteenth century, the bulk of the Italians arrived after the American Civil War had ended.

To measure the record of such a nationality in the culture of another requires avoidance of a racial explanation for progress, as well as over-emphasis on the role of any given nationality. But pitfalls are difficult to escape. Lawrence A. Kimpton, former Chancellor of the University of Chicago, once cautioned historians about possible distortion in immigration research:

> There are too many people who enter the field with ready made conclusions, obtained from their local household gods rather than their laboratories, and proceed to gather facts and footnotes to substantiate it. . . . We so often find a social scientist of a minority group who gathers data about the difficulties of other minority groups . . . the second-generation immigrant historian who writes of the woes of the immigrant in America . . . and there is a resulting selection and emphasis. The trace of a tear is there; a cause lurks in the background.[11]

Kimpton might have added that "immigration history," frequently written by immigrants themselves, also seeks to prove a partisan thesis. Such accounts applaud the nationality upon which the author has done his research, which he seeks to present as more important than any other. These works are freighted with long lists of immigrants. Another limitation is their exaggeration of the achievements of Greeks or Italians or Germans who have "made good." To avoid an excess of racial zeal in writing immigration history is, thus, to count oneself fortunate.

The writing of the West's immigration history should not be further postponed, for its sources become more elusive as each year passes. Because foreigners have been assimilated so rapidly west of the Mississippi River, loss of national identification has been the rule rather than the exception. This was not the case in the large eastern cities. In fact, other studies have repeatedly focused attention upon the slow acculturation of the Italian in Boston, New York, or Philadelphia. Yet, standing in vivid contrast to

[11] Letter to author, November 29, 1955, enclosing his speech, "The Social Sciences Today."

the once current notion that Italians were unassimilable is their virtual ethnic disappearance out west. Acculturation proceeded so rapidly that the story of western immigrants can be constructed only with difficulty. Their record is hidden and sometimes inacessible. Manuscript letters, journals, and memoirs have been subjected to the hazards of house cleaning, fires, removals, and indifferent treatment at the hands of a generation that hardly knew its grandfathers, a generation that often consigned their yellowed letters to incineration. Almost all of the Italian, French, and German language press in California has been wiped out by the attrition of time. Whole runs of newspapers have been used to wrap garbage by those who knew no better. The historian must consequently build his description partly from fugitive sources.[12]

Why focus upon only one nationality—and why only west of the Mississippi? Not all immigrants settled in large eastern cities. Yet too many studies measure acculturation in a city environment amid conditions quite different from those pertaining in the West. The gaps that exist in our understanding of the rural immigrant are, thus, an obvious reason for undertaking this research. Yet, to include within the covers of a single book all the nationalities that played a part in the shaping of the American West would be an overly ambitious undertaking. Even to describe the record of Mediterraneans would be a formidable task; hence I have chosen the Italians, a neglected group whose record is manageable and whose language I understand. This is not primarily a statistical study. Based only in part upon census reports, it is, rather, an interpretation of the role of these people as it is revealed in a variety of sources. When necessary to support generalization, this study reaches outside the geographical area of its coverage and ranges widely in time. The story has been pieced together from thousands of scraps of information scattered throughout the United States and Italy.

12 Regarding the scarcity and past abuse of documentation in far western immigration history, see William Mulder, "Through Immigrant Eyes; History at the Grass Roots," *Utah Historical Quarterly*, Vol. XXII (1950), 34–49; and Andrew F. Rolle, "America Through Foreign Eyes," *Western Humanities Review*, Vol. IX (Summer, 1955), 261–64.

With perhaps one exception, this is the first book to deal solely with a foreign nationality west of the Mississippi. Although Kenneth O. Bjork's *West of the Great Divide: Norwegian Migration to the Pacific Coast, 1847–1893* is organized differently, his is a parallel account. Most state histories say next to nothing about their foreign populations, which is an indirect tribute to the rate of assimilation.

Today few Americans are immigrants. Now that defensiveness with respect to the immigrant experience has faded, studies may appear less full of emotion, pride, and prejudice than those written in the past. With each successive generation of historians, new patterns of interpretation supersede the old. The new immigration history no longer breathes so much of the spirit of apology and filiopietism or of the nativist bigotry of the past. A study of one nationality, in this case the Italians, hopefully will provide insights into the general immigration movement. Non-apologetic histories of minorities are needed that do more than stress outworn clichés about racial melting pots, disillusionment, or esoteric immigrant contributions to American life. As one writer puts it:

> From the interpretive view, possibly the outstanding question is the relation of immigration to westward expansion and the Turner frontier thesis. . . . Inevitably the fact of immigration must be somehow placed in an understandable relationship with the fact of the frontier. . . . As Americans moved west, Europeans moved west also. But, although historians have recognized that European immigration was organically connected to the American conquest of a continent, no substantial effort has been made to clarify the relationship of the two movements.[13]

This book treats the story of only one nationality out west. Yet, my ideas about immigration, although not provable in all particulars, do represent a theory of immigration history. Hopefully this point of view provides an alternative to earlier beliefs about the immigrant. My findings, however at variance with prior view-

[13] Richard C. Haskett, "Problems and Prospects in the History of American Immigration," . . . *A Report on World Population Migrations as Related to the United States of America*, 59–60.

points, have generated some insights that do not exclude earlier research. Although this book is partly thematic in structure, I have also felt a responsibility to tell the actual story of the Italians in the American West. It is difficult both to be interpretive and to provide a narrative chronicle. Yet, by examining the immigrant record state by state, it is possible to make some new generalizations. The book's first chapters look into the eighteenth-century experience of adventurers, priests, and itinerant travelers before examining the major migration out west.

Old World and New

I

WHY THEY LEFT: *The European Background*

GUGLIELMO FERRERO began his penetrating *Life of Caesar* with the statement: "A century before Christ, Rome was already the first Mediterranean power." The history of the Italian people is steeped in the richness of a lengthy past. From her days of antiquity through the Renaissance, Italy's history created the unique memory of a proud and powerful heritage never quite erased from the Italian consciousness. For the inhabitants of Italy, however, this sense of glory receded as the country approached modern times. One of the last nations to achieve independence, Italy had failed to keep pace with her splendorous past. The morning of the Roman Empire and the noon of the Renaissance far outshone the dusk of Italy's nineteenth-century *Risorgimento,* or "resurrection," as a united country.

Before the *Risorgimento* brought Italy a tardy unification, she was plagued by foreign armies tramping over her countryside. Throughout much of the nineteenth century, Italy was at the mercy of a reactionary Austria or an invading France. Such foreign interventions were bound to provoke an eventual exodus. Political repression created prominent exiles, among them the political philosopher Filippo Mazzei, as well as Mozart's librettist Lorenzo Da Ponte, and the patriot Giuseppe Garibaldi, who for a time sought asylum in the United States. Most Italians, however, moved to the New World for reasons other than political. The whole tide of events seemed to flow against them at home. The gap between Italy's expectations and reality discouraged individual enterprise.

Social, economic, and political conditions usually best explain why immigrants left their native land in search of new homes. From the eighteenth to the twentieth centuries, conditions on the Italian peninsula encouraged the departure of hundreds of thousands of persons for the farthest reaches of the Western Hemisphere. A glance at the Italy of past epochs helps one to understand not only why immigrants left but also the role of this nationality in the New World.

Periodic famines were almost endemic, even in Italy's breadbasket provinces. Furthermore, unprecedented taxation (at one time twenty-two different taxes were levied upon landholdings) and widespread unemployment caused perennial discontent. Land was hopelessly restricted to monopolistic owners, and in overpopulated provinces the soil belonged to the nobility; tenants were frequently leaseholders or landless agricultural workers who labored for a pittance. Landlords demanded high rent and a sizable proportion of peasant crops, leaving little for these laborers to live on in the winter months. The phrase *"chi ha prato ha tutto"* (whoever has land has everything) summed up the fact that by the nineteenth century a dynastic land elite monopolized Italy's future.

In contrast to this unattainable land stood the sparsely settled, unclaimed, distant American West. The vastness of America, a vision of hope, extended inland from her eastern shores for three thousand miles. Whereas in the Old World land was scarce and men were many, in the New World there was much land and few men. With this concept in mind, Father De Smet, the renowned frontier priest, wrote:

> In my visits to the Indian tribes, I have several times traversed the immense plains of the West. . . . Every time I have traveled over these plains, I have found myself amid a painful void; Europe's thousands of poor, who cry for bread and wander without shelter or hope, often occur to my thoughts. "Unhappy poor," I often cry, "why are ye not here? Your industry and toil would end your sorrows. Here

you might rear a smiling home, and reap in plenty the fruit of your toil." Yes, this void exists; and when I say it must be filled by an industrious and perserving [*sic*] population, I concur with the experience of all travelers.[1]

For centuries Italy's peasants struggled with a parched, stubborn, and eroded soil. Poor rainfall, lessened by the many high mountain barriers, further reduced the tillable acreage. Small peasant villages, their topsoil drained away by centuries of erosion, dotted the land—cliff-hanging, barren, rocky remnants. Elsewhere, scorched and sandy plots of terrain, perennially lacking in water, made the growing of crops at best marginal. In the south, rain was either unpredictably scarce or so abundant as to cause floods. In the nineteenth century, peasants living in its swamps and marshes were at the mercy of cholera, which ravaged the villages of Italy.

Except for Portugal, no country in Europe had a lower consumption of meat per inhabitant. In some of Italy's southern provinces the peasant diet consisted of little more than bread and water, with macaroni available a few times a week and meat only once in a while. Statistics dramatize the difference between the standards of life in Europe and in America. In 1880, the average Italian each year consumed only 28 pounds of meat, at a time when the United States led the world with a consumption of 120 pounds per capita. Italy had a deficit of 5,000,000 bushels of wheat that year while the United States enjoyed a surplus of 150,000,000 bushels.[2] The Italians, traditionally great eaters of *pasta* products, had every incentive to look enviously toward the United States, and particularly toward the agricultural areas of the American

[1] H. M. Chittenden and A. T. Richardson (eds.), *Life, Letters and Travels of Father Pierre-Jean De Smet, S.J., 1801–1873*, II, 647. There were relatively few Italians in the United States before 1820, and probably little consciousness of America or of its western expanses prior to that date.

[2] As late as 1947, the United Nations Relief and Rehabilitation Administration noted that 60 per cent of the Italian diet consisted of cereals, principally wheat from which *pasta* is made. Meat still formed only about 3 per cent of the average diet. See Muriel Grindrod, *The Rebuilding of Italy: Politics and Economics, 1945–1955*, 164–65.

West, where their most desired foods—grain and meat—were to be found in abundance.[3]

For prospective immigrants, the alternative to this affluence was to stay on in a country where life not only was increasingly debased but social apathy prevented the correction of inequality. How the poorest sections of Italy felt about their plight was obvious after 1870. Only with difficulty could uprisings of starving *contadini* be suppressed by the governments which followed the union of Italy that year. Throughout the 1880's bread riots broke out in many cities as well as in the rural districts of Lombardy, Calabria, and Sicily. In these provinces peasants living below a subsistence level joined the indignant unemployed of the cities in violent revolt. During that decade these demonstrations, however, ended in frustrating governmental repressions, as did later outbreaks in Milan against grain shortages and a tax on flour milling.[4]

The disparity between relative wealth in Italy's north and abject poverty in the south remained unmistakable. Carlo Levi, in his book *Christ Stopped at Eboli*, poignantly describes the wretched living conditions among the peasants of Lucania in southern Italy:

> The peasants' houses were all alike, consisting of only one room that served as kitchen, bedroom, and usually as quarters for the barnyard animals as well, unless there happened to be an outhouse. . . . On one side of the room was the stove; sticks brought in every day from the fields served as fuel, and the walls and ceiling were blackened with smoke. The only light was that from the door. The room was almost entirely filled by an enormous bed, much larger than an ordinary double bed; in it slept the whole family, father, mother, and children. The smallest children, before they were weaned, that is until they were three or four years old, were kept in little reed cradles or baskets hung from the ceiling just above the bed. When the mother wanted to nurse them she did not have to get out of bed; she simply reached out and pulled the baby down to her breast, then put

[3] *The West from the Census of 1880*, 10–11.

[4] Maurice F. Neufeld, *Italy: School for Awakening Countries*, 39; Daniel L. Horowitz, *The Italian Labor Movement*, 35.

him back and with one motion of her hand made the basket rock like a pendulum until he had ceased to cry.

Under the bed slept the animals, and so the room was divided into three layers: animals on the floor, people in the bed, and infants in the air. When I bent over a bed to listen to a patient's heart or to give an injection to a woman whose teeth were chattering with fever or who was burning up with malaria, my head touched the hanging cradles, while frightened pigs and chickens darted between my legs.

Concerning the peasants' feelings about America, Levi writes:

The Kingdom of Naples has perished, and the kingdom of the hopelessly poor is not of this world. Their other world is America. Even America, to the peasants, has a dual nature. It is a land where a man goes to work, where he toils and sweats for his daily bread, where he lays aside a little money only at the cost of endless hardship and privation, where he can die and no one will remember him. At the same time, and with no contradiction in terms, it is an earthly paradise and the promised land.[5]

Another Italian writer, Danilo Dolci, has also described the discouragingly hopeless attitude of Sicily's peasants. If he today finds an inexorable fatalism in them, one can well imagine their instinctive distrust of "progress" on the Italian peninsula. Not even neighbors could be trusted in such a society. The government was always regarded as by its nature an enemy. There was no idea of co-operative enterprise, no belief in the possibility of agricultural improvement or indeed of any progress at all. One prerequisite of social reform is the capacity to look forward, and in Sicily the lack of this ability undoubtedly presented the biggest obstacle of all— the dialect did not even possess a future tense.

Furthermore, most of the Italian people during the late nineteenth century had no feeling of involvement in the process of unification. Indeed, in Italy's provinces the rural multitudes, wedded to parochial loyalties, were often against national unity.[6] All too often the aristocracy did not comprehend the peasantry.

[5] Carlo Levi, *Christ Stopped at Eboli,* 121–23.

[6] Nello Roselli, *Mazzini e Bakounine, 12 anni di movimento operaio in Italia, 1860–1872,* 16, 38.

Frequently the politicians did not understand the city masses. And monarchs did but little to alleviate the misery of the people. At a time when the national focus should have been directed toward internal improvements, Italy's lethargic and inefficient bureaucracy concerned itself with colonial aspirations beyond the ken of the Italian people—only to be thwarted in various attempts to build up overseas colonies in North Africa and in the Mediterranean.

After 1878, partly as a result of the Congress of Berlin, Italy began to feel self-conscious about her lack of colonies. With the English guarding Gibraltar and Suez, the Mediterranean aspirations of Italian politicos came alive. In Eritrea and Abyssinia, Italy saw a last chance to carve out an African "sphere of interest," as the large powers now labeled their colonialism. In 1887, Italy sent a poorly prepared army into Abyssinia.

But, following fifteen years of almost constant fighting, Italy was able to retain only narrow strips of land (Eritrea and Somalia) along the coast of the Red Sea. In 1912, after a war with Turkey, the Italians took Tripoli on the south shore of the Mediterranean. The cost of these military adventures, however, reduced Italy almost to bankruptcy. Never a rich country, she increased taxation to support armaments expenditures. Since these taxes fell largely on the poor, hundreds of thousands of Italians were further encouraged to leave their homeland.

The power struggle between pope and king also had discouraging effects. For decades the country was hampered by this unsatisfactory church-state relationship. Critics of the church summarized their feelings by the phrase *"Siamo sotto le unghi dei preti."* (We are under the talons of the priests.)[7] Oppressed thus by the church and by burdensome taxation for the maintenance of a growing army and navy, Italy's poor suffered. Usurious rates of interest on loans rose as high as 50 per cent.

Italy's inability to mechanize, added to her feeble economic growth, industrial lag, and unimaginative leadership, intensified the appeal of the outside world to her workers. In the overcrowded

[7] Frederick H. Wright, "The Italian in America," *Missionary Review*, Vol. XXX (March, 1907), 197.

cities, delayed industrialization and uneven economic advance was the rule. Healthy economic growth does not flourish in times of political disorder and floundering national purpose. A hostile social climate augurs, instead, meager opportunity and few jobs. Such events as the cholera epidemic of 1887—plus an apathetic national mentality, monarchical problems, constitutional crises, and misunderstanding between classes—created widespread public frustration.[8]

In addition, Italy suffered from ineradicable physical handicaps, among them earthquakes, droughts, floods, malaria, and depleted soil and mineral resources (especially coal and iron). As the population after the turn of the century reached a density of 113 persons per square mile, vast tracts of land, located sometimes in pestiferous swamps and inaccessible mountain ranges, remained uninhabitable.[9]

Depressed by a psychology of scarcity, little wonder that whole villages became depopulated, or *spopolati*, as provincials grew accustomed to a migrant life. During 1900 an estimated million workers spent up to two months annually working away from their families in other provinces. In time whole towns were literally split in two, half their population in Italy, the rest on the other side of the ocean. In 1901 the mayor of the South Italian town of Moliterno, introducing Italy's visiting prime minister, said: "I greet you in the name of eight thousand fellow citizens, three thousand of whom are in America, and the other five thousand preparing to follow them."[10]

Romantic sentiment, often based on myth, came to be enmeshed in the powerful attraction of the New World. Whereas the potential immigrant was ready to renounce the traditional and the conventional, cultured Americans admired the antiquity of Italy. From an early date they held, almost as wry counterpoint, symbolic and sentimental notions about Italy that have been care-

8 Roberto Tremelloni, *Storia dell'industria Italiana contemporanea, passim.*

9 William E. Davenport, "The Italian Immigrant in America," *Outlook*, Vol. LXXIII (January 3, 1903), 29–30.

10 Edward Corsi, *In the Shadow of Liberty*, 20.

fully described by Van Wyck Brooks. Although few immigrants came to America before the mid-nineteenth century, the Italianate influence was well known there. By the end of the eighteenth century Mediterranean styles of art and architecture had emerged in the eastern United States as the Napoleonic fashion for things Roman spread—a vogue manifested in such places as Jefferson's Monticello estate.[11]

One should not overlook the role of adventure in the decision to go to the New World. Indefinite attitudes based on feeling and mood especially influenced romantic young adventurers who headed for the American West. More tangible factors relating to the young, however, included their desire to escape military conscription, parental domination, and rural immobility. Far from restraints and traditions of all sorts the West represented the least controlled of environments. Its flamboyance and very adolescence appealed to youthful spirits. So did the incredible "Westward Movement." This frontier challenge of "the known meeting the unknown" produced a particular fascination. Louis Adamic, a Yugoslav, described how the writing of James Fenimore Cooper, with its legendry of Indians and cowboys, acted as a magnet: "my chief motive in emigrating was not the hope of economic betterment, but a desire for excitement and adventure."[12]

The search for the primeval, a recurrent theme in man's literature, had motivated the New World's earliest explorers from Ponce de León onward. Constantine Panunzio, in his recollections, reiterated Adamic's pull of adventure. For Panunzio, the freedom of the West and "the call of the sea was in my very soul," he wrote. "Two things only" he "seemed able to picture: the vast stretches of virgin lands and the great, winding rivers. I had read something of the Indians. . . . I got the idea that America was a . . . great country, vast in its proportions, vaguely beautiful." The myth that the American West represented a "Garden of the World" appeared early in the immigrant mentality, a state of

[11] See Paul R. Baker, *The Fortunate Pilgrims: Americans in Italy*; and Van Wyck Brooks, *The Dream of Arcadia: American Artists in Italy, 1760–1915.*

[12] "The Land of Promise," *Harper's*, Vol. CLXIII (October, 1931), 619.

mind that stimulated immigration. "Among the hundreds of myths cherished by the peasants," writes Carlo Levi, "one stands out among the rest by providing the perfect avenue of escape from grim realities. . . . It is their version, magical and real at the same time, of an earthly paradise, lost and then found again: the myth of America." Immigrants coupled the myth of the primeval with a rising level of expectation at home. Levi points out that, as early as 1853, the villagers of Vasto, a town in the Abruzzi region, protested deforestation of their land and threatened, because of the danger to "our pastures," to emigrate to California.[13]

The Italian vision of the Golden West, with its cowboys, saloons, sheriffs, whisky, and Indians, became even more firmly implanted in the immigrant mentality after 1910. December 10 of that year saw the New York *première* of Giacomo Puccini's *La Fanciulla del West*, based on David Belasco's *The Girl of the Golden West*. Naive and cliché-ridden though it may seem today, opera lovers did not consider it a parody of the "wild West," as the region was later pictured in Western films. Instead, the opera suggested endless prairies and rugged mountains in the shadow of which even a cowgirl saloonkeeper and schoolmistress named Minnie could find a place in the sun. For those who chose to believe, *The Girl of the Golden West* presented a valid picture of its heroine, as Puccini's *Madame Butterfly* made them believe in Cio-Cio-San and her Japan. A nostalgic duet ended with the refrain:

> Goodbye, beloved country
> Goodbye, my California
> Mountains of the Sierra, snows, goodbye!

Immigrants thus subconsciously had hopes of adventure to reinforce their conviction that, because the homeland promised little economic or political reform, they should leave. It became natural to look for greener pastures across the seas.

Southern Europe simply offered too few inducements for the city unemployed, young or old, and these came to look toward

[13] Constantine Panunzio, *The Soul of an Immigrant*, 60, 64; Carlo Levi, "Italy's Myth of America," *Life*, Vol. XXIII (July, 1947), 84–85.

foreign shores for their vision of the future. Depending upon the district in Italy in which immigrants were born, wages were from two to five times less than those in America. A comparison of daily wage scales prevailing in 1880, between San Francisco Chinese and Italians at home, illustrates the differential that became such a large factor in the departure of many from Italy.

Occupation	San Francisco Chinese	Neapolitan Labor
Shoe cobblers	Lire 7.25	Lire 2.50
Tailors	7.75	2.80
Cigar makers	5.75	3.00
Leather workers	6.25	2.75
Cabinet makers	4.50	2.40

In 1903, Sicilian *braccianti*, or common laborers, were paid the equivalent of twenty-five cents for twelve hours of work.[14]

In America, conversely, foreign-born laborers were sorely needed to buttress the growing agricultural and industrial system. Throughout most of the late nineteenth century, Italian workers in the United States could count on earning wages of about $1.50 per day. These laborers were to play a critical role in constructing the railroads, tunnels, bridges, waterworks, and farm system of the new continent. Everywhere in this prodigal land, there was much to do. With smoking factories to man, roads to build, houses to erect, and forests to clear, the immigrant was overwhelmed by the challenge. The land seemed to yearn for improvements of permanence. Terrain never before worked had yet to yield itself to the plow, as wilderness woods and hills provided the lumber with which to construct a civilization out of barrenness.

Is it a coincidence that Frederick Jackson Turner, progenitor of the frontier theory of history, was strongly influenced by the Italian scholar, the political economist, Achille Loria? Turner read his seminal *Analisi della proprietà capitalistica* (Turin, 1889) soon after its publication. And from Loria's book he borrowed the concept that "free," or unoccupied, land "was the key to a nation's

[14] Egisto Rossi, *Gli Stati Uniti e la concorrenza Americana*, 710; William D. Foulke, "A Word on Italian Immigration," *Outlook*, Vol. LXXVI (February 20, 1904), 459–61.

economic growth and that with the thickening of population the economy inevitably shifted to more complex forms." In a note which he wrote to Turner from Padua during 1894, Loria in turn acknowledged that Turner's "admirable paper on the frontier in American history" had provided "many citations important to the support of my economic theses."[15]

There has been much confusion concerning what Turner thought of the immigrant on the frontier. How did he actually feel about the foreign element in American life? Although Turner may not have stressed the impact of immigration and of the European background on America, it was a factor in his thinking. As a boy at Portage, Wisconsin, where Turner was born in 1861, the future historian "witnessed the transformation of German and Scottish and Welsh immigrants as they prospered amidst the cheap lands of frontier America. These scenes never faded from Turner's memory." Indeed, they helped to convince him "that the United States did differ from Europe, and that cheap lands helped account for that difference."[16]

One of Turner's earliest essays went beyond stressing the importance of the environment in the history of the West, asserting that the European heritage had remained strong: "Our heritage is to be understood as a growth from European history under the new conditions of the New World. How shall we understand American history without understanding European history?" Turner believed that "what the Mediterranean Sea was to the Greeks, breaking the bond of custom, offering new experiences, calling out new institutions and activities, that the ever retreating Great West has been to the eastern United States directly, and to

[15] Loria to Turner, Feb. 17, 1894, a.l.s., Huntington Library, San Marino, California, is pasted inside Turner's copy of Loria's *Analisi della proprietà capitalistica*; Ray Allen Billington, *America's Frontier Heritage*, 11, 239; and Lee Benson, "Achille Loria's Influence on American Economic Thought: Including His Contribution to the Frontier Hypothesis," *Agricultural History*, Vol. XXIV (October, 1950), 182–99.

[16] Ray Allen Billington, *The American Frontier* (Washington, 1965), 6, cites Turner to Carl Becker, a.l.s., Dec. 16, 1925, and other correspondence regarding Turner's youth, from Turner Papers, Huntington Library, San Marino, California.

the nations of Europe more remotely."[17] Turner, in short, believed that the frontier produced an American in whose character "coarseness and strength combined with acuteness and intuitiveness; that practical inventive turn of mind, quick to find expedients; that masterful grasp of material things, lacking in the artistic but powerful to effect great ends; that restless nervous energy; that dominant individualism working for good and evil and withal that buoyance and exuberance that came with freedom."

For immigrants who never heard of either Turner or Loria the evolution of a frontier philosophy was beside the point. Even exploitation of the primitive earth was not so much their goal as was the uplifting of new land. Sigmund Freud's *Civilization and its Discontents* discusses this vital creative human urge in terms that Italians well understand: "Beauty has no obvious use; nor is there any clear cultural necessity for it. Yet civilization could not do without it." The Italians provided a humanizing ingredient in a harsh industrial society. Today, as one looks at the impressive artistic mosaics they fashioned in the New York subways, or the terrazzo and statuary work these immigrants left behind, their almost lyrical desire to improve America's beauty is apparent.

From 1860 to 1870 only 12,000 Italians left their homeland for the United States. Italy's agricultural depression of 1887, however, made unemployment acute; decreasing the need for farm hands, it markedly stepped up expatriation. By then Italy had an excess of births over deaths of 350,000 per year. By 1906, despite heavy emigration, there was still an annual surplus of eleven per thousand persons in births over deaths. In the years of this century before the First World War, 8,500,000 Italians emigrated abroad. Although some 2,400,000 of them later returned home, a net total immigration of over 6,000,000 persons occurred at a time when Italy's population consisted of only 35,000,000 persons. Most Italian emigrants arrived in the United States in the years from 1880 to 1924, during one of the greatest—and last—waves of immigration of all

[17] F. J. Turner, *The Early Writings of Frederick Jackson Turner* (Madison, 1938), 71–83.

30

times. As they sought new moorings in a promised land, a veritable emigration fever gripped these masses.[18]

The majority of Italians en route to America came from the countryside and had not seen a major city before reaching embarkation points. After 1880, the ports of Genoa, Naples, and Palermo became great human expatriation centers. To discourage vast crowds from milling about these ports, steamship companies were forbidden to advertise more than the bare details of sailing dates. Across the ocean, as many as fifteen thousand Italians reached Ellis Island in a single day. In 1880 steerage passenger rates from Naples to New York were only $15.00; they grew to $28.00 by 1900.[19]

The federal census of 1900 recorded that since 1820 (no immigration records were kept before that date) some 20,000,000 newcomers had entered the United States and that one-third of the nation consisted of foreign-born residents or the children of foreign-born. United States immigration reached its crest in 1907, when 1,285,000 foreigners arrived. For years, the annual number of arrivals from abroad passed the million mark. From 1900 to 1914 13,500,000 immigrants came to America. In 1901 alone half a million persons left Italy. In the single year 1913, one person in forty departed from that country.

Italian-born persons would one day become the second-largest foreign element in the United States. In 1910 the federal census counted 1,343,000 Italians here. With their native-born children, they numbered that year well over 2,000,000 persons. In the following decade another 1,109,524 appeared. They forged a living link between their homeland and America as millions of Italians flowed into United States ports.

Relatively few of these immigrants were highly trained or very literate. The more nearly illiterate the peasant, the more he

18 Confederazione Generale dell'Industria Italiana, *Annuario di statistiche del Lavoro*, 404–405; Denis Mack Smith, *Italy, a Modern History* (Ann Arbor, 1959), 240.

19 J. F. Carr, "The Coming of the Italian," *Outlook*, Vol. LXXXII (February 24, 1906), 421.

thought of America as a New Eden. For the common laborer the New World promised to turn one's personal thorns into garlands. Occasionally Congressional action slowed the tide of immigration. In 1882, Congress excluded paupers, criminals, and other undesirables; in 1885, foreign contract labor was shut out, as were additional bad risks. By 1917, a literacy test was required for adult immigrants. These restrictions represented an economic and social reaction to the tremendous increase in immigration after 1880 and the shift in its origins to south-central and eastern Europe. From 1911 to 1915, 67.4 per cent of America's immigrants came from these areas. In 1921, following a slackening during World War I, the United States drastically restricted immigration, establishing an emergency national quota. Then, in 1924, a permanent quota policy of restriction, supported by American labor, stopped the flow of unorganized, cheap manpower. Despite the slowdown in emigration to the United States, by 1950 the number of Italians who had in-migrated had increased to 4,776,884.

A "new immigration" thus settled upon the United States, dissimilar from the earlier invasion of Nordics. In 1898 there were, for the first time, more immigrants from Italy than from any other land, and more than twice as many Italians as Britons. Prior to the arrival of most Italians, the American West had already been visited by thousands of German, Scandinavian, and English folk. Its railroads had spread westward in large measure by dint of Irish brawn. Now a new nationality would enter this scene. An explosive release of energy seemed to characterize the masses of immigrant peasants about to be transformed.

Before World War I, the ratio by sex of Italian immigrants entering the United States was about eighty men to every twenty women. Because of unknown conditions abroad, and the lack of money with which to make the trip, emigration long remained preponderantly male, mostly single male. After the war, a growing familiarity with life abroad, including all its dangers and challenges, as well as human emotional and sexual needs, gave a new impulse to female immigration. Thereafter whole families increasingly migrated together.[20]

32

Even prominent persons considered emigration or actually went abroad, not only to America. Among these were Mazzini, Foscolo, Rosetti, Da Ponte, Pareto's father, and the great Garibaldi, who, after twelve years in the Argentine and a period of residence on Staten Island, could call himself an American. Cavour too had once considered going to America. Even Mussolini, unemployed during 1909–10, had planned to emigrate there.

The English writer D.H. Lawrence believed that migration occurred not so much because immigrants sought a new freedom or economic opportunity, but because they wanted to drift away from a sense of authority inherent in the parenthood structure of Europe. Intuitively and perceptively Lawrence wrote about the immigrant growing a "new skin" and "sloughing off the old skin."[21]

Much later than Lawrence the Italian writer Cesare Pavese described Americans of the preindustrial era as men who had re-established contact with the land. Sensitive Europeans of his sort, restless, trapped, and strangulated by masses of people, admired the Jeffersonian concern for the soil, for region—for *paese*, or native haunts. It was in the cities of Italy, rather than in America, that Pavese felt uprooted and alienated. And he saw in the writings of William Faulkner, Sherwood Anderson, and Louis Bromfield the American allegiance to soil, rather than a revolt against village origins. Had Pavese immigrated, America would have represented liberation from being uprooted in the culture of his own homeland. Logical or not, his writings are pervaded by an obvious search for a new start amid things primitive. This represents an attitude that is traceable to the immigrant experience.

In the American West, especially, visitors and immigrants alike sometimes experienced a rebirth. One Italian wrote that there he was, indeed, "born again," and that he would have "to take up as much as possible of the garb and language, of the habits of thought and of the nature and temperament of an alien race. . . . It was the

[20] Anna Maria Ratti, "Italian Migration Movements, 1876 to 1926," *International Migrations*, II, 451–52; Smith, *Italy*, 239–41.

[21] *Studies in Classic American Literature* (New York, 1923), 6, 76.

beginning of a new life. A new mind and a new heart were, with or without consent, to grow up within me."[22]

In an age when immigration restrictionists strongly influenced United States policy, there were also those Americans who applauded the decision of Italians to emigrate. After the turn of the century, one commentator wrote: "The Italians have been driven away from home by poverty. Who would leave beautiful Italy of his own choice?"[23] Yet another of their champions observed: "It is the intelligence, not the stupidity, of the peasants that is bringing them to us."[24]

In the United States, the period following the Civil War was, of course, a great era of continental expansion—one which saw a burgeoning migration that eventually brought the frontier movement of the American people to a close on the shores of the Pacific. This period of striking national vigor coincided with peak in-migration from 1870 to 1910. In those decades America's agricultural frontiers, as well as the industrial regions of the country, attracted the new immigrants.

Central to the movement of peoples into this continent there remained the subconscious vision of the land conjured up in their minds. As previously noted, a large part of this vision involved the American West. Andrew Carnegie told Samuel Gompers that a poem inspired his father to leave Scotland for America:

> To the west, to the west, to the land of the free,
> Where the mighty Missouri rolls down to the sea;
> Where a man is a man if he's willing to toil,
> And the humblest may gather the fruits of the soil.
> Where children are blessings and he who hath most
> Has aid for his fortune and riches to boast.
> Where the young may exult and the aged may rest,
> Away! far away, let us hope for the best
> And build up a home in the land of the west.[25]

[22] Gallenga, *Episodes*, 1.

[23] Jane E. Robbins, "Italian Today, American Tomorrow," *Outlook*, Vol. LXXX (June 10, 1905), 382.

[24] William E. Davenport, "Italian Immigration," *Outlook*, Vol. LXXVI (February 27, 1904), 527.

34

In seeking further reasons why immigrants were attracted to the New World, one should never underrate the impetus of idealism. Among the Italians, as with other immigrants, the old clichés seemed true, although time worn by the sentimentality of too many writers. One of these ideas was that every American could rise to the top, regardless of origin or religion. Another source of hope was the belief that America was a refuge for the unfortunate and maltreated in an atmosphere of equality. Trite as it may seem, the American tradition of fair play and equal opportunity unlocked the immigrant heart.

An example of this reasoning can be seen from the correspondence of Dr. Paolo de Vecchi. In a letter to a fellow physician, this founder of California's Italian-Swiss Colony argued: "In this country, the aristocracy of wealth is not an aristocracy, because it does not have traditional privileges." What one needed to succeed in America, De Vecchi claimed, were ambition and an educational background suited to one's goals. He believed, therefore, that it was the widespread ignorance of Italy's Calabrian peasants which must be blamed for their employment at the level of Negro labor in the American South. Because they had come to America debased intellectually, they enriched others rather than themselves. Neither racial decadence nor American heartlessness led these peasants to be employed on the same ranches as Indians; it was the lack of educational opportunity in the homeland that had flawed their future. But in America, De Vecchi continued, such handicaps could be remedied. For him, America remained the land of opportunity, of unexampled possibilities for success. This was the message he sent home for compatriots to read. The effect of such reasoning should not be underestimated.[26]

[25] This poem, by Charles MacKay, quoted in William Carlson Smith, *Americans in the Making . . .*, 19. Another version reads:
> To the West! to the land of the free.
> Where the mighty Missouri rolls down to the sea.
> Where the prairies, like seas where the billows have rolled,
> Are broad as the kingdoms and empires of old.

[26] Paolo de Vecchi, *Due lettere al Prof. Angelo Mosso a proposito dell'ultimo suo libro "La Democrazia nella religione e nella scienza."* De Vecchi excoriated

At first the talented immigrants whom De Vecchi wanted in the western vineyards stayed home. Prior to the vast "new immigration" of the late nineteenth century, the United States attracted occasional priests, adventurers, and wealth seekers, a few intellectuals and merchants, and some failures at home. Not many educated persons or merchants were among these immigrants. A very few upper-class members of the professions, willing to retrain themselves, joined less fortunate immigrants. In addition to ignorance of the language, a cultured immigrant faced many other disadvantages. Because America was known as a nation where one did not need to be a member of a profession, a country where the ignorant also got wealthy in a few years, it attracted not the educated and rich but, more often, the illiterate and poor.

Increasingly, holdouts and diehards who had been barely far enough away from home to lose sight of their village bell tower became less apprehensive about emigrating. The caution of a few, however, never entirely disappeared. These were filled with doubts about leaving—especially for *il distante Ouest*. Even after selling their huts and farm animals, peasants from southern Italy rarely had enough money for the journey, however cheap the steerage rates. Just getting to New York was a major financial strain.

In 1892, according to United States Bureau of Immigration statistics, Italian immigrants brought into the country an average of only $11 per person. That same year, on the eve of a United States financial panic, the average amount taken back by each returning Italian was $250. By 1901, Italians sent home an estimated three hundred million lire of remittances annually. In the town of Basilicata, while its population declined steadily, the increase of postal savings rose from nine million lire in 1900–1901 to fifteen million lire in 1905–1906.[27]

In addition to money, the Italians shipped home an unending

Mosso's condemnation of America, which, he charged, was based on a quick tour of the country.

[27] Industrial Commission, *Reports* XV, lxxiv; Napoleone Colojanni, "Homicide and the Italians," *The Forum*, Vol. XXXI (March, 1901), 63–68; R. F. Foerster, *The Italian Emigration of Our Times*, 448–49.

stream of packages containing food, tools, gadgets of various sorts, clothing, and other gifts, all to mark their prosperity in the New World. Whereas in their homeland, village women wore black dresses to avoid the expense of laundering, in America one's clothing changed to brighter colors—something the immigrant wanted known back home. Bare feet took on shiny shoes; soiled clothes gave way to new. Tons of immigrant-bought rarities, sometimes obtained with money buried in backyard Mason jars, got loaded onto ships each Christmas.

Only the immigrants themselves could not return—not if they hoped for greater riches. The possibility of never again seeing the faces of loved ones created deep emotional conflicts. Pasquale d'Angelo, an immigrant who came to be called the "pick and shovel poet," wrote a moving account of how, bound for the New World, he left his weeping mother behind:

> Sobbing, she threw her arms about me and pressed me to her breast. In the darkness of her tight embrace, eyes closed, I wept. We both wept there on the steps. She kissed my lips again and again. Her warm tears fell on my face. I was sobbing, "I will return soon, we will return soon." But no. Her mother's fears foretold the truth. I never returned. Again she embraced me, as she did when she would cradle me to sleep on her breast. Again she kissed me. And so we remained for a long, long while until a tranquil peace came upon us.[28]

Migrants like D'Angelo nevertheless felt impelled to leave Italy. For him departure in 1910 was almost a compulsive act:

> Our people have to emigrate. It is a matter of too much boundless life and too little space. We feel tied up there. Every bit of cultivable soil is owned by those fortunate few who lord over us. Before spring comes over our valley all the obtainable land is rented out or given to the peasants for a season under usurious conditions, namely for three-fourths, one-half or one-fourth of the crops. . . .
> But now there was escape from the rich landowners, from the terrors of drought, from the spectre of starvation, in the boundless Americas out of which people returned with fabulous tales and thousands of liras—riches unheard of before among peasants.[29]

[28] Pasquale d'Angelo, *Pascal d'Angelo, Son of Italy,* 52.
[29] *Ibid,* 48.

No matter how rich they found the new land to be, a temporary sense of loneliness gripped D'Angelo and countless other emigrants. It is, therefore, no wonder that most of those who arrived on the eastern tidewater of the United States were content simply to reconstruct replicas of hometown villages along the city blocks of their "Little Italys." D'Angelo put it this way: "We fellow townsmen in this strange land clung desperately to one another. To be separated from our relatives and friends and to work alone was something that frightened us, old and young. So we were ready to undergo a good deal of hardship before we would even consider breaking up the gang."[30]

Today it is difficult to imagine how lonely and uninformed the immigrants were concerning conditions beyond the eastern seaboard. Few reliable sources of information were readily available to them, including books. One of the best-known guides, Edward H. Hall's *Travelers', Miners', and Emigrants' Guide and Handbook,* was published in London in 1867. While it gave instructions concerning how newly debarked persons could go west from New York City, it is safe to assume that most immigrants, even if they could read English, never saw its pages. Instead, they were confused about anything but life in an eastern city. An old immigrant song hints at their mood as they were dumped on American soil:

> Trenta giorni di barca a vapore
> e nell 'Merica siamo rivati . . . .
> (Thirty days on a steamship
> and in America we arrived . . . .)

Preparation for events beyond the sea voyage and landing were minimal.

Most immigrants intuitively distrusted the unfamiliar. They had to develop a sense of trust, despite an old adage to the contrary: "*Fidati era un buon uomo—non ti fidare era meglio di lui,*" or "Trust was a good man—Don't Trust was better than he." An observer wrote: "As soon as they step outside of the Italian colony they are almost as helpless as babies, owing to their lack of knowledge of the language, customs and laws of this country." He went

[30] *Ibid.*, 85.

38

on: "That is one of the fundamental reasons why these people, in the open air, working in the fields—prefer the gray life of the slums; anything rather than to be separated from the rest of their countrymen. It is the instinct that makes all living creatures band together in time of storm."[31]

In the large cities obvious factors held back acculturation—a major impediment was too much access to the native language. Stores where immigrants did their daily shopping were operated by Italians whose customers were all Italians. Poles and Serbs also patronized merchants who spoke their homeland tongues. While "upward mobility" occurred, east or west, it was impeded whenever there was too easy access to foreign stores, newspapers, physicians, and churches.

D'Angelo, speaking of departing the large eastern city to go westward, wrote: "When a laborer leaves one locality for another, he always does so for some fancied betterment and not with the idea of touring the country. . . . And deep in his heart a man hates to go around begging for a job to be greeted with a sneer or a turned shoulder."[32] He continued: "High railroad fares are usually what keep laborers near this hell-hole metropolis. Going to a distant job is a gamble."[33]

Yet restless immigrants, of the sort that could never be content in a crowded urban environment, took the gamble. To pass beyond the squalor of the eastern cities toward the grandeur of the West's prairies and mountains was finally to separate oneself from memories of Europe. To a degree such thinking may have been escapism. Critics of immigration in the homeland thought abandoning one's native soil was an illusionistic opiate. But the call of virgin lands acted like a magnet.

Furthermore, many of the immigrants had farm backgrounds. Of the 880,908 Italians who migrated abroad in the period 1891 to 1910, more than half—or 452,059—were farmers.[34] In the years

[31] Enrico C. Sartorio, *Social and Religious Life of Italians in America*, 18–19.

[32] D'Angelo, *Son of Italy*, 119–21.

[33] *Ibid.*, 100.

[34] Shepard B. Clough, *The Economic History of Modern Italy* (New York, 1964), 138.

1860 to 1900, when immigrants swelled the growth of America's cities by almost 36,000,000 persons, agricultural workers helped increase its farm population by about 9,000,000 in forty years. The Italians among these were unskilled and from rural stock, often dispossessed *contadini*. In 1901 an observer noted the character of this immigration:

> Our immigrants as a whole are a peasant population, used to the open, with the simple habits of life. . . . Practically all the immigration from Austria-Hungary . . . is from the country, as is also the immigration from Italy. The Italian mendicant, who is seldom seen here, is a member of a highly specialized class.[35]

The move beyond the confining steel and concrete skyline of the eastern city was complicated. To reach farm country not only required money, which the newly arrived Italian did not have, but involved traveling great distances in a totally unfamiliar land. When D'Angelo decided to go westward, he recorded these memories: "We had about two hours to get ready. We all went to get our bundles and our one valise in which we had our common possessions. These consisted of pots, four old tin plates, rather yellow-looking, some spoons and forks for use in case we should ever dare to cook macaroni. Years afterwards, when I had learned some words, I named this same battered valise our 'culinary panoply.' "[36]

The danger of being fleeced was also real. "Many an immigrant headed for Independence, Louisiana was put on a train for Independence, Missouri."[37] Payment of a fee—or *"bossatura"* to job brokers (*padroni*)—added to the burden of moving out of the eastern cities. Yet, in the first decade of the twentieth century almost half a million Italian male immigrants became farm laborers.[38] "On the farms they showed what hard work and intensive cultivation could do to make abandoned farms bloom. They

[35] Kate Holladay Claghorn, "The Changing Character of Immigration," *Public Opinion*, Vol. XXX (February 14, 1901), 205.

[36] D'Angelo, *Son of Italy*, 103.

[37] Lawrence Pisani, *The Italian in America, a Social Study and History*, 67, 70.

[38] *Ibid.*, 83–84.

proved that supposedly worthless land, sandy or pine brush, could be reclaimed."[39]

Although the earliest immigrants did not move farther inland than perhaps 150 miles west of New York, surprising statistics reveal the measurable effect of later migrants. Nearly 60 per cent of Arizona's population in 1870 was foreign-born. That year more than half of the men aged twenty-one and over in Utah, Nevada, Arizona, Idaho, and California had been born abroad. St. Louis, Denver, and Salt Lake City were full of foreigners. San Francisco was peopled by more Italians than any other foreign group. Perhaps appropriately it bore the name of their fellow countryman, Francis of Assisi.

The immigrant's move inland, whether as farmer, railroad worker, miner, or lumberjack, became more than evident. One authority writes that "every state in the Union gained by the net migration of foreign-born whites. In absolute terms the largest gains occurred in the urban and industrial populations of the Northeast and the North Central divisions. In relative terms, the highest increases were in the North and West, and particularly in the Dakotas."[40]

About the foreign migration westward a historian of the Middle West has written:

> The Western States, in proportion to their total population, had proved amazingly attractive to the immigrants. Though over 19,087,000 of the 1900 count (including those with only one foreign-born parent) lived east of the Mississippi River, 7,112,000 were in the States (including Louisiana and Minnesota) to the west of the same line. In the eleven Mountain and Pacific States they were 47.6 percent of the total population, the figure reaching 61.2 in Utah, 57.3 in Montana, and 54.9 in California. Nevada also had a majority. Kansas and Missouri alone of the West North Central group had less than 40 percent of alien parentage, while the percentage in North Dakota was 77.5, in Minnesota 74.9, and in South Dakota 61.1. In round numbers Minnesota had 1,312,000, Iowa 958,000, California

[39] *Ibid.*, 249.
[40] Taeuber, *Changing Population*, 63, 310.

815,000, Missouri 741,000, Nebraska 530,000, Texas 472,000, and Kansas 403,000. Aside from Texas the numbers, as well as the percentages, in the West South Central States were low.

In 1900 the twenty-two states west of the Mississippi contained 6,000,000 inhabitants of immigrant stock, all of whom had arrived since 1860.[41]

Closely related, then, to the larger movement of peoples to our eastern shores was the penetration of immigrants drawn to the waters and cities of the West—persons who sought a richer life beyond the mountains. Some of them exhibited a spirit of independence, even of rebellion, and determined to change the routine of their lives. To examine the migrant's exposure to an eastern environment alone is to look at only one side of the immigration mosaic. Subsequent chapters will, therefore, describe migration from the eastern seaboard to the Pacific.

[41] Fred A. Shannon, "A Post-Mortem on the Labor–Safety-Valve Theory," *Agricultural History*, Vol. XIX (January, 1947), 31–37.

The Explorer-Pioneers

II

FROM EXPLORATION TO MIGRATION

As THE LEWIS AND CLARK EXPEDITION inched its way into the upper Missouri country during 1804, its members unexpectedly met a western foreigner. This was Antoine Tabeau, a little man who held out his hand to them and said, in English with a French accent: "Welcome, gentlemen, to the Upper Missouri." A succession of Frenchmen, Spaniards, and Italians had already been to the Far West from the time when Francisco Vásquez de Coronado undertook a journey in 1541 which led him into today's central Kansas in search of the fabled land of Quivira. Early trappers, scouts, and residents with names like Vigo, Bossu, Bougainville, and Miranda graced the mysterious West with their presence for decades before most "Americans" had arrived. From earliest times to the present, therefore, the stereotyped image of the Italian immigrant in America has not quite rung true.

Aside from the exploits of Columbus, the story of the Italians in North America begins with an account of those priests, soldiers, and adventurers who went into the Spanish Southwest as early as the sixteenth century. In that vanguard was Fray Marcos de Niza —or Fra Marco da Nizza (1495–1558)—a colorful son of Savoy in the service of Spain. This cleric's exciting, if inaccurate, observations about present-day Arizona and New Mexico led to the mounting of Coronado's famous expedition, which penetrated the mainland northward from Mexico. More than a century after Niza had wandered aimlessly throughout the Southwest, Eusebio Francesco Kino (sometimes Chino or Chini), a priest-explorer-cartographer, appeared on Spain's Sonora frontier. From 1681 to 1711 he made major improvements in the mapping and settlement of the farthest reaches of Spain's colonial empire, from the Colorado River to the Gulf of Mexico. In 1965, Kino's statue was unveiled in the United States Capitol at Washington, a symbol of the numerous Jesuit "Black Robes" who contributed their learning, and in some cases their lives, to Spain's empire.[1]

Anxious to give these Italians proper importance, the trails-historian Herbert Eugene Bolton entitled a section of his *Rim of Christendom* "The Sons of Italy," and wrote about them:

> The Black Robe story is one of Homeric quality. The missionaries were the adventurers of the seventeenth and eighteenth century, successors to the conquistadores of an earlier day. They traveled vast distances, coped with rugged nature and the fickle savage, performed astounding feats, won amazing victories over mountains, rivers, hunger, cold and thirst.[2]

Leaving behind a homeland that was among Europe's most picturesque, these men of God went out among the heathen unescorted. Whatever their shortcomings, these failings died with them in the deserts they tried to tame. In times of trial they seemed always unafraid. Without their contribution to knowledge about the approach-routes to California and the American Southwest, it would have taken decades longer to occupy.

Italians also took part in the exploration of the Pacific coast.

---

[1] The original version of this volume included three chapters on the activities of these precursors. See Appendices A–C.

[2] The best portrayal of Kino is Herbert Eugene Bolton's *Rim of Christendom*. Another biography is Rufus Kay Wyllys, *Pioneer Padre, the Life and Times of Eusebio Kino*. See also Eugenia Ricci, *Il Padre Eusebio Chini, esploratore missionario della California e dell'Arizona*; and Kino's own *Favores Celestiales*, translated and edited by Bolton as Kino's *Historical Memoir of Pimería Alta*. See also Bolton's *The Padre on Horseback*; and Frank C. Lockwood, *With Padre Kino on the Trail*. Other testimonials to the record of the Italian Jesuits appear in Peter M. Dunne, *Pioneer Black Robes on the West Coast*; and the same author's *Early Jesuit Missions of Tarahumara*. See also Luigi Villari, *Gli Italiani negli Stati Uniti*, 1–5. See Appendix B.

Here various non-clerics either recorded or participated in colorful adventures. The traveler Dr. Giovanni Francesco Gemelli Careri (1651–1718) undertook a round-the-world voyage of five years and five months duration, the last phase of which took him eastward across the Pacific aboard Spain's annual Manila Galleon voyage. He left behind a unique account of travel along the Lower California and Mexican shoreline. The first Italian to anchor on the California coast was probably Captain Alessandro Malaspina, who in the years 1786–88 made a controversial scientific voyage around the world in the service of Spain. Paolo Emilio Botta, son of the historian Carlo Botta, was yet another early visitor to California, arriving on the French vessel *Héros* in 1827. The story of these and other early Italians in the Southwest is not, however, generically connected to the later overland migrations that are the subject of this book.[3]

OTHER EARLY ITALIANS in the New World found themselves, like Botta, in the service of France. Among these was the soldier of fortune Henri de Tonty (or Tonti). Part of his right arm was blown off by a grenade in the Sicilian Wars, and Tonty came to be known as "the man with the iron hand." He was associated with La Salle in the exploration of the Mississippi River basin and of the Illinois country. Tonty was also a fur trader who, under Governor Frontenac, engaged in large-scale trading with the Iro-

[3] On Gemelli Careri see Henry R. Wagner, *The Cartography of the Northwest Coast of America to the Year 1800* (Berkeley, 1937), 139; William L. Schurz, *The Manila Galleon* (New York, repr. 1959), 29, 239–40, 253, 267, 384; William H. Wallace, "Journal of the Great Voyage from the Philippines to America," *Journal of American History*, Vol. II (4th Quarter, 1908), 585–86; a translation of Careri's narrative is in Awnsham and John Churchill, *Folio Collection of Voyages and Travels* (London, 1704), IV, 1–606. There is an even larger literature about Malaspina, the basic source being *La vuelta al mundo por las corbetas Descubierta y Atrevida al mando del capitán de navio D. Alejandro Malaspina desde 1789 á 1794*. The California portion of this has been translated and edited by Edith C. Galbraith as "Malaspina's Voyage Around the World," *California Historical Society Quarterly*, Vol. III (October, 1924), 215–37. Regarding Botta, see his *Observations on the Inhabitants of California, 1827–1828*, ed. by J. F. Bricca, a fragment of his *Viaggio intorno al globo, principalmente alla California ed alle isole Sandwich*. See Appendix B.

quois during the 1690's. He knew how to turn hostile Indian tribes into his allies. At Mobile Bay he carried on successful peace negotiations with the Chickasaw and Choctaw, winning their confidence by his courage and honesty. He also brought hundreds of French into the Middle West. Louise Phelps Kellogg, an historian of the upper Middle West, has stated: "He was respected and beloved by all, and was the true founder of Illinois." Had there been a unified Italy at the time, the opportunity to recruit a Tonty into France's officialdom might never have existed. France was fortunate to have the loyalty of such a foreigner. No nation could have asked for a man more forceful and vigorous, and La Salle wrote that his "energy and address make him equal to anything."[4]

It is difficult to ascertain how many Italians served France in the New World before the loss of her North American empire to the British. Several thousand in one way or another probably came to the West under French auspices. Soldiers and political exiles were in the Italian and Carignan Regiments in Canada, the latter raised by the Prince of Carignano as early as 1644. Some Piedmontese members of these military units remained in America, settling in what is now Louisiana. John Law, the Scottish financier who became involved in a French colonization scandal known as the Mississippi Bubble, tried to recruit Italians in 1720 for his Mississippi Company. That year some 250 of them shipped out to New France via Agaden, France, from Genoa, Italy.[5]

By the end of the eighteenth century many Italians had adopted permanent residences in both Spanish and French Louisiana. As fishermen, farmers, soldiers, or political figures, they integrated themselves into the colonial society of these regions. A certain François Marie Reggio became in 1796 royal standard-bearer of

---

[4] Francis Parkman, *La Salle and the Discovery of the Great West* (Boston, 1869), 117–18. See also L. P. Kellogg, *The French Regime in Wisconsin and the Northwest;* as well as John Carl Parish, *The Man with the Iron Hand;* Giovanni Schiavo, *Four Centuries of Italian-American History,* 85–90; Henri de Tonty, *Dernieres découvertes en l'Amérique Septentrionale de M. de la Salle . . . .* Emilio Goggio, *Italians in American History,* 3. Today only a town in Illinois and Tonti-town in Arkansas, perpetuate Tonty's name geographically. See Appendix C.

[5] Schiavo, *Four Centuries,* 77.

the New Orleans *cabildo*, or town council. A Venetian, Giovanni Gradenigo, presided over the trustees of the Church of the Immaculate Conception at Opelousas, where his descendants are still prominent. The Sarpy family, whose Italian origins are remote, are also in Louisiana as early as the eighteenth century. Peter Sarpy navigated the first keelboat on the Missouri River. He and his brother, John B. Sarpy, were associated in the 1840's with both the Missouri Fur Company and the American Fur Company at St. Louis. In what was then called the Old Southwest, Louisiana's earliest Italians became so rapidly assimilated with the French and Spaniards that they lost their identity. Because some changed their very names, it is difficult to identify with certainty the provenance of Louisianans whose ancestors came from Italy.[6] The eighteenth century, however, saw the establishment of a cosmopolitan frontier in the Mississippi Valley that featured a sizable Italian penetration.

In 1783, twenty years after France lost her empire in the New World, the Mississippi region fell into the hands of the newly organized United States of America. The struggle by which the American West was won from England also involved Italians of both foreign and native birth to whom insufficient attention has been paid. The patriots who fought the American Revolutionary War beyond the Mississippi included Italians.

Francesco Vigo (baptized Giuseppe Maria Francesco Vigo) ultimately became aide-de-camp to George Rogers Clark, American commander in the West during the Revolution. This man's little-known career reads like an adventure story. Born at Mondovi in 1747, Colonel Vigo was a Piedmontese. At an early age he ran away from home and enlisted in the Spanish Army. After a tour of duty in Cuba he was transferred to New Orleans and, by 1772, to St. Louis, then under Spanish control. While there, he made the acquaintance of the Spanish lieutenant governor, Don Fernando de Leyba. Though Leyba was interested in transacting business at St. Louis, he could not afford to jeopardize his official position by

[6] Giovanni Schiavo, *Italians in America Before the Civil War*, 80.

such trafficking. Vigo, after being discharged from the Spanish military service, entered the fur trade. Next he formed a secret partnership with the governor under which he acted as his business agent.[7]

Vigo became a vigorous Indian trader and also bartered goods with other Europeans in the Mississippi Valley. He thereby met an increasing number of American colonials, including the Virginian, George Rogers Clark. Though only twenty-six years old, Clark became commander of American forces in the West during the American Revolution. Clark, who co-operated with the Spanish commander at St. Louis, was to become a close friend of Vigo's.

Toward the end of 1778, when British and American forces came to blows with one another in the Old Northwest, Vigo decided to join Clark in a campaign against the British. Clark gathered together at Fort Pitt and Wheeling a band of some 175 tough frontiersmen and descended the Ohio to Fort Massac. Then he crossed Illinois, and in July, 1778, wrested Kaskaskia and other British fortifications, including Cahokia and Vincennes, from the English. Vigo, who exercised great influence over Clark's volunteers, also played a notable part in the final fall of Fort Vincennes. He allowed himself to be captured by a group of Indians friendly to the British and to be turned over by them to General Henry Hamilton, commander of the Vincennes garrison. Although technically a prisoner, Vigo was allowed the run of the fort, during which time he observed its defenses and convinced its inhabitants that American forces would soon attack the fortress. The English foolishly released Vigo on the promise that he would retire to St. Louis; instead, he journeyed northward toward the American forces in the Mississippi Valley.

On February 2, 1779, Vigo reached Kaskaskia, where Clark had quartered his force. He convinced Clark that no time should be lost in attacking Vincennes, then held by only a few British troops. Vigo not only gave Clark this valuable intelligence; he ad-

[7] Richard C. Garlick, *Italy and the Italians in Washington's Time*, 84. Vigo had another silent partner, Emiliano Yosti, an Italian land speculator and stone quarry owner, about whom little else is known.

vanced Clark personal funds to undertake his historic march back across southern Illinois. Vigo also raised money from local traders —principally Frenchmen—who had turned against the British. On one occasion Vigo cashed an eight thousand dollar draft of Clark's at a time when Virginia currency was not easily accepted by western merchants.[8]

Vigo, during his march with Clark through torrential rains that inundated many valleys, never lost faith in his commander. At times they and their men waded for hours through water that reached their waists. Holding precious powder horns and firearms high above them, they pushed on toward their goal, Vincennes. On February 23, 1779, they completely overwhelmed General Hamilton's startled British forces. Vigo remained with Clark during the rest of the Revolution.

Although most writers acknowledge that Vigo shares with Clark responsibility for the memorable campaign that ended British influence in the Northwest,[9] both men fell into obscurity after their victory in the West. Clark became an unrewarded frontiersman and Indian fighter who even toyed with the idea of defecting to the Spanish in the lower Mississippi area. As for his Italian friend Vigo, although he visited President Washington in 1789, and briefly became a negotiator with the Indians for the new United States government, he did not within his lifetime receive reimbursement for his personal financing of Clark's critical expedition against Vincennes. In fact, Vigo died there in 1836 a pauper; his undertaker was unable to collect twenty dollars necessary to bury him. Forty years later, in 1876, the United States government finally repaid his heirs some fifty thousand dollars for their ancestor's role in helping to win the American Revolution in the West.[10] In 1941, President Franklin Delano Roosevelt, as if to recognize belatedly that Vigo's career had been too long

[8] Goggio, *Italians*, 4.

[9] Garlick, *Italy and the Italians*, 84–100.

[10] Schiavo, *Four Centuries*, 124–28. There is today a county and township in Indiana named for Vigo and a Vigo Street in the city of Vincennes. See also Bruno Roselli, *Vigo, a Forgotten Builder of the American Republic*; and Roselli's *Francesco Vigo, una grande figura storica fra gli Italiani degli Stati Uniti.*

eclipsed, issued a declaration which read: "To Colonel Francesco Vigo, a patriot of Italian birth, the United States are indebted, next to Clark, for the liberation of the Northwest regions."[11]

Many other adventurers from Europe followed Vigo into what was then the American West. Explorers, traders, and priests were, in a sense, government officials. Sometimes they were in the formal service of France or Spain, or later, of the United States. But the adventurer usually arrived under his own sponsorship. Independent spirits, on occasion members of the European nobility, were drawn to the West both for its natural splendors and because of scientific interests. Among these foreigners were the German princes Paul of Wurtemburg, Carl of Solm-Braunfels, and Maximilian of Wied.

Even before these Germans came west, Count Luigi Castiglioni[12] and Count Paolo Andreani, both Milanese, reached what was then the farthest western frontier. The interests of both men were primarily scientific; in 1783, Andreani had made one of the first European balloon ascensions in history. In the summer of 1791, some years after his experiments in aeronautics,[13] he explored the Lake Superior region. While at Le Point he made observations to test whether the earth was a true sphere or not, a subject then much discussed among naturalists.

By birch canoe Andreani visited Grand Portage; he has been called the first European to circumnavigate Lake Superior. His measurements of latitude and longitude seem to have been both accurate and useful to later travelers. Like Castiglioni before him, he visited George Washington and Thomas Jefferson. For President Washington he brought a copy of the Italian poet Vittorio Alfieri's "Ode to America." Much taken with the western theme, Andreani, in a letter of March, 1808, to Jefferson, offered to pre-

---

[11] Quoted in Carlo Sforza, *The Real Italians*, 117.

[12] Castiglioni published a two-volume work on the natural resources and plant life of North America, *Viaggio negli Stati Uniti dell'America Settentrionale fatto negli anni 1785, 1786 e 1787 . . . .* See Howard R. Marraro, "Count Luigi Castiglioni, an Early Italian Traveller to Virginia (1785–1786)" *Virginia Magazine of History and Biography*, Vol. LVIII (October, 1950), 473–91.

[13] Carlo Castelli, *Il viaggio aereo dell'illustre Cavalier Don Paolo Andreani.*

pare a description of his experiences in the Louisiana region before Lewis and Clark's time. He also, however, made some abusive remarks about Americans which aroused even Washington's ire.

Perhaps the most important fact about Andreani was his presence in the West as early as 1791. He fits into the pattern of those foreign observers, drawn toward the outer fringes of North American settlement, who by their writings and experiences attracted later immigrant settlers to it. Andreani left an account of the fur trade which was preserved in a work by a fellow aristocrat, the Duke de la Rochefoucauld, who wrote several volumes of *Travels*. Unfortunately, the major portion of Andreani's journal seems to have been lost.[14]

Among the Italians prominent in the settlement of Louisiana was Orazio de Attelis, Marquis of Santangelo, a restless spirit and accomplished agitator who had participated in revolts in Tuscany, Naples, and on the Island of Elba. In 1824 he came from Spain to what was then the West. After he had taught languages for a time in New York, he went to Mexico, where he became involved in further political controversy. Forced to leave Mexico in the 1830's, De Attelis traveled to New Orleans. There he opened a school and published a weekly, *El Correo Atlantico*. During some twenty years in the United States he engaged in controversy after controversy as a pamphleteer. He championed the detachment of Texas from Mexican control, associated himself with Sam Houston's fight to free Texas from Mexico, and backed Henry Clay against James K. Polk in the presidential election of 1844. Excoriating Mexicans and Americans alike, he spoke of President Polk as an "ambitious and mileficent [*sic*] demagogue." De Attelis finally returned to Italy to participate in the revolutionary uprisings of 1848.[15]

[14] G. H. Smith, "Count Andreani, a Forgotten Traveler," *Minnesota History*, Vol. XIX (March, 1938) 34–42; Schiavo, *Four Centuries*, 257–58; François de la Rochefoucauld-Liancourt, *Travels Through the United States of North America*, I, 325–35; and T. L. McKenney, *A Tour of the Lakes* (Baltimore, 1827), 263.

[15] Howard R. Marraro, "Pioneer Italian Teachers of Italian in the United States," *Modern Language Journal*, Vol. XXVIII (November, 1944), 555–82; Schiavo, *Four Centuries*, 169, 264, 270. A biography of this amazing man, who

One finds the names of Italians in early Louisiana associated with a wide variety of pursuits. In the medical profession Doctor Francesco Antommarchi of New Orleans was at one time Napoleon's personal physician on the island of St. Helena. Pier Antonio Maspero and Pietro Bello were barometer and thermometer manufacturers. At Bayou Plaquemine a Triestene, Giovanni Questi, from 1819 onward, operated a ferry. Louis Reggio became a river pilot. Francesco Vigo's own nephew, J. H. Vigo, owned a saloon in New Orleans in 1838. It is impossible to name all the Italians who settled along the lower Mississippi, but it is known that their numbers increased steadily, especially after the European revolutions of 1848.[16]

Frederick Law Olmsted in his *A Journey in the Seaboard States* described a colony of Italian exiles who had settled at Natchitoches in a period when Louisiana swarmed with romantic adventurers of every type.[17] Within Claiborne County, a Count de Leon in 1833 founded, near the present-day town of Homer, a religious community which lasted until about 1870. The Italians in Louisiana organized other religious and patriotic organizations. Among these were "I Moschettieri di Monte Vernon" and various "Società di Mutua Beneficenze." Chapters of the Mazzini movement were also formed in New Orleans and some larger towns.[18]

One Italian in Louisiana, Captain Salvatore Pizzati, became enormously wealthy. Born in Sicily in 1833, he arrived in New Orleans on the eve of the Civil War and began a maritime career that was to involve him in widespread shipping activities. He was a shrewd and skillful financial entrepreneur who transported thou-

became an American citizen, is N. Cortese, *Le venture Italiane ed Americane di un Giacobino molisano.*

[16] Schiavo, *Four Centuries,* 303–304. By 1850 they numbered about 1,000 in Louisiana; Bureau of the Census, *Compendium of the Seventh Census,* 116. Unless specifically mentioned as emanating from another source, all census statistics are drawn from the federal censuses of the year for which a population figure is offered.

[17] F. L. Olmsted, *A Journey in the Seaboard Slave States* (New York, 1856), II, 282–86.

[18] Schiavo, *Four Centuries,* 163; Joseph Rossi, *The Image of America in Mazzini's Writings,* 15–30.

sands of boatloads of fruit from Central America. About 1880 he sold a veritable flotilla of vessels to the United Fruit Company for a handsome profit, after which he owned or supervised other forms of business, including the Columbian Brewery, and the Southern Insurance Company. He also operated a plantation of fourteen thousand acres, planted with citrus trees, and invested in banks and other commercial and industrial institutions. After the turn of the century, toward the end of Pizzati's life, he built and endowed a New Orleans orphanage, designed to care for destitute Italian waifs. In his lifetime he was easily one of the wealthiest Italians in the United States.[19]

The Italians in the lower Mississippi Valley improved their status steadily, and some of them, as if to assert their loyalty to the South, fought on the side of the Confederacy during the Civil War.[20] Participating also in the rebuilding of their new homeland after the war, the Italians developed a virtual monopoly in the fruit, vegetable, fish, and oyster trades of Louisiana. Their climb upwards is illustrated by the travel account of Italian writer and traveler, Giulio Adamoli, who described the ornate residence of a rich Italian on Lake Ponchartrain as a place where one might meet some of the most illustrious persons in the South.[21]

From an early date New Orleans made room for Italian culture. After the 1820's, musical events and operatic stars were sponsored there quite regularly. Gasparo Spontini's rarely produced opera *Vestale*, once thought to have received its American *première* in New York City in 1925, had actually been staged at New Orleans as early as 1828. In 1836 alone Bellini's *Norma* received ten performances there. The great soprano Adelina Patti made her debut at New Orleans in 1855, when not yet eighteen years old. The magic of her voice was to bring her back for many seasons as the toast of the American operatic scene. She and her contralto sister, Amelia, sang frequently at New Orleans, especially during the

[19] G. B. Cassignoli and H. Chiariglione, *Libro d'oro degli Italiani in America,* 342–46.

[20] Ella Lonn, *Foreigners in the Confederacy.*

[21] "Letters from America," *The Living Age,* Vol. XXV (April 1, 1922), 36.

1860's with the Ghioni and Susini Italian Opera Company, as well as with the Italian Company of the Grand Theatre of Mexico.[22]

As growers of cane sugar, corn, and strawberries, the Italians of Louisiana generally prospered. At first, because they could not pay the forty dollars per acre asked for swampy or forest-covered land, they worked a few acres on a share basis. Their system of sharing resembled the Tuscan *Mezzeria*, familiar throughout central Italy. Under this scheme owners divided land into tracts, each of which they assigned to a separate family. The owners furnished needed seeds or tools for cultivation. Each cultivator was expected to till a few acres of land on which he produced onions, carrots, celery, beets, or other vegetables. At the end of each season, part of the produce was credited to him and part to a landlord who deducted rent or other advances—at least until the sharecropper became a landowner.

Eliot Lord, an early interpreter of Italian activity in America, wrote about Italian gardeners at Independence, Louisiana, in 1905:

> Fifteen years ago there was not an Italian family in this settlement on the main line of the Illinois Central Railroad, sixty-two miles north of New Orleans. Now there are at least one hundred and sixty thriving Italian families in the township, and their work has made Independence the 'blue ribbon' strawberry shipper of Louisiana, if not of the country at large. The railroad and bank reports for the season of 1904 credit the berry growers and pickers of Independence with the shipment of two hundred and seventy-five carloads of berries of unsurpassed quality to St. Louis, Chicago, Cincinnati, and the southern markets, with a money return of $700,000.[23]

"There is not," Lord asserted, "a single one of the cities of this country yet reached by the Italians where there is available market land near by that is not now receiving vegetables and fruits as the produce of Italian labor."[24]

[22] Ronald L. Davis, *A History of Opera in the American West* (Englewood Cliffs, N.J., 1965), 8, 10, 16, 19.

[23] Eliot Lord (ed.), *The Italian in America*, 127.

[24] *Ibid.*, 123.

The Louisiana Italians bought up land abandoned by Americans and, by digging drainage canals, converted sticky mud bogs into excellent farm soil. In a very few years, former sharecroppers who had become landowners were developing into people of means. In Arkansas and Louisiana they raised vegetables of all sorts, as well as peaches and apples. These Italians grew in their ability to master climate and competition. Even limited success, indeed, seemed spectacular to them. Above all, they were hard-working, and few of the quarrelsome lazzaroni who worked for the railroads lived among them. In fact, work was such an imperative that until 1911 the school year at Independence, Louisiana, closed in March so that children could pick strawberries.[25]

Louisiana attracted more Italians than any other state west of the Mississippi except California. Utilizing direct sailings between Mediterranean ports and the Gulf of Mexico, by 1900 their numbers increased to almost 17,500. They came mostly from Calabria and Sicily. The language they evolved among themselves—a mixture of regional dialects and English—is almost incomprehensible to either an Italian or an American. These South Italian vegetable farmers scattered over the entire southern portion of Louisiana, but New Orleans became their center. After the turn of the century its famed French market came to look more Sicilian than French. Louisiana once boasted as many as five Italian newspapers, one of which remains in existence.[26]

By 1910, Louisiana had more than twenty thousand Italian-born residents, about half of whom worked in sugar cane and cotton production. As tenants they cultivated parcels of land which were usually assigned by landowners to a single family. Because they shared their labor, some of these immigrants were eventually able to buy land of their own. If an Italian raised strawberries he

[25] See Alexander E. Cance, "Immigrant Rural Communities," *The Survey*, Vol. XXV (January 7, 1911), 587–95; Lord, *Italian in America*, 128.

[26] Newspapers listed in Louisiana Historical Records Survey, *Louisiana Newspapers, 1794–1940* (Baton Rouge, 1941), include the *Correo Atlantico, Il Monitore del Sud, Gazetta Italiana, L'Italo-Americano,* and *La Voce Coloniale.* George P. Rowell, *American Newspaper Directory* (New York, 1895), 327, also lists the *Gazetta Cattolica,* founded in 1890.

did not hesitate (in those days before immigration restrictions) to call upon the help of friends and relatives as far away as Italy itself. For years during the cane-cutting season—*La Zuccarata*—thousands of Italians arrived in the American South each year from their homeland. Sometimes railroad and construction workers from up north also joined them in the harvesting of crops.[27]

The best results were obtained by thrifty immigrants when they actually came to own the land they farmed. While some Italians were exploited as day laborers, enough of them had experienced sufficient tenancy and peonage to become eager to strike out on their own. These, therefore, relied on the "boss" or "padrone" system only as long as they needed the help of a "middleman" to find employment. In short, the hard workers among them sought to achieve prosperity in the quickest possible time.

THE RECORD OF THE ITALIANS who entered the Mississippi Valley stands in contrast to the notion that immigrants formed a static, non-mobile, introverted group which preferred to huddle together in large urban centers. The Italian's success in agriculture makes it obvious that his role as a city laborer has been overstressed. Admittedly, the majority of immigrants did remain in the large cities of the East Coast, but a significant number transcended this stereotype and pushed westward. Indeed, the farther west they went, the more colorful and individualistic their story seemed to become.

[27] Alberto Pecorini, "The Italian as an Agricultural Laborer," *Annals*, American Academy of Political and Social Science, Vol. XXXIII (January–June, 1909), 162.

III

JOURNEY TO THE WEST: *Settlement in the Northern and Southern Mississippi Valley*

AMONG THE EARLIEST FOREIGNERS to appear in the northern Mississippi Valley was a proud and haughty middle-aged Italian dressed like the model frontiersmen in James Fenimore Cooper's *Leatherstocking Tales*. Brooding and lonely, this foreigner is said to have influenced Cooper's vision of that noble breed. He was Giacomo Constantino Beltrami, whose wanderings further help to modify the stereotype of the Italian in America. An Indian agent with an Italian name, Major Lawrence Taliaferro, helped outfit him. He described Beltrami as more than six feet tall, of commanding appearance, proud of bearing, and very quick to anger.[1]

Clad in buckskins, moccasins, and a soft felt hat, Beltrami was the first notable Italian to venture as far west as the Dakotas and Minnesota. During his trip, he sought the sources of the Mississippi. Beltrami learned that the actual origins of rivers are difficult to pinpoint on a map, especially by persons who first enter virgin areas. Yet a magnetic attraction leads such men to chart rivers and to blaze wilderness trails. Following the Louisiana Purchase, these explorer-types sought to associate their names with new western discoveries. Would-be pathfinders came out of backgrounds far removed from the primitive regions that attracted them. They

[1] "Autobiography of Major Taliaferro," Minnesota Historical Society *Collections*, Vol. VI (1894), 240–42.

59

included foreigners like Beltrami, who went into the woods alone in search of the primeval.

A native of Bergamo, Beltrami had been a judge during the Napoleonic regime in northern Italy. He came to America in 1823, a recalcitrant political exile of the Napoleonic Wars. As an increasing number of persons spilled over the Alleghenies into the Mississippi Valley, Beltrami, after embroilment as a civil servant during the French occupation of Italy, sought a new start in America. He interested himself especially in its geography. This at a time when most trails into the West remained unopened. His consuming interest was to discover the headwaters of the Mississippi.

Like Beltrami, other travelers attached themselves to official expeditions or joined parties of fur trappers to insure their personal safety. After making his way beyond Pittsburgh, Beltrami, therefore, wisely accompanied Major Stephen H. Long's United States topographical expedition from Fort St. Anthony (later Fort Snelling) as far as Pembina in present-day North Dakota. Of all the earliest governmental expeditions that had yet visited the region west of Lake Superior, Major Long's was the most important.

Although Beltrami appreciated the opportunity to accompany this party, he soon fell into a serious argument with Major Long at Pembina. Long did not think highly of the visitor, as he later recorded: "He has recently published a book entitled 'La Decouverte des Sources du Mississippi,' which we notice merely on account of the fictions and misrepresentations which it contains." After Long sold Beltrami a horse, the Italian angrily struck out on his own, traveling, however, with the help of friendly Chippewa and Ojibway Indians. Before Beltrami reached the northernmost sources of the Mississippi, he discovered various remote lakes and rivers within what is now Minnesota. He was, in spite of Long's criticisms, a linguist and jurist of note, with a quite good foreign reputation as a geographer and explorer. In fact, he was to write the earliest geographical descriptions of Minnesota's Red and Turtle Lakes. Beltrami had fortunately been "briefed" as to the nature of this primitive country by the already mentioned Indian

agent at Fort St. Anthony, Major Taliaferro, a man of wide experience in the wilderness. He had voyaged down the Ohio with
Taliaferro, then up the Mississippi to Fort Snelling, where he
joined the Long expedition.

After following Indian trails with two Ojibways and a half-
breed interpreter, Beltrami reached the confluence of the Thief
and Red Lake rivers. Journeying mostly by canoe, at the mouth of
the Thief River he made the mistake of dispensing with the services of his half-breed interpreter. Soon thereafter a party of hostile
Sioux attacked. After one of the Ojibways was wounded in the
arm with a rifle ball, the fickle Indian companions deserted the
demanding Beltrami, leaving him to make his way alone along the
Thief River. But Beltrami, inept at canoeing, quickly tired, up-
setting and drenching his provisions—including a side arm and
sword. As he waded waist deep in the river's icy waters, dragging
his canoe behind him for miles, Beltrami held an imaginary "con-
versation with the fishes beneath" to keep his spirits up. As he
described his ordeal:

> A storm which commenced before mid-day continued till night. Not-
> withstanding this, however, I did not relax an instant but to take my
> food. I saw the hand of providence in the physical and moral vigour
> which supported me during this dreadful conflict. In the evening
> . . . my bear skin and my coverlid, which constituted the whole of
> my bed, were completely soaked; and what was worse, the mould
> began to affect my provisions.[2]

Once the river became narrower and deeper, Beltrami was forced
to learn how to navigate his boat when shallowness did not permit
wading. However, he preferred to return to the use of a dragrope
whenever possible. He did not have the stamina necessary to
maneuver the canoe hour after hour through treacherous rocks
and falls. One can imagine Beltrami's elation when, after days of

---

[2] Quoted in Warren Upham, *Minnesota in Three Centuries* (4 vols., Mankota,
Minnesota, 1908) I, 373. Regarding Beltrami see also Theodore Christianson, "The
Long and Beltrami Explorations in Minnesota . . . ," Minnesota History *Bulletin*,
Vol. V (November, 1923), 249–64; Richard G. Wood, *Stephen Harriman Long,
1784–1864, Army Engineer, Explorer, Inventor* (Glendale, 1966), 126–29.

grueling travel, he met a canoe party of Ojibways. One of these agreed to take him back to Red Lake. At Little Rock, or Gravel River, Beltrami engaged a second half-breed guide. They left Red Lake and made a series of long portages southward between various lakes and streams and eventually reached Mud Lake. Later Beltrami encountered a lake that had no visible outlet which, with an eye to posterity, he named Lake Julia for the Countess Giulia Medici Spada.[3] From this area the Turtle River flows southeastwardly; Beltrami called this stream the Mississippi, believing Lake Julia to be the source of that great river, the "Father of Waters." From near-by Cass Lake he voyaged down the Mississippi to Leech Lake.

Near that place Beltrami's short temper again exploded. He had engaged an Ojibway subchief, Cloudy Weather, to lead him out of the region only to become impatient over the Indian's impassiveness as well as his stubborn slowness. Taliaferro tells the story as follows:

> The chief took our Italian friend in his canoe, and turned down stream. Indians are proverbially slow, hunting and fishing on the way; Beltrami lost all patience, abusing his Indian crew, made many menaces, etc. The "Cloud" tapped him on the hat with his pipe stem, as much to say "I will take you to my father safe, if you will be still."[4]

This time Beltrami fortunately took the hint. At Fort St. Anthony that settlement's inhabitants believed Beltrami had perished. Returning safely, he was greeted with pleasure by both Taliaferro and Joseph Snelling, son of the founder of Fort Snelling. Beltrami appeared with clothes fashioned from the wilderness, his original wardrobe torn into shreds. His head, by his own description, was "covered with the bark of a tree, formed into the shape of a hat and sewed with threads of bark." His outer clothing was composed entirely of "skins sewed together by thread made of the muscles of animals, which completed the grotesque appear-

[3] Villari, *Gli Italiani*, 11.
[4] Quoted in Upham, *Minnesota*, I, 361.

ance of my person."[5] After several days of rest Beltrami, on October 3, 1823, set out down the Mississippi by keelboat to St. Louis. In December he reached New Orleans, sure that he had made the definitive and true discovery of the sources of America's major river.[6]

Beltrami was, however, to become embroiled in a controversy that would make his actual explorations form only a small part of his career. The scholarly altercations which followed comprise the bulk of his story. Beltrami spent the winter of 1824 in New Orleans, where he published in French a volume which bears the English title *The Discovery of the Sources of the Mississippi and of the Bloody River.*[7] He next traveled extensively in Mexico. At London in 1828 he published *A Pilgrimage in Europe and America Leading to the Discovery of the Sources of the Mississippi and Bloody River; with a Description of the Whole Course of the Former and of the Ohio.* Two years later he published several volumes on Mexico in Paris.

Beltrami's books concerning his travels in the United States were not well received by American critics. He had written harshly of his relationship to Major Long and other prominent explorers. Long's own *Narrative* retaliated by referring to Beltrami's observations as both inaccurate and misleading, making him out to be an eccentric.[8] Beltrami, in turn, paraphrased Lafayette, who supposedly told him that the Americans "will never forgive my having been able to do, all by myself, what their numerous and powerful expeditions had attempted in vain."[9]

For years Beltrami bullheadedly combatted those American

[5] J. C. Beltrami, A *Pilgrimage in Europe and America* . . . , II, 481.

[6] An excellent summary of Beltrami's travels is in Upham, *Minnesota,* 372–75. See also the biographical account by A. J. Hill, "Constantine Beltrami," Minnesota Historical Society *Collections,* Vol. II (1860), 183–96.

[7] *La découverte des sources du Mississippi et de la Rivière Sanglante.* See J. C. Beltrami, A *Pilgrimage in America* . . . (Chicago, 1862).

[8] See William H. Keating, *Narrative of an Expedition to the Source of St. Peter's River, Lake Winnepeek, Lake of the Woods, etc., Performed in the Year 1823 by Order of the Hon. J. C. Calhoun, Secretary of War, Under the Command of Stephen H. Long, U.S.T.E.,* I, 314.

[9] Quoted in Schiavo, *Civil War,* 96.

explorers and geographers who doubted his theories. In 1825 he published a pamphlet entitled *To the Public of New York and of the United States* and subtitled "Read me entirely, and without prejudices, or do not read me at all."[10] All too clearly a partisan attempt to induce Americans to accept "his" discovery of the sources of the Mississippi, the pamphlet accused the editor of the Philadelphia *National Gazette* of prejudice in favor of Major Long and of "being malicious and rude." It only gave rise to further controversy. Beltrami was not only of a quarrelsome disposition; he was seriously disadvantaged, having explored a region which government expeditions had officially mapped. His equipment could not possibly match that of the United States topographical engineers under Major Long. Beltrami's trip had been of only several months duration, compared with the deliberate, less spectacular observations made by Long's party. His book, however, aroused so much popular interest that it is said to have influenced two prominent authors, Hector Chateaubriand and (as noted previously) James Fenimore Cooper, who based some of their descriptions of Indians and frontiersmen upon it.

The fact that Beltrami's report on the sources of the Mississippi appeared before Long's account aroused permanent antagonism in geographical circles. In 1832 another controversy broke out when Henry Rowe Schoolcraft, the naturalist and Indian authority, announced that *he* had discovered the real source of the Mississippi, a lake which he named Itasca. Both Long and Schoolcraft considered Beltrami an amateur. Actually, the argument over who discovered the sources of the Mississippi has never been fully settled, and Beltrami's claim has received surprising support by later generations.[11] After his death in 1855, Beltrami's home

[10] Reproduced in *The Magazine of History*, Vol. XL (1930), 173–202. See also E. C. Gale, "A Newly Discovered Work on Beltrami," *Minnesota History*, Vol. X (September, 1929), 261–71.

[11] See Schoolcraft's *Narrative of an Expedition Through the Upper Mississippi to Itasca Lake, the Actual Source of This River*. In 1881 argument over the source of the "Father of Waters" broke out again and came to include repudiation of even Schoolcraft's notions. Lake Glazier, visited that year by Captain Willard Glazier, was named as a new source. See Pearce Giles, *The True Source of the Mississippi*. Glazier mentions Beltrami in his *Down the Great River*.

town, the city of Bergamo, honored him as a great explorer and called him "the true discoverer of the sources of the Mississippi." A United States Geological Survey report also credited Beltrami with this distinction. In Minnesota a large county in the northern part of the state (comprising Red Lake and Turtle Lake) has borne his name since 1866. An island in Lake Agassiz is also named after him, as is Lake Beltrami.[12]

Despite Beltrami's temperament, and the controversy that raged around him, it is obvious that his visit to the early West was important. Beltrami was more than a follower of other men's trails. In the tradition of earlier controversial foreign travelers, including the Counts Castiglione, Andreani, and Arese (to be discussed), he helped chart for Europeans the New West which he visited.[13]

Minnesota

Several decades after Beltrami's exploratory trip, other Italians came into Minnesota to farm, to mine its rich soil, and to missionize its inhabitants. As was the case elsewhere, the earliest whites to arrive on this frontier were Jesuit priests who established churches and schools. Among them was Father Francis de Vivaldi, who in 1851 accompanied Bishop Joseph Cretin to St. Paul, where they erected the first Catholic diocese in Minnesota. Another priest, Father Demetrius de Marogna, founded colleges at St. Cloud, in 1857, and at St. John's Lake in 1866.[14]

[12] In 1865 a large volume commemorating his life and work, *Giacomo Constantino Beltrami—Notizie e lettere pubblicate per cura del Municipio de Bergamo e dedicate alla Società Storica del Minnesota*, was published at Bergamo in Italy. Later Beltrami's grandniece, Eugenia Masi, published another eulogy in Florence. See her *G. C. Beltrami e le sue esplorazione in America*, as well as her "*Notizie di G. C. Beltrami sugli indigeni Americani*," in *Atti del XXII Congresso degli Americanisti*. Other Italian writings on Beltrami are A. Lami, *C. Beltrami e la scoperta delle sorgenti del Mississippi*, and G. Capsoni, "*Costantino Beltrami e la scoperta, delle sorgenti del Mississippi*," *Annali Universale di Statistica* (July, 1869).

[13] Beltrami was probably ignorant of the fact that as early as 1798, David Thompson, geographer for the Northwest Company, had traversed the region which he had "explored." See William W. Folwell, *A History of Minnesota* (4 vols., St. Paul, 1921–30) 111; Schiavo, *Four Centuries*, 260–62; and Schiavo, *Civil War*, 94–100.

[14] Schiavo, *Four Centuries*, 295.

Later in the nineteenth century, as Minnesota became an important mining area, Beltrami's compatriots flocked there in search of livelihood, partly because of recruiting abroad by state immigration societies. Among the immigration groups in the western states there were to be founded a Minnesota Emigration Society, an Iowa Board of Immigration, a Nebraska Board of Immigration, the California Immigrant Union, and the Oregon State Board of Immigration. Through reports and pamphlets these semi-official organizations sought prospective immigrants.

The last quarter of the century saw the opening of Minnesota's Mesabi and Vermilion ranges. Men, supplies, and equipment poured into the state. The investment of new mining capital led to an expansion of job opportunities for all immigrants. Picks, wielded by foreigners, tearing loose the rich rocks of America, could be heard throughout the Mesabi Range. As in the coal mines of Kansas, Italians mined metalliferous outcroppings of the subsoil, favoring open-pit mining over tunneling into the Vermilion Range. From 1875 to 1881, as the number of Italian miners who entered the United States quadrupled, Minnesota became a magnet for them, and their makeshift dwellings dotted its torn-up landscape.[15]

From 1880 to 1890 the population of Minneapolis bolted upwards from 46,887 to 164,738, while St. Paul grew from 41,473 inhabitants to 133,146. The number of Italians in Minnesota would increase to almost 10,000 in 1910. As early as 1882 the small settlement called Tower, among the first permanent mining camps in Minnesota, was in operation. At such Minnesota towns Italian miners helped increase the state's iron ore tonnage from zero as late as 1880 to fifteen million tons by 1902. In 1910 there were almost 10,000 native-born Italians in Minnesota. That year those who lived in the state's fifteen largest cities helped to form over 8 per cent of its population.

Immigrant descriptions of life in middle western mining towns are not easy to find. To contrast the differences between Italy and

15 Lord, *Italian in America*, 99–100, offers statistics on the high proportion of North Italians among the miners.

the coal mining community of Union City, Indiana, Antonia Pola has the main character of her novel *Who Can Buy the Stars?* think about them:

> The ugliness of the mining camp stared at her and assaulted her senses as she walked along the rickety wooden sidewalk. The shabby cottages were of the same homemade architecture as those of Cartonville [also in Indiana] and other mining camps she had seen in her ten years in America. Almost every little house had at the back a plot of ground cultivated as a vegetable garden, with occasionally a geranium plant or an anemic rosebush. But the vacant property and the country around was uncultivated and full of weeds of an uninteresting shade of green. This was May, when ordinarily nature displays a magnificence of green and flowers. In this coal country, everything was colorless and full of dust.
>
> She thought of Italy in flower from February to November. Visions of the hills of Piedmonte, at this time intensely alive with brilliant green, of prairies washed by the dew, of emerald seas of early hay waving under a friendly breeze, and of wild flowers nodding gently by the country roads, made her heart contract.[16]

Although the majority of the Italians in Minnesota engaged in mining, some joined railroad gangs recruited and formed at Minneapolis, St. Paul, and Duluth. Still others became truck farmers outside these cities.

By 1906 there were Roman Catholic Italian parishes at Hibbing and Eveleth. In the Vermilion Range towns from Ely to Calumet, however, one parish per community served the Irish, Germans, Slavs, and Italians. An assimilative role was played by such interethnic congregations. Similarly, immigrant businessmen performed a mediating function by forming partnerships, especially between Italians and Slavs. A statistical study of the careers of fifty prominent businessmen who had come to the Minnesota ranges before 1901 reveals that 58 per cent of them were foreign-born.[17]

---

[16] Antonia Pola, *Who Can Buy the Stars?* 104; on Italian miners in Minnesota see Industrial Commission, *Reports*, XVI, 205, 292, 297–302.

[17] Timothy L. Smith, "New Approaches to the History of Immigration in

Across the Mississippi in neighboring Wisconsin the successful Vernon County community of Genoa was settled by Piedmontese as early as 1863. These immigrants, who had originally settled in Galena, Illinois, cleared heavily timbered lands considered unfit for farming. They bought these cheaply and on them raised barley, rye, corn, wheat, hops, and even, somewhat precariously, tobacco. These immigrants, who were also first-rate dairy farmers, worshiped in a stone church built with their own hands. Like the Italian farmers at near-by Cumberland, Wisconsin, their Americanization proceeded so rapidly that they were rarely referred to as foreigners. As they learned to use modern machinery, they came to own some of the largest farms in the Middle West.[18]

Iowa

A precursor of the several thousand Italians to settle in Iowa was another foreigner who does not fit the stereotype of the Italian in America, Samuel Mazzuchelli. At the age of twenty-four this son of a wealthy Roman banker renounced his family's riches to come to the New World as a Dominican priest. In Iowa, and also in Illinois and Wisconsin during the 1830's, he became a gentle apostle for whites and Indians alike. For years he roamed the plains and forests, equipped only primitively and undergoing perils of every sort, including hunger. On one occasion he was reduced to making a meal out of "a prairie rat of very bad odor."[19] On the frontier, Mazzuchelli came to be known as "Father Kelly," a name given him by his Irish parishioners. A philologist as well as a missionary, he published an almanac of the Chippewa language in 1833, which was probably the first book printed in Wisconsin. He also wrote the first volume published in the Sioux language. Like other clerics who ministered to the trappers, traders, and Indians of the West, Mazzuchelli was both a man of

Twentieth Century America," *American Historical Review*, Vol. LXXI (July, 1966), 1269–70.

[18] A. E. Cance, "Piedmontese on the Mississippi," *The Survey*, Vol. XXVI (Sept. 2, 1911), 779–85; Industrial Commission, *Reports*, XV, 538.

[19] Rosemary Crepeau, *Un Apôtre Dominicain aux Etats-Unis, le Père Samuel ... Mazzuchelli*, x.

learning and a servant of God. For years he was the only priest from the waters of Lake Huron and Michigan to those of the Mississippi River, across the prairies and forests of Wisconsin and Iowa. The design of the old state capitol building at Iowa City is attributed to him. Mazzuchelli ultimately set down his ideas about the West in a volume published in Switzerland.[20]

While European interest was whetted by foreign men of the cloth who went west, absorption with the frontier was never confined merely to the religious. A secular traveler whose visit to the Iowa region was fleeting but significant was Count Francesco Arese, a Milanese. In 1837–38 this aristocrat made a trip, described in a book entitled *A Trip to the Prairies and in the Interior of North America*.[21] After a close association with Napoleonic sympathizers in Italy and France, and following a tour with the French Foreign Legion in Algeria, Arese arrived in the United States as an exile during the middle of the national financial Panic of 1837. He mingled socially with Prince Louis Napoleon, Henry Clay, and the prominent Chouteau family of St. Louis. At age thirty-two he undertook a trip up the Missouri River to what is now the western portion of the state of Iowa, near Council Bluffs. About his first encounter with Indians in central Iowa, Arese wrote:

> I much preferred seeing them in lithographs. The first time I saw Indians and was really, so to say, in contact with them, they caused me to feel such disgust and fright (in Italian I would say *ribrezzo* . . .) as seemed unconquerable; and I should never have suspected that within three months I should be glad to sleep between two In-

[20] Schiavo, *Four Centuries*, 249. In 1836, Mazzuchelli (1806–64) opened with prayer the first session of the Wisconsin territorial legislature; see Crepeau, *Un Apôtre*, xi. Mazzuchelli's *Memorie storiche ed edificanti di un missionario apostolico . . .* (2 vols., Milan, 1844; Lugano, 1845). See also Luca Beltrami, *Padre Samuele Mazzuchelli, missionario domenicano nell'America del Nord dal 1829 al 1864*. A surprising number of books about the West were reprinted in French and Italian. Cf. Louis L. Simonin, *Le Grand-Ouest* (Paris, 1869), reprinted at Milan in 1876 as *Il Far-West degli Stati Uniti*.

[21] Edited and translated by Andrew Evans. See also R. Bonfadini, *Vita di Francesco Arese*; and Lynn M. Case, "The Middle West in 1837, Translations from the Notes of an Italian Count, Francesco Arese," *Mississippi Valley Historical Review*, Vol. XX (December, 1933), 381–99.

Life among the American Indians as seen by an Italian artist. About 1880.

dians (males, of course), side by side so as to keep warm during a night of North wind.[22]

Like Beltrami before him, Arese tried hard to adapt himself to the western environment. From the Iowa region he traveled, on horseback and by canoe, into the Vermilion River country of present-day South Dakota. He ventured through the land of the Sioux and made his way into southwestern Minnesota via the St. Peter's River to Fort Snelling, where Beltrami had been. Arese returned east through Wisconsin and Michigan to Montreal and Quebec.[23] In a day when travel west of St. Louis was still exceed-

[22] Arese, A *Trip*, 66.
[23] A map showing Arese's travels appears in *ibid.*, opposite xxiv.

ingly rough, indeed sometimes dangerous, Arese made a unique six-thousand-mile trip. Like other aristocrats who visited the West, he was excited by the frontier:

> When speaking of America one might certainly find something bad to say of her, and especially is it easy to sharpen one's wit by finding objects of ridicule here—that is a commodity not lacking: but if one has only just a tiny bit of candor, he must put his conceit in his pocket and, European as he may be, say that This is an astounding country, magical, miraculous; and that ever so many things here must be seen to be believed.[24]

The impressions which Arese, Beltrami, and Mazzuchelli took back to Europe helped to shape Italian attitudes toward North America.

Long after Arese visited the cutting edge of the frontier in that summer of 1837, other Italians crossed the flatlands of Iowa to help settle the region. These foreigners were mostly small farmers. By 1860 the average cost of an acre of farm land had reached $16.32. To raise cash they worked in the primitive towns emerging out of the treeless expanses of Iowa: Des Moines, Council Bluffs, Sioux City, and Davenport. As immigrants accumulated capital, they bought property both inside and outside these communities. Later they acquired the expensive farm machinery needed to become successful farmers. By 1910 there were almost six-thousand Italians in Iowa. With their children, who made up a still larger number, these were not temporary visitors like Arese, spellbound by the enchantment of the West. They intended to become permanent settlers.

Italians established a newspaper, the Des Moines *Tribuna Italiana*, and even named a few Iowa towns and counties, among them Aetna, Mount Aetna, Como, Florence, Garibaldi, Genoa, Genoa Bluff, Milan, Palermo, Paoli, Parma, Turin, Verona, Marengo, and Verdi.[25] As these urban centers sprang up, they attracted specialized labor, serviced the surrounding countryside,

[24] *Ibid.*, 173.
[25] Pauline Cook, "Iowa Place Names of Foreign Origin," *Modern Language Journal*, Vol. XXIX (November, 1945), 622.

provided their residents with comforts and necessities, and attracted more immigrants. In addition to economic power, these towns were among the agencies by which America transformed itself from frontier rurality to urban maturity.

Iowa's foreign-born settled in considerable numbers in the state's northern half. In Hamilton County, for instance, by 1880 they made up one-third of its population. The federal manuscript census that year showed that almost half the farm operators in that county were foreign-born.[26]

Missouri

A larger number of Italians were attracted to Missouri than to either Minnesota or Iowa. Easy access to St. Louis, one of the principal gateways to the West, accounts for the migration there of large numbers of foreigners of all nationalities. Amid its cosmopolitan environment the Italian felt more at home than in the Iowa towns of Yankee origin. The French language, if not the Italian, continued to be spoken in Missouri, and the European tradition was everywhere evident.

In addition to a sizable number of Italian traders and land speculators who followed Vigo and his partner, Emilien Yosti, Italian priests also made their mark in St. Louis. They were in the same tradition of self-sacrifice as Father Kino in the Spanish Southwest and Father Mazzuchelli in the Old Northwest. These were headed by Father Felix de Andreis, a Piedmontese. His group of Lazarists had landed at Baltimore in 1816 and walked as far as Pittsburgh. From there they took a flatboat to Kentucky. In 1817 they reached Perryville, eighty miles south of St. Louis, where they built the Seminary of St. Mary, the first Catholic institution of its kind west of the Mississippi River. A pioneer outpost, this rough-hewn log establishment blended into its curriculum the training of divinity students, the chopping of wood, and farm work for the seminarians.[27]

[26] Allan Bogue, *From Prairie to Corn Belt, Farming on the Illinois and Iowa Prairies in the Nineteenth Century*, 15–16.

[27] Schiavo, *Four Centuries*, 244.

Giuseppe Rosati, an unusual Italian priest who accompanied De Andreis across the Atlantic, succeeded him upon his death in 1820 as Lazarist Superior in America. Rosati achieved this post after helping to found what later became St. Mary's College. He also taught courses there in logic and theology.[28] Rosati became coadjutor bishop of Louisiana in 1824 and later Bishop of St. Louis. This post entailed supervision of religious activities from Arkansas and Missouri to the Rocky Mountains. In 1829, under Rosati's patronage, the Jesuits founded St. Louis University. The priest himself also founded the first school for deaf mutes west of the Mississippi in 1839, and he helped found St. Louis Hospital. Besides supervising the erection of St. Louis Cathedral, he established thirty-four churches in Missouri and went on to found convents, schools, and orphan asylums throughout the Mississippi Valley.[29]

Bishop Rosati operated at the epicenter of that increasing movement of foreign Catholic missionaries into the Far West. It was, in fact, Rosati who authorized the much better known Belgian Jesuit, Father Pierre Jean De Smet, to go into the Northwest Indian areas. In the wake of this decision there was to follow the organization of more missions, schools, and parishes throughout the Rocky Mountains and the Oregon Territory.[30]

Following Italian clerics into nineteenth-century Missouri were a number of farmers who came from Sunnyside, Arkansas, in the 1890's, to take up lands at Montebello and Verdella. Because of the poor soil and a lack of supervision at the two spots, some of these dispersed and sought employment with local mines and railroads. Others, however, became producers of wine, fruit, vegetables, "small grain," and cotton near both communities.[31]

[28] Goggio, *Italiano*, 10. See also Robert F. Trisco, *The Holy See and the Nascent Church in the Middle Western States, 1826–1850*, in which Bishop Rosati's activities are discussed. On page 179, a Count Vincent Piccolomini-Arragona of Florence is quoted as stating (in 1839) that he had spent ten years in the United States in "scientific pursuits." Father Mazzuchelli is mentioned on 260 and 262.

[29] Schiavo, *Civil War*, 301, 316.

[30] Gilbert J. Garraghan, *The Jesuits of the Middle United States*, passim. Schiavo, *Civil War*, 315–16.

[31] Industrial Commission, *Reports*, XV, 506.

In 1898, still other Italians who had worked in the Arkansas cotton fields settled at Knobview, Missouri, about a hundred miles south of St. Louis. There, the St. Louis and San Francisco Railroad offered them property on most encouraging terms. After making a "down payment" of only fifteen dollars per forty acres, the Italians were allowed to pay the balance five years later. Less desirable state-owned lands also became available to them at three dollars per acre, with eight years to pay at 7 per cent interest.[32] Fifty families among them could scrape up only one thousand dollars in cash, but with this they bought abandoned bottom land on which they built small wooden houses and laid out farms. In these early and difficult years immigrants lived in empty barns or stables. Potatoes, which Italians traditionally dislike, formed the chief staple of their diet. Like the settlers at Montebello and Verdella, some of the men among them had to take jobs in the Illinois coal mines. Others became railroad workers, not returning to Knobview until they could pay off their land and buy farm implements, horses, and cattle.

Within ten years, however, most of these agriculturists had prospered. By marketing tomatoes, apples, grapes, and dairy products, in 1922 their landholdings averaged thirty acres in size and yielded a profit of eight thousand five hundred dollars per year. Six years later these immigrants shipped over one hundred carloads of grapes under the auspices of the Knobview Grape Grower's Association. That town's Italians formed the Ozark Grape Corporation headed by one of their number, David Gentilini. Utilizing careful techniques of cultivation, Knobview's Italians steadily increased the production of grapes. They paid special attention to plowing their fields deeply so that the roots of their vines would have ample furrow space in which to grow. In the bottom of each hole they dumped such fertilizers as they could find—manure, oak leaves, and loamy trash of any kind. With all this they mixed good earth. Set in such soil, a vine had vitality and ventilation below as well as a reservoir for holding moisture. These Italians paid special attention also to pruning and spraying and

[32] E. Mayor des Planches, *Attraverso gli Stati Uniti*, 248.

sought expert advice from the Missouri Fruit Experiment Station at Mountain Grove.[33]

Another farm community in Missouri helps to dispel the notion that the Italians turned their back upon agriculture. This was Marshfield, some twenty-five miles from Springfield. The town was settled by farmer-miners who had saved their hard-earned wages to buy farm lands on which they raised corn, hay, and wheat. According to a government report, by 1910 this colony had become more successful than a near-by German community.[34]

After 1875 there was another Italian agricultural settlement in southwestern Missouri, the unique Waldensian community at Monett. Members of this Protestant sect, after departing the overcrowded valleys of northern Italy, first settled in Uruguay. A few of these moved to Monett where they became affiliated with the Presbyterian Church, forming a colony of about one hundred members. This group resembled an even larger Waldensian colony at Valdese, North Carolina, established later, in 1893. Both groups sought religious freedom in a new land.[35]

Still another Italian enclave was located at Pilot, Missouri. There, after 1880, the Big Muddy Coal and Iron Company employed many Italians as miners. In 1892 this same company sent a group of them to work in its mines at Fredonia (today Cambria), Illinois.[36] By 1920, Italian-born persons in Missouri numbered almost fifteen thousand. Three-fifths of these lived in St. Louis. If one were to count the second generation, this figure would be approximately doubled. Some were engaged in trading, vending, and operating small businesses. Others became fruit wholesalers and restaurant operators. (A large, well-known St. Louis Italian restaurant is Garavelli's.) Most Italians, however, were unskilled

[33] Allen E. Drayer, "Italy in the Ozarks," *American Fruit Grower*, Vol. XLIII (September, 1923), 14; Drayer, "Italians in Knobview," *The Interpreter*, Vol. II (April, 1923), 15–16; Industrial Commission, *Reports*, XXI, 377; Cance, "Immigrant Rural Communities," *The Survey*, Vol. XXV, 591. Giovanni Schiavo, *The Italians in Missouri*, 151–54 is a summary of activities at Knobview.

[34] Industrial Commission, *Reports*, XXI, 369, 374.

[35] "The Waldensians in America," *Mennonite Life*, (April, 1950), 23.

[36] Dolores M. Manfredini, "The Italians Come to Herrin," *Journal of the Illinois State Historical Society*, Vol. XXXVII (December, 1944), 317–28.

laborers drawn also to Kansas City's factories, into construction crews, and into local industry.

At St. Louis they launched several newspapers. At its peak *La Lega Italiana* had a circulation of 16,500. A Republican weekly, *Stampa Italiana*, reached 8,100 readers by 1931. The Italian center of the city was its Fairmount Heights district. East or west, those who lived in cities continued to cultivate small garden plots, sometimes raising flowers, *basilico*, and other herbs in old tomato cans and window boxes. Amid the furrows of small garden patches, they planted lettuce, beans, and the indispensable *pomodore* for *pasta* sauces.

In Missouri, as elsewhere in the Middle West, an increasing number of Italians turned to farming. Located usually just outside the city limits, they breathed the fresh air of the countryside and came to feel some of the freedom which they prized in such an environment.[37]

Troubles and Successes Southwestward

After the Civil War the American Southwest, a land of cotton, sugar, and subsistence agriculture, seemed alien in every way to the immigrant's past. If he were a tradesman or artisan, the South offered fewer opportunities than elsewhere to practice his skills. Its labor force mixed into the emotional struggle of white and Negro. There the immigrant faced competition with depressed labor and confronted a humid climate unlike that of Europe. In the American North, immigrants were warned not to migrate southward; this advice undoubtedly cut down the number of foreigners who moved into the trans-Mississippi South.

Yet the southwestern states maintained active immigration bureaus from the 1890's onward. Furthermore, the South, since the days of La Salle and Tonty, possessed a lingering cosmopolitanism. Although seemingly inhospitable to immigrants, it

[37] Industrial Commission, *Reports*, XVIII, 343; Lord & Thomas, *Pocket Directory of the American Press* (Chicago, 1919), 646; N.W. Ayer, *Directory of Newspapers and Periodicals* (Philadelphia, 1931), 1236–38.

attracted some, and these continued the Spanish and French tradition of earlier generations. In the 1880's there were more
Italians in Louisiana and Arkansas than any other foreign group,
as their padrones brought increasing numbers to work on the Mississippi levees. By 1885 the Yazoo Delta's first Italian agricultural
colony had settled at Friar's Point, Coahoma County, Mississippi.
Other immigrant groups fanned out through Washington and
Bolivar counties and westward across the Mississippi River.[38]

Alfred Stone, a leading Delta planter and writer, was widely
supported by his fellow planters in predicting that heavy Italian
migration to the region would eventually displace that of Negroes.
To prove his white supremacy ideas, Stone, a racist, used as evidence the success of the Italians as cotton-choppers, especially in
Arkansas.[39] Their largest center in Arkansas was at Sunnyside, in
Chicot County along the Mississippi River in the southeastern
portion of the state. After 1895, five hundred immigrant families
settled there on an island opposite Greenville, Mississippi, along
the west bank of the river. Austin Corbin, a northern "philan-
thropist" who owned the Long Island Railway, made this settlement financially possible.

Instead of settling his colony with Italians from the big cities
of the United States, Corbin reached an agreement with the
Mayor of Rome, Prince Emanuele Ruspoli, for the direct transportation of immigrants to his new colony via New Orleans. These
workers, sent up the Mississippi by steamers of Corbin's own
Anchor Line, debarked at Sunnyside. Most knew not one word of
English; many had never even been on a farm. Befuddled and
confused, they could be made into useful workers only under a
padrone, or boss-rule, system, the details of which will be described
later. Bakers, tailors, and shoemakers fresh from Italy were utterly
dismayed when Corbin supplied them with "agricultural implements, draft horses, seeds, houses, stores, warehouses, gins, presses,

[38] New York *Tribune*, January 2, 1884.

[39] Alfred H. Stone, *Studies in the American Race Problem*, 102, 115–23, 188–
208.

carts, a railroad, a steamer," and even cotton baling equipment. Their "benefactor" also provided the Italians with a school, a church, and a telegraph office.[40]

Corbin's venture was a mixture of humanitarianism and hard-nosed Yankee enterprise. Although his American foremen treated workers with a tyrannical attitude carried over from dealing with Negroes, the Italians rose to the challenge of toil and heat. For a time the shaky colony prospered. In competition with local Negroes, with whom they worked as cotton-choppers, they showed a surprising production record. Individual Italians produced an annual average of 2,584 pounds of lint cotton per working hand while the Negroes averaged only 1,174 pounds. "They planted the banks of streams which had never before known the touch of a plow," including "ditch banks and fence rows," cultivating every square foot of soil on which they paid rent.[41]

As if to explain why the Italians outproduced the Negroes at a ratio of two to one, a contemporary observer wrote that whereas Negroes were sometimes indolent, intemperate, and lacking in thrift, the Italians were "hard, patient workers, willing to do any kind of work, and to do it thoroughly." He pointed out that, although they consumed "large quantities of their sour wine, they are not an intemperate people."[42] When competing with Negroes, Italians worked incessantly, out of a sense of competitive pride. In some localities they were able to produce a crop half again as great per acre. One Negro complained about all this: "Fo' Gawd in Heaven, dat Dago en his wife en fo' chillun wuz pickin' cotton by de moonlight. I do' 'no' how it looks to you, but I calls dat er under-handed trick myse'f."[43]

[40] Claghorn, "Agricultural Distribution," in *Reports*, XV, 505–506.

[41] Alfred H. Stone, "Italian Cotton Growers in Arkansas," *Review of Reviews*, Vol. XXXV (February, 1907), 209–13; Claghorn, "Agricultural Distribution," in *Reports*, XV, 505–506. Giovanni Preziosi, *Gli Italiani negli Stati Uniti del Nord*, 98; "Settlers in Tontitown," *Interpreter*, Vol. VIII (January, 1929), 55–58.

[42] Emily Fogg Meade, "Italian Immigration into the South," *South Atlantic Quarterly*, Vol. IV (July, 1905), 217–23.

[43] Foerster, *Italian Emigration*, 368.

Italian domesticity at Sunnyside exemplifies their life elsewhere as well. A colorful account of that community describes its houses as "literally covered with strings of dried butter beans, pepper, okra," as well as "corn, sun-cured in the roasting ear stage." In order to save money, the people made meat a luxury, substituting *verdura*, which included *cicoria*, *escarola*, and dandelion greens. The Italian used all three in salads or soups. *Per fare bella figura*, or to make a good showing, they dressed their children neatly and kept their huts clean. In their woodsheds was "enough fire wood, sawed and ready for use, to run the family through the winter months."[44]

Sunnyside, however, was never well drained, and it remained dangerously malarial. Just as Corbin was about to provide for pure water and proper sanitation, he died. Settlement of his estate took so long that Corbin's projects were unduly jeopardized. Depressed cotton prices in 1895 helped defeat the Sunnyside colony. Meanwhile, there was an alarming increase in the colony's mortality rate. In two months of 1896 there were 130 deaths, a high proportion of them among the women and children. During 1897–98, therefore, a majority of the Italians abandoned Sunnyside in panic. In the autumn of 1899, 80 of the colonists died within one month. Others returned to Italy, and some moved to South America, Alabama, and places farther west. Of the forty families that remained, few prospered.

According to standard accounts, until quite recently unchallenged, the colonists were charged loan rates of interest as high as 10 per cent, and were, in addition, bilked of their money by *padroni* and even by the physicians who attended them. After Corbin's death in 1897, Sunnyside became a commercial venture whose inhabitants were looked upon as a source of profit. Had Corbin lived, he might have brought about one of the most successful experiments in the history of American agriculture. But the death of Sunnyside's major sustainer helped spell its doom, at least as he had envisioned the colony. Those Italians who remained at Sun-

[44] Alfred H. Stone, "The Italian Cotton Grower: The Negro's Problem," *South Atlantic Quarterly*, Vol. IV (January, 1905), 45.

nyside were each reduced to paying seventy-five cents per month merely to get a priest to say Mass for them on Sunday.[45]

Another, more successful, version of the Sunnyside story has also arisen. The executors of Corbin's estate leased its lands to O.B. Crittenden and Company of Greenville, Mississippi, across the river from Sunnyside. He and his partner, Leroy Percy, were experienced in the precarious operation of cotton growing and one authority maintains that their skills in plantation organization and management proved decisive in the eventual success of the Italian colony. Its owners, ultimately, called Sunnyside a model agricultural colony. A crop rent system was adopted, each tenant being charged an annual seven dollars per acre rental, with supplies and medical care dispensed through a plantation store. Crittenden and Percy bought Sunnyside's whole annual crop, and, by 1903, the plantation still had fifty-two Italian families living there; that year Crittenden and Percy claimed to have paid these immigrants thirty-two thousand dollars beyond rents and various other expenditures.[46]

Despite the failure of the Sunnyside colony, after the turn of the century the Italian's successful competition with the Negro was given national publicity. In addition to Stone other writers stressed the theme of white immigrant superiority:

> If the colony located at Sunnyside . . . was a failure at first, it is no sign that Italians cannot succeed in agriculture. Immigrants, largely from other industries, placed in competition with Negroes in production of a crop that they knew absolutely nothing about, under foremen accustomed to drive slaves, in a swamp country—hot and sickly to newcomers—attacked by malarial fever and losing a large number of the first settlers, it is not to be wondered at that failure was threatened. But success has come even in that case, where failure stared all in the face.[47]

[45] Stone, "Italian Cotton Growers in Arkansas," *Review of Reviews*, Vol. XXXV (February, 1907), 209–13; Claghorn, "Agricultural Distribution," in *Reports*, XV, 506; Des Planches, *Attraverso*, 142.

[46] This paragraph is based upon Robert L. Brandfon, "The End of Immigration to the Cotton Fields," *Mississippi Valley Historical Review*, Vol. L (March, 1964), 591–611.

Still another article read: "the white man, in the person of the Italian immigrant, has proved his ability to more than meet the Negro upon his most favored ground." Its writer continued: "Measured by whatever standard may be applied, the Italian has demonstrated his superiority over the Negro as an agriculturalist. . . . From the garden spot which the Negro allows to grow up in weeds, the Italian will supply his family from early spring until late fall, and also market enough largely to carry him through the winter. I have seen the ceilings of their houses literally covered with strings of dried butter beans, pepper, okra, and other garden products, while the walls would be hung with corn, sun-cured in the roasting-ear stage. In the rear of a well-kept house would be erected a woodshed, and in it could be seen enough fire wood, sawed and ready for use, to run the family through the winter months. These people did not wait till half-frozen feet compelled attention to the question of fuel, and then tear down the fence to supply their wants." Like other critical writings, this one, reflecting white bias, seriously questioned the Negro's work habits.[48]

At times Negroes, indeed, seemed wasteful and inefficient. Writers thus professed to see a great contrast between their work and that of the Italian, "so jealous of the use of every foot for which he pays rent that he will cultivate with a hoe places too small to be worked with a plough and derive a revenue from spots to which a Negro would not give a moment's thought. . . . I have seen them walk through their fields and search out every skipped place in every row and carefully put in seed, to secure a perfect stand. I have seen them make more cotton per acre than the Negro on the adjoining cut, gather it from two to four weeks earlier, and then put in the extra time earning money by picking in the Negro's field. . . . the frugality and thrift of the former offer a contrast to the latter's careless, spendthrift ways."[49]

[47] J. L. Coulter, "The Influence of Immigration on Agricultural Development," *Annals*, American Academy of Political and Social Science, Vol. XXXIII (January–June, 1909), 154.

[48] Stone, "The Italian Cotton Grower: The Negro's Problem," *South Atlantic Quarterly*, Vol. IV (January, 1905), 42–47.

[49] J. F. Carr, "The Italian in the United States," *World's Work*, Vol. VIII (October, 1904), 5402.

About this Italian capacity for labor another observer wrote in 1904: "His entire family will often work all day long, and far into the night. He can live on what any other man, except a Chinaman, would starve on; and his success is so general that there are few Italians who do not have a bank account, and send money regularly to Italy."[50]

In the aftermath of the Sunnyside colony, the Italians began other communities in Arkansas and Missouri. More important, a new leader arrived to minister to them. This was Father Pietro Bandini, a young Italian priest sent to America at the urging of the Bishop of Arkansas. Father Bandini energetically interested himself in the plight of his stranded countrymen. Assembling them together in a meeting, he told his new charges:

> I have promised God that I would save you, and save you I will. Where is the coward who would balk at the difficulties? Where is the materialist who will whimper if he must go without food now and then, or sleep, as our ancestors did, under the starry heavens? You are my flock, and I, your God-given shepherd, will lead you into the sheepfold. Follow me at once.[51]

Father Bandini led them away from Sunnyside and arranged for the survivors of that colony to buy land at Knobview (Montebello [Montevallo?]), Missouri.

But Father Bandini wanted some colonists to remain in Arkansas. In 1898, after some shrewd negotiation with the St. Louis and San Francisco Railroad, he obtained an option on nine hundred acres of Ozark land in the northwest corner of Arkansas, where that state touches Kansas and Oklahoma. The tract was at an elevation of fifteen hundred feet, six miles west of Springdale, where the railroad stopped. The railroad sold the immigrants this terrain for only one dollar per acre. They believed that its location along the railway would increase its value and settled on its rocky, brush-covered soil. The colonists cut logs from the near-by forests and built homes there. Father Bandini helped them to construct

50 John T. Faris, *The Romance of Forgotten Towns* (New York, 1924), 322.
51 Quoted in *ibid.*, 324.

a stone chapel, and he inspired Italy's Queen Margherita to send accessories for this church. Father Pietro, as he was now called by his flock, cared for a myriad of details. From Italy the priest imported seed, trees, flowers, tools, and even insect larvae to combat local pests.

Although the soil first seemed barren and unproductive, some of them recognized this grayish ground as similar to a certain type of terrain in their homeland. After a few years of difficulty Father Pietro's Italians were successful in dairying, grape-growing and fruit-raising. With their spiritual leader making the arrangements, fifty families thus established a community which they named Tontitown in honor of Enrico Tonti (Henri Tonty), symbolically called "Father of Arkansas." Bruno Roselli, an Italian journalist who wrote an article about Tontitown, was inspired by its appearance:

> Right and left of me was Italy. The houses were built tight and compact, with green shutters and red roofs. A crooked path, a coquettish pergola, a row of old kitchen jars made into flower pots, proclaimed the *Italianità* of the place where a drab and grubby existence was not thought to be an unavoidable element of farming life. The merry festoons of the vine, running from tree to tree and from end to end of the farms, reminded me of happy days of barefooted intimacy with the children of the *contadini*, pursuing a multitude of many-hued butterflies and dreams.[52]

To finance the purchase, at fifteen dollars per acre, of added land for the colony, its men worked in local zinc mines and in the near-by Oklahoma coal pits while their womenfolk tended house. Similar to sweathouse conditions in the large cities of the North, wages in these mines amounted to only one dollar for a twelve-hour day. Low pay and cold quarters were, however, not the only difficulties encountered by Italian colonists during the winter of 1899. A cyclone destroyed their first crop of strawberries and vegetables, forcing them to live off polenta, or corn meal, so familiar in the old country.

[52] "Settlers in Tontitown," *Interpreter*, Vol. VIII (January, 1929), 56–58; Industrial Commission, *Reports*, XV, 506.

Further difficulties came to Tontitown. Inhospitable and resentful neighbors set fire to a schoolhouse the Italians had built for their children. Infuriated, Father Pietro, a former Italian army officer, took a rifle in his hands and made a reasoned appeal to the nativist raiders. He also announced that sentinels would be placed on guard around the settlement. His defensive preparations made a strong local impact, insuring future friendly relations.[53]

Under this inspired mentor, Tontitown's Italians showed a willingness to improve their lot. Studying United States Department of Agriculture reports, they learned the latest methods of crop rotation and scientific agriculture in planting vineyards, fruit orchards and grain. Their onions, string beans, cow peas, and apples became known throughout the Ozarks. Tontitown grew into almost a model agricultural community. By 1912, three creameries, a broom factory, a brickyard, and a blacksmith and cobbler's shop further diversified the town's commerce. Before his death in 1917, Father Bandini went back to Italy where he attracted the attention of the pope, the prime minister and the queen mother, all of whom promised to help direct future emigration away from the old city-channels of settlement toward the western United States.[54]

Aside from a small pocket of settlements in Conway County, one other Italian colony in Arkansas deserves mention. This was St. Joseph, some seventy miles from Little Rock near Center Ridge, consisting of about 150 persons from Campobasso, Italy. Each family cultivated from 40 to 160 acres of land. The community, however, gained some notoriety when, on an inspection trip during 1912, the Italian ambassador to the United States discovered that there were seventeen-year-old husbands and thirteen-year-old wives living there. He learned, indeed, of a seventeen-year-old girl who was the mother of three children.[55] As early marriages followed the custom of the American South, this should not have disturbed the ambassador. But he wearied of complaints

[53] Anita Moore, "Safe Way to Get on the Soil: The Work of Father Bandini at Tontitown," *World's Work*, Vol. XXIV (June, 1912), 215–19.

[54] Des Planches, *Attraverso* 213, 253–56.

[55] Brandfon, "The End of Immigration to the Cotton Fields," *Mississippi Valley Historical Review*, Vol. L (March, 1964), 604–605.

by Italian colonists throughout the South. At Marathon, Mississippi, the ambassador encountered an irate crowd that bemoaned the high prices they paid for food and other supplies at company stores. Work was hard to find, he was also told, and the heat, disease, and impure water had grown unbearable. He advised these malcontents to move elsewhere.

In Arkansas, although Italian immigrants became well known, even by 1910 there were less than two thousand of them in the state. Yet, compared with other foreign groups, the Italians constituted a measurable minority. Particularly at Tontitown they flavored the life of one of America's most inward-looking non-cosmopolitan states.

The Italian government did what it could to discourage immigration into the deep South. In 1905 a widespread yellow fever epidemic led Italian authorities to route departing immigrants toward Texas. Better wages up north and the desire of immigrants to return to Italy hastened the end of colonization into the Black Belt. Once large industrial plantation units, such as those run by Crittenden and Percy, came into operation, tenants, immigrant or non-immigrant, found it more difficult to become landowners.

After 1906 one does not hear of many more attempts to attract Italian colonists into the American South. That year Scottish backers of a Deltic Investment Company, however, assigned fourteen 200-acre plots in Louisiana to Italian immigrants. This was in the nature of an agricultural experiment. During the next year that company sponsored a recruiting trip to Italy by the editor of the Memphis Italian newspaper, *Corriere Italiano*. The company hoped to attract fifty Italian families, offering prospective migrants $150 toward their sea fare to New Orleans, as well as housing upon arrival. The experiment, however, failed after the expenditure of some $15,000. This, again, illustrated the South's lack of attraction for immigrants. The Scots themselves, while enterprising and persistent, were to experience great difficulty in protecting plantation investments.[56]

[56] W. Turrentine Jackson, *The Enterprising Scot; Investors in the American West After 1873* (Edinburgh, 1968), 275.

The new restrictions of anticontract labor laws (particularly the Foran Anti-Contract Labor Act of 1885), further curtailed southern immigration. After experiencing the 1907 ravages of the boll weevil epidemic, numerous discouraged immigrants surrendered their cotton fields to Negroes.

The inauguration of direct steamship service between Naples and New Orleans had dramatized the westward transcontinental connection via the Southern Pacific Railroad to California. From the early 1900's onward through the period of the Immigration Act of 1924, Italians down south were diverted elsewhere—but not before encountering difficulties that went beyond the discomforts of which they had complained to their ambassador. Discrimination was about to descend upon these immigrants in other parts of the United States as well.

Acculturative Problems

IV

ACCUSATIONS: *Discrimination and Criminality*

THE ITALIANS, whether in the East or in the West, encountered nativist discrimination. An immigrant slogan of the day ran, "America beckons, but Americans repel." While it can be argued that intolerance was less pronounced in the West, no one could claim that it was less rampant in the South—even west of the Mississippi. Not only did the natives openly hurl insults at foreigners, but immigrants there seemed frequently at the mercy of human forces beyond their control. In a state like Arkansas or Louisiana, exploitation of foreign laborers was common. In the 1890's, cotton mills paid commissions of twenty-five dollars for each immigrant family brought into a company town. Wages of fifty cents were paid a mother or her children for an entire day's work. On occasion workers could earn only fifteen cents for as much as thirteen hours of backbreaking labor under unhygienic conditions. In an atmosphere of debased labor, large and small cotton-growers alike were guilty of abuses against workers. One of the most important planters in the South, the already mentioned O.B. Crittenden, was once arrested for mistreating his Italian cotton-pickers.[1]

The ignorant whites and Negroes with whom Italians had to compete proved to be no more tolerant toward the newcomers than did southern employers. Field hands down south hated the idea of an Italian family working from sunup to sundown—even

[1] Preziosi, *Gli Italiani*, 96–99.

into the night, when the moon lighted up the Arkansas and Louisiana landscape. Discrimination did not always originate with native Americans. The age-old discriminatory padrone system of work control actually originated in the Mediterranean world. It resembled the seventeenth-century practice of indentured servitude that had brought many Americans to the eastern tidewater. Carl Wittke has likened the padrone system to feudal serfdom, a phenomenon with a non-American connotation, unlike respectable—because American—indentured servitude.

Although there was less practice of the padrone system west of the Mississippi than in the eastern United States, it was sometimes used at Omaha, Kansas City, St. Louis and Denver to recruit mining, railroading, and agricultural labor. The padrone usually negotiated a single contract for the men working under him. In 1864, in part because of the shortage of miners during the Civil War, and because the demand for cheap labor remained strong, Congress passed an act to encourage the immigration of laborers. Although it was rescinded four years later, there was no formal enforceable prohibition against the search for labor in foreign countries. For decades, agents regularly sent manpower, under contract, to the United States. Until 1885, when the importation of contract laborers was definitely ended by law, the quest for "captive workers" in Europe had vigorously continued. Charlotte Erickson suggests that large numbers of immigrants did not respond to this recruitment; yet every attempt was made to get them to come under contract.

Contractors, taking advantage of widespread illiteracy, particularly in southern Italy, sent laborers to the American West under exploitative conditions. These folk were often former peasants accustomed to meager fare and hard work. Of those who came from northern Italy, only 11.4 per cent were illiterate, compared to the 57.3 per cent illiteracy rate for Italian southerners.[2] These taller, fair-haired northern people were those who gave the padrone the most trouble, because they demanded higher wages and better

2 This was one reason why the United States Immigration Commission kept separate statistics for North and South Italians.

90

working conditions. Both northern and southern Italians, however, were paid less than native Americans when herded about in gangs by *padroni*.

Oscar Handlin pictures the padrone as "shielding the laborer against the excesses of employers."[3] More often, the padrone acted as the representative of the contractor in handling the most gullible and ignorant immigrants. In collusion with contractors, he drew up self-serving contracts binding them to a working period of from one to seven years; he furnished transportation to their place of work; he was the middleman who represented the workers to the employer and the employer to the workers. Consequently, his opportunities for corruption were unusual. The buzzard-like padrone hired the immigrant (who frequently arrived in America without his family) at a fixed rate and expected to profit from whatever wage he obtained for him above that rate. In many cases he paid immigrants what he saw fit. He not only demanded commissions from both laborers and employers but made money out of furnishing them food; he could even exact a commission from wages which workers sent back to Europe; and he might also finagle a cut out of the steamship passage of those returning homeward.

Strong critics of the padrone system eventually excoriated its practices: "There are people who would like to keep him [the Italian] out of this country; it would be more reasonable to keep out the contractor." The writer believed it was the contractors who were "systematic law-breakers," whereas a laborer was "usually faithful to the letter of his engagement, even when he feels wronged or deceived." As to the contractor, he frequently repudiated "the terms of the contract either as to wages, or hours of labor, or the very nature of the work. Contractors have been known to promise employment, to pocket their fees, and then to lead the men to lonely places and abandon them." A parallel source of complaint concerned working conditions: "At sunset the work ceases and the men retire to a shanty, very much like the steerage of a third-class emigrant ship." Immigrants were some-

[3] Handlin, *Uprooted*, 29.

times packed together in unclean and narrow berths. "The shanty where the Chicago National Gas-Pipe Company huddled its Italian workmen, near Logansport, Ind., was blown down by a wind-storm and several men were killed. Neither the number nor the names of the dead were known, as Italian laborers are designated only by figures." The brutality of padrones was a frequent source of complaint: "The contractor is a strongly-built, powerful man; he has acquired the habit of command, is well armed, protected by the authorities, supported by such of his employees as he chooses to favor, and, sad to say, by the people, who are hostile to the laborers." Certain contractors actually armed their guards with Winchester rifles to prevent laborers from running away. Like a government, they could fine workers or beat and punish them for resistance to authority. On Sunday contractors could keep them at work and one was known to tax his men in order to make birthday presents to his wife. "A feudal lord would not have expected more from his vassals."[4]

The swelling number of immigrants, however, gave them a group security which made the padrone's position increasingly untenable. Living with their own kind reinforced mutual courage. Once the foreigner learned that contracts signed in Europe were unenforceable in American courts, they tore up these contemptible documents, to which they had agreed only in order to reach the New World. Even if the immigrant had signed a contract after landing in the United States, he could always run away to the West, especially when labor conditions grew unendurable. Opposition by the Italian government also helped to break down the controversial system which flourished in the decade 1870–80. To sidestep the immigrant's reliance upon *padroni* and other conniving labor brokers, Italian officials set up an immigration bureau that helped speed them on their way better informed.[5]

After 1885, the padrone, as noted, legally lost his ability to exact forced tribute from immigrants or to prey upon his countrymen.

[4] S. Merlino, "Italian Immigrants and Their Enslavement," *The Forum*, Vol. XV (April, 1893), 183–90.

[5] Industrial Commission, *Reports*, XV, lxxxiv.

Ultimately the padrone was relied upon as an employment broker by only the most illiterate immigrants. After an increasing number of workers joined labor unions, this freed them even more from the padrone. A survey of Italian workmen in Chicago in 1896 showed that they worked for *padroni* an average of only eleven weeks and four days after reaching America. If the padrone was an honest labor broker, he could, of course, save the immigrant from a variety of pitfalls; but most *padroni* were primarily engaged in enriching themselves.[6]

Although immigrants eventually were freed of the padrone system, yet another device existed by which employers could bilk them. This was the company store, or commissary, located close to the foreigner's place of work. Debt-ridden immigrants were forced to use the contractor's "pluck-me store," where laborers sometimes even had to purchase "the straw on which they sleep." Prices for food staples ran as high as 100 per cent above the cost of the goods to the seller, with the quality as bad as the price was high. About it D'Angelo wrote:

> The commissary system prevails throughout this country. In its most extreme workings it results in perpetual peonage of the unlucky laborers who get caught. Usually the lure is high wages and free transportation to some distant locality. My own uncle, Giuseppe d'Angelo, was attracted to a place in Florida where he was held eight months before he was able to effect an escape. The food they gave him was vile and the living conditions were unspeakable. The laborers—white-men—were guarded by ferocious Negroes with guns which they used at the least excuse. And this in free America. No wages are paid, and the men are told that, instead of expecting any, they themselves are in debt to the company.[7]

D'Angelo went on to give a superior description of bookkeeping techniques employed in a company store run for the immigrant traffic: "Each man has a small book in which are marked the prices of the objects he buys. The Commissary man also keeps a

[6] Carr, "The Italian in the United States," *World's Work*, Vol. VIII (October, 1904) 5402.

[7] D'Angelo, *Son of Italy*, III.

book. And it is his book that counts, not the laborer's. If you try to save money and spend very little you will find when pay day comes that you are charged with as much debt as someone else who ate his fill."[8]

IT IS IRONICAL that foreigners are sometimes more intolerant of one another than their native-born "enemies." In America tension between immigrants themselves was common. As the legendary monopoly of Irish workmen and policemen was threatened by hordes of south Europeans, outbreaks among them mounted. Yet, out west there was less of the interforeign tension that plagued New York's German and Polish Jews or existed in the Pennsylvania mines, where riots among the Hungarians, Swedes, Italians, and Irish frequently broke out.

Among the Italians themselves the age-old tension between North and South never quite disappeared, in the New World or in the old country. The historical differences between northern and southern Italy are striking. Whereas the Italian North has evolved within the European cultural mainstream, southern Italy remains a neglected and backward area. Centuries of misery shaped the life of its immigrants, while those from North Italy enjoyed a more industrialized, cosmopolitan environment that boasted closer contacts with Switzerland, France, and Germany.

Progressive North Italians, who had provided much of the leadership during Italy's national unification, or *Risorgimento*, traditionally assumed an attitude of superiority toward southern Italians. Many Piedmontese, Lombards, and Venetians, furthermore, arrived in the United States before the Calabrians, Neapolitans, or Sicilians. At first, indeed, Italian immigration to the United States came mostly from the North. By 1876, northern Italy had sent 85 per cent of the country's annual immigration abroad. Added to a serious agricultural slump in the 1880's, demographic, economic, and psychological factors modified the traditional South Italian's love of homeland, fear of travel, and ties to a patriarchal and agricultural way of life. Southern Italy increas-

[8] *Ibid.*, 112.

ingly became an exploited colony of its northern industrial complex. This tended to intensify emigration out of the Italian South. From Sicily, the Abruzzi, Calabria, and Campania came a new flood into the United States.[9]

North Italians resented the fact that the swarthier, short-statured southerners so often represented the "typical Italian" in the American mind. They also disliked the inferior cultural impact that these southern folk, who came from economically depressed areas, made in America. The very North Italians who looked down their noses at the southerners were called "tight" and "mean" by the former.

> The men of the North were pictured somewhat in the same stereotype as the American Yankee, as more shrewd and enterprising, cold in nature, and a little too concerned with money, but, nevertheless, the source of monumental movement and progress. The men of the South were viewed as more genial and easygoing, more in love with life and with nature, in disposition good natured and sunny. The United States Immigration Commission used to keep separate figures for North and South Italians, although they made no such divisions in the case of people from any other country.[10]

With good cause the South Italians frequently resented the distinction made between them and their northern compatriots. Yet, the fact that it persisted suggests some basis for making such a distinction.

It was generally believed that North Italians possessed a higher standard of education than those from the South. In the period from 1899 to 1910, government reports indicate that three times as many North Italians as South Italians were professionally trained persons. As noted, less than 12 per cent were illiterate, as compared to more than half of those from the South who arrived in the United States. The North Italians, who had perhaps twice

---

[9] From 1876 to 1900 northern Italy provided more than two-thirds of the total immigration to the United States, a ratio that shifted markedly after the turn of the century. See M. R. Davie, *World Immigration, With Special Reference to the United States*, 111; and Mack Smith, *Italy, a Modern History*, 241.

[10] Pisani, *The Italian in America*, 50–51.

as much money upon arrival, seemed more aggressive about finding a place in the sun—particularly the western sun. They generally met easier acceptance, in part because of their literacy. The
Italian who could not read or write seems to have been an exception in the West. In 1901, one study notes, 63.14 per cent of the
Italians who reached California were from northern Italy. By
1904, some 73 per cent of them came from the Italian North.
Whereas only 2 per cent of the Italians who went to the western
states in 1901 were South Italians, 88 per cent of those who
reached the North Atlantic states that year were from the Italian
South. In 1903 the figure for southerners is 86 per cent versus 1
per cent.[11]

In her provocative analysis of antiforeign sentiment in New
England, Barbara Miller Solomon points out the distinction
which immigration restrictionists made between North and South
Italians. Even intellectual leaders like William Dean Howells dif-
ferentiated between Italians born in the North and in the South.
The first was said to have an appealing "lightness of temper." The
second was spoken of as only a "half-civilized stock," although it
sometimes produced "real artists and men of genius." Henry
Cabot Lodge, Boston Brahmin that he was, excepted from his
criticism the northern, or "Teutonic," Italian, who had Germanic
blood and belonged "to a people of Western civilization." Other
racially minded restrictionists found the South Italian too conservative and slow to change the ways of his forefathers. Forgetful
of the Visconti and Sforza families of northern Italy, Americans
thought of the southerner as more violent, addicted to stiletto and
revolver, quarrelsome, feuding, and even murderous. As long as
the South Italian remained within his quaint but colorful peasant
environment, he was believed capable of escaping pauperism and
criminality, but let him come to the slums of America and, according to racists, he soon fell prey to debased behavior.[12]

[11] *Abstracts of the Reports of the Immigration Commission*, 64 Cong., 3 Sess.
Sen. Doc. 747, I, 97. See G. E. di Palma Castiglione, "Italian Immigration into
the United States," *American Journal of Sociology*, Vol. XI (September, 1905),
196.
[12] Barbara Miller Solomon, *Ancestors and Immigrants* . . . , 164, 166–67.

If the North Italian met less discrimination, it was because he could pass himself off as less different from native Americans than his compatriot from southern Italy. "Differentness," particularly in the use of language, was at the heart of intolerance in America, east or west. There was hardly anything more pathetic than an Italian, northern or southern, who could not speak, read, or write the English language. Because English was difficult to learn, uneducated immigrants transformed words into their own equivalent, as one writer observed:

> *Bum* has an Italian plural, *bummi*. *Rag, bar, car* become *raggo, barro, carro*. *Job, basket, shop,* and *mortar* are changed to *jobba, basketta, shoppa,* and *mata*; *grocery* to *grosseria,* and *customer* to *cos-tu-me*. *Business* is hardly recognizable as *bi-zi-ne*; and no one could guess that *Bokeen, stracinosa, sediolo, rai-ro-de,* and *elettricosa* stand for *Hoboken, station house, City Hall, railroad,* and *electric cars*.[13]

H. L. Mencken, whose *American Language* discusses this transposition of words, points out that the "new language" which immigrants created was of real value to them. Many spoke only local dialects, some mutually unintelligible except by those from the same region who flocked together. Their "American-Italian" jargon, furthermore, described terms unfamiliar in the homeland. Among these were *visco* for whisky, *ghenga* for gang, *loffari* for loafers, *blacco enze* for blackhand, *grinoni* for greenhorns, *ruffo* for roof, and *gliarda* for yard. The word fight they changed into such forms as *faitare, faiti, faitato, faitava, faito,* and *faitasse*. The Italians of the West used *ranchio* for ranch, a word seldom heard in the East. "You bet" became *you betcha*; a son-of-a-gun was called a *sanemagogna*; job was transformed into *giobba,* along with lynch into *linciare*. The latter term was one which no immigrant cared to utter loosely.

Discrimination was deeply rooted. Nativists not only feared that the flood of cheap labor into the United States would lower the standard of living; they also dreaded the foreign power of the

---

[13] Carr, "The Italian in the United States," *World's Work*, Vol. VIII (October 1904), 5399.

Catholic Church—to which Italians belonged in great numbers. Both the church and immigration seemed to threaten the established order, especially in the large eastern cities. There, corrupt political machines lived off the foreign vote. Against the evils which "patriotic" nativists saw in the inundation of immigrants, they erected a powerful psychological barrier designed to influence large segments of the population. The American Protective League, an anti-Catholic organization of the 1890's, used existing political parties to foment distrust of immigrants in the Middle West. Attempts were made by its adherents to prevent the sale of property to south Europeans. A.P.L. newspapers bannered their "patriotic" hate doctrines from Galesburg, Illinois, to Denver, Colorado.[14]

Reuben Gold Thwaites, a chronicler who ventured into the Ohio Valley at the turn of the century, observed an example of such discrimination in the Middle West. He encountered a "tall, raw-boned, loose-jointed young man, with a dirty, buttonless flannel shirt which revealed a hairy breast." This individual, unemployed as a result of the influx of foreigners into local coal mines, was vociferously anti-immigrant: "I tell ye, sir, the Italians and Hungarians is spoil'n' this yere country fur white men; 'n' I do'n see no prospect for hits be'n' better till they get shoved out uv't!" Thwaites, however, felt that this critic was projecting other anxieties onto foreigners in general and wrote: "What new fortune will befall my friend when he gets the Italians and Hungarians 'shoved out,' and 'things pick up a bit,' I cannot conceive."[15]

While one can point out that there was less discrimination against foreigners out west, one should not close his eyes to the fact that, befuddled as the immigrants often were, they were subjected to indignities. Sometimes they would be fleeced of their worldly possessions, even by fellow countrymen. Hotelkeepers, stationmasters, cabbies, baggage handlers and restaurant owners

[14] Discussions of political nativism are in Ray Allen Billington, *The Protestant Crusade, 1800–1860*; Theodore Maynard, *The Story of American Catholicism* (New York, 1941); and Donald L. Kinzer, *An Episode in Anti-Catholicism: The American Protective Association* (Seattle, 1963), 91.

[15] Thwaites, *On the Storied Ohio* (Chicago, 1903), 69.

charged travelers exorbitant prices. People would give them false directions, cheating them out of precious savings. An immigrant traveling through a terminal city like Chicago, St. Louis, or Omaha was well-advised to stay away from saloons, billiard parlors, or houses of ill repute; scoundrels of every description lay in wait for such prey. Newcomers were wise to head the suggestion of more experienced migrants that, before continuing westward, they rest for a few days in a tavern—not allowing strangers to rush them into the long and confusing journey.

Out of the predicament faced by these newcomers, immigrant mutual aid societies and traveler's-aid groups were formed in many localities.[16] To prorate the risks of immigrant illness or to share their expenses of death, the Italian government partly subsidized such protective organizations as the Italian Typographical Union, the Rapallo Lawyers' Association, and the Italian Athletic League. For immigrants, these associations also evoked elements of the nostalgic—uniting them and making them conscious of similarity of background. If immigrants had not encountered discrimination, they would never have founded or joined such groups.

There can be no denying that through the period when immigrants were gaining a foothold on the land of their adoption, vilification continued to be aimed at the immigrant from southern Europe in particular. The western states, which had been most lenient in permitting aliens the right to vote immediately after declaring their intent to become citizens, began to withdraw such privileges after 1875. The Dakotas were the last states whose constitutions granted aliens, in 1899, full rights of suffrage. By the turn of the century only half of those states that had extended the privilege retained it. For some nativists "Europe, according to sanctified American myth, was a center of corruption; the conflicts of class which had marked its history were now appearing on American grounds; therefore the immigrant must be the carrier of the dreaded contagion."[17]

[16] Charlotte Erickson, *American Industry and the European Immigrant, 1860–1885*, 86, 104.
[17] Cushing Strout, *The American Image of the Old World*, 110; Kinzer, *Episode*, 15.

The racist assumptions of such exclusionists as the Boston Anti-Immigration League were even imbibed by historians of the nineteenth century, as well as by the general public. Both read the anti-immigrant diatribes of the daily press. The Anglo-Saxon cult of superiority flavored the writings of at least two major western chroniclers. The American frontier's most important interpreter, Frederick Jackson Turner, showed occasional ethnic prejudices, as did West Coast historian Hubert Howe Bancroft, whose writings depicted a great Aryan march to the Pacific coast. Neither Turner nor Bancroft knew quite how to depict the immigrant story in their writings. A case might have been made by more sympathetic interpreters that blended the immigrants' search for opportunity on the frontier with abandonment of Europe's feudal background. Asiatic authority Owen Lattimore, who has studied frontiers in other parts of the world, believes that Turner could not believe that it was the immigrants' leaving the European environment of special class privilege—rather than the frontier itself—that explains his democratization in the West. The immigrant himself, Lattimore believes, demolished ideas about aristocracy and its hereditary landed nations. These concepts apparently never occurred to either Bancroft or Turner.[18]

Public discrimination against south and east European immigrants waxed and waned. With a rebirth of restrictionist doctrines and racism after the Spanish-American War, social pressures on non–English-speaking foreigners generally grew stronger. What Richard Hofstadter calls a "mystique" of white Anglo-Saxonism swept the country. Its powerful grip on the nation continued into the 1920's. Obsession with the idea of inferior ("old-stock" immigrants) versus superior "races" led even educated Americans to elevate Teutonic peoples over the "new immigrants," often of darker complexion.[19]

Yet, occasional voices spoke out against intolerance. As early

[18] Owen Lattimore, *Studies in Frontier History, Collected Papers, 1928–1958* (London, 1962), 489–90; Gilman M. Ostrander, "Turner and the Germ Theory," *Agricultural History*, Vol. XXXII (October, 1958), 258–61.

[19] Richard Hofstadter, *Social Darwinism in American Thought*, 172.

as 1849, Melville's *Redburn* called for an America that would be not merely a "narrow tribe of men," but whose "blood is as the flood of the Amazon, made up of a thousand noble currents all pouring into one." Much later Theodore Roosevelt championed the immigrant "melting-pot" concept, although with Nordic overtones. His was still a generation in which the superiority of Aryans was celebrated, but which at times defended immigration as an enriching national policy. This defense appeared in popular magazines before and after the turn of the century: "This Italian, this Slovak, this Jew is different from the Yankee. Suppose he does not become a Yankee all at once? Is that any ground for contempt or fear of him? Is not a character that is a bit firmer than wax worthy of respect?"[20]

Encouraged by fluctuations in public mood, the Italians looked forward to acceptance by American society. They tried to place quickly behind them the years of trial and privation, but some discrimination, especially in the American South, was bound to continue. In Louisiana the Italians unwittingly got in the way of white demagogy. Unschooled in the racial prejudices of the South, they awkwardly interfered in various attempts to hold down Negroes. Themselves a minority group, they were attracted to southern Populism in the 1890's. The Populists proposed "that both whites and Negroes look with less prejudice at their mutual problem of making a living."[21]

Coming so soon after the South's Reconstruction era, the conduct of Louisiana's Italians did not please white supremacists. At a time when the Knights of the White Camellia and the White League flourished, Italians (like most other foreigners) remained outside the pale. Unassimilated into southern culture, they had no reason to look back with nostalgia upon the ante bellum past and seemed impervious to anti-Negro feeling. Indeed, when the Populists threatened southern Democrats, the Italians joined the

[20] "The Making of Americans," *Outlook*, Vol. LXXIV (August 22, 1903), 971.

[21] George E. Cunningham, "The Italian, a Hindrance to White Solidarity in Louisiana . . ." *Journal of Negro History*, Vol. L (January, 1965), 25.

former in various parades against anti-Negro legislation. In opposing anti-Negro discrimination, the Italians obstructed the political objectives of southern Democrats who wanted "to rally all whites around the common cause of white supremacy."[22] The Italian bloc openly opposed the discrimination program of the Choctaw Club, New Orleans' political machine. This aroused the animosity of the city's newspapers, particularly the *Times-Democrat*. The Italians' ignorance of the depth of southern racial feeling helped bring on mob violence against them in 1891.

Discrimination was frequently entwined with accusations of criminality. The racial tension of the day turned public attention on the weaknesses of foreign minorities, damaging their reputations and making them all subject to suspicion. In the 1890's, New Orleans became a center of difficulty for Italians. Its *Daily Picayune*, however, likened the Gulf of Mexico to another Mediterranean Sea, which furnished "every possible facility for their maritime operations in fish and fruits."[23] The Italians had become economically important, and the *Daily Picayune* congratulated them for their progress from fruit-peddlers on the city's streets to controllers of much of the growing fruit trade with Latin America. This rapid rise in economic status would lead to trouble. A foreign outbreak at New Orleans, in fact, assumed the proportions of an international episode. In 1890 a series of Sicilian crimes, partly in the nature of vendettas, occurred. They were due primarily to the interference in the local fruit trade of various *capi mafiosi*, or Mafia chieftains, of the secret Black Hand (*Mano Nera*) society. Among these avaricious Sicilians were Antonio and Carlo Matranga, originally from Palermo, who allegedly levied tribute on every banana freighter that came into the harbor. Various Italian competitors who tried to muscle into this lucrative traffic were dumped into canals with their throats cut, or found virtually decapitated. Others became the victims of bombs, shotguns, and daggers.

Although a number of Mafia suspects were tried for these

[22] *Ibid.*, 26.
[23] New Orleans *Times-Democrat*, November 12, 1890.

crimes, none were convicted. This led the public to believe that bribery had impeded the course of justice. Then came an even greater shock. On March 15, 1890, while investigating such criminal charges, New Orleans Chief of Police David Hennessy was murdered. This followed upon disclosures of complicity by two rival Sicilian dock-working gangs. Yet none of the witnesses could identify the assassins, although more than forty Italians were arrested the day Hennessy died. The New Orleans *Times-Picayune* reported that they "were as dumb as clams."[24] Suddenly the timidity of the law enraged public opinion. In frontier vigilante fashion a New Orleans mob took justice into its own hands.

Edgar H. Farrar, a prominent white supremacist, headed a "Committee of Fifty" to "suppress the Mafia" and to hunt out Hennessy's assassins. Nine suspects were brought to trial. On March 12, 1891, six of these were acquitted, and a mistrial was declared for the other three. The *Times-Picayune* was indignant, inviting "all good citizens" to a mass meeting "to take steps to remedy the failure of justice in the Hennessy Case." Its readers were exhorted to "come prepared for action," and the newspaper published a list of prominent Louisianans who endorsed its call to duty. In the opinion of the *Times-Picayune* there was no doubt that the Sicilians then cowering in the city jail were linked to criminal elements. In this instance, a lynching was virtually advertised beforehand in the New Orleans press.

On March 15, 1891, one year after Police Chief Hennessy's murder, a mob seized eleven of these unsuspecting Sicilians and hanged them. Included were the nine who had been tried and two others who had not. The *Times-Picayune* congratulated the mob, moralizing that "desperate diseases require desperate measures." The paper reported proudly that when the mob left the parish prison eight culprits lay dead on its blood-stained floors and "behind the crumbling walls of the gloomy old prison another lay dying on a stretcher near where he had been shot."[25] The police

24 *Ibid.*, October 16, 17, 19, 20, and 21, 1890.
25 *Ibid.*, March 4, 8, 10, 14, 15, 1891.

ultimately arrested more than one hundred Italians in an anti-foreign delirium that swept New Orleans.[26]

When news of this event reached Italy, national indignation reigned. The Italian government directed its minister to the United States, Marchese Rudini, to demand that the lynchers be punished and that an indemnity be paid. American Secretary of State James G. Blaine explained that the lynchings had received public approbation in New Orleans, including the approval of many law-abiding Italians. Blaine pointed out to the Italian government that it was, therefore, difficult to achieve restitution and that indemnification was primarily a matter of state jurisdiction. Nevertheless, President Benjamin Harrison apologized, calling the affair "an offense against law and humanity." As to the Mafia, obviously involved, it protected its own members by hiring the services of Thomas J. Semmes, one of the country's most spectacular criminal defense attorneys.

After a sharp exchange of diplomatic notes, during which the Italian government charged that the United States had avoided its responsibility to protect foreign nationals, Italy withdrew her minister at Washington. Then it was discovered that eight of the eleven jail inmates who had been killed were naturalized Americans. After urging by President Harrison, Congress voted twenty-five thousand dollars to be distributed among the survivors of the other three non-American dead. Italy then restored diplomatic relations. In this case the presence of Italy's sons in the mid–United States led to an incident of such intensity that it hindered relations between the two countries. The incident also illustrated that xenophobia was not yet dead.

There was yet another lynching of Italians in the town of Hahn-

[26] On this episode see Thomas A. Bailey, *A Diplomatic History of the American People* (New York, 1942), 449–52; John E. Coxe, "The New Orleans Mafia Incident," *Louisiana Historical Quarterly*, Vol. XX (October, 1937), 1067–1110; J. A. Karlin, "The Italo-American Incident of 1891 and the Road to Reunion," *Journal of Southern History*, Vol. VIII (May, 1942), 242–46. See also Lord, *Italian in America*, 128; Frederic Sondern, Jr., *Brotherhood of Evil, the Mafia*, 58–62; J. S. Kendall, "Who Killa de Chief?" *Louisiana Historical Review*, Vol. XXII (January, 1939), 492.

ville, St. Charles Parish, Louisiana, on August 9, 1896. Once again the United States government paid an indemnity. The sum of six thousand dollars went to the survivors of three victims, described as subjects of Italy's King Humbert.[27]

Whenever the Italian government learned of discrimination against its nationals, as in still another lynching of five Italians at Tallulah, Louisiana, in 1899, it tried to discourage emigration. Unable, however, to slow down this flow abroad, Italy accepted the fact that America remained a safety valve, even an escape hatch, for its surplus population. Ultimately the Italian government shifted its attention toward helping emigrants to achieve acculturation in a new environment by establishing a general emigration office whose branches reported news of latest conditions in the New World. The government also sought to reduce swindling and mistreatment of its emigrants by stipulating that no one could recruit or sell them steamship tickets without a license. Agents had to deposit as much as one thousand dollars security and sign an agreement to protect immigrants from exploitation. The Italian government gave the Society for Italian Immigrants, located in New York City, thousands of dollars and instructed its consulates in the United States to offer immigrants their good offices.[28]

The New Orleans lynchings encouraged charges that the Mafia, described as a sinister and secret "international terrorist organization," was behind much criminal activity in the United States. Exaggerated accounts of Mafia power resulted from the failure of immigrants to report crimes in their midst. They concealed these crimes primarily because they feared arrest. Although the Mafia was responsible for much organized crime, one writer points out how, in the late nineteenth century, "the organization in its Americanized form was just as unknown in Italy as Tong Warfare of the American type was in China."[29] The very term "Black Hand" originated in America. In Sicily the Mafia, or Onorata Società,

[27] Cunningham, "The Italian, a Hindrance to White Solidarity in Louisiana, 1890–1898," *Journal of Negro History*, Vol. L (January, 1965), 31–32.

[28] Pisani, *Italian in America*, 50–51.

[29] R. A. Schermerhorn, *These Our People: Minorities in American Culture*, 250.

was once a regulatory organization—designed to punish, in vigilante fashion, criminals escaped from the law. In the United States the organization was corrupted by second-generation criminals reared in the slums of the eastern cities. Luigi Barzini writes: "The theory of an international Mafia with headquarters in Sicily and branches in the United States is comforting and plausible. It helps explain mysterious events, accounts for strange loyalties and alliances, and sometimes justifies the impotence of the police."[30] But these suppositions are supported more by folklore and reputation than by evidence.

Perplexing is the fact that the Mafia as a formal organization does not exist. There are no Mafia headquarters, no Mafia offices. The Mafia has no written statutes, no lists of members, no fixed rules. The question of who becames a Mafia leader is an obscure matter of family prestige, influenced by personality and force, and never the result of balloting. The Mafia can be defined as a haphazard collection of men and groups, each working independently in local situations but co-operating with each other to control its interests in the economic life of an area.

There is, thus, not just one Mafia but instead an endless network of Mafias. There is an old Mafia and a new Mafia, a rural Mafia and an urban Mafia. Originally considered an "honorable society," the Mafia grew out of a deep distrust of foreign rule in Sicily, which lasted without a break for twenty-five centuries. This expresses itself today in the organization's obvious sullenness; Sicilians do not act like mainland Italians. Strong disrespect for government developed over the years into a sort of resistance movement against established law.

There are sharp differences between the old and new Mafia societies. The old Mafia was not originally a criminal organization. Despite murders and occasional violence, it was capable of restraint and even gallantry. The "best families" of the Sicilian provinces often headed up the old Mafia. The new Mafia is pure gangsterism.

[30] Luigi Barzini, Jr., "The Real Mafia," *Harper's Magazine*, Vol. CCVIII (June, 1954), 40.

Actually, crime had not been so rampant in Italy as in certain parts of the United States. In 1889 an American observer pointed out that Italian laws forbade the departure of criminals, or even persons accused of criminal activity, from Italy, and added: "I have now lived for over three years on the outskirts of Alassio, a town of six thousand inhabitants, about half way between Nice and Genoa. Theft here is rare, burglary unknown; so that we have slept for weeks with doors unlocked and even open. . . . A murder has not been known here for fifty years. . . . crimes produced by lust are almost unknown."[31] Yet the Mafia blackened the reputation of all Italians in America. Most of these deeply resented, indeed loathed, the ill-repute with which the Al Capones and Lucky Lucianos were to tar them. Honest and law-abiding immigrants considered the criminal syndicates a product of the American slums. Accusations of criminality against an entire nationality they thought unfair. The average American remained quite unaware that the incidence of criminal convictions among Italian immigrants in the United States long remained approximately the same as that for other foreign-language groups and was even less than that of native-born persons. Italian homicides, however, received heavy attention in the press. Somehow, southern Italians, especially, seemed more dramatic in committing gangland crimes, and these evoked the bugaboo of the avenging, bloodthirsty Italian. Because it was partly rooted in truth, nothing could erase this image.[32]

In the early years of this century the headlines in metropolitan newspapers frequently "trumpeted the tale of Italian blood lost incessantly: 'Caro stabs Piro . . . Cantania murdered . . . Ear Biting Crime . . . Rinaldo Kills Malvino . . . Gascani assaulted . . . Vendetta near Oak Street.' "[33] In 1912, the Italian ambassador to the United States, on an inspection tour of the American South, reported a lingering, indeed pervasive, prejudice, particularly against Sicilians, at New Orleans:

[31] Eugene Schuyler, "Italian Immigration into the United States," *Political Science Quarterly*, Vol. IV (September, 1889), 480–95.

[32] Schermerhorn, *These Our People*, 250.

[33] John Higham, *Strangers in the Land*, 160.

To hear these gentlemen, all our Sicilians are ostensibly affiliated with secret societies, all are ready to commit havoc because of hatred or a vendetta spirit. They would—furthermore—use any means, including firearms, stilettos, and even poison.[34]

Continued discrimination caused great resentment in Italy. A standard volume on America, written by Vito Garretto, complained that "this shameful discrimination" was designed to keep cheap labor out of the country. Garretto felt that a Celtic-Anglo-Germanic superiority complex was at work, directed against Latins, Slavs, and other minorities. For the Italians, whom he portrayed as hard working, and never "congenital alcoholics" like the Irish, to suffer such indignities was intolerable. Garretto advised Italian immigrants to migrate toward the American West instead of remaining, cramped and inhibited, in the murky air of America's eastern big cities. He believed that in such dank environs the children of immigrants were inevitably tempted away from the honest folkways of their forebears onto avenues of crime. In short, his book put the blame for the potential criminality of Italian-Americans on the United States environment itself. Another writer, Napoleone Colojanni, saw criminality not as a question of race but, rather, as linked with ignorance and lack of education.[35]

Nativism, mixed with the undeniable criminality of some immigrants, seriously damaged their acculturative progress. A coterie of Italian criminals, unwanted in Italy itself and flourishing in an atmosphere of lax law enforcement, helped to produce a stereotype which decent Italians sought to escape. How much this desire may have influenced some of them to forsake the soot of the cities for cleaner western vistas, forests, and plains is, of course, unmeasurable. Yet, the desire to lose themselves in a new environment must have helped immigrants decide to move westward. The ganglands in which criminals operated were then in the large

[34] Des Planches, *Attraverso*, 7.

[35] Vito Garretto, *Storia degli Stati Uniti nell'America del Nord, 1492–1914*, 440–41, 459; Colojanni, "Homicide and the Italians," *The Forum*, Vol. XXXI (March, 1901), 63–68.

cities; not until the first third of the twentieth century were accusations of Italian criminality heard in the cities of the West.

Flight from the unfavorable image of criminality, therefore, helped stimulate the westward migration of the Italians. One authority was sure that criminal Italians would never go to the American countryside and, consequently, violence among Italians would remain "largely the result of overcrowding and the close competition of city life."[36]

Most of the Italians who moved inland were not concerned with crime. Instead, a certain spontaneity moved them out of the East. Whether ditchdiggers, artisans, or farmers, they sought the promise of those words engraved on the base of the Statue of Liberty. In a desire to restore their "image," the Italians demonstrated remarkable resilience. About this quality John Horne Burns, an American of Boston Irish stock who was in Naples during World War II, observes: "Unlike the Irish who stayed hurt all their lives, the Italians had a bounce-back in them."[37]

[36] Meade, "Italian Immigration into the South," *South Atlantic Quarterly*, Vol. IV (July, 1905), 217–23.

[37] *The Gallery* (New York, 1947), 69.

V

"BE PATIENT WITH US": *The Italian on the Land*

ONE OF THE CLICHÉS about the Italian immigrant is that he was best suited to a big city environment. Although traditional *contadini* were not farmers in the sense of the word today, they came to America as town-dwelling farm-laborers. In many cases they had worked for absentee owners rather than as independent peasants, but their background was the soil. And a man's occupation tells the historian something of his views of society, of his home and circle of friends, of his aspirations, and of the sort of person he was. Immigrants who came from a life spent out-of-doors could not escape rural attitudes and viewpoints. If at times they seemed ill at ease, this was part of the ungainliness of farm folk throughout the world. The life they had known had been simple and uncomplicated. On the landed estates of their homeland, farm implements had been primitive, based upon the *"zappa,"* a wide mattock, and rude axes and plows inherited from Roman times. However difficult the peasant's life, however stubborn the land he tilled, Italian love of the soil was deep and pervading. Some immigrants had, of course, rejected the old farm society and its rural outlook. These could never be budged out of a city. After the turn of the century, one immigrant who felt himself bound to a city life recalled: "A very large proportion of the working classes are in communities from which they are not at liberty to move with ease." Yet, he noted: "The working class in the country lives and fares far better than any working class in any part of the world."[1]

Although some immigrants shunned farm labor after arriving in America, others would have worked the soil had they been able so to arrange their lives. A government immigration report evinces this depth of feeling for the soil:

> there is not an Italian cafone doing unskilled work on a railroad grading who, at the sight of an American farm, with a white-fenced and red-roofed house, with a revolving windmill, capacious stables and outhouses, with extensive fields where crops are growing and maturing, or of a pair of robust American horses behind a plow, or a well-filled cart of produce, or a herd of cows, sheep, or swine, or of a court well stocked with poultry, does not feel the nostalgia for his old calling and a strong attraction to the soil, which he would like to till again in that diversified and intensive way for which he is so famous. . . . He is often ignorant, however, of the laws governing the proprietorship of land, and he has no hint at all of the homestead law by which, after a few easy formalities, he could obtain 160 acres of government land at once.[2]

Unfortunately, statistics regarding the occupations of immigrants are infrequently complete. In particular, the occupational categories of the census are skimpy as to details about agricultural, as opposed to industrial, workers. Not until 1943 was there published an occupational breakdown even of the Thirteenth United States Census (1910). That study throws light, however, upon the large number of foreigners involved in agriculture. Of 10, 851,581 males (aged ten years and over) engaged in agriculture, forestry, and animal husbandry (1910), some 6,567,826 were of native parentage, while 1,323,166 were of foreign (but non-Oriental) parentage; 1,038,945 were foreign-born whites. The number of Italians among these millions of farmers of foreign background is difficult to discern. That there were more than is commonly supposed seems obvious.[3]

---

[1] Eli Ginzberg and Hyman Berman (eds.), *The American Worker in the Twentieth Century*, 90.

[2] Industrial Commission, *Reports*, XV, 496–97.

[3] Consult Alba M. Edwards (ed.), "Appendix B of Hitherto Unpublished Thirteenth Census Occupation Statistics," in *Sixteenth Census of the United States (1940), Comparative Occupation Statistics, 1870–1940,* 159.

"Out of rural Italy into urban America"[4] was a phrase that came to be applied to the Italians. Because Italians were infrequently engaged in farming, Americans came to believe them unfitted for agriculture. Yet, perhaps 80 per cent of the Italian immigrants came from a farm background. Of these no more than 20 per cent moved back into agriculture. On this score, the statistics conflict. One study estimates that "while 67 percent of all the laboring Italians of the United States were engaged in agriculture at home, only 6.60 percent were actually engaged in agriculture in this country."[5] Another study estimates that only some 15 per cent of the Italians who came to America became full-time farmers, although 85 per cent of Italy's immigrants listed "agriculture" as their major occupation before they left.[6]

Even in the big cities love of the soil persisted. Herbert Gans, in his *The Urban Villagers* (New York, 1962), called the Italians of Boston almost village-minded immigrants. Rudolph Vecoli, like Gans, found in his study of Chicago Italians that, although settled on the city blocks of that metropolis, former peasants congregated with immigrants from the same province or village. They excluded outsiders, who might be untrustworthy. Their emotional attachment to regional dialects, in fact, hindered assimilation in the large cities. Further to demonstrate their rurality, in New York they went out to the end of the subway lines in search of cheap land on which to raise vegetables and goats. There and elsewhere in the East, this quest for the near-rural endured for a surprisingly long time.

The attraction of the land and of a country environment was always strong in the Italian. The tug of old friends engaged in agriculture exerted a constant influence. With friend helping friend, immigrants frequently located among former neighbors from across the sea. Mutual reassurance was vital. Together, immi-

[4] Antonio Mangano, *Sons of Italy, a Social and Religious Study of the Italians in America*, 32, 60.

[5] Pecorini, "The Italian, an Agricultural Laborer," *Annals*, American Academy of Political and Social Science, Vol. XXXIII (January–June, 1909), 158.

[6] Nathan Glazer and Daniel P. Moynihan, *Beyond the Melting Pot, the Negroes, Puerto Ricans, Jews, Italians and Irish of New York City*, 187.

grants could work toward conquering the hardest handicaps. The first of these was financial. More immigrants might have gone into agriculture if they had not arrived after the federal government and the railroads had already dispensed large, cheap tracts of land. As a consequence, Italians resorted to finding bits and pieces of land discarded by others. Some of this property was located on the outskirts of cities. Run-down farms in need of refurbishing formed yet another source. Truck farming, the origins of which are usually little known, often began in this way. In such an environment it has persisted until today, when cities have gradually enveloped the countryside around them.

That it was good business for the American farming community to welcome the Italians into its midst is part of the message of a 1906 government report:

> Lately the *American Agriculturalist* published an article from one of its subscribers in Ohio, in which the writer says that if an American farmer wishes to grow rich, he must take . . . an Italian family on his farm. He describes the work of 'his' Italian family and compares it to that of a family of ants or bees. . . . It is useless to deny that the better class of Italians are living under the shadow which bad city conditions are casting. . . . This movement to the plow ought to be started by Italians and encouraged by the Americans friendly toward them, and by the Italian government, as the surest means of following and protecting Italians abroad.[7]

After the turn of the century Gustavo Tosti, Italian consul general in New York City, also observed that many Italians were better suited to agricultural life than to work in crowded cities. He strongly urged their dispersal throughout the United States. Yet he sensed the inherent difficulties in such a shift. "Our immigrants must leave the congested cities and seek a purer atmosphere in agricultural work," he counseled. He felt that a basic question was how to transform immigrants into small landowners. Some could find employment during only a few months of the year. While at harvest time there was much demand for labor, enforced idleness during other seasons drove them back to industrial cen-

[7] Industrial Commission, *Reports*, XV, 498–99.

ters. "The only way to get at the root of the question," the Consul General believed, was "to transform a large proportion of our immigrants into landowners or farmers."[8]

Some farm workers came from villages in the poorest parts of Italy—Calabria, the Abruzzi, Sicily—where a man could exist on five cents per day. His food might consist of polenta, macaroni, vegetables, bread, cheese, chestnuts, wine, and little or no meat. In America the immigrant would eat food in every way superior to his non-immigrant neighbors. Saving in other wants, he bought the best cuts of meat, large and well-baked loaves of bread, olive oil, sausages, and the finest cheeses. Statistics gathered in 1912 indicate that the Italians spent more for food than any other nationality earning less than $900 per year. This included native Americans.[9] About 1890, one immigrant reported: "You could get a four-hundred-pound hog for $4; then there was enough meat and lard to last the winter and well into spring. . . . If you went into a butcher shop and bought a few pounds of pork or beef, you got free of charge all the tripe and lungs you wanted. . . . you could step into a saloon, buy a glass of beer for a nickel, and eat your fill off the free counter."[10]

The foreigners' preoccupation with food provided only part of the unique color which their way of life generated. Their arrival in the West was acted out in scenes of indelible human interest. The vitality and energy with which they attacked the future was memorable. After unloading at some water-tank railway station, a host of children would jump off an immigrant train—followed by bales of bedding, old trunks, roped suitcases, boxes of clothing, bags of Italian bread, macaroni, salamies, and clanging bundles of cooking utensils. Sometimes a mother unloaded a baby carriage in the middle of a sandy vineyard or orchard, and occasionally even a heavy stove made its appearance at trackside.

Then there followed the job of getting settled on the land, all

[8] Gustavo Tosti, "Agricultural Possibilities of Italian Immigration," *Charities*, Vol. XII (May, 1904), 474.

[9] Isaac Hourwich, *Immigration and Labor*, 261.

[10] Ginzberg and Berman, *American Worker*, 41.

of which made it necessary for "the Italians to save their money piously." One account stated: "It is a rare rainy day that finds any Italian family penniless; but now the cry goes up that these newcomers do not spend enough and they lower the standard of living." At a time when this sort of criticism was frequently heard, apologists for the immigrant also pointed out: "A fat Italian or a drunken Italian is a comparatively rare sight."[11]

At first, the Italian transported his relatively simple methods of cultivation to the New World. A study of Italian farmers, centered in the 1890's, stated: "In scattering manure from wheelbarrows women and boys are seen using their bare hands." The same survey pointed out, however: "As soon as an Italian can save a sufficient amount of money he buys a horse. Until then he relies upon a wheelbarrow. . . . A goat is frequently the source of the milk supply. Nearly every Italian keeps a pig and chickens for his own use." The Italian's economy was everywhere to be seen, as the same report observed: "They [even] collect leaves from the public streets for bedding for their animals."[12] The Italian utilized every inch of ground. He crowded incredible activity into a small plot, which he at first rented. If his land included an orchard, the immigrant planted tomatoes, beans, or potatoes between its trees. He cultivated small vegetables between large vegetables and berries. By turning over fresh furrows of soil that had never seen the sun, he utilized ground for two or three crops. Green peas and onions or early cabbage and kale might be followed by sweet corn and tomatoes. The immigrant's front yard, ordinarily used by Americans for flowers and a lawn, might be planted with grapes, berries, and vegetables.[13]

But the Italian yearned most to be master of his own land and home. To possess the land was the real test of a man's worth. Any sacrifice was endurable to reach that goal. Frugal to a fault, the Italian discarded nothing. Emily Meade's Italian farm study re-

[11] Robbins, "Italian Today, American Tomorrow," *Outlook*, Vol. LXXX (June 10, 1905), 383.

[12] Emily Fogg Meade, "The Italian on the Land," *United States Bureau of Labor Reports*, 486.

[13] *Ibid.*, 487.

iterated the foreigner's sacrifices and privations: "When an Italian purchases wild lands he spends his leisure time grubbing it out and getting it ready for cultivation. . . . He pays for the digging of a cellar and for a pump and gives his note or notes, made negotiable by the signature of a freeholder, to the builder who puts up the house." Miss Meade described a first generation immigrant "who a few years ago had practically nothing" and who bought a farm for $1,500 which was covered with weeds and which was unprofitable. He cleared the land and paid off his mortgage from the first year's crop of berries alone. Later, out of further profits, he "purchased a farm of 20 acres on the main road for $700, and has erected one of the best houses of the vicinity, at a cost of $3,500, spending $1,100 of this amount for plumbing, which included a hot water heating apparatus, a well-equipped bathroom, and a steam pump for the house and barn."[14]

There were various ways in which a settler could obtain public land. A series of nineteen land laws, called pre-emption acts, were passed by Congress between 1801 and 1841. These made available up to 160 acres of public land to squatters over the age of twenty-one upon considerations of residence and improvements. In 1862 Congress legislated the Homestead Act in order to induce settlers to migrate into the trans-Mississippi West. This act provided that the head of a family could acquire a quarter section of land consisting of 160 acres, settle it, cultivate it for five years, and then acquire title to the land. But such a family head must be a citizen, or must have declared his intention to acquire citizenship. By 1890 the land made available under this act had been largely settled. In 1873, Congress had also passed the Timber Culture Act, the first of several laws designed to encourage preservation and utilization of forest lands. This act granted 160 acres of treeless lands to settlers who were encouraged to plant trees on them.

For immigrants the settlement even of public lands proved expensive, however. In the Dakotas, by the 1880's interest on money ran as high as 60 per cent a year. Although few city dwellers had the money needed to succeed as farmers, wages in frontier

[14] *Ibid.*, 502, 510.

regions remained higher than anywhere in Europe. In the four states from Kansas on the south to North Dakota on the north, furthermore, farm employment rose two-thirds in the decade from 1880 to 1890. In those years increasing numbers of hopeful immigrants moved westward.

Because of the immigrant's frugality, when he got "way out west," where there was frequently a surprising and appallingly low degree of self-sufficiency among farmers, he was at a real advantage. The Italian farm worker's reliance on himself alone stood in contrast to the dependency of neighbors upon supplies and equipment from town, thereby draining off precious cash. The Italian, who had little or no money, simply "made do." This remarkable ability to live within one's means helped to make up for lack of funds and experience. Though economically poor, the Italian came to the New World with a determination not typical of native Americans, pampered by the richness of their surroundings.

One ought to remember that the Italian's homeland was predominantly an agricultural country. The laboring force had been traditionally attached to agriculture. In the year 1908 almost ten million Italians out of a total of twenty-five million above the age of nine were engaged in agriculture in the homeland. As late as 1954 over eight million people, or 42.4 per cent of Italy's working population, still worked in agriculture.[15] As previously noted, however, the various United States censuses are vague as regards the occupational categories of immigrants. Furthermore, certain nationalities are popularly identified with a particular occupation or industry. Census statistics tend to reinforce what one scholar calls "a sort of stereotype that conceals more than it reveals."[16] Although census statistics make the Italian appear to be mainly an industrial worker, the Census of 1890 showed that many Italians were gardeners. Italian women (in contrast, say, to the Japanese) were not heavily engaged in agriculture but worked as hairdressers, seamstresses, and mill hands. Italians were also engaged in large numbers as marble-quarry workers, miners, wood choppers, fisher-

[15] As against 31.6 per cent in industry. See Grindrod, *Rebuilding of Italy*, 163.
[16] E. P. Hutchinson, *Immigrants and Their Children, 1850–1950*, 70–71.

117

men, musicians, barbers, restaurateurs and saloonkeepers, peddlers, and railroad laborers. A high proportion were confectioners,
silk mill employees, charcoal burners, stonecutters, cooks, distillers, hatmakers, tailors, boot and shoe makers, and printers.[17]

As of 1920, 41 per cent of the nation's foreign farmers were to
be found in six states: South Carolina, Minnesota, Wisconsin,
Texas, Michigan, and California. Of these, 140,667 were foreign-
born farm "operators." There were probably two and a half times
as many actual "farmers"; of these farm "operators," 13,000 to
18,000 were Italians, the greatest concentration of them being in
California, New York, New Jersey, Louisiana, and Colorado—
three of these states west of the Mississippi River. The following
table[18] pictures part of this situation statistically:

Region	Italian Farm Owners	Italian Tenants	Per Cent of Owners	Per Cent of Tenants
West North Central	422	170	71.28	28.72
West South Central	1,555	936	62.42	37.58
Mountain States	1,576	304	83.83	16.17
Pacific States	3,195	1,703	65.23	34.77

Foreign-born farmers enjoyed an increasingly high proportion
of land ownership, although they could not usually afford the most
fertile farm tracts: "The best farms left by the native-born are
rented to other native-born who would rather till the good soil of
another than struggle with poor soil of their own. The foreign
born take the marginal land hoping that their energy and muscle
will overcome other handicaps."[19]

It is easy to underestimate the cost of setting up a midwestern
family farm in the nineteenth century. As early as the 1850's, it

[17] *Ibid.*, 138.
[18] Edmund de S. Brunner, *Immigrant Farmers and Their Children*, 4, 256–59.
[19] *Ibid.*, 37.

cost as much as $5 per acre to have the prairie sod broken up by contract laborers. An average 100-acre wheat-corn farm required an investment of at least $100 in implements and tools. In addition, a breaking plow, reaper, and thrasher—a minimum of implements—cost at least $375. A few draft animals, hogs, and poultry might well cost an additional $200. It would have been hard to start such a farm for less than $1,000, which would *not* include the cost of about forty acres of land. For the poor, immigrant or not, therefore, farm ownership was out of the question, at least for a number of years. Cheap land existed, but it was usually raw and undeveloped, with no possibility of yielding an immediate livelihood. Thus, without the moderate capital needed to transform the land into profitable farms, immigrants were sometimes debarred from farming or ranching.[20]

Regarding the many problems faced by immigrant farmers, Archbishop John Ireland wrote: "The greatest misfortune that fell to the lot of Catholic immigrants coming to America forty or fifty years ago was that they were allowed to be huddled in cities where, as a rule, nothing was possible to them but to be made hewers of wood and drawers of water, instead of being induced to occupy the fertile lands of the Western States, where independent homes were to be won with little cost and labor."[21] As to the cost of setting oneself up in farming, Archbishop Ireland commented: "We consider that, if the immigrant had $300 of his own on arriving upon his own land, he would get on well with our assistance, provided he is industrious and understands farm work."[22] Ireland became a leader in the Irish colonization movement. The Archbishop went westward in the late 1870's and negotiated with various railroads for the sale of land to immigrants in Minnesota. There he formed numerous Catholic settlements, primarily Irish. Except at Tontitown, the Italians never enjoyed such dynamic clerical leadership as did the Irish.

[20] Clarence H. Danhof, "Farm-Making Costs and the 'Safety-Valve': 1850–1860," in *The Public Lands, Studies in the History of the Public Domain*, ed. by Vernon Carstensen, 264–69.

[21] Shannon, *Catholic Colonization*, 39–40.

[22] Egisto Rossi, *Gli Stati Uniti*, 228.

In those parts of the West where shelter against harsh weather was desperately important, an immigrant could purchase a pre-fabricated house, rather than build it with his own hands. In the 1880's such houses were available for $150, in a single-story model, and $250 for a double-story one. Egisto Rossi, who wrote a hand-book for Italian immigrants, recommended purchase of such transportable houses, to be shipped to the West by railroad. They were not, however, very popular, nor was organized colonization by Italians. Yet Rossi was able to state: "The immigrant colonies of the Far West . . . are a good example of economic redemption beside which there is no equal in any other nation."[23]

One writer has discussed the influence of foreigners upon American agriculture in terms of various "cultural islands" in the South with "non-Southern agricultural backgrounds which carry on farming programs that depart in varying degrees from the types of farming traditional in the area." These "tell-tales of immigrant settlements," or distinctive "island remnants" of foreign agricul-tural innovation, are still characterized by low incidence of ten-ancy, constant farm improvements, a good "live-at-home" pro-gram, considerable manual work done by farm operators, small relief rolls during depression periods, and very little reliance on outside credit.[24]

After the turn of the century, occasional spokesmen for the immigrants became convinced that they should become farmers in such colony-type communities. One advocate of agricultural colonies believed that work on farms was "too unstable" and the wages paid "too small to attract even a foreign peasant. The Italian can do better in the city or on rough railroad work," he suggested. Furthermore, the treatment and accommodations which the im-migrant got as an itinerant farm worker were "far from being ideal, even for him." A "colony-approach," such as existed at St. Helena, an Italian community near Wilmington, North Carolina,

23 *Ibid.*, xvi.

24 Walter M. Kollmorgen, "Immigrant Settlements in Southern Agriculture: A Commentary on the Significance of Cultural Islands," *Agricultural History*, Vol. XIX (April, 1945), 69–78.

would, he felt, serve such immigrants best. There, three hundred North Italians, mostly Venetians, specialized in growing tobacco, grapes, beans, strawberries, and lettuce. Named after Queen Helena of Italy, the colony "rested upon both a sound philanthropic and economic base."[25]

Another champion of colony settlement contrasted the distribution of western Italians with those clustered in the East: "In the agricultural and mining country west of the Mississippi the distribution is more uniform," he wrote. "In Nevada there are Italians in every county, and in California there is only one county where there are none. In Colorado, Wyoming, Montana and Louisiana they are well scattered. Considered in regard to their destiny it will be found that results vary from two-tenths of one Italian in one hundred square miles in Oklahoma to twelve Italians to one square mile in Rhode Island." The writer applauded the attempt of the Italian ambassador, Baron des Planches, who, working with the Gould railroad interests, had sought to widen the distribution of Italian farm immigrants. He quoted a prediction of Ambassador des Planches: "Once they own little farms here they will become endeared to this country, and will not be tempted to return to their own country."[26]

If many of Italy's immigrants ended up in industrial rather than in agricultural pursuits, the reason was partly that the late nineteenth and early twentieth centuries presented unusual opportunities for the working man in America's largest cities. Italian migration reached its height at a time when the greatest need for unskilled industrial laborers existed. Into the 1870's the wages offered by its mills and mines outdrew those available on the average American farm. If there was a large influx of north Europeans to the farms of the Middle West, this could be partly explained by the fact that these immigrants had relatives there, and such precursors helped to bring them into established farm communities.

[25] Felice Ferrero, "A New St. Helena," *The Survey*, XXIII (November 6, 1909), 171–80.

[26] Frederick Boyd Stevenson, "Italian Colonies in the United States: A New Solution of the Immigration Problem," *Public Opinion*, Vol. XXXIX (October 7, 1905), 453–56.

Also, in those earlier years, America's bountiful crops stood in sharp contrast to poor harvests in Europe. Penniless south European immigrants who came along in the 1890's and later, and who did not know the language of a new country, often found it easier to remain with semiliterate compatriots in America's foreign colonies, locked safely inside the very eastern cities where their ships had landed.

The heavy concentration of Italians in urban areas was, thus, not due to their ineptitude as agricultural settlers but to the economic opportunities available in cities for propertyless workers. Yet their dispersion as truck gardeners indicates a leaning toward agriculture whenever they could afford to be so involved. Of course, not all immigrants wanted to leave the eastern coastline for the Far West—not while they could dig subways, or cut stone in quarries, or engage in mill work, or blast, cut, and grade railroad beds, or labor in eastern coal and iron works.

Bruno Roselli, an Italian journalist who visited New York in the 1920's, considered it an act of some courage for immigrants to leave the safety of settled tenement districts, however crowded, dark, or well-nigh pestilential: "Would they dare leave the costly protection of their only American friends, Mike the barkeep and Mr. Pinkus the landlord?" Roselli, however, urged Italians to head west: "You are unsuccessful and unhappy here. You cannot compete in business with the Jew, while your ignorance of English puts you at a disadvantage with the Irishman. Get away from such competition, and let us see whether your strong arms will not bring abundant riches out of the soil. . . . You are born of a race of pioneers, which lacked opportunities in Europe, and fails to find them here when in cities crowded with craftier peoples, but thrives when facing the obstacles of nature."[27]

Those immigrants who, albeit tardily, followed the frontier tradition by heading westward, formed a minority of their immigrant group. There is good reason, however, to believe that this was a selective minority, frequently composed of strong-willed persons who took a chance upon finding success rather than remaining

[27] "Arkansas Epic," *Century*, Vol. XCIX (January, 1920), 378.

behind in the ghetto environs of the eastern city. Robert G. Athearn, a historian of the West, writes of the hardihood of these chance-takers:

> Those who today talk about the intrepid pioneer and his ever-west-ward movement, despite Indian dangers and a generally forbidding country, should take into account the European farmer who, know-ing little English and less geography, was plunked down upon a prairie farm by the rising American business man. The newcomer was no ax and long-rifle man; he was a transplanted farmer and he wanted no more than to pursue his profession. . . . The new agrarians modified the frontier's characteristics not only by virtue of their numbers, but also by their culture. They were not, as a rule, the covered-wagon pioneers. They came by train, frequently straight from immigrant ships.[28]

There was a difference in the regional backgrounds of these "non-city immigrants." By 1909 some 80 per cent of the Italians engaged in agriculture had come from predominantly rural south-ern Italy and Sicily. Only 20 per cent had come from the more industrial northern Italy. Yet more than 50 per cent of those engaged in agriculture in the United States were North Italians rather than South Italians.[29]

Many of these North Italians were better educated than those who came from southern Italy. A few were even graduates of Italy's *scuole techniche* (much like technical high schools). They, therefore, were in a stronger position to compete than their south-ern compatriots. Yet, it is a mistake to claim that no illiterate peasants came to western America from the Italian North.

The Italian, North or South, loved the land with the same sort of affection he reserved for his family. In foul or good times, his forebears had worked it patiently for generations. Despite the fact that he arrived after the best free lands of the West were gone, he sought to learn the new mechanized techniques of American agri-

[28] R. G. Athearn, *High Country Empire, The High Plains and the Rockies* (New York, 1960), 172, 202.

[29] Pecorini, "The Italian as an Agricultural Laborer," *Annals*, American Acad-emy of Political and Social Science, Vol. XXXIII (January–June, 1909), 158; and Grindrod, *Rebuilding of Italy*, 226.

culture. Even immigrants who remained in the large cities cultivated small garden patches or raised poultry. Others left dangerous
and unhealthy industrial jobs in order to return to agriculture. On
the farm the Italian produced the cheeses he wanted, grew grapes
for his wine and *basilico* for his *pasta*, and butchered young pigs
for *salsiccia*, or sausage.

Merle Curti's study of Trempeleau County, Wisconsin, in the
1870's illustrates how foreign farmers pushed on to better land
once they could afford it. Indeed, non–English-speaking immigrants there "moved on in higher percentages than the native-
born."[30] Although too few Italians reached the farm, the success
of those who did was slow but sure. One of them summed up this
progress in a poignantly optimistic plea for tolerance.

> Wait at least twenty years and see what sort of Americans we shall
> become. Just now we are ignorant. We are poor. We are slow-
> minded. But so would you be if you had begun life as a peasant in a
> backward country. Give us the same opportunity to grow that your
> fathers had, and we, too, shall soon have mind as well as muscle. Be
> patient with us, for we find that the oppression of centuries is hard
> to overcome. All that you can give us now, in the day of our weak-
> ness, we shall pay back with interest when the day of our strength
> is here.[31]

Denying the stereotype of the Italian as a non-farmer, Edward
Corsi, commissioner of immigration, wrote: "As farmers they
stand alone in the cultivation of fruit and vegetables, as witness
their highly successful farming ventures in Vineland, Fredonia,
Canastota, and Valdese." Corsi continued: "The Italian who
comes from the soil is finding his way back to the soil. He has been
returning to the farm more and more in late years."[32]

In marked contrast to those Italians who had tolerated selfish
padroni, the more ambitious rebelled against paternalism in any

[30] Merle Curti, *The Making of an American Community: A Case Study of
Democracy in a Frontier County* (Stanford, 1959), 443.

[31] Quoted in Herbert N. Casson, "The Italians in America," *Munsey's Magazine*, Vol. XXXVI (October, 1906), 122–26.

[32] Edward Corsi, "Italian-Americans and Their Children," *Annals*, American
Academy of Political and Social Science, CCXXIII (September, 1942), 100–106.

form. This was the sort of immigrant who struck out westward where he was beholden to no one. "The further west you go," wrote one writer in 1904, "and the smaller the colonies become, the better for the reputation of the Italians."[33]

[33] Konrad Bercovici, *On New Shores*, 86–87.

Italy Out West

VI

TRAVELERS TO *"Il Grande Far Ouest"*

NOT ALL FOREIGNERS in the West were settlers. Wandering visitors, among them journalists, political exiles, and adventurers, sometimes followed or preceded the immigrants. After the Civil War, as political conditions became more stabilized, greater numbers of tourists traveled to America. The development of steam navigation made ships speedier and travel more comfortable. The opening of the railroads also made it possible for sojourners to extend what might once have been a visit along the East Coast, or to the Gulf region, or to the Great Lakes, into a trip to *"il grande Far Ouest."*

The West, however, aroused ambivalent feelings among early Italian travelers. The writer Antonio Gallenga (L. Mariotti), who in 1838 ventured to Nashville and Louisville (then still considered West), was struck by many contrasts. The verdant hills, covered with tall forests of oak, ash, cedar, and maple, were wantonly laid waste by the American inhabitants. Gallenga, who observed this prodigality over a period of three years, wrote: "The Americans were soon to outstrip the very worst savages in Europe in their senseless and ruthless detestation of trees." He saw patches of Indian corn "growing to a height and luxuriance to which even the richest flats of my native North Italian region have nothing to compare. Flocks and herds, though ill-tended, were glorious." Gallenga also found the majesty of the land in stark contrast to the uncouth frontiersmen. After watching one of these—a militia general, aged forty, who despoiled the carpet of a lady's living room with his spit—Gallenga recorded all too literally: "I do not think that revolting sight was needed to thoroughly disgust me with the West. But it was the last drop in a brimful cup, a cup that was fortunately soon to pass from me." Yet, the thrills of riding at a full gallop down corduroy roads, the openness of the countryside, the sheer wonder of the West's vistas and its opportunities, could not keep from impressing such foreigners.[1]

In the homeland most Italians gained their first notion of the West through accounts written by such travelers, either as books or in letters. Preoccupied with problems at home, few knew what went on abroad. Carlo Vidua, a traveler to St. Louis in the 1820's, commented upon the relative public safety on the American scene. But he found the roads wretched: "One can travel safely night and day, except for the risk of breaking one's neck or being stuck in the mud when it rains, because the roads are not really roads, but trails in the midst of woods or prairies." Occasionally, a key book gave Italians a vision of the West, albeit distorted. Andrew J. Torrielli, who has made a study of Italian opinion of America, describes Gustavo Strafforello's *Il Nuovo Monte Cristo*, published in Florence in 1856, as the "fantastic adventures among California gold seekers of a young Irishman, Dick Murphy, besides whom Edmond Dantè pales into insignificance." We do not know, however, if its author ever traveled to the West. Such writings have no great importance today, but they do indicate the degree of continuing interest abroad in the American West.[2]

What was the West that these books pictured? First it was big, very big. Books of travel told how, out beyond the Missouri, the monotonous roll of the Great Plains extended over western Kansas, Nebraska, most of the Dakotas, and the eastern portions of Montana, Wyoming, Colorado, and New Mexico. These plains formed the slope of a vast Cordilleran Plateau which, broken only

[1] Gallenga, *Episodes*, 197–210.

[2] Torrielli, *Italian Opinion on America*, 17; Joseph Rossi, "The American Myth in the Italian Risorgimento: The Letters from America of Carlo Vidua," *Italica*, Vol. XXXVIII (1961), 165.

by intermittent mountain peaks, reached westward to the Rockies. Within this region lay some of the principal mountain masses of North America, the foremost of these being the Rocky Mountain chain itself. Still farther beyond the mountains a complex geographical system, with deeply forested valleys and outlying plateaus of buffalo grass or mesquite, occupies part of Montana, Wyoming, Colorado, and New Mexico, as well as Idaho. Located on yet another plateau beyond the hundredth meridian are the western portions of New Mexico, Colorado, Wyoming, and much of Utah, Arizona, and Nevada, up to California's Sierra Range.

In the 1860's, when travelers reached the Omaha region, they began to feel that they were on the edge of a vast, generally arid, frontier. Beyond that point the savagery of the West had not yet been tamed or well described. It seemed to yearn for such description, asserted Italian geologist Giovanni Capellini. Accompanied by a French scholar, Jules Marcou, he wrote of his misgivings about this wide land of plains and rivers. Capellini was professor of geology at the University of Genoa and Bologna. An early exponent of Darwinian ideas, he did significant work as a paleontologist and had helped establish the discipline of prehistoric archaeology before his trip to the American West. Although fascinated by the West, Capellini in 1863 confessed to a moment of uneasiness about what lay ahead while crossing the Missouri River between Council Bluffs and Omaha at night:

> While my friend and the driver advanced to explore the ground, I remained to guard the baggage. Apart from other inconveniences, we also lacked torches. Unexpectedly, an individual drew near and advanced to ask me where we were going at so late an hour. I confess that before learning his intentions I had put my hand to my revolver; but this gracious gentleman was lost like us, and wishing to find some means of getting to Council Bluffs simply wanted to inquire if we were on our way back there.[3]

[3] Quoted in Oscar Handlin (ed.), *This Was America* (Cambridge, 1949), 249. The original is in Capellini's *Ricordi di un viaggio scientifico fatto nell'America Settentrionale* (Bologna, 1867).

Impressed by the necessity for self-protection, Capellini sought a permit to carry a weapon:

> The commandant to whom I applied was a certain Bassett. Two mounted guards, ragged and unarmed, were at the foot of the staircase that led up to the military headquarters. In the middle of the office was Mr. Bassett, stretched out on a stool with his feet extending onto the desk on which a bottle of whiskey kept company with an inkstand and a human skull. The last-named object was shaped like a well and designed as a glass, not for drinking purposes, at least not at the moment, but to hold sand![4]

Upon reaching Omaha, Capellini sauntered into the offices of the city's newspaper, the *Nebraskian*. He did not seek publicity but wanted old newspapers in which to wrap fossil specimens that he had collected. On the next morning he was startled to read "a full account of the geologist's life, hailing him as a pioneer in the opening of the West."[5] Capellini was so pleased to learn that he was already well known to many people that he commented most favorably in his book, *Ricordi di un viaggio scientifico* (Bologna, 1867), on the degree of cultural awareness beyond the Mississippi.[6]

Not all travelers to the West liked what they saw. A contemporary of Capellini, Antonio Caccia, traveled to California during the Gold Rush and, in his book *Europa ed America, scene della vita dal 1848 al 1850*, lamented the discourtesy of the inhabitants. He admired the countryside but not its inconsiderate residents. On the Mississippi River, for example, river boat races upset him. Although these contests caused many terrible accidents, Americans would not give them up. Caccia found the citizens particularly hardheaded about such matters.

Lieutenant Colonel Ferri-Pisani, Corsican aide-de-camp to Prince Napoleon on his Civil War tour of the United States, also displayed mixed feelings about the West. On the one hand, the

[4] Handlin (ed.), *This Was America*, 287–88.

[5] Torrielli, *Italian Opinion*, 139–40.

[6] In 1895, as rector of the University of Bologna and an Italian senator, Capellini won the Hayden Prize of the Philadelphia Academy of Science. The citation called him "one of the most illustrious geologists of the world." *Ibid.*, 18.

Colonel was indignant about the "curiosité brutale" of westerners; yet he paid grateful tribute to their hospitality.[7]

One of the most amusing of all travel accounts was *Un viaggio nel Far West Americano*, by Giovanni Vigna del Ferro, who was in the United States for four years beginning in 1876. Accompanied by Jehan Soudan, a French journalist, Vigna del Ferro in 1879 obtained train tickets from the railroad financier Jay Gould and left for the West with a chest full of provisions and a case of precious old burgundy. The presence on his train of a troupe of actresses, including the celebrated Sarah Bernhardt, as well as La Bernhardt's sister, Jeanne, and the actress Marie Colombier, greatly enlivened his journey. He accompanied them from Buffalo to Toledo to St. Louis and then toward Omaha. There he crossed the swollen Missouri and, on *"le alte praterie,"* or high plains, the traveler found the "noble Indians" reduced to drunken sots, the buffalo largely decimated, and the plains covered with the carcasses of steers who had died during the previous harsh winter.

Vigna del Ferro's contact with Sarah Bernhardt's troupe of actresses permits a brief comment on the alleged "gallantry" of Italians in the West. As compared to the coarse, often untutored, characters whom women sometimes encountered on the frontier, Italian visitors scored rather favorably. An early account by a western lady traveler concerned a "Monsieur R." who though "only an Italian gardener," impressed her as having "very polite manners, and who may be said to have seen a little of the world." She described him as "tall and majestic in person," quick to make "very elegant bows to Madame C." The suitor "spoke English enough to assure her he had the highest esteem for her, and would marry her tomorrow if she would consent."[8]

Gallenga thought American men so harassed by the workaday world that they neglected their women. He, therefore, found

[7] Camille Ferri-Pisani, *Lettres sur les Etats-Unis*, cited in Henry T. Tuckerman, *America and Her Commentators* (New York, 1864), 369. See also Ferri-Pisani, *Prince Napoleon in America*, 1861.

[8] Richard Flowers, *Letters from Lexington and the Illinois* (London, 1819), repr. in R. G. Thwaites (ed.), *Early Western Travels*, X (32 vols., Cleveland, 1904–07), 132.

"ladies' men" to be "terribly scarce in America. Yankees come home worn out from their work," he observed, "debased by greed, unfitted for ladies' company." Their lack of polish and companionship, therefore, threw a spotlight of acceptability upon the foreign man, whom Gallenga considered more gallant and more "willing to devote himself to women, to humor them, to take some interest" in them.[9]

En route to Reno from Omaha, Vigna del Ferro enjoyed the train ride but deplored the cooking; instead of whetting his appetite, western foods made him sick. He had, therefore, brought along various cans and boxes of tuna, mortadella cheese, sardines, and butter. The party stopped at Cheyenne, Denver and Leadville. For several weeks Vigna del Ferro left the train with members of the group and camped out in southern Colorado and northern New Mexico. He disapproved strongly of the extermination of the Indians and, in fact, applauded their fighting back—as in Custer's last stand. This was a most unpopular judgment to be voicing at this particular time. He also visited Apache camps along the Río Grande, giving the Indians whisky, which they called "water of the devil."

At Leadville, then the center of the West's mining frontier, Vigna del Ferro found a ratio of thirty men to one woman. He thought its muddy streets might be improved if both men and women did not rely almost entirely on horses for transportation. His account speaks of law and order and of lynch law, recording the presence of only a few Italians working in the mines. He believed Leadville would not grow large because the town was more than 10,000 feet in elevation, and he thought domestic animals, including dogs, could not live there. He spoke of pneumonia as the order of the day and revolvers as the order of the night. When the party reboarded the train at Cheyenne its members went to Ogden, and then to Salt Lake City. He visited the Mormon Tabernacle and moved on to Virginia City in Nevada

[9] Gallenga, *Episodes*, 54.

Territory, inspecting the Comstock Consolidated Virginia Mines, "the most productive in the world."

Passing through Reno, Vigna del Ferro went on to San Francisco, which he described as the city with the "greatest Latin element in the United States"; he was enthusiastic about the fact that four-fifths of its fishermen were Genoese. Its fish venders he described as mostly from Lucca. They also operated boarding stables for Italian vegetable and flower growers who brought their produce to market from the surrounding countryside. As he visited Italians in the West, this particular traveler found mutual aid societies still in operation, as well as uniformed lodges of the Bersaglieri and Garibaldini. In many homes hung pictures of King Victor Emmanuel, King Humbert, Queen Margherita, Cavour, and Mazzini. With his French friend, Vigna del Ferro ultimately returned to New York and reboarded the French vessel *L'Amérique*, which also took Sarah Bernhardt back to Europe. Extracts of his account were reprinted in a New York Italo-American newspaper, *La Patria.*

Carlo Gardini and other travelers referred in their accounts to the popularity of opera throughout the American West. Modern historians have commented upon the whole place of culture on the far western frontier, a subject closely related to the immigrant story.[10] Diaries and travel accounts like Gardini's challenge the conventional view of life beyond the mountains. Far from stressing the primitive and hell-roaring aspects of western life, they devote attention to the activities of men who thirsted for culture, who read widely and regularly, who supported performances of plays and musical events. Frontier existence was not, as depicted in the television and movie scripts, all violence. Despite admitted lawlessness, life in the West was influenced fully as much by merchants, bankers, farmers, artisans, educators, and musicians as ever by vigilantes and outlaws.

Bernhardt and other performers, among them Edwin Booth,

[10] See Walter Rundell, Jr., "The West as an Operatic Setting," in *Probing the American West*, 49–61; Davis, *History, passim.*

Salvini, and Ristori performed throughout the West. Each of them, for example, traveled to Central City, some thirty miles west of Denver, to perform at its famed opera house. Despite the bruising, uncomfortable trek up the canyon by stagecoach, these itinerants felt a sense of duty toward their remote but appreciative audiences.[11]

Gardini, who visited the United States four times between 1878 and 1886, spoke of Americans treating Italian opera divas as though they were queens. Out west sorely spoiled entertainers traveled in special railroad cars equipped with pianos, private dining rooms, and salons. At Cheyenne, Gardini encountered an opera troupe that had covered 13,000 miles in three months, giving eighty-five standing-ovation performances. He attended their version of Donizetti's *Lucia di Lammermoor*, which featured a chorus of more than sixty Italian singers from London's Covent Garden Company. The conductor was a Maestro Arditi, composer of the popular "*Il Bacio*," or "The Kiss." Gardini described the Cheyenne Theater as well appointed, and its audience as well dressed, in addition to being attentive. "The touching melodies of Donizetti," he recalled, "heard in a still wild region where only a few years before ferocious Indians like Sitting Bull and Crazy Horse roamed, left an indelible impression upon my mind."[12]

Travel accounts by foreigners almost invariably dwelt upon the Indians ("*i pelli rossi*"), the variety and grandeur of the western country, and dramatic adventures experienced en route to the West. A hell-raising book that conforms to a pattern that we might call "the foreign-Western" is L. Simonin's *Il Far-West degli Stati Uniti, i pionieri e i pelli rossi*. The author visited the United States five times in the period 1859–75. Although Simonin was conscious of the disappearance of the covered wagon era, his work is full of allusions to the skeletons of whites massacred on the plains, raging fires on the prairies, buffalo hunts, revolvers, Indian funeral pyres,

[11] On this theme examine Andrew F. Rolle (ed.), *The Road to Virginia City*; and Louis B. Wright, *Culture on the Moving Frontier*; as well as Fred A. Shannon, "Culture and Agriculture in America," *Mississippi Valley Historical Review*, Vol. XLI (June, 1954), 3–20; Davis, *History*, 36.

[12] Carlo Gardini, *Gli Stati Uniti, ricordi di Carlo Gardini*, I, 80–83.

An Italian artist's idealization of a cowboy roping a steer. About 1880.

scalpings, and such intriguing matters as the plural marriages of
Mormons. Simonin's book included a sentimental tribute to the
West as a melting pot and to the "new American race" which he
found there:

> By the words "American race" I do not intend only the Anglo-
> Saxon from which the Yankees derive (these do not forget to revel
> in this fact on occasion), but also each nationality that has emi-
> grated to the United States: Germans, French, Italians, Belgians,
> Scandinavians. Each has learned how to bend to the environment in
> which they are destined to live; and each, having come from the four
> corners of the world, now form but one people.[13]

We know little about Simonin personally. He spent most of his

[13] Simonin, *Il Far-West*, 35. The original Italian reads: "E per razza Americana intendo qui non solo la razza anglo-sassone da cui dipendono i Yankees (essi
non dimenticano di gloriarsene all'occasione), ma anche ogni razza emigrata agli
Stati Uniti: Tedeschi, Francesi, Italiani, Belgi, Scandinavi. Tutti sanno bentosto
piegarsi all'ambiente in cui sono destinati a vivere, e tutti, venuti dai quattro canti
del mondo, non formano in breve che un solo popolo."

American visit in Colorado, and some of his descriptions of that territory are exceptional. In 1867 he wrote another book, about mining, entitled *La vita sotterranea,* published in English in London in 1869. Simonin based part of his work upon interviews with the mulatto Jim Beck, who lived among the Sioux until his death in 1867.[14]

The fascination of encountering these "original western types" produced legendary overtones in foreign travel accounts. Gardini wrote of attending an Indian sideshow in St. Louis, where such "notorious and bloodthirsty" types as Texas Jack, Texas Ned, and Buffalo Bill performed side by side with their former enemies, the Indians. After they had "spread such terror in the past," he wrote, "I saw them not only applauded, but, because of their athletic ability and *bravura*, they enjoyed the full admiration of the spectators."[15]

The violence of western life intrigued foreign travelers, particularly writers. The more bizarre an adventure, the greater potential reader interest. Gardini met a man who claimed to have been scalped by the Indians but who, after lying quietly on the ground, was left by them as dead. This individual, he reported, managed to "pick up his scalp" and, somehow, to get it to grow onto his head again. This description defies belief, although Gardini maintained that there were other instances of persons whose scalps were sewn back into place.[16] On another occasion a Texas lynching of a Negro horrified Gardini, who wrote: "Seized by the terror of the affair, I retired into my railroad car out of fear that, looking outside, I should actually view the cadaver."[17] Unusual people, institutions, customs and folkways remained especially intriguing to foreigners.

Because it was possible in America for illiterates to rise quickly to positions of wealth, Gardini was shocked to

[14] *Ibid.,* 128–29.
[15] Gardini, *Gli Stati Uniti,* II, 16.
[16] *Ibid.,* 199.
[17] *Ibid.,* 304.

read in an American newspaper that at Leadville there lives a young man named John L. Morrisey, who neither knows how to read or write; he does not even know how to tell time, and he has assembled three million dollars. A few years ago he had no other money than his wages as a miner.

Gardini went on to tell that Morrisey became the developer of the Crown Point Mine, in which he found a vein of ore so rich that it provided him with an income of eighteen thousand dollars per month.[18]

Finally, a traveler like Gardini was bound to be impressed by the spirit of western independence, especially when he viewed it in the following touchingly dramatic context:

> In the dining room of my hotel, at a table near mine, there sat down a little girl who could not have been more than nine or ten years old; with a serious expression she ordered soup and ice cream. The waiter, amazed to find this girl alone, asked her if he should bring food also for her father. "Oh no," she replied in a resolute voice. "I am alone; my poor father died a few days ago."

Gardini confessed to a sense of shock over the episode. Yet, he stated, doubtless having in mind the traditional Italian love of children: "It is not rare to find in America, even among such young persons, so proud and independent a spirit as to surprise visiting foreigners, especially Italians."[19]

Gardini was one of the few Italians not to complain about the food he encountered. Most travelers, foreign or not, did not think highly of the cuisine, especially that served on western railroads. "I too had been led to believe," wrote Gardini, "that in the stations of the railroad to the Pacific one ate badly: the cuisine is not, obviously, our refined Italian type or even French, but, whether at Grand Island, where I ate an evening meal, or at Sydney, where I breakfasted, I found certain excellent dishes—Antelope beefsteak and Prairie Chickens, at almost all meals, are both delicious and healthful."[20]

[18] *Ibid.,* 114.   [19] *Ibid.,* 93–94.   [20] *Ibid.,* 76–77.

Whenever available, Italian boardinghouses were a boon to weary travelers. During the last quarter of the nineteenth century one could find these institutions in Denver, Cheyenne, Salt Lake City, and Sacramento. They catered to foreigners and native Americans alike. There, lonely immigrant boarders, who had left women and children behind in the old country, lived alongside travelers. The boardinghouse provided sorely needed washing, mending, cooking, and those other amenities which only a woman can properly furnish. Men without women, these immigrants came to look upon the western boardinghouse as a home away from home. There Italians found gaiety, laughter, familiar food, and consolation. The boardinghouse environment, with its wine and smoke-filled atmosphere, so similar to the sounds and smells of the homeland, provided reassurance and allayed anxieties in a strange, new land.

The boardinghouse was also a place of entertainment. There the Italians sang songs that had survived in their hearts. Good will filled the air as Sicilians sang a cantilena while the Piedmontese chanted "*La Violetta.*" For card players it was a clubhouse, where *briscole* was regularly played in the kitchen. The Piedmontese, instead, played "*morra,*" the finger-guessing game. Each of these games reflected, in some sense, the regional characteristics of Italians. Luigi Villari has summarized these local attributes:

> The Piedmontese is aristocratic, reserved, hospitable, steady, and industrious, while the Lombard is quick, businesslike, rather noisy and fond of chatter, and active. The Venetian is gossipy, lazy, artistic and not particularly honest. The Tuscan is hard-working, sceptical, courteous, slow, conservative, but not exclusive, full of family affection, and frugal to the point of niggardliness. The Roman is reserved and dignified, but averse to hard work, and his passions frequently lead him to deeds of violence. In the South there is a considerable difference between the Neapolitans and the Sicilians. The former are gay, of great natural intelligence and adaptability, artistic, loquacious, superstitious, utterly wanting in self-respect, vicious, fond of a quarrel, especially if it ends in the law courts, and much given to

outward show. They are often cruel and cowardly, but in great emergencies they can rise to a height of self-abnegation and heroism which has rarely been equalled. The Sicilian, on the other hand, is silent, and has more dignity than the Neapolitan; he is more gentlemanly in manners and appearance, but he is vindictive and savage, and intolerant of all restraint.[21]

To return to the subject of immigrant boardinghouses, they sometimes accommodated twenty or more regionally diverse persons, with perhaps two or three to a bedroom. Crowding was inevitable. There was a common bathroom; guests used kitchen and hall successively as dining room, smoking room, and living room. These places especially attracted persons who did not intend to establish themselves permanently in the locality. Those anxious for news from home came here to exchange scraps of village information. Rather than assemble in saloons to share their confidences, Italians preferred the more confined protection of the boardinghouse.

Surely the most flamboyant and arrogant of all Italian travelers out west was the "patriotic exile" and cosmopolite Colonel Leonetto Cipriani. Cipriani lived in a kind of dream world of stimulated excitement. As early as 1833–34, he had traded goods at New Orleans and in the Caribbean. On a later voyage to New York he enjoyed as shipboard companions the notorious "dancer" Lola Montez and the Hungarian patriot Louis Kossuth. Obsessed with dreams of conquest and glory, the mustachioed Cipriani, a cultured nobleman, six feet four inches tall, made various western journeys, the most remarkable of which was a covered wagon trip in 1853 from Missouri to California. Cipriani was the first Italian to record crossing the plains in a covered wagon. Furthermore, his is one of the earliest accounts of a transcontinental cattle drive. Cipriani's acid reactions appear in his *Avventure della mia vita*, published many years after his death.[22] For Cipriani's 1853 wagon

---

[21] Luigi Villari, *Italian Life in Town and Country* (New York, 1902), 36.

[22] See Ernest S. Falbo (ed.), *The California and Overland Diaries of Leonetto Cipriani . . . from 1853 Through 1871*.

expedition to California he bought cattle and surveying instruments to make "a personal railroad survey of the West." His caravan left St. Louis in mid-1853 with twenty-four men, twelve wagons, five hundred cattle, six hundred oxen, sixty horses, and forty mules. On an investment of thirty-five thousand dollars, Cipriani hoped to earn two hundred thousand dollars upon arrival in California. After a trek over the plains of almost six months, including, for him, an insufferable diet of beans and flapjacks, visits with the Mormons, Indian encounters, stampedes, and other hazards of the trail, he got his caravan to California, but realized only a modest profit.

In his *Avventure,* Cipriani kept alluding to the crass materialism of Americans. He considered them, especially on the trail west, to be unscrupulous profiteers. When near the outskirts of Fort Lawrence, Kansas, Cipriani decided not to enter the fort, *"non volendo avere nessun rapporto con quei cannibali."* Engaged in *"un gran giro"* to avoid Fort Lawrence, he met on this detour the buckskin-clad son of Marshal Andrea Massena, Duke of Rivoli, Prince of Easling, who was living among the Indians. Cipriani called him "one of the best of the Napoleonic generals," and recorded that Massena was happy "and would not return to Europe for a million." As to the reputation of the commandant of Fort Lawrence, Cipriani warned that, though people called this officer a gentleman, *"in quel paese bisogna guardarsi anche dai gentiluomini, perche quel titolo e del tutto relativo."* At Fort Bridger, Cipriani did praise a Major Fitz-Hugh of the local army complement as a likable man.[23]

Cipriani hated the commanders of the army's western forts, particularly the commandant of Fort Kearney. He found it inexcusable that this individual had sold him barrels of rotten flour and other unusable supplies while crossing the plains. Cipriani remonstrated in his memoirs, observing that in business a person who sells rotten goods can be punished by law. To sell such goods "to a ship about to leave for the Indies, or to a caravan that must traverse the continent, is an infamous irreparable act, which could

[23] Leonetto Cipriani, *Avventure della mia vita,* II, 103–104.

even expose those thereby wronged to die of hunger," he wrote. Cipriani's was an extreme case of phobia toward the country through which he traveled. When he reached Chimney Rock—traditional resting place for parties on the Oregon Trail—he refused to carve his name on its sandstone base because so many *American* names were already there.[24] He did, however, chisel his name, six inches high, on "Solitary Tower Rock" with the following inscription: "Colonello Leonetto Cipriani—16 Luglio, 1853–Tiberio's tomb–Roman St. Angelo Castle–Tiber River," because it reminded him of the monumental Castel Sant'Angelo in Rome.[25]

Cipriani seemed to be as much an enigma in his own country as in the United States. By 1859 he somehow achieved the rank of major general in the Italian Army, however, and went on to become governor general of the Romagne District. After the peace of Villafranca that year, he imagined that he had been politically slighted and chose once more to exile himself from Italy. But he returned to Italy eventually and in 1865 was made a senator. If we can believe him, in 1871 he allegedly retraced his 1853 western covered wagon route by Pullman car. Cipriani died in 1888 at his Italian castle, Bellavista, near Centuri.[26]

One of the fullest of the late nineteenth-century Italian travel accounts was that of Palermo-born Francesco Varvaro Pojero. He wrote *Una corsa del nuovo mondo*, at both the observational and philosophic level. An experienced author of European adventure stories and, like Cipriani, a minor nobleman, Varvaro had read De Tocqueville's and Dickens' travel accounts before embarking for the New World. Like Cipriani and other Latinate travelers, he too was critical, even flip, about much of what he saw during his three-month stay. At first, Italian critics like Varvaro were dismayed by American traits and character. Then they warmed to the country and its people, as he himself observed:

> Presumptiousness, boastfulness of manners, inspire a great aversion

24 *Ibid.*, 100–102.
25 *Ibid.*, 103. Cipriani's activities in California are mentioned in a later chapter.
26 Telesforo Sarti, *Il parlamento subalpino e nazionale*, 52.

to all those who first encounter Americans; but, after a long stay in their country, under such defects one finds very solid values, such as good will, honesty, intelligence, ingenuity, and industry, which traits turn aversion into admiration.[27]

Varvaro felt, however, that there was almost too much democracy and lack of manners in the United States. This showed itself in countless minor ways. He resented men who stood in the presence of ladies with their hats on and with their hands in their pockets. The Far West seemed to magnify such gaucherie even more than the eastern part of the country. He also found the existence of a single class of travel on trains degrading. On more than one occasion the journalist resented his fellow travelers and he recalled especially an "impertinent" seventeen-year-old passenger who argued with his father at the top of his lungs. At Denver, Varvaro was nettled by the discourtesy of a mysterious occupant of his theater box. When he found that this creature (with whom he was involuntarily to spend the evening) was his lady companion's coachman, Varvaro exploded. He could not disguise being offended by what he called a basic lack of American courtesy. The niceties which he habitually extended to women were simply missing out west. Always a "lady's man," he found American women comely, even beautiful, but frequently lacking in delicate manners.

Conversely, Varvaro approved of other American practices. One of these was directness in law enforcement. He even applauded vigilante action in the absence of law. At Canon City, Colorado, a lynching taught him that Americans were intolerant of slowness in the law and that they did not believe in shielding criminals. One wonders whether Varvaro would have been quite so approving if the lynching had been that of an Italian—an event which had in

[27] *Una corsa nel Nuovo Mondo,* I, x, 266. Translation is mine. Original text: "La presunzione, millanteria, la ruvidezza dei modi ispirano una grande avversione a tutti coloro che per la prima volta si mettono in contatto col popolo Americano; ma quando, dopo un lung soggiorno del paese, sotto questi difetti si trovano pregi tanto solidi quanto la buona fede, l'onestà, l'intelligenza, l'ingegno, l'operosità, all'avversione succede spesso l'amirazione."

144

From *Harper's Weekly* (1891)

The mass lynching of eleven Italians in the parish prison at New Orleans in 1891 was the first of a series of antiforeign outbreaks during that decade. The mob was led by the district attorney and other prominent citizens.

From *World's Work* (September, 1904)

An Italian celebration shortly after the turn of the century in Arkansas, commemorating September 20, which corresponds to the American Fourth of July.

Indian Boys' Band trained by Italian priests near the turn of the century. St. Ignatius Mission, Montana, a Jesuit establishment.

Cataldo Mission, Cataldo, Idaho, was built without nails in 1848 by Jesuits, using native Indian Christianized labor.

Ravalli, an early Montana stage stop, about 1890. It was named for the
Jesuit Italian priest Father Anthony Ravalli. Note cowhand in
woolly chaps at left.

From *World's Work* (September, 1904)

The Italian public school at Tontitown, Arkansas,
at about the turn of the century.

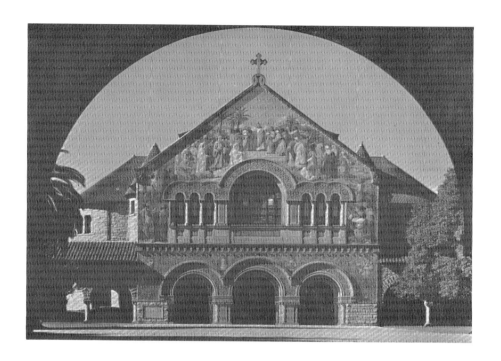

Stanford University's chapel in Palo Alto, California, is an outstanding contribution of Italian architectural motifs to American culture.

Charles A. Siringo, of Italian descent, became a famous cowboy, Pinkerton detective, and author. First published in 1912, A *Cowboy Detective* went through many printings. This illustration is from the 1915 edition printed at Santa Fe, New Mexico.

1891, as noted previously, caused a break in the diplomatic relations between the United States and Italy.

As Varvaro's westward-bound train passed caravan after caravan of covered wagons, he was sorry for these overland immigrants who would have to travel for weeks across the plains before reaching their promised land. He found the monotony of the prairie country annoying and compared his feelings at his first view of the Rocky Mountains with the sensation one feels when a ship sights land after many days at sea. Varvaro also expressed compassion for the Chinese, whom he first saw at Denver, a race which he described as despised by most Americans. At Green River, in western Wyoming, he was served by Chinese wearing azure tunics over which their pigtails "cascaded nobly." Each time he saw one of these "Celestials," a doleful sense of pity was aroused in him.

Varvaro arrived in the Far West only a few days after the Custer massacre. He reported American indignation against Indians and, in particular, Sitting Bull, whose Sioux were under sharp public disapproval. This traveler found it sad that the Indian would be unable to continue his nomadic life. Along with the Chinese and the Negro, here was, to his mind, a third race that obviously had to struggle mightily to find a place in American society. Each of these races he somehow found pathetic, living as they did in "the land of the free and the home of the brave."

At Salt Lake City, Varvaro met Brigham Young. He only with difficulty accepted the fact that Young's power seemed to be total and absolute. To a stranger, the ability of one particular Mormon chieftain to defy even the federal government was more than impressive. Varvaro did not believe that Brigham Young was truly loved by his people, although the Mormons respected his financial abilities and dutifully followed his leadership. As to polygamy, the visitor found it amusing that Indian tribes near by (he mentioned the Utes, Shoshones, and Snakes) should also be addicted to multiple marriages, a practice which the whites carried on in the name of Christianity! Like Baron Hübner, in his *Passegiata intorno al mondo* (Turin, 1873), Varvaro predicted, quite incorrectly, that Mormonism might well die along with its founder, partly because of what Europeans considered to be its bizarre social practices.

At Virginia City, Nevada, Varvaro met an Italian immigrant who told him that if his intention was to make money out west he had best avoid mining. "If you wish to sell coffee, or sugar, or almost anything else, that is fine, but stay away from mining," he counseled his countryman. Varvaro's informant had himself become a fruit vendor and found it hard to believe that Varvaro had come west simply to observe the scenery and not to seek his fortune too. Here were two different levels of foreignism, albeit both Italian, confronting one another. Varvaro's compatriot sold him an orange from Los Angeles for eight cents and therewith ended the brief encounter. When he did not give back any change for a twenty-five–cent piece, the journalist objected. The fruit vendor's reply was: "We do not out here calculate small fractions of change in business dealings. In fact," he added, "we do not have any change smaller than ten cents in general circulation." Varvaro tried hard to find this understandable: "It is natural in a country where silver looks down upon copper and not only copper but paper money as well." From Ogden onward gold and silver did, indeed, dominate the currency picture, he wrote.

Varvaro traveled onward to San Francisco. After visiting the standard tourist sights of California, he retraced his route eastward to Chicago. Only occasionally did he come in contact with immigrants, and he was much their cultural superior. The education and background of a traveling writer bore little resemblance to that of immigrants he encountered along the way. This was one reason why such highly literate travelers could not settle permanently in the New World. On the one hand, the educated foreigner was, as Gallenga stated, a welcome peculiarity; yet such a person found it difficult to habituate himself to the crudity of the American environment. Gallenga pointed out that if a cultured visitor could keep his temper, he "brought with him novelty and variety," as well as "oddities and peculiarities" that were widely appreciated in the United States. "A foreigner, in short, was the lion of a season in American circles," and, Gallenga wrote, "fore-

146

most along all aliens were Italians," partly because of a widespread natural sympathy among Americans for the revolutionary struggles which they had experienced against foreign tyranny.[28] Gallenga, however, like other Italian intellectuals, had to confess that he could not stay in America:

> I was not fit for American life. The education which had made me an Italian patriot and driven me out as a political exile had done nothing to prepare me for the lot of the ordinary emigrant.[29]

Both the traveler and the immigrant, however, encouraged people back in their homeland to come to America. In drawing other migrants to the New World, the accounts of individual travelers were as effective as letters written to Italy by immigrants themselves. The effect of personal testimonials, especially when glowing in enthusiasm, cannot be overestimated. Letters would sometimes be read by almost every literate villager. They, indeed, had the effect of virtually depopulating remote rural areas; whole families were drawn from Italy as a result of letters from the New World. A lonely and downhearted country boy could hardly resist a trusted relative's self-justifying descriptions of the richness of America, of its limitless expanses of land, and of the fairy tale prosperity encountered there. Those immigrants who had secured land were especially enthusiastic about the cattle, oxen, and horses which they could never have afforded back home. As they stocked new farm plots with pigs, chickens, and other livestock, they naturally boasted of their success. Not all letters, of course, were full of good cheer and enthusiasm. Disillusioned persons expressed their intention to return home. All too few immigrant letters, so highly revealing of their mood, have, however, survived.

Frequently the mothers, sisters, and aunts of immigrants saved only the money and photographs that accompanied letters. These were clumsily written in the crude confines of sod shanties and mining shacks, and flowed back to the old country in an uninterrupted stream. A good summary of the importance of letters is provided by the son of some Italians who went to Colorado:

[28] Gallenga, *Episodes*, 110.   [29] *Ibid.*, 215.

Each month one of my father's brothers sent a letter home. They were letters which my father read avidly—as, for that matter, did all the villagers. They used to gather in my grandfather's house whenever one of the magical missives from the New World arrived, listening again and again to the incredible accounts of America which the letters contained, nodding to themselves, muttering aloud, occasionally giving vent to delighted incredulous exclamations.[30]

A typical letter might read:

> I urge you to consider coming to America before it is too late. I myself have no intention of returning to Italy. In a year or two I hope to be able to send for the rest of my family. There is plenty of work here and the pay is good.[31]

An immigrant wrote to a parent: "Father Alfonso used to tell me fabulous stories about Paradise. If he is still living, tell him that I have found Paradise in America and that it is infinitely better than he supposed."[32]

THE INFLUENCE OF BOTH "America letters" and travelers in enticing immigrants to the New World cannot be overestimated. Immigrants too, excited by the material wealth they saw on all sides, filled their accounts to the homeland with appealing descriptions. As the western environment became more refined, travelers began to note particulars that were less frontier-like. On an inspection trip, undertaken after the turn of the century, the Italian ambassador, Edmondo Mayor des Planches, frequently made mention of such American phenomena as chewing gum, sandwiches, the phrase "high standard of living," saloons, barbecues, spitoons, whirlwinds, parlor cars, snow fences, geysers, baseball, oil derricks, deserts, stock raising, poker games, and quick lunches. No one of these items possessed great significance, but they dotted the accounts of other travelers as well. And, in general, they were not characteristic of Europe.

After 1900 a diffused image occurred in the writings of travelers.

[30] Jo Pagano, *Golden Wedding*, 4.
[31] Angelo Pellegrini, *Americans by Choice*, 194.
[32] *Ibid.*, 100.

As America became less regional and more national, the emphasis of such accounts came to transcend local environment, following prevalent American social patterns. One such selection illustrates this tendency.

Writing in 1929, the Countess Irene de Robilant, a brilliant commentator, was shocked by the narrowmindedness of the Middle West. Influenced by the criticisms she read in Sinclair Lewis' *Main Street*, she found portions of the country no less than stultifying insular: "It is the Spoon Rivers, the Gopher Prairies and the Zenith Cities that feed the continent and, along with the millionaires, form the greater part of public opinion in the West, the electoral campaigns and even determine the election of presidents." In contrast to this, she found the Far West full of hope and promise. Once one left behind the "monotonous grain fields of Kansas and Oklahoma," things felt spiritually more comfortable. In the Hispanic orbit of New Mexico, Arizona, and California, the mesa and pueblo heritage awakened one's Latin perceptions. While the countess deplored mistreatment of the Indian, as had other Italian observers, the American West proved itself a place of fascination and excitement. The countess took special delight in recounting the story of a Hopi Indian who, enriched by oil revenues, traveled to Denver to buy an automobile for his family. He ended up buying a hearse, which he found more spacious than any other vehicle, for her a touching tidbit. Foreign travelers, although sometimes mixed up about the West, were well read and usually eager to describe as much as possible a fascinating new subject. The Countess de Robilant was, for example, aware of the writings of the anthropologist Bandelier, of the novels of Jack London, and of the fine descriptions of nature by both John Wesley Powell and John Muir. Intrigued more by the newness of the West, with all its spaciousness and potential, such a writer dwelt hardly at all upon the immigrant theme but, instead, seemed fascinated by life on the farthest edge of a continent.[33]

[33] Irene di Robilant, *Vita Americana, passim.*

VII
ONTO THE PRAIRIES AND BEYOND

AT FIRST GLANCE the seemingly strange and arid region beyond the
Missouri hardly appears capable of offering hospitality. In its
southern portion it is a dry and wrinkled land of cacti and piñon.
To the north lies a cold, remote area where livestock, since the
days of the buffalo, have each winter pawed the snow to find
bunch-grass fodder. Sloping plateaus break off, leaving behind
craggy mesas and cliffs hundreds of feet high. In this rocky region a few sizable streams cut deep below the surface; much of
the water supply is absorbed by the parched valleys through which
they flow. While the thirsty land could support cattle and sheep,
it succored few men willingly.

Despite these handicaps of climate and topography, settlers
were drawn both to the open range and onward to the high mountains which flanked the sun-bleached prairies. Immigrants too
penetrated them in search of mining, farming, or ranching jobs.
The trails of the West widened, and all sorts of people turned foot-
paths into roads. They hammered together cabins and outsheds
alongside the brush "wikieups" of former trappers. In time countless new city-dots appeared on western maps, connected by railroad tracks.

After the 1870's the plains resembled a great sea and the trains
became ships as the immigrant tide burst beyond the Mississippi
Basin. Native-born farmers who moved westward made it possible
for others to obtain farms more cheaply. When town lots, rather

than prairie land, began to command higher prices, more reasonably priced farm plots acted as an incentive for immigrants to replace original western settlers. Few, however, realized that the relatively low price of prairie land formed only a minor portion of the cost of farming. Still, the land attracted, and settlers headed toward it, mostly by railroad—a major factor in opening up the West to immigrants.

Along with the Irish, Russians, Hungarians, and Austrians, the Italians constituted part of the labor force on the western railroads. As the roads built west, they sorely needed this immigrant labor, both to lay tracks and to erect wayside stations, water tanks, and supply depots. Railroad growth after the Civil War was little short of spectacular, reaching fifty-two thousand miles in 1870. Throughout the depression years of the 1870's, construction diminished but moved ahead once more after 1879. During the eighties, railroad investment prospects looked good again, as the national economy turned upward until 1887. Then it dipped briefly, only to boom once more until 1893.

By 1880, the railroads laid 93,000 miles of track, opening 10,000 miles in that year alone. In 1887, they built a record 13,000 miles. By 1890 trackage stretched along 166,000 miles. Total track in operation doubled from 1877 to 1892. The Great Northern road reached Everett, Washington, from St. Paul in 1893. By then the Northern Pacific too stretched to the Pacific Ocean. The Southern Pacific, building eastward from San Francisco, had reached New Orleans in 1882. During these years both the Union Pacific and Atchison, Topeka and Santa Fe were also expanding.

The Gould railroad interests were among the first to visit Italy in search of manpower. At various times Jay Gould virtually controlled the U. P. and A. T. and S. F., as well as Kansas Pacific, Missouri Pacific, Texas and Pacific, Denver Pacific, and other western railroads. His recruiters lured immigrants to the West, offering land grants secured from the federal government. Italians who broke their ties with the East at the Union Depot in Chicago usually traveled toward the northern plains via the Northern Pacific and Great Northern railroads. Those who went into the southern plains boarded the Rock Island and eventually transferred to the Santa Fe, Southern Pacific, or Kansas Pacific. Some traveled into the central plains and Rockies via the Burlington, Union Pacific, and Denver Río Grande Western systems.[1]

The success of the Illinois Central Railroad's colonization began the process of railroad-directed western settlement. As the railroads pushed into unsettled regions, millions of acres were opened to cultivation. Large-scale colonization could never have been accomplished without the western railroads. The railroads needed the immigrants as much as the immigrants needed them. One of the most successful immigration programs was run by the Northern Pacific Railroad, which, in 1870, brought principally Scots, Dutch, Norwegians, Swedes, and Germans to the West, and some Italians as well.

After 1875 the railroads were decisive in settling colonies of immigrants in specific communities. At Milwaukee, in the 1880's, Italians founded a small colony of railroad workers near the yards of the Chicago and Northwestern Railroad, many of them having been recruited by a "New York Labor and Construction Company." In a state like Minnesota, railroad recruiters actually determined the location of farms, towns, and centers of trade. The railroads not only took people westward; they marketed crops, extended credit on those crops, and assumed the functions of banks, credit bureaus, and colonization societies. The West bustled with immigrants.[2]

During a great railroad boom that lasted from 1879 to 1883, a veritable "construction frontier" reached beyond the tier of states west of the Mississippi into the Rockies. In the Dakotas, during

---

[1] For discussions of immigrant labor in building American railroads, see Paul W. Gates, *The Illinois Central Railroad and Its Colonization Work*; Richard C. Overton, *Burlington West: A Colonization History of the Burlington Road*; James B. Hedges, "The Colonization Work of the Northern Pacific Railroad," *Mississippi Valley Historical Review*, Vol. XIII (December, 1926), 311–42; Robert E. Riegel, *The Story of the Western Railroads* (New York, 1926). For routes of travel see Carl F. Kraenzel, *The Great Plains in Transition* (Norman, 1955), 248ff; and Industrial Commission, *Reports*, XV, 411.

[2] Shannon, *Catholic Colonization*, 85, 255, 279.

the single year 1880, one railroad alone added 724 miles of track. The Denver Río Grande Western built 400 miles of track in Colorado in 1881, and planned another 800 miles. That road advertised widely for ten thousand workers at wages of $1.25 to $1.75 per day. British, French, and Italian labor agents saw to it that this demand did not go unfilled.[3]

Statistics concerning the number of Italians engaged in railroad construction are impressive. On the eve of the twentieth century the Union Pacific employed about two thousand, and the Great Northern fifteen hundred to nine thousand. Some eight hundred usually worked for the Wabash, eleven hundred for the Chicago and Northwestern, and fifteen hundred for the Chicago, Milwaukee, and Puget Sound. By 1902 the Canadian railroads alone employed over six thousand Italians, half of whom worked for the Canadian Pacific.[4]

The attractions of immigrant labor for railroad construction continued beyond 1900. From 1908 to 1909 over nine thousand Italians secured jobs on railroad lines to the West. They sometimes did not return to the point of origin when their jobs were finished, remaining in the West, where the climate was generally warmer and where all-year employment as section hands could be found.[5] Most Italian rail workers emigrated as single men; the majority were in their late teens and early twenties. Although predominantly unskilled, their status was transient. Not all immigrant laborers were willing to put up with long hours of toil—setting rails and ties in the sweltering heat of the sun or in the damp and clammy drizzle of winter. Thus other jobs lured them away from manual labor at "track's end."

To work on a railroad gang meant privation and discomfort. In an atmosphere of backbreaking pick and shovel work, where muscular brawn and dripping sweat were the order of the day,

[3] Erickson, *American Industry*, 76; Gerd Korman, *Industrialization, Immigrants and Americanizers* (Madison, Wisconsin, 1967), 27.

[4] Foerster, *Italian Emigration*, 359. Fuller evaluation of the immigrant role in building the western railroads is called for in Haskett, "Problems and Prospects," in *World Population Migrations*, 60–61.

[5] Industrial Commission, *Reports*, XVIII, 340.

tempers grew sharp. There was controversy over wages and hours, poor accommodations, and rivalry with other minorities, particularly the Irish, Scandinavians, and Germans, as well as Slavs and even Hindus. Each strove to impress the gang boss, upon whose good opinion jobs depended. Disputes over the merits of whisky versus wine could end in bloodshed during a Saturday night of violence.

Furthermore, there was little opportunity to display those traits for which Italian males were noted: impressing the opposite sex with their strength and potency. Such exhibitionistic activity requires a receptive circle of admiring females. These lonely and bronzed men who laid tracks along western America's railroad lines missed the warmth of family and relatives, the close-knit affectionate nightly gatherings for which Italian life was famous —with familiar card games, the smell of Turkish tobacco, strong coffee, and Chianti bottles.

It almost seemed as though immigrant life, particularly out west, consisted of a series of improvisations. To service the immigrants there came to America a small army of merchants who had been tradesmen in Italy and who emigrated along with some of their best customers. These merchants supplied home-style foods, including olive oil, cheeses, and salamis. European recipes called for involved formulas of cure, grind, and blend; most dishes were heavily spiced and some were doused in wine. St. Louis, Denver, and Salt Lake City merchants became heavy buyers on the national spice and condiment market.

The farther west the immigrant went, the more he had to pay for his specialties. The bilking of railroad workers was common. Sometimes the execrable food served in construction camps was hardly fit to eat. One contractor operated a saloon at each end of a tunnel which his men were boring. When they had no money, he accepted bank checks at a discount of ten cents on the dollar.

Because railroaders were a turbulent lot, agents tried to secure men with families—persons more likely to be sober and industrious. These might eventually settle on lands through which a road was building. All such roads, especially western ones, needed

154

the cheap labor which the immigrant offered. Also, the railroad could earn further money by supplying him and his family—an added incentive for encouraging large-scale colonization.

A gang of immigrant laborers from one particular village in Italy frequently worked on the same construction project. The Sicilian boss of a maintenance or construction crew usually favored his fellow immigrants; a Tuscan would employ natives of Florence or Siena. It was a good idea not to mix nationalities. To avoid squabbling in railroad construction camps, even North and South Italians were, at times, kept separate from one another.

From water boy to roadmaster, the work remained hard and the hours long. But this was the kind of employment in which even illiterates could excel. Little training was required, and immigrants could begin almost immediately to earn wages and to save money to bring other members of their family to America. Furthermore, this type of work, which kept the immigrant away from confining urban crucibles, meant a sort of freedom for him.

Immigrants frequently were influenced to remain on the railroad by close friendships with their fellow nationals. Thus, old friends hung onto track-repairing jobs to the end of their days. Others were "birds of passage," who planned to rush home to waiting parents and loved ones with newly found riches. By working twelve to sixteen hours per day, they put aside a nest egg for retirement in Italy. For these people America was truly the land of ceaseless toil.

On occasion the railroads overbuilt. They reached into remote areas years before substantial traffic revenue existed. When freight and passenger business failed to materialize, profits were usually insufficient to pay interest on the bonds that had financed construction of the railroads. Then some of them would either go into bankruptcy, or would reorganize their capital structure, to reduce indebtedness. This usually meant unemployment for rail workers. Bankruptcy of one or two major roads could, indeed, lead to regional and even national financial panics. In what historian Ray Ginger has called an "age of excess," the railroads tended to lead the country into overexpansion. After 1887, and again in 1893, when railroad construction seriously slowed down, thousands of workers became rootless migrants; mines and mills laid off men and cut back production as the demand for farm products fell and prices declined.

Even in good times those Italians who brought along young brides preferred farm jobs to construction work along lonely stretches of railroad track. Such immigrants usually stayed on in Kansas, Nebraska, and the Dakotas until financially independent enough to buy farms and to start their own businesses. Ample quantities of cheap railroad land helped ease their lot. The railroads, having built their lines, sought to settle the surrounding land by luring settlers. Some of the most successful of these had virtually no education, and they worked their way up in life by determination and native shrewdness.

Moving from mine to mine and from farm to farm, immigrants frequently shifted jobs. While the Italians moved less than some other nationalities, by seasonal migrations they hoped to gain better pay and better work. In general, there were jobs for those who wanted to work hard.

The railroad trip west usually was an ordeal. In crowded emigrant cars, poorly designed for human traffic, hard wooden benches served as seats. Straw pallets were laid out at night for sleeping. One washed in tin basins located at the rear platform. Overpriced snacks, consisting of smelly cheese or old eggs and dry bread, were available at most wayside stations. As the train rattled over uneven trackways, women, especially, found travel toward new frontiers wearing. Railroad personnel seemed singularly uncooperative—indeed, almost abusive at times. The trip by locomotive grew long and hot as America's plains stretched tediously and interminably ahead. An unwatered wilderness, from which Indians and the remaining buffalo looked on at the startled passengers, separated raw towns like Dodge City and Omaha. Yet, the new transcontinental railroad, crowded and smelly with passengers, was the only link between what Robert Louis Stevenson called "wayside stations in the desert."[6]

[6] R. L. Stevenson, *Across the Plains* (London, 1892).

In the late 1880's an Italian woman, "with only a sack of bread to last her until she reached her uncle out west, an immigrant's identification tag pinned to her dress," was one of countless travelers who got lost. She ended up in a city whose name she never did learn, and where, not understanding the directions concerning a change in trains, she spent a day and night in the station. "Believe me," she recalled, "I was scared. I couldn't speak one word of American. I didn't know what to do, and I sat in the station waiting for someone to tell me." When she reached Colorado she again got mixed up in her directions:

> Those darn fools on the train, they put me off at the wrong station again before I got to Coalville. I didn't have anything to eat for almost two days. . . . No clothes, no money, no nothing. I can never forget.[7]

Working for the railroads, of course, was not the only endeavor that attracted the western immigrant:

> The industry of the Italian laborer and the benefits to this country which accrue from his work cannot be disputed. He tills the soil, builds railroads, bores mountains, drains swamps, opens here and there to the industry of American workmen new fields which would not perhaps be opened but for his cheap labor.[8]

The wages which such persons received in America were crucial to their recruitment. Throughout most of the nineteenth century, the average weekly earnings of adult male Italians varied from $9.61 to $11.28, compared to an average wage of $13.89 for native Americans.[9] Competition between immigrant groups helped keep wages down, but the rate of pay remained far superior to that in Europe. Whereas a carpenter in 1880 could earn only $4.18 per week in Italy, his pay in the United States was as high as $12.00. A baker in Italy earned $3.90 versus $8.00 to $12.00 here. A horseshoer there received $3.50 but $12.00 to $25.00 out west. A com-

[7] Pagano, *Golden Wedding*, 20–22.

[8] Merlino, "Italian Immigrants and Their Enslavement," *The Forum*, Vol. XV (April, 1893), 184.

[9] Pisani, *Italian in America*, 91.

mon laborer in Italy received as little as $2.00, but $6.00 to $9.00
in the West.[10] While the American cost of living was sometimes
higher than that in Europe, thereby reducing the real wage advantage, immigrants were still attracted by such pay.

Some Italians, following earlier waves of Swedish, Norwegian,
and German immigration, arrived on the plains in near penniless
condition. By the 1880's they (along with the Hungarians, Poles,
Russians, Greeks, and other east Europeans) had to accept employment which others sometimes did not want. It has been noted
that they rarely had the money with which to buy land, that some
of the choicest lands had already been allotted; thus they failed to
reap the benefits of the American homestead system. Therefore,
those who worked for the railroads lived a will-o'-the-wisp existence that often saw them settling at "rail's end"—wherever a railroad stopped its construction.[11]

In America's job hierarchy the newer immigrants from southern
Europe replaced the north Europeans after 1880. To forestall
trade unionism, employers sometimes encouraged national rivalries. Replacing Germans and Swedes who settled out west, the
Italians were looked upon as potential strikebreakers. Yet, immigrants seem to have been used less frequently as scab laborers
there than, say, in the bituminous coal fields of the East. Occasionally they were imported to break western strikes, organized
into gangs or crews subject to the discipline of English-speaking
foremen, or "*bossas.*" Government immigration reports spoke of
"progressive displacement" when immigrants entered the bottom
job ranks as earlier arrivals moved upward on the scale of desirable
occupations.[12]

More strange than the labor system was the West's geography.
No part of Italy resembled the bleak western prairies, their monotony relieved only by intervening groves of wood. Invariably, immigrants found the flat, open plains uninviting. Trailing along
stock and farm equipment, they pushed out onto the cold prairies,

[10] *The West from the Census of 1880,* 23.
[11] Riegel, *Story,* 239.
[12] Erickson, *American Industry,* 108–10; 118–19.

158

attempting to bring untamed lands under the plow. Hoping to find some river bottom that might remind them of the homeland, they built fires on the dirt floors of abandoned log shanties that offered poor protection against the driving sleet of winter. At night, snow would sometimes drift in across beds and blankets and through ill-fitting chinks between the logs. To keep warm, three or four persons might sleep in the same rude bed. Amid the darkness of crude surroundings, a toughening process went on that transformed the immigrant into a pioneer.

Kansas

Only a few Italians were among the earliest settlers in Kansas. Of these, clerics predominated. From 1836 to 1840, Brother Andrew Mazzella labored to bring Catholicism to the Indians near today's Leavenworth and Pottawatomie (now in Nebraska). After 1848 a Piedmontese Jesuit, Paul M. Ponziglione, wandered between Kansas and Wyoming for forty years as a missionary to the Indians. He built seven churches in Kansas.[13]

In large measure the story of the Italians in Kansas is that of a racial group drawn to its southeastern corner by a growing bituminous coal industry. After 1878 the first mines were near the towns of Pittsburg and Scammon. Italian miners came there in 1880 as strikebreakers. Cast in this role by employment agencies, they were originally unpopular. Eventually they became a decisive factor in the labor market. By 1907 they constituted the largest group of foreign-born miners in Kansas. Sixty per cent of the miners in the state were aliens and 25 per cent of these were Italians. Because they, like the Yugoslav miners of southeastern Kansas, were few in number, assimilation was relatively easy.[14]

Largely from northern Italy, these miners numbered thirty-five hundred by 1910. Unlike their fellow countrymen in the coal fields of Pennsylvania, they had in most cases been miners in their homeland. A Federal Immigration Commission concluded that

[13] Schiavo, *Four Centuries*, 167, 252.

[14] Industrial Commission, *Reports*, VII, 14, 27; William F. Zornow, *Kansas, a History of the Jayhawk State* (Norman, 1957), 183, 305.

their productivity was "largely due to the better class of workers being pushed farther west by the influx of less desirable immigrants in the districts nearer the Atlantic Seaboard."[15] This same commission determined that these Italians had established an early and high rate of property ownership. More property and homes were owned in Kansas by Italians than by any other immigrant group. Towns like Chicopee were settled almost entirely by Italians. Other settlements, including Pittsburg, Frontenac, Osawatomie, and Mulberry also had sizable Italian groups living in them. At Pittsburg, Kansas, they established a semimonthly labor journal, *Lavoratore Italiano*. Although these Italians were predominantly miners, some of them settled in or near cities like Topeka or Kansas City as storekeepers or truck gardeners. The foreign-born Italians in Kansas never numbered many more than thirty-five hundred; but, as elsewhere, statistics do not tell the full story.[16]

Immigrants of all nationalities settled in Kansas at a time when the cities of the Middle West grew spectacularly. During the decade from 1880 to 1890, while New York City increased from 1,911,629 to 2,507,414 inhabitants, Kansas City bolted from 55,781 to 132,710 persons. Fantastic health claims by railroad and land agents influenced the migration to Kansas. Some of these went so far as to claim scientific proof that "rain follows the plow," that "rainless geographical belts retreat before the march of civilization," and that the climate was so salubrious that an old Kansas resident found he could not die. He finally did so by moving to Illinois!

Train fare to Kansas and elsewhere in the Middle West was, fortunately, low. In 1870, an immigrant traveling from New York City to Emporia paid only $21.35 for transportation. It took eight days and nine nights to go this nineteen-hundred–mile distance by rail. Land was obtainable in Kansas that year for $1.50 per acre, and unskilled laborers were paid wages of about $2.00 per day.[17]

---

[15] Industrial Commission, *Reports*, VII, 37.   [16] *Ibid.*, 27.

[17] Alan Conway (ed.), *The Welsh in America: Letters from the Immigrants* (Minneapolis, 1961), 131.

Kansas Italians did not participate strongly in the extensive wheat farming for which the Middle West became noted in the late nineteenth century. Large-scale investments for machinery were required. Also, wheat farming demanded mastery of special agricultural techniques as yet outside the ken of newly arrived immigrants. Crops were different from those of the old country. So were methods of agriculture. Farm machinery was not only costly; it was baffling to the uninitiated. Most immigrants remained small truck-farmers, cultivating vacant lots on the edge of some midwestern town. They were unable to live wholly off the soil, as they had in Italy, and the staples they bought dissipated hard-earned capital.

In a rural atmosphere it was difficult to reproduce a community life similar to Europe's agricultural environment. Whereas a peasant might have previously lived in some hamlet while he cultivated a small family plot near by, in Kansas houses seemed to be a long distance from each other, a factor which made foreign wives, especially, feel lonely and isolated while their husbands were off tilling the soil. Once the Italian mastered the technique of working that soil, he proved as good a farmer as any of his neighbors, an achievement which usually helped his local standing; seldom did it seem to arouse jealousy.

Many Italians settled at Kansas City, Kansas, as well as at Kansas City, Missouri. By 1920 they constituted the third-largest group of foreign-born there, after the Germans and Russians.[18] One writer describes them as follows:

> The majority of Kansas City's North Side Italians minded their own business, paid their bills, went to Mass, sent their children to school, and deported themselves in the manner of good citizens everywhere. Many of their houses were unpainted, were drab, and covered with soot, but inside was neatness, and cheer, traces of art and religion, and above all, music.[19]

Regrettably, however, Kansas City's North Side also sheltered an

[18] Roy Ellis, *A Civic History of Kansas City, Missouri* (Springfield, Missouri, 1930), 37.
[19] Giovanni Schiavo, *Missouri*, 106.

underworld of racketeers and hoodlums in the city's "Little Italy" district. Among these criminals were four Italians, Michael la Capra, Adam Richetti, Charles Gargotta, and Johnny Lazia.

Lazia's career forms the heart of a seamy era in Kansas City's history. For in the 1930's this soft spoken, amiable, and dapper young man became the political boss of the North Side. By 1928, Lazia had eliminated the power of an Irish boss, Michael Ross, ruthlessly abducting a number of Ross's lieutenants. Before Lazia challenged Ross, the Italians of the North Side had virtually no political organization. They seemed proud to escape satellite status under Irish bosses. With the North Side Democratic Club under his control, Lazia was in a position to make an alliance with Thomas J. Pendergast, whose political machine controlled Kansas City. Pendergast (whose sister Mary had married an Italian, William C. Costello) became genuinely fond of the seemingly modest Lazia.

Lazia's appearance was deceptive. Mild mannered, wearing rimless glasses and spats, and carrying cane and gloves, he gave an impression of kindliness. He spoke good English, chewed gum incessantly, told humorous stories, and was superficially polite. Lazia apparently kept tough visiting criminals from Chicago and St. Paul "in line" for Pendergast, employing ruthless and cruel methods and dumping his gangland victims along Jackson County's roadsides. Lazia himself rode in a chauffeured bulletproof car and had a personal bodyguard named Big Charley Carollo. Although married, Lazia was frequently to be found alone in a cottage on Lake Lotawana.[20]

Lazia's power derived in part from Kansas City's Italian complex, which was congested into a relatively small area east of Market Square. By 1929 some 85 per cent of the residents in the "Little Italy" district were of Sicilian origin. Even before the first World War some twelve to fifteen thousand persons of Italian descent lived there, squeezed between the Negroes and the Irish. This created an atmosphere of racial antagonism as in other large

[20] Maurice M. Milligan, *Missouri Waltz, the Inside Story of the Pendergast Machine by the Man Who Smashed It* (New York, 1948), 33, 106–107, 119–33.

American cities. Members of the Mafia were possibly responsible for various unsolved murders. In this environment early in his life Lazia, who never advanced in education beyond the eighth grade, had attracted the attention of local businessmen. He studied law on his own and seemed headed for a legal career when, at the age of eighteen, he was caught in a robbery attempt. Although sentenced to fifteen years in the Missouri Penitentiary, Lazia served less than a year. He was released in 1917, partly because of intervention on his behalf, and partly because of the wartime atmosphere of clemency.[21]

Having profited from political influence, Lazia turned to similar activities—lending money to friends, keeping youngsters out of jail, trading real estate, and managing gambling and bootlegging enterprises. Nicknamed "Brother John," he robbed the rich but supported local charities, gave to down-and-out panhandlers, and simultaneously ingratiated himself with Pendergast's power structure. He somehow avoided arrest, although he was once indicted, with various others, in a liquor conspiracy. But he obtained freedom when his bodyguard, Carollo, "took the rap" instead. During 1928, Lazia led Kansas City's Italian community in a successful election campaign against Irish opponents, centered upon a "home rule" bond issue. By the use of force, personal charm, and unusual organizational and executive abilities, Lazia built up a strong political following. Soon he even grew to have a voice in naming men to the Kansas City Police Department. From this there flowed gambling and liquor concessions as well as police tolerance of organized vice.[22]

By the summer of 1934, Lazia was thirty-seven years old and at the peak of his power. The Italian dictator Benito Mussolini had recently bestowed the Order of the Crown of Italy upon his protector, Pendergast. As one dictator rewarded another, Pendergast had derived considerable strength from a political alliance forged with Lazia as boss of Kansas City's North Side. Just as Quantrill

[21] William R. Reddig, *Tom's Town: Kansas City and the Pendergast Legend* (Philadelphia, 1947), 248–51; Milligan, *Missouri Waltz*, 103–107.

[22] Reddig, *Tom's Town*, 251.

and the James Boys once ruled the countryside around that city, Pendergast and Lazia now ran it internally, in concert with other petty dynasts. Because federal authorities were investigating income tax evasion charges against Lazia, Pendergast had written to Postmaster General James Farley on his behalf. Then, quite suddenly one sticky July day, Lazia was machine-gunned by unknown assailants. Various key figures attended the funeral. Among these were Boss Pendergast, as well as the city's police director and even Mike Ross, whom Lazia had unseated. The murder was never officially solved, but was probably the work of a rival gang. Upon Lazia's death his bodyguard, Carollo, seems to have become Kansas City's crime czar; he ultimately served long sentences at the Leavenworth and Alcatraz penitentiaries.[23]

Nebraska

In thinking of Nebraska the immigrant scarcely comes to mind, unless one has read Willa Cather's charming descriptions of its "French farm country" in her *O Pioneers* (N.Y., 1913) or Mari Sandoz's graphic account of her crusty immigrant father in *Old Jules* (Boston, 1935). It is difficult to believe that a Mediterranean influence ever existed in so remote a region. In the midst of America's heartland, Nebraska would be the last place one would expect to find Italians.

Yet, the immigrant record, especially in Nebraska's largest city, has been substantial. By 1863 an Italian colony was already clustered around the outskirts of Omaha. While working on the Union Pacific Railroad, the single men among them lived in boardinghouses. The heads of families moved into a colorful district called "Dago Hill," located near such other immigrant areas as "Sheelytown," "Polack Hill," and "Little Bohemia." There Italians operated lunchrooms and stores, and bought land for vegetable gardens. By 1888 they had founded the "Dal Cenisio All'Etna Lodge" and later the "Omaha Italian Club." During the decade 1901–10, when the great wave of Italian immigration to the United States reached a crest of 2,044,877, almost 2,500

[23] Milligan, *Missouri Waltz*, 10, 103–107.

Italians arrived in Omaha. This was an increase of more than 400 per cent over the previous decade. Throughout this period railroads continued to add maintenance crews and shopworkers to their staffs, while packing plants and stockyards also expanded payrolls.

Social acceptance in a city like Omaha became more of a problem for immigrants than life in the country or in a small rural town. They, however, integrated themselves reasonably quickly into their environment. During the Trans-Mississippi and International Exposition of 1898, a group of Omaha Italians who were eager for acceptance drew attention to their presence in Nebraska by attempting to pilot a flotilla of Venetian gondolas from the Ohio River up the Missouri. After reaching Cairo, Illinois, they encountered severe ice in the river. Because of this and the chilly weather, they abandoned the expedition and returned to Omaha by a much-publicized train ride. After 1915 the Italians of Omaha published their own newspaper; *Il Progresso*, a weekly, had circulation by 1931 of 5,785. These were, of course, tiny papers when compared to Edward Rosewater's Omaha *Bee* or William Jennings Bryan's *World-Herald*, both of which had catered to immigrants in battles against the American Protective League in the 1890's.[24]

The immigrant's role in a city like Omaha proved to be different from his acculturation in a country environment. Observers could detect among Omaha's residents of Italian descent (12,000 by 1940) the type of cohesion that characterized immigrants in a large metropolis. The immigrant experience there was not completely dissimilar to the ethnic enclaves in large metropolitan communities. An unspoken spirit of clannish solidarity, particularly among South Italians, pervaded the life of the Omaha Italians—a spirit similar to that found at Kansas City, Minneapolis–St. Paul, and San Francisco. In these urban concentrations, immigrants yearned to create a political force as quickly as possible. In Omaha, under the leadership of James J. Piatti, a Wil-

[24] The most helpful book on the Italians in Nebraska is Work Progress Administration, *The Italians of Omaha*, 23–27; Ayer, *Directory*, 1236–38.

sonian Democrat, the Italians played an important role as early as the election of 1912. Whereas the Irish had held many municipal posts from the 1890's onward, henceforth the Italians listened to their own leaders, generally voting Democratic. Until the eve of World War II the local "Sons of Italy" organization took a strong part in the political life of Omaha.[25]

The Dakotas

The sparsity of population in the north central prairie states of North Dakota and South Dakota is reflected in the small numbers of Italians who went there. The Dakotas had only 135,000 people in 1880. Then several years of good rainfall shot the population up to 330,000 by 1883. Even by 1910 the total number of these immigrants was only several thousand. Compared with that of persons of Scandinavian origin, Italian influence in the Dakotas has been negligible. A few settled near Sioux Falls. Others named a village in that locality Dante. Basically, Italians avoided the Dakotas, whose Badlands they considered, with good reason, especially inhospitable. At a time when the Italian population of most western states increased, the Dakotas lost about 50 per cent of their original Italian settlers. A severe drought between the censuses of 1910 and 1920 dramatized for them the climatic alternation between blinding snow storms and devastating drought. In some northern counties of the Dakotas rainfall averaged twenty inches a year, but the water was too poorly distributed to ensure regular harvests. Flax cost $1.50 a bushel and wheat $1.00 a bushel. A penetratingly hot sun and choking dust withered both crops and men in a treeless countryside. Conversely, hailstorms in midsummer and early autumn pelted farms, stripping new plants of their leaves and causing widespread damage. Italian farmers were, furthermore, unused to handling such crops as alfalfa, wheat, beets, barley, oats, and potatoes. This was a region unsuited to the raising of a few vegetables on a small farm, the normal Italian pattern. Unable to engage in intensive agriculture that required capital and machinery, the Italian farmer often departed after only

[25] *Italians of Omaha,* 103–109.

a short residence. In a region where farms extended for miles, he was again overwhelmed by the gigantic proportions of an extensive agriculture which he did not understand. It is little wonder, then, that section hands on the railroads which crossed the Dakotas continued on west in search of the timbered hillsides and water so treasured in the old country. Too often the railroads had promised settlers land that bore no resemblance to the dry and treeless wastes which could support no farmer—immigrant or otherwise. For those who stayed on and learned to live in temperatures of thirty degrees below zero, the Badlands held less terror as the years passed. Those who came to believe that the climate steadily got better could buy land from others who had departed for as little as $15.00 per acre. As late as 1910, incidentally, more than half of the United States farm population lived on land unoccupied five years before. Few white Americans felt any attachment to a plot of land. They moved repeatedly, and still do so. Although the moving van has become an American symbol, the Italians had no such background.[26]

Farmers who left their land behind, however, characteristically neglected the work necessary to keep farms productive. Immigrants moved onto foreclosed farms, unplowed for years; old orchards had to be pulled up and replanted, fences rebuilt, dry wells redrilled. In fact, newcomers frequently found a costly rehabilitation of most older farms necessary. Some of this land, especially along the Minnesota border, proved to be rather good farm country, with better distribution of rainfall than elsewhere. Good-natured settlers who were not afraid of work even learned to call the area home.[27]

SHIFTING ABOUT from place to place, restless western immigrants came to know two or three "homes" in their lifetimes. Whenever labor conditions worsened, or agricultural lands became depleted

---

[26] *Guida degli Stati Uniti con particolare riferimento alla opera svoltavi degli Italiani*, 115.

[27] Lewis F. Crawford (ed.), *History of North Dakota* (3 vols., Chicago, 1931), I, 417.

by the blowing away of rich topsoil, or the knee-deep grass of the prairie turned brown during droughts, immigrants sold out and sought more fertile lands farther west. Persons who lost their farms in the financial panics of 1873 and 1893 moved on as far as California, where their descendants live today.

VIII
HIGH IN THE SKY: *Colorado*

Long before Colorado achieved statehood in 1876, it was known as a region of great mineral wealth. In addition to its silver and gold mines the state had a rich tableland. Fertile and well wooded, it would produce fine crops when properly irrigated. The area was bound to attract foreigners. In fact, European newspapers once described Colorado as the "Italy of Western America."[1] It rightfully became known to most Europeans as the most mountainous of all the American states, with more peaks within its borders than any other.

The first Italians to head for Colorado's precipitous slopes were from one of the most mountainous regions of Italy, Liguria. From Genoa the four Garbarino brothers started out for Colorado when it was still an untamed wilderness. In the spring of 1859, attracted by rumors of gold, they accompanied an ox-train that left St. Louis, loaded with mining implements, including shovels, gold pans, cradles, and materials with which to build sluices. After only a few days' travel they were met by what they believed to be friendly Indians. Trading ensued, and, little suspecting treachery, the party with which the Garbarinos traveled bedded down for the night. They were awakened by the sound of horses' hoofs. The Indians had stampeded nearly all the animals, including "four fine saddle horses" belonging to the Garbarino brothers. Because their con-

[1] Henry S. Lucas, *Netherlanders in America, Dutch Immigrants to the United States and Canada, 1789–1950*, 431.

voy lost most of its work horses, provision had to be made for replacing these animals. The Garbarinos were among various persons sent back to the Missouri settlements to acquire new horses. For a time it did not appear that they would ever reach Colorado.

After an uncomfortable return journey the Garbarinos eventually saw the Rocky Mountains and, by summer, the mouth of Clear Creek. They were to found a successful family in Colorado. At the site of the present-day city of Golden, one of the brothers, Charles, settled down in what was then a stormy mining camp. Two other brothers, Joseph and Antonio, wandered around other mining camps until they stopped at Georgetown in 1860. The fourth brother, Louis, ultimately made his home at Boulder, among miners lured by gold strikes at Central City, Black Hawk, Russell Gulch, Georgetown, Empire, and other mining camps, as well as the discovery of silver at Leadville. In 1870 the Garbarinos had achieved enough remuneration from mining to send for still another brother.[2]

In Colorado, Italian clerics again appeared at an early date. By 1867 a group of Neapolitan Jesuits, displaced by revolutionary activities in Italy, came to found the Colorado–New Mexico Mission of the Jesuit order. From Santa Fe, New Mexico, they moved northward into the San Juan Valley. There, the Conejos Mission having already been founded, Father Salvatore Persone and Brother Cherubin Anzalone assumed charge of the mission.[3]

The arrival of these priests accompanied the movement into Colorado of secular compatriots who during the 1880's came to work on the Denver and Río Grande Western Railroad as well as in the new state's mines. Demand for their labor was so great that a labor syndicate at Denver employed agents in Italy to toss circulars into village huts that glowingly advertised working conditions in Colorado. The prospective immigrant, however, had to pay his own passage; he also deposited three, five, or ten dollars, and

---

[2] The account of the Garbarino brothers is based upon a statement by their niece printed in Giovanni Perilli, *Colorado and the Italians in Colorado*, 25.

[3] A fuller treatment of the activities of this order is in the section on New Mexico. See J. M. Espinosa, "The Neapolitan Jesuits on the Colorado Frontier, 1868–1919," *Colorado Magazine*, Vol. XV (March, 1938), 64–73.

agreed, in his contract, to pay his "importer," or padrone, 20 per cent of his wages for three years.[4]

The story of one particular migrant to the Rocky Mountain West illuminates that of others whose experiences were similar. This was Adolfo Rossi. During 1881, when only in his early twenties, Rossi headed westward from New York by rail for the Colorado mines. The Denver, South Park and Pacific Railroad (control of which was later bought by the Union Pacific) paid his fare and that of seventy other young Italians. At Denver, Rossi found a city in great contrast to those in Italy. Its streets were largely unpaved, its sidewalks made out of boards; log houses and tents dotted the outlying districts. He was astonished that a large number of men wore beards, women drove buckboards, and cowboys actually wore furry leather chaps. In the belief that he had been hired as a timekeeper, Rossi went to work at a railroad camp eleven thousand feet in altitude, on one of the highest spurs in the Rocky Mountains. Various of his fellow workers thought they had been engaged as cooks, carpenters, and blacksmiths. Instead, Rossi included, they were all put to work clearing and leveling a roadbed of forest and rock so that railroad tracks could be laid across mountainous terrain. Their pay was $2.50 per day, with room and board included. Many miles removed from civilization, they made the best of their unexpected, backbreaking predicament.

Rossi's group also complained about the impossibly bad food and crude log cabins without doors or windows. Some of them had fortunately brought along musical instruments, and they began to play and sing homeland melodies. Much to the amusement of their Irish laboring companions, the Italians, with flute, trombone, and accordion, whiled away leisure hours in the wilderness. Rossi correctly surmised that this was the first time that particular area of the world had ever heard such sounds from mortal man.

Rossi did more than play a musical instrument. He went on to become a waiter at the nearest mining town in a restaurant that

[4] Denver *Labor Enquirer*, January 19, February 9, 1884.

served buffalo and mountain-goat meat. In an Alpine atmosphere the nights were cold and crisp, and Rossi flourished, both in health and fortune. He was soon tanned and bronzed by the sun. Next, a railroad agent offered him a job at company headquarters in Denver. Part of his work was to visit remote construction crews. At one labor camp Rossi found that Italian workers had devised two new dishes. They named the first of these *stufatino alla Colorado*; it consisted of wild game surrounded by a mushroom sauce. The second dish they called *polli delle Rocciose,* or Rocky Mountain chicken—which actually consisted of fat squirrels, roasted over a bed of glistening coals. This food stood in contrast to the boiled bacon, potatoes, and kale of the Irish workmen. In a land where whisky and beer reigned supreme, the Italians found it difficult to find wine. But, despite troublesome shortages, they were able to build a rough facsimile of the cuisine they had once known in their homeland.[5]

The advance of the Italians into the high mountains was due mostly to the way in which the Colorado mines boomed in those years. In the decade from 1880 to 1890, Denver alone increased its population from 35,029 to 106,773 inhabitants. The sound of picks and shovels was everywhere, as inexperienced Italians began to supplant English, Welsh, and Cornish workmen. Slovaks, Poles, Ruthenians, and Russians also made up a new talent pool. They not only overran the labor market of Pittsburgh in the East, but thrust their hammers and drills into the hardrock of western America in search of gold, silver, iron, lead, and copper. Cemeteries in Leadville, Butte, Central City, and other mining camps of the Far West are today filled with Italians who arrived in those years and who also entered the field of granite and freestone quarrying as softstone cutters, stone dressers, slate planers, and stonemasons.[6]

The resultant effect of the new manpower upon this country's working population can hardly be overestimated. In "the old

[5] Adolfo Rossi, *Un Italiano in America, passim.*

[6] See Rowland T. Berthoff, *British Immigrants in Industrial America,* 1790–1850, 55, 61, 81.

days," almost everybody worked, or tried to, and the hundred years before 1910 was compounded by an avalanche of immigrants that averaged three million per decade. Most of these sought manual labor at subsistence wages. Production—on the farm, at the steel mills, along the expanding railway systems—was the key to the economy and to employment. Even small cyclical changes at the production level caused serious economic and social repercussions.

The competition of too many inexperienced laborers, who suddenly had to learn how to use dangerous explosives and complicated machinery, accompanied prejudice and labor agitation against them. It was in Colorado that the Italians experienced the most serious tension they were to encounter in the Far West. In the 1880's even the Italian Jesuit establishment at Pueblo almost had to close its doors because of local ill-feeling. Additional bitterness accompanied the remonstrances of Italians themselves against unsatisfactory working conditions in mines, smelters, and along railroad lines. In 1882, five hundred discontented immigrant laborers of all nationalities congregated at Denver to protest a number of broken promises made by mine operators. That city's Italian consul complained to the Denver *Republican* of April 20, 1882, about the unfair treatment they had received. Prolonged concern over the welfare of workers led these immigrants to form an Italian Protective and Benevolent Association, with headquarters at Denver. Soon thereafter a *Circolo Italiano* was formed as a response to their social needs.[7]

It was the misfortune of too many Italians in Colorado to be engaged in mining—a highly competitive, cyclical industry which placed workers at the mercy of forces beyond their control. Immigrants not only became embroiled in protracted controversies with mine owners and managers. Occasionally they lost their lives in the process. From 1880 to 1914, Colorado was rocked with some of the most explosive labor disputes in the West's history. The Italians comprised only a small factor in this violence, yet they were in the very center of a truly large labor conflagration.

[7] Quoted in LeRoy R. Hafen, *Colorado and Its People*, II (2 vols. New York, 1948), 111.

Throughout the 1890's serious labor disputes against immigrants mounted in Colorado's southeastern coal districts. In the Trinidad mines violence accompanied this mood. In Gilpin County a group of Italian Tyrolese silver miners came into competition with Cornish pickmen. Until the Cornish adjusted to their new competitors, there was conflict. About this accommodation one of the "natives" of Central City remembered returning to his mountain home in the late nineties after its "golden age" had passed. His accustomed amber home brew had given way to the red Chianti of Italy, and "names ending in 'ini' appeared on store signs where once were the names of Polyglase and Trelawney."[8]

Tension between laborers, immigrant and non-immigrant, resulted mostly from the importation of "cheap workers" by big mining corporations. In an age before large-scale unionization, immigrants aroused the jealousy of other workers because they could live on a small income and were willing to work in the mines for lower wages. Whenever mining experienced one of its characteristic slumps, violence was apt to erupt. At Gunnison in 1890 and at Denver in 1893, Italians were lynched, as a witness of the latter murder graphically recalled:

> The victim had been working on the South Oak road at Alpine tunnel, and in an altercation with a contractor named Hoblitzell, had shot and mortally wounded him. The Italian escaped, but was captured later during the day and taken to Gunnison, where he was given a preliminary examination the following evening. The sheriff and district attorney feared for the safety of the culprit, so he was placed in a room on the second floor of the courthouse, where it was thought he would be better protected. Everything was quiet up to midnight and it was thought there would be no trouble. A few minutes after twelve, however, the guard heard a light rap on the door and, thinking it was one of the guards, unlocked the door to see what was wanted and found himself staring into a small flock of six-shooters. He was overpowered, the prisoner hastily removed, and a short time later was swinging at the end of a rope from the sign of Kelmel and Allison's livery stable on Tomichi Avenue. A few days

[8] Lynn I. Perrigo, "The Cornish Miners of Early Gilpin County," *Colorado Magazine*, Vol. XIV (May, 1937), 98–101.

later, the town was somewhat stirred by the report that 300 Italians were on the way to burn the town in retaliation.[9]

Although the Italians never carried out this rumored threat, Gunnison's residents believed them capable of doing so. Colorado violence was not, of course, restricted to acts against the Italians. The writer of the above account naively recorded: "In the first nine months after I arrived, there had been no less than six shootings and murders, all of which ended fatally, one lynching and one legal hanging."[10] The fact that this incident involved a foreigner, and thus seemed exotic, was probably the main reason it was recorded for posterity. Similarly, the account of so startling an event as a quadruple-murder in Denver by four Italians during 1875 had fascinated local newspaper readers.[11]

The swashbuckling atmosphere of frontier towns encouraged violence among potential delinquents. As late as 1880, Leadville, then only about two years old, had some three hundred saloons; its four dance halls and five theaters were never empty. A spirit of turbulence, rather than justice and order, formed the tide of life that surged upward into the Colorado Mountains. In an environment of adventurers, gamblers, and ne'er-do-wells, where gangs of rustlers shot it out on the streets of cow towns, miners could hardly expect to be spared violence. In 1895 in the southern Colorado coal fields a group of miners slew six Italian workers implicated in the death of an American saloonkeeper. In 1900, four others met their death at Walsenburg.

Italians sometimes found themselves embroiled in the quarrels of others. In 1899 a strike at Lake City, Colorado, grew out of a mining company's requirement that single men must be boarded in its dormitories. When the Italians, goaded by native miners who hated such "boarding house requirements" as much as they, refused to accede to this stricture, the operators gave all concerned

---

[9] George A. Root, "Gunnison in the Early 'Eighties,'" *Colorado Magazine,* Vol. IX (November, 1932), 204–205.

[10] *Ibid.,* 205.

[11] See D. J. Cook, *Hands Up; or Twenty Years of Detective Life in the Mountains and on the Plains* (Norman, 1958), 12–38.

notice of termination of employment. Then the Italians refused to leave the premises, whereupon "the company," over the protest of the local Italian consul, told the single men they had three days in which to leave. Married persons were ordered to move elsewhere within one month. A serious strike followed these announcements.

At other times strikes were caused by poor safety conditions. Miners complained that tunnel inspection was a farce, that protective cages were not being used to lower them into dangerous shafts, that mines with immense stopes had hardly a timber in them. What was worse, because of poor ventilation, miners frequently had to be carried out of tunnels unconscious or dead from the effects of gas.

These abuses were bound to drive miners into the arms of unions. One immigrant stated that he joined the mining union at Cripple Creek "because I saw it would help me to keep in work and for protection in case of accident or sickness, for the union is just like any other secret order that way."[12] After the turn of the century a Socialist journal, *Wayland's Monthly*, objected violently to the deportation of laborers in the Colorado mines by military authorities. These forced evictions had included Italians. Among them, at Trinidad, on March 26, 1904, were Josef Paganni and Adolfo Bartolli, editor and publisher of *Il Lavoratore Italiano*, a labor journal that had stirred up trouble against mine operators. Also ousted from that mining camp was William M. Wardjon, national organizer of the United Mine Workers of America. *Wayland's Monthly* reported what it considered to be further extralegal outrages:

> On May 19, eighty Italian strikers were marched from Berwind to Trinidad by a troop of cavalry. They had refused to register in Berwind. . . . The men complained that the march of eighteen miles over the mountains on a hot day caused them great fatigue and that some of them dropped by the wayside, but they were cursed and driven on by the mounted soldiers. They were given water, but no food, neither on the march or at Trinidad. On arrival at military headquarters they were photographed in groups and registered ac-

[12] Ginzberg and Berman, *American Worker*, 63.

cording to the Bertillon system, then turned loose. . . . On May 22 ten men, who had been arrested on various charges during the previous fortnight were placed on board a southbound Colorado and Southern train at Trinidad and taken across the line into New Mexico, in charge of an officer and a squad of soldiers. They were ordered not to return to the coal-mining district during the prevalence of martial law.[13]

Immigrants thus participated vigorously in the conflict that marred labor-management relations early in this century. During the 1904 Cripple Creek strike, Colorado's governor declared martial law and ordered the state militia to destroy the Western Federation of Miners. Similarly, four years later, Nevada's governor, during the Goldfield, Nevada, strike, supported mine owners in an attempt to drive the union's membership out of that state.

Foreigners detested the notion that they were the chattels of mine or mill owners, dependent upon them for jobs, homes, food, and even schooling. Having fled the feudalism of the past and made the break westward, they felt an impatience with the status quo that did not permit them gracefully to tolerate discrimination in the high mountains. As Americans in transition, they possessed a freedom of choice unrooted in a particular locality. Despite Colorado's labor violence, the western scene represented an open, fluid society.

Early in this century, spurred by Socialist talk of building a classless society, western immigrant miners grew to have a great interest in trade unions. In this attitude they differed, as one authority puts it, from native Americans who regarded trade unions as "un-American." Typical was the way in which the Italians became involved in attempts to unionize the Rockefeller-owned Colorado Fuel and Iron Company Works at Trinidad and Pueblo and in a variety of similar causes. An especially tragic altercation took place on April 20, 1914, at Ludlow, Colorado. There, in a tent colony established at that mining camp, the Italians participated in a heated demonstration over wages, hours,

[13] U.S. Commissioner of Labor, "Class Conflict in Colorado," an extract from a report, in *Wayland's Monthly* (April, 1907), 56–58.

and working conditions. A pitched battle with the mine operators followed. The state militia was called out to quell the outbreak. Troopers raked immigrant and non-immigrant strikers with machine gun fire and burned the entire Ludlow tent camp to the ground. Two Italian women and thirteen children were burned to death. President Wilson interceded with a proposal to end this strike, and eventually the state of Colorado paid the Italians damages for the incident, thereby accepting partial responsibility for the deaths caused. Because of serious adverse publicity against the Standard Oil Trust after the Ludlow outbreak, John D. Rockefeller, Sr., hired a public relations man, Ivy Lee, to try to improve his image.[14]

Immigrant involvement in labor disputes was inevitable at a time of great strife for the United States union movement. They joined first one and then another labor organization. In 1907, Italians had participated in a strike launched by the Western Federation of Miners in the iron ranges of Minnesota. After the failure of the 1907 Minnesota iron strike, the Western Federation of Miners, however, gave up industrial unionism and returned to the fold of the American Federation of Labor. Inexperienced immigrants eventually turned to the Industrial Workers of the World as an organization that encompassed all laborers, not just craft workers. In 1910 only 15 per cent of the Italian iron workers in the United States had been miners before, and they especially felt the need for union protection. From 1912 to 1914 the Italians also became involved in copper mining disputes in Montana. Industrial unionists struck again in 1918 within the Minnesota iron pits. A successful strike, it made the high-water mark of the I.W.W., soon to experience reversals that would lead to its ultimate dissolution.[15]

[14] Perilli, *Colorado*, 41–42; Percy C. Fritz, *Colorado, the Centennial State* (New York, 1941), 370–79. A Socialist account of the Ludlow massacre and other mining violence is in the fiftieth anniversary issue of *La Parola del Popolo* (December, 1958), 98–116; Moses Rischin, "The Jewish Labor Movement in America," *Labor History*, Vol. IV (Fall, 1963), 230.

[15] Selig Perlman and Philip Taft, *History of Labor in the United States, 1896–1932*, IV (4 vols., New York, 1935), 388–90; Fred Thompson, *The I.W.W., Its*

Eventually, new economic pursuits partly replaced the gold and silver mining for which Colorado had been famous. This had the effect of diversifying immigrant activity. After the turn of the century, Marble, Colorado, for example, became a center of important quarrying and marble-cutting operations. There Italian artisans worked its pure white stone into final form, polishing it by hand. At Marble, in fact, they processed the largest block of marble ever quarried—one hundred tons in weight—and it now occupies an honored place in the nation's capital as the Tomb of the Unknown Soldier.

Another aspect of the Italian impact upon Colorado has been the influence of the Missionary Sisters of the Sacred Heart. Their leader, Mother Frances Xavier Cabrini, became the first American to be canonized as a saint by the Roman Catholic Church. In 1904–1905 this "Saint of the Immigrants" founded at Denver the Queen of Heaven Institute and directed the building of a succession of schools and orphanages in other western states. Despite the decline of the Italian population, her work still survives.[16]

The Italian-born population of Colorado reached a peak of 15,000 in 1910. If one counts the second generation, they then numbered some 40,000, enough persons to support various newspapers. Among the Italian papers published in Denver from 1885 onward were *La Stella, La Nazione, Il Risveglio, La Capitale, Il Roma,* and *La Frusta. Il Vindici* was a monthly and *La Voce del Popolo* a weekly with a circulation of 15,595 by 1931. At Trinidad *Il Corriere di Trinidad* had a circulation of 3,500 in 1919. By the 1950's the only surviving papers were *Il Risveglio,* at Denver, and *L'Unione,* at Pueblo. The latter reached a circulation of 16,291 in 1931.[17]

First Fifty Years, 1905–1955, 101–104. A good analysis of mining and labor turmoil is Vernon H. Jensen's *Heritage of Conflict: Labor Relations in the Nonferrous Metals Industry up to 1930.*

[16] See Sister M. L. Owens, "Frances Xavier Cabrini," *Colorado Magazine,* Vol. XXII (July, 1945), 171–78; Theodore Maynard, *Too Small a World; the Life of Francesca Cabrini.*

[17] Perilli, *Colorado,* 38; *Foreign Language Publications,* 1; Schiavo, *Four Centuries,* 170; Lord and Thomas, *Pocket Directory,* 646; Ayer, *Directory,* 1236–38.

Colorado's Italians settled in some incredibly remote locations. Only a mile from Julesburg is a place known as "the Italian's Cave." This is an artificially enlarged subterranean cavern with the ruins of a two-story stone building at its mouth. Its walls, more than two feet thick, are pierced with weird loopholes. This for a time was the home of a French Canadian, Jules Reni, founder of Old Julesburg. The place, with its primitive water system, seems to have been built by Umberto Gabello, an Italian miner. Gabello amassed a sizable fortune in the gold fields at Cripple Creek. He lived a hermit's life in his cave-house, avoiding contact even with neighbors. Some considered him mad; others believed him to be a sorcerer. After he died, esoteric symbols were found carved on the walls of his dwelling, giving rise to the notion that he considered it a temple of the sun.[18]

In Colorado, as elsewhere, it is not easy to recapture the spirit and daily life of immigrants whose records have been destroyed. When available, however, first-person accounts are useful. Here is such a fragmentary description of conditions around 1900:

Uncle Dominic lived in Coalville, a coal camp situated in the coal fields of south-central Colorado. It was a settlement of perhaps eighty or ninety company shacks, in which lived the miners and their families. The country around was mountainous and barren. Rockton, the nearest town, was four miles away, reached by a dusty, bumpy road. Here stood the railroad station, from which traveled, once a day, a freight train to Coalville—with a caboose for passengers—to pick up the coal. . . . To hear my father describe it, there was nothing barren about Coalville in those days, however. The miners were mostly Italian and Polish, with a sprinkling of Welsh, Swedes, and native-born Americans. . . . The miners were paid according to the amount of coal they dug, and the best of them averaged no more than fifty or sixty dollars a month. In turn they had to pay the company exorbitant rent for the shacks in which they lived, and the high prices charged at the company store for foodstuffs kept them indebted to the company. As a result, there was considerable dissatisfaction, especially among the Americans; but the Italians and Poles,

[18] Work Progress Administration, *The Oregon Trail* (New York, 1939), 78.

remembering the poverty which they had known in the old country, were, on the whole, content.

A real sense of unity developed in such mining camps as the writer goes on to describe:

> The Italians in the coal camp . . . were like one great family held together by the mines, and when anyone of them left, his departure was mourned like that of a brother. . . . Everyone in Coalville attended the farewell gathering, even the superintendent of the company.[19]

In the cold and rugged environment of the mining camps, housing and food, especially in winter, meant much, as this same author recalled:

> The great roaring fire in the pot-bellied stove in the wintertime, with the mist on the windows and the snow-covered mountains; the frosty cellar, with its sacks of spidery potatoes and onions and the cans of spareribs and Italian pork-sausage preserved in lard; the sound of the wind whirling around the corners of the house. . . . the great cauldrons of blood-red spaghetti, the pots of stews, the platters of fried potatoes and peppers, the redolent loaves of bread browning in the oven.[20]

In 1910 the Colorado State Board of Immigration made a strong bid for Italian farmers to settle in the state.[21] Those who arrived clustered around the farming community of Welby, north of Denver. There they engaged in fruit growing, dairying, and the cultivation of celery. These agricultural products they shipped into the Colorado capital, where the demand for them grew as the population increased. One rather minor but locally well-known by-product of the Italians in Colorado is Merlino's Cherry and Raspberry Cider, made by a pioneer family that settled in Cañon City.

Italians left certain geographical marks on the high and rocky land of their adoption. At the head of the Gunnison River,

[19] Pagano, *Golden Wedding,* 9–10, 39.
[20] *Ibid.,* 36.
[21] Higham, *Strangers,* 113.

Italian Peak (sometimes Italia Mountain) has been named for them; so has Como in Park County, a town occupied after 1879 by Italian coal miners. In 1907 the Italians obtained passage by the state legislature of an act making Columbus Day a legal holiday. Other holidays also continue to be celebrated. An outstanding annual event among the Denver Italians, as elsewhere, is the feast of San Rocco, which commemorates the life of a priest who begged money from the rich with which to help heal the sick.[22]

In Colorado, despite poor working conditions and serious competition, the Italians were able to integrate themselves into the state's society. The widespread industrial warfare they encountered did not permanently flaw their future. The Rocky Mountain West provided them with a gratifying time of growth, a time to build and a time to plant their roots deeply in the soil.

[22] See *Denver Post*, August 23, 1955.

IX

PIONEERING IN THE INTERMOUNTAIN REGION

BEYOND THE ROCKIES and east of the Cascades lies the Intermountain West. Migration moved rapidly from the Great Plains into this extensive land-locked area in the second half of the nineteenth century. Before a frontier of settlement could develop, trappers, traders, explorers, and men of the cloth roamed the high country from Colorado westward to Utah. Italian priests were among those who penetrated the region, and their activity came to be centered upon the Indian tribes that lived in western Montana and beyond. In the Rocky Mountains and on the Great Plains these men, most of whom were foreigners, wore the black robes of the Society of Jesus, and they thereby recognized neither territorial nor geographical boundaries. Since the sixteenth century, when Francis Xavier attempted to missionize Japan, the Jesuits had manned outposts as far away as Goa in India and along the Zambesi River in East Africa. America formed only a part of the worldwide activities of the Jesuit order.

Missionizing the Indians of western America, however, was an important part of Jesuit operations. In 1831, and again in 1835, 1837, and 1839, Indians from western Montana had traveled eastward to St. Louis in search of "the white man's book of heaven." These Flathead–Nez Percé "delegations" were led by French-speaking Iroquois who asked the Jesuits at St. Louis College to open a permanent mission among the Pend d'Oreilles, Kutenais, Spokanes, Kayuses, and Kettles as well. In 1840, after red men had repeatedly asked that "Black Robes" be sent to teach them the ways of the whites, the Belgian Jesuit Father Pierre Jean De Smet made his well-known reconnaissance journey to the tribes beyond the Rocky Mountains on the far side of the Continental Divide. Following that trip De Smet returned to St. Louis to appeal for volunteers with which to Christianize these distant tribes. Although De Smet occupied the center of the western missionary stage, he was not one of those frontier Jesuits who spent a lifetime among the aborigines. He was, rather, chief creator, financier, and staffer of the Jesuit missions in northwestern America.[1]

Eventually, De Smet's call for help aroused action in Europe. From Italy, traditional recruiting ground of the Jesuits, eager young clerics responded. Large numbers were not needed. In 1841, the first of these Jesuits, a twenty-nine-year-old Roman named Gregorio Mengarini, reported to Father De Smet at St. Louis. That year De Smet, Mengarini, and a party consisting of Father Nicholas Point, three lay brothers, and some Canadian mule-drivers and mountaineers traveled westward out of Missouri. On April 30 they left the future jumping-off place of such western parties—Westport. Near the Kaw Indian village on the Kaw River they were joined by a party of about fifty immigrants, the first organized group to cross the Great Plains to California. Of the initial meeting between the two groups, John Bidwell, leader of the overland party to California, later wrote:

> Finally a man came up, one of the last to arrive, and announced that a company of Catholic missionaries were on their way from St. Louis to the Flathead nation of Indians with an old Rocky Mountaineer for a guide, and that if we would wait another day they would be up with us. At first we were independent, and thought we could not afford to wait for a slow missionary party. But when we found that no one knew which way to go, we sobered down. . . . otherwise probably not one of us would ever have reached California.[2]

[1] On this score see Gilbert J. Garraghan, *Chapters in Frontier History*, 136–37.

[2] John Bidwell, *In California Before the Gold Rush* (Los Angeles, 1948), 15–16, contains references to the Bidwell-Bartleson party and the Jesuits who accompanied them west as far as Soda Springs. A Protestant, Bidwell wrote of Father De Smet, "He was genial, of fine presence, and one of the saintliest men I have ever

The "old Rocky Mountaineer" was Thomas Fitzpatrick, veteran of the trail and a guide of wide experience, having conducted Marcus Whitman and his wife across the plains to the Oregon country in 1836. Fitzpatrick was assisted by John Grey, another frontier hunter, and several trail-blazing teamsters. These assistants of De Smet guided both groups on a five-month trip across the plains and over the Rockies. The Jesuit equipment consisted of four two-wheeled carts and a wagon drawn by mules. The priests themselves rode saddle horses. At a cutoff within present-day Idaho, Fathers De Smet and Mengarini bade the Bidwell-Bartleson group farewell. Traveling on toward Fort Hall and the Snake River country, the Jesuits headed into western Montana.

Eventually the priests—all three of them foreigners—reached the Bitter Root Valley, where the Flatheads, or Selish Indians, lived. In the area which the Lewis and Clark expedition had traversed thirty-six years before, located between present-day Stevensville and the later Fort Owen, they built a rude log construction whose cracks they chinked with clay. They named the lonely place St. Mary's. This was not only Montana's first mission and church; it became a point of departure from which further missionary activity was launched. After De Smet left him in charge at St. Mary's, Mengarini was to spend the next ten years among the Indians.

Mengarini was a remarkable man. Later to become President of Santa Clara College in California, he grew so adept at using the Selish and Kalispel languages that the Indians ordinarily could not tell the difference between his speech and theirs. Most of all he enjoyed the trick of passing himself off as a member of their tribe.[3] A basic source concerning the early history of what was then called "Old Oregon" is a narrative which Mengarini himself wrote.[4] Mengarini became the foremost authority on the language and

known, and I cannot wonder that the Indians were made to believe him divinely protected." See also Albert J. Partoll (ed.), *Mengarini's Narrative of the Rockies . . .* "Sources of Northwest History, Number 25," a pamphlet.

[3] Lawrence B. Palladino, *Indian and White in the Northwest*, 79.

[4] Edited by Partoll, in *Mengarini's Narrative of the Rockies.*

culture of the Flatheads. He published A *Selish or Flat-Head Grammar* (New York, 1861), printed in Latin and never superseded.[5] As early as 1846 he began work on A *Dictionary of the Kalispel or Flat-Head Indian Language,* published in 1877 at St. Ignatius, among the first of the Jesuit missions in Montana.[6]

There are criticisms that could be levied against the Jesuit record. In some cases their labors were not long-lasting. While they relieved the sufferings of native converts, the Indians on occasion reverted to their earlier aboriginal state, influenced only superficially by the education and training given them by European mentors. Yet, these early clerics made almost superhuman attempts to understand the Indians. They were responsible for the first Indian grammars written in Montana. In 1879, Father Alexander Diomedi, who worked among the Kalispels in the upper Columbia River and Coeur d'Alene regions, wrote his *Sketches of Modern Indian Life.*[7] He operated his own press and also printed *Smiimii Lu Tel Kaimintis Kolinzuten,* a Kalispel book of scripture. Diomedi wrote with much detail, producing, in addition, a Kalispel *Dictionary,* the joint effort of his fellow priests at St. Mary's Mission over more than three decades.[8] The book, printed in three volumes, required three years of time (1876–79) to print.[9]

Another skilled linguist was Father Philip Canestrelli who in 1894 published A *Kootenai Grammar.* Designed for the use of missionaries, the Canestrelli grammar was published in Latin, a language which the Jesuits had been required to learn. Anthony Morvillo's A *Dictionary of the Nez Percé Language,* printed at St.

[5] Latin title: *Grammatica Linguae Selicae.*

[6] "Silver Dick" Butler, an early Montana printer, helped install at St. Ignatius a press that was brought to Montana in 1876. Butler worked for several years on the dictionary, using Italian boys to set the type. This early press was sent to the Gonzaga University Museum at Spokane, Washington, in 1898.

[7] Not, however, published until 1894.

[8] Andrew F. Rolle, "The Italian Moves Westward," *Montana, the Magazine of Western History,* Vol. XVI (January, 1966), 20.

[9] Schoenberg, *Jesuits in Montana,* 29. Examples of this early Jesuit printing in the Northwest are reproduced in Wilfred P. Schoenberg, *Jesuit Mission Presses in the Pacific Northwest.*

Ignatius Mission in 1895, is another example of the work in which Mengarini and Canestrelli engaged. These Jesuits reveled in the chance to unlock the Indian languages through the grammars and missals they published.

Mengarini and De Smet were the first white residents of the Mission Valley near present-day Missoula. In 1844, they here built St. Ignatius, a mission whose wooden buildings were eventually rebuilt as brick and stone structures designed to keep out the harsh winter cold. Later Father Joseph Bandini joined them at St. Ignatius, which is still a sizable Jesuit establishment.[10]

Father De Smet's biographer called Mengarini "a man of tried virtue and gentle nature, a skillful physician, a musician of no mean order and a remarkable linguist." Like Father Peter Prando, Mengarini was skilled in folk medicine and Indian herbalism, while Father Ravalli administered medicine of all sorts, including vaccination. Mengarini even wrote professional articles for ethnographic and anthropological journals printed in America.[11]

The frontier brought out, in both Mengarini and Ravalli, unusual powers of perception and a tenacity to face its harshness in loneliness. For a Roman accustomed to a Mediterranean climate, the winters of the American Northwest were fierce. In 1844, Father De Smet, desiring to visit Mengarini, wrote to explain why he could not do so:

> One of the Kalispels offered to carry a message to St. Mary's on snowshoes, so I wrote Father Mengarini, saying, among other things, "I have done what I could, with prudence to come to you; but I have found insurmountable barriers in the snows of the Coeur d'Alene

[10] Part of the artistic decoration of St. Ignatius was the work of Brother Joseph Carignano, S. J. (1853–1919). Born in Turin, he decorated chapels and churches at Missoula and elsewhere in Idaho and Montana. By profession a cook, he stole time from his pots and pans to devote to his painting.

[11] Titles of Mengarini's articles are listed in the footnotes of his *Narrative*. See Mengarini to De Smet, dated June 28, 1842, in De Smet's *Voyages aux Montagnes Rocheuses chez les tribus indiennes du vaste territoire de l'Orégon . . . par le R. P. De Smet*, 251–53. See also P. J. De Smet, *Western Missions and Missionaries*; R. P. Laveille, *Le P. De Smet, 1801–1873*; and Robert I. Burns, *The Jesuits and the Indian Wars of the Northwest*, 50.

mountains and the over flowed rivers, and now finally the ice stops me on Clark's Fork."[12]

Later, De Smet learned that Mengarini himself "had only escaped with the greatest difficulty from the snow and water, and that twelve of his horses had perished in the 'evil forest.' "[13]

These missionaries were, furthermore, never completely free from Indian depredations. Mengarini once described the history of his mission as largely "an account of Blackfeet inroads and Flathead reprisals." Pacification of the predatory, indeed murderous, Blackfeet posed a persistent problem. In fact, had not pestilence decimated the Blackfeet the year before the Jesuits arrived, their mission would have failed. Even after the mission was established, the Blackfeet boldly raided it at night and drove off horses and mules.

Indians repeatedly troubled the area adjoining the mission. Mengarini's *Narrative* describes a typical Indian battle between the Flatheads and their mortal enemy, the Blackfeet.

> Lodges had been set up in various places, and behind these the Flatheads would make their last stand if beaten in the field. A hillock separated us from the plain, but we could hear the whizzing of the balls as they passed over our heads. No cry was raised during the battle, but we heard the reports of the rifles nearer and nearer, and knew that our warriors were hard pressed. I had no sooner reached the thicket than I raised my hands to heaven and prayed fervently. The battle lasted nearly all day. . . . as the sun was sinking in the west our victorious warriors returned, bearing with them the bodies of the four slain. The enemy, leaving twenty-four upon the field, had sought safety in their camp.[14]

From 1841 to 1850, Mengarini taught these Flatheads the catechism, organized an Indian band, played games with them, studied their folklore, and practiced medicine among them. It seems remarkable that a priest fresh from Europe could adapt himself so readily to the rugged life of a frontier as yet unvisited

[12] Chittenden and Richardson, *Life, Letters and Travels*, II, 466.
[13] *Ibid.*
[14] Mengarini, *Narrative*, 8.

by white men. But Mengarini and De Smet were in the tradition of Father Kino of the Southwestern Spanish frontier more than a century and a half before. In Montana, as in Arizona and New Mexico earlier, Jesuits labored against great odds to missionize the Indian.

Montana's earliest history is in part the story of a handful of such frontier priests—often Italians—and of their material and spiritual achievements. Founding missions, churches, and Indian schools, printing dictionaries and grammars, and attempting to convert their charges to Christianity were their major objectives. They were not interested in bringing Italian settlers with them. Whenever members of the order were killed by Indians this seemed to spur on the recruiting of replacements in Italy. Some seventy Italian Jesuits, priests, seminarians, and lay brothers reached the Northwest between 1840 and 1900.[15]

The northwestern Jesuits were, for their time and place, generally highly educated men. Father Congiato had been vice president first at a College of Nobles in Italy and of the College of Fribourg in Switzerland, as well as of a small Jesuit college in Bardstown, Kentucky. After his Indian career ended, he would become president of San Francisco College, later the University of San Francisco. Giorda had taught at an Italian seminary, Canestrelli at the Gregorian University in Rome. Diomedi was a former tutor at the Jesuit Roman College. Imoda taught at the College of Nobles in Naples. D'Aste had pursued mathematical studies at the University of Paris. Cataldo had studied in Sicily and Belgium; Prando at Rome and Monaco; Rappagliosi in Italy, France, and Belgium. Palladino had studied in Italy, Austria, and France. And Vanzina was prefect of San Francisco College before beginning his seventeen years among the northwestern Indians.[16]

Father Gregory Gazzoli came from the most important family among the Italian northwestern Jesuits. Described as "urbane and talented," he belonged to the Roman nobility. Gazzoli's uncle was

---

[15] Letter to the author from Anthony P. Via, S. J., Jesuit Historical Archives, Oregon Province, Mount St. Michaels, Spokane, Washington, November 30, 1955.

[16] Burns, *Jesuits*, 48, 55.

a cardinal, and he himself had been baptized by Pope Pius VII. Such a social background, with its ease of life, did not, however, deter Gazzoli from becoming, in 1850, a missionary near Lake Coeur d'Alene. He and Father Ravalli ran a two-man mission there for years and, along with Cataldo, exerted their influence to keep the Indians from going on the warpath.[17]

These Jesuits were an international brigade composed not only of Italians but also of Austrians, French, Germans, and Belgians. Late in 1846, Father De Smet set out for the third time on a final journey from the Rocky Mountains to St. Louis, never again to return as an active field missionary. While he was the impresario of the Jesuit effort on the frontier, men like Mengarini were its ultimate executors. But Mengarini, ordered first to the Willamette Valley in Oregon and then to Santa Clara, California, in 1850, was only one of them.[18]

The Italian Jesuits worked among all the tribes of the Northwest. Father Grassi (who came to prefer a year-around diet of pancakes and bacon over any other kind of food) lived among the Blackfeet, Gros Ventres, Kalispels, Okanagans, Chelans, Yakimas, and Umatillas. Father Caruana worked among the Yakimas; Guidi among the Kettles; Morvillo with the Nez Percés; Imoda among the Blackfeet; and Palladino among the Flatheads.[19]

Most of them having been born during the Napoleonic Wars, their lives were to transcend the Victorian era, and they were to live beyond it in the American wild West. The life spans of these priests were remarkable: De Smet, for example, lived from 1801 to 1876; Joset, 1810–1900; Cataldo, 1837–1928; Accolti, 1807–78; Ravalli, 1812–84; Congiato, 1816–97; Palladino, 1837–1927; Caruana, 1836–1913. Most of these priests arrived after the Turin Province of the Jesuit order assumed control of the American northwestern missions in 1854.

Some among them were recruited from Italy earlier by De Smet.

[17] *Ibid.*, 153, 401, 425.

[18] Before his death at Santa Clara, California, in 1886, Mengarini assembled a series of memoirs about his activities as one of the founders of St. Mary's.

[19] Burns, *Jesuits*, 53–54, 409, 426.

Father Anthony Ravalli, a native of Ferrara, landed on the Pacific in 1844 at Fort Vancouver in the company of Father Michael Accolti. He was to spend the rest of his life in the West.[20] Ravalli thereby turned his back upon what would have been a brilliant European career. Having entered the Jesuit order at fifteen and studied medicine, surgery, art, philosophy, and the natural sciences, Ravalli had taught at Turin. Described as facile and cordial, he was Montana's first physician, druggist, and medical authority. Ravalli could handle a plane, a foot adz, a carpenter's saw, a dress stone; he could lay brick, do a mason's work, make furniture, set a horseshoe, forge and temper iron; he moulded his own candles and was a good musician and painter. He was, furthermore, jovial, energetic, and outgoing. His only shortcomings were genuine difficulty in learning various Indian dialects and general laxity in maintaining Indian discipline.[21]

Ravalli reached the Bitter Root Valley in midsummer of 1845 to carry forward the work of Mengarini and De Smet. He replaced Father Peter Zerbinatti, who soon thereafter drowned in the Bitter Root River. After 1845, laboring almost alone at St. Mary's, Ravalli constructed "an unlikely baroque structure ninety feet long and sixty feet high . . . built of hewn timber, completely without nails."[22] He made virtually every article necessary for church ceremonies. Ravalli transported a set of European buhrstones by pack horse to St. Mary's via Fort Colville, some three hundred miles away. This, Montana's first grist mill, operated by water power, greatly improved the diet of the padres. They, like the Indians, had existed largely upon dried buffalo meat, fish, tallow, roots, berries, and a few vegetables. With Father Mengarini, Ravalli also constructed a primitive sawmill. He next invented a small still to extract alcohol for medicinal purposes from the camas

[20] Accompanying De Smet and Ravalli on this trip, in addition to Accolti, were Fathers Peter Zerbinatti and the Swiss Joseph Joset, as well as Brothers Vincent Magi and John Nobili.

[21] "Father Ravalli—Missionary, Pioneer, Teacher," *The Daily Missoulian* (Missoula), March 8, 1904, based upon an article, "Father Ravalli," in *Anaconda Standard,* June 16, 1895; Burns, *Jesuits,* 72, 193.

[22] *Ibid.,* 192.

root and sugar out of potatoes. From his small log dispensary he vaccinated Indians, performed amputations, and concocted powders and medicines out of the crudest of materials. Ravalli's immediate superior was Father Jerome d'Aste, a Genoese displaced by the Revolution of 1848.[23]

These self-exiled clerics received mail from their homeland about once a year. Even to keep up this contact, and to seek provisions, they had to send Indians some eight hundred miles to Fort Vancouver. In addition to his duties among the Flatheads, Ravalli spent time with the Coeur d'Alene Indians in today's north Idaho panhandle. Although later (1860–63) assigned to the Jesuit College in Santa Clara, California, he was eventually allowed to return to western Montana in the mid-1860's, where he ministered to gold miners during the rush into the Sun River country. In 1866 he had the pleasure of reopening St. Mary's mission, closed since 1850. By the late sixties, whites were entering western Montana in greater numbers. For decades Ravalli, in boots and a long overcoat, with a breviary in his pocket, medicines and surgical instruments in his saddlebags, was a familiar figure as he rode an Indian pony through the winter snows and summer heat to minister to the sick and injured. Toward the end of his life the priest became so ill that he could not tend the little drugstore inside the log cabin built near St. Mary's which was the first one in the Northwest.

For forty years Ravalli carried on his labors without returning to his homeland. He retained a lingering love for the land of his birth. Once, when asked if he ever felt the desire to return there, he answered, "Yes, and I could have had that pleasure. But then the sacrifice would not have been complete." He lowered his head after this remark, weeping and sobbing like a child.[24] Something of the forbearance that typified this pioneer's character appears in a letter written by him to Miss Narcissa Caldwell a few months

[23] Helen A. Howard, "Padre Ravalli: Versatile Missionary," *The Historical Bulletin* (January, 1940), 33–35; Palladino, *Indian and White*, 59–60. Wilfred Schoenberg, *Jesuits in Montana, 1840–1960*, 16–17.

[24] Palladino, 59–60.

before his death at St. Mary's Mission in 1884. He had been confined to his bed for several years. In order to minister to the sick he had himself carried out of St. Mary's on a black deer-thong pallet. Despite his pain, he wrote, "Not for it shall I desist from blessing my God, because I am certain that He will not send me tribulations, which without His help, I could not endure."[25]

Held in high regard, this Italian established a reputation which led to the permanent affixing of his name on Montana's landscape. Ravalli County and the town of Ravalli, a station on the Northern Pacific Railroad, were named in his honor.[26]

The career of another highly literate Piedmontese further illustrates Jesuit influence in the Northwest. This was Father Giuseppe Giorda, who, like Gazzoli, was born of a noble family and had done pastoral work in Corsica. Giorda followed in the Ravalli missionary tradition. In 1865, Father Giorda visited one of the wildest of western mining towns, Virginia City, after founding St. Peter's Mission on the Missouri and working among the Coeur d'Alene Indians. He hoped to establish a church at Virginia City. The existence of an atmosphere of violence, prohibitive prices and lawbreakers did not rule out the need for religion. During had been ruined for future use. Governor Meagher then asked to find a chapel in which to celebrate Mass. After searching throughout the town, the priest was on the verge of abandoning his efforts when unexpected help came to him.

On Christmas Eve news of his unsuccessful attempts to find space reached a local barroom. Several of its leading customers, after raising their glasses on high, contacted the forceful Irishman who was acting governor of Montana—General Thomas Francis Meagher. The governor, a striking figure with a bulbous nose and curled locks of hair, agreed to help collect gold so that Father

[25] Fr. A. Ravalli to Miss Narcissa Caldwell, June 16, 1884, a.l.s., Montana Historical Society, Helena, Montana.

[26] I am indebted to Anne McDonald, former curator of the Montana Historical Society, for an appraisal of Ravalli's importance. An official account of his activities and those of his associates appears in Garraghan, "The Oregon Missions," in *The Jesuits of the Middle United States*, II, 236–392. See also Palladino, *Indian and White*, 64–76.

Giorda could rent an already engaged theater at the corner of Wallace and Jackson streets. As helpers of every variety began to transform the theater, the actors performing there were persuaded that they needed a rest during the holiday season. All gaudy pictures and signs were removed. A large cross was hoisted over the door, and decorative evergreens were brought into the building. Next, Virginia City's residents constructed an altar, communion railing, and confessional. For Catholics the preparations seemed as exciting as the Gold Stampede at Last Chance Gulch.

A midnight Mass followed. The service was so crowded that worshipers knelt at the door in the inclement weather. After Mass was over, the proprietor of the theater complained that his building had been ruined for future use. Governor Meagher then asked him to set a price on the structure. Meagher personally collected another offering of gold dust on a Delft plate with spoons in it to scoop up the gold. The governor, expressing the wish that Father Giorda might make Virginia City his home, handed the proceeds to the amazed Torinese priest. By this time Giorda was in tears. The Mass he had celebrated introduced Montanans to their first urban church.[27]

Soon thereafter Giorda, although he regretted that he spoke the English language indistinctly, was chosen chaplain of the Second Session of the Montana Territorial Legislature.[28] From 1862–66 he was superior-general of the Montana Jesuits. Giorda, as noted, also founded St. Peter's Mission among the Blackfeet, later headed by another Italian, Father Joseph Damiani. In 1877, Father Cataldo replaced Giorda as superior after Giorda had served in that capacity again. According to Pope Pius IX, Giorda next refused a bishopric—and in a "uniquely modest" manner. Giorda preached his sermons in six languages, among them Nez Percé, Flathead,

---

[27] See *Montana Post*, December 23, 1865; F. X. Kuppens, "Christmas Day, 1865 in Virginia City, Montana," *Illinois Catholic Historical Review*, Vol. X, (July, 1927), 48–53; also Palladino, *Indian and White*, 307–308. For an account of the environment, see Rolle (ed.), *The Road to Virginia City*. At Hell Gate another Italian, Father Urban Grassi, established a church for white men in 1863. See Merrill G. Burlingame, *The Montana Frontier* (Helena, 1942), 300.

[28] *House Journal*, 2 sess., *Montana Legislature for 1866* (Helena, 1867), 9.

and Blackfoot. The Indians called him Roman Head and thought him excessively kind, for which reason they made him an intermediary during the Nez Percé War of 1877. Like Mengarini, Morvillo, Canestrelli, and other fellow Jesuits, Giorda made significant contributions to Indian linguistics. In the years 1877–79 at St. Ignatius Mission he helped Mengarini bring out his Kalispel *Dictionary*; with Father Joseph Bandini he also published *Narratives from the Holy Scripture in Kalispel* (1879).[29]

Giorda had gone to Virginia City at a time when the territory was filling up with whites. Soon the Jesuits were to labor with a new Caucasian constituency. But before that day arrived, missionization of the Indians went on for years. Among the leaders of its last stages was Father Joseph Cataldo. He was born in Sicily the year Queen Victoria ascended the British throne. Andrew Jackson was then president, and Lincoln was twenty-three years old. Cataldo taught at the Collegio Massimo in Palermo when Garibaldi exiled the Jesuits from the Kingdom of the Two Sicilies, closing down and nationalizing their colleges. With ninety members of his order, Cataldo left his native land in 1860. He completed further studies at Louvain, Belgium, and went on to Boston in 1862 for six months; in 1863 he traveled to California by sea and taught briefly at Santa Clara College. Then Cataldo volunteered for service in the Jesuit Rocky Mountain missions. In September, 1865, he set sail from San Francisco for the Columbia River. With Father Giorda as his guide, he traveled up that river, portaging over The Dalles, then went by horse to Walla Walla. Cataldo was to spend the next sixty-three years among the Indians.[30]

From 1865 to 1928, Cataldo was active in Idaho, Washington, Montana, Oregon, Wyoming, and Alaska. He mastered twenty languages, European and primitive. From 1877 to 1893 he was superior-general of the northwest Jesuit missions. Although originally a sickly person, Cataldo developed a strong physique. Rob-

[29] "Father Giorda Revisits Helena," *Daily Rocky Mountain Gazette* (Helena), III, June 8, 1870. Giorda died in 1884. The details are in Schoenberg, *Jesuits in Montana*, 20–21; Burns, *Jesuits*, 385.

[30] George F. Weibel, *Rev. Joseph M. Cataldo, S.J., a Short Sketch of a Wonderful Career*, 1–6.

ert I. Burns calls him a "soldierly figure," if at times combative and petty.[31]

In 1877, Cataldo got into trouble with various Protestants and with several government officials, among them General O. O. Howard, army commander of the Department of the Columbia. The dispute was over whether Chief Joseph of the Nez Percés should return to a government reservation. Cataldo, however, ultimately acted as a peacemaker in the Nez Percé War of that year, as did Ravalli, who exerted every effort to keep the Bitteroot Flatheads peaceful. Cataldo was known among the Indians as *Kaoushin,* or Broken Leg. Father Paul Ponziglione of the Missouri Jesuits recorded Chief Joseph of the Nez Percés' opinion of Cataldo. Ponziglione visited the Nez Percé and Ponca Indians in 1879 and quoted the chieftain as stating: "Cataldo is my friend, he is a good man, all my people love him and I would wish very much to see him once more."[32] Ponziglione, incidentally, was the son of an Italian count; he had taught at the Jesuit college in Genoa until arrested by Sardinian revolutionists in 1848. He then went into exile as a missionary among the Osages, Chippewas, Foxes, Kaws, Arapahoes, and Cheyennes.

Father Cataldo, still alive in 1928 at the age of ninety-two, was to end his years covered with honors. In 1881 he was the founder of Gonzaga University in Spokane, as well as, for a time, in charge of the Jesuit missions in Alaska. Cataldo Mission at Cataldo, Idaho, perpetuates his name.[33]

Few temporal rewards were to come to those Italians whose names formed the list of pioneer clerics who came to the American Northwest—Grassi, Zerbinatti, Diomedi, Carignano, Caruana, Congiato, Damiani, Folchi, Griva, Imoda, Tadini, Bandini, Prando, Rappagliosi, Tosi, Canestrelli, Cataldo, D'Aste, Gazzoli, and Palladino among them.[34] These Italians dotted the countryside

[31] Burns, *Jesuits,* 371.

[32] *Ibid.,* 377–78, 409, 425, 457.

[33] Weibel, *Rev. Cataldo,* 26, 32–35.

[34] A Genoese, the Rev. Lawrence Palladino, S.J., became the author of a significant volume in the history and culture of the West. His *Indian and White*

with wooden mission churches whose white painted interiors reflected the culture pattern from which they had come. Their log missions were rough on the outside but delicate within. The Cataldo Mission, St. Mary's, and St. Ignatius in Montana, represent the tangible results of a far-flung missionary system rivaling the Spanish California mission chain of adobe and brick. These northwest missions, carefully wrought and rustic, are the surviving evidences of a system created by dedicated men.[35]

Once California was added to the missionary responsibilities of the Jesuits, Father Accolti, superior-general there, shifted the resources of the northwestern missions to that more promising state. Cataldo, Congiato, Mengarini, Palladino, Caruana, and Grassi thus ended their years teaching at Santa Clara or San Francisco colleges. But they were remembered in Montana, from where the Flatheads once sent a delegation all the way to California to beg Father Mengarini to return.[36] As these worn-out "Black Robes" died, their places were taken by a different type of Italian.

MONTANA'S LATER IMMIGRANTS came to live there not because it was a center of Jesuit activity but to find work and to raise their children. The territory lay about new northern routes of railroad travel, rich both in mineral resources and in long stretches of unoccupied land. Because settlers were scarce, a Montana Immigration Society was formed in 1872, four years before the embattled General Custer fell at the Little Big Horn. On May 2 of that year an entry in its record book read: "We want merchants, mechanics, laborers, farmers, miners, stockgrowers, and consumers of all

in the Northwest, reprinted many times, is a forceful account of the interaction of two racial stocks. Palladino was also professor of Latin and Greek at St. Ignatius College, San Francisco, and at the University of Santa Clara, as well as President of Gonzaga University. See Helen Fitzgerald Sanders, *A History of Montana* (Chicago, 1913), 1031–32.

35 For further details regarding these Italian-built missions, see William L. Davis, *A History of Saint Ignatius Mission*, 14, 122–28; and William N. Bischoff, *The Jesuits in Old Oregon, 1840–1940*, 217–19.

36 Burns, *Jesuits*, 48, 66–67.

kinds."[37] This invitation also predated Montana's great copper and coal strikes. By the 1880's an entrepreneur named Christian Yegens brought the first Italian-Swiss immigrants into the Billings area to work in its coal mines, as they were to do at Red Lodge, in Carbon County.[38]

On September 18, 1899, a newspaper fragment appeared in the *Weekly Missoulian* which speaks for itself under the heading "Political": "It is claimed that some four hundred Italians took out their naturalization papers in Silver Bow County a couple of days ago, under the direction of their bosses, so as to have the right to vote on the first day of October. In this, each party charges the other with fraud. But the facts proven by the registry office shows the super-human efforts being put forth to carry the elections." Italians were beginning to be a political factor in western Montana.

The biggest Italian community in Montana was at Meaderville, a copper mining camp on the outskirts of Butte. There, in the 1890's, the Anaconda Copper Mining Company began to hire Italian, Cornish, and Finnish labor in quantity. Miners who had worked in Minnesota's Vermilion Range or in the coal sumps of Cartonville, Indiana, now built small houses near Butte's slag pits, surrounded by growing piles of earth. Several hundred North Italians formed a ragged town, which they called Meaderville, around the tailings of Butte. Rough and raw when they arrived, the immigrants gradually softened that great mining camp. They established their own eating places, grocery stores, and recreation.

[37] Record book of the Montana Immigration Society, a MS at the Montana Historical Society, Helena, dated March 22 to April 7, 1872; see also Helena *Weekly Herald*, April 4, 11, 25, and May 2, 9, 23, 1872.

[38] As late as 1955 these North Italians, according to the *Carbon County News*, Vol. XXXII (August 18, 1955), participated in an annual "Festival of Nations." The Italian contribution consisted of celebrating a "Festival of Oranges," the Carnivale d'Ivrea, said to have originated in Ivrea, Piedmont, during the year 1200. This paper stated: "The people of the town, so the story goes, were ruled by an evil baron. Finally a young bride killed the baron and brought the townspeople his head. Every year the townspeople hold a carnival in which the oranges symbolize the baron's head. A bride is chosen queen of the festival and rides through town on a colorful float, throwing candy and oranges to the crowd. The bride, played by Mrs. Joe Alberi, wore her wedding dress from Italy."

They worshiped in St. Helena's Parish, where only Italian was spoken, and at near-by Walkerville also established a sizable Italian community.

At Butte, as elsewhere in the West, the shortage of women so seriously affected the community that, in the 1890's, when Dominic Foresco, a resident of Meaderville, needed a wife, he advertised for such a companion in the city's press. Foresco announced that he would be personally "on display" at Butte's main intersection for three hours daily. The next day he appeared at the corner of Park and Main streets, wearing a white carnation on his lapel. But, he was arrested for disturbing the flow of traffic after his presence gathered large crowds. When Foresco was released from jail, numerous prospective brides met him outside, for they had learned that this particular foreigner owned some twenty thousand dollars worth of government bonds.[39]

At Meaderville a storekeeper, Dominic Bertoglio, became one of the foremost Italian leaders. Bertoglio, a Piedmontese, had worked in the mines of Wisconsin and Arizona before going to Butte in 1892. With a capital of only $160 he opened the Bertoglio Mercantile Company. It was an immediate success. In time he became one of the founders of the Spokane Telephone Company, active also in the affairs of the Tivoli Brewing Company and the Patent Plow Point Company of Detroit, Michigan, as well as the owner of considerable mining property. By 1910 there were more than a dozen members of Bertoglio's family in business at Meaderville.[40]

Another successful Butte Italian was Vincent Truzzolino, who engaged in the business of manufacturing a most un-Italian product—"hot tamales." He also became financially involved in managing mining and real estate properties. Truzzolino was, like Bertoglio, a prominent Republican. He ended his days in wealth, having shipped thousands of his tamales all over Montana.[41]

[39] Work Progress Administration, *Copper Camp, Stories of the World's Greatest Mining Town, Butte, Montana*, 4.

[40] See Sanders, *History*, III, 1503–04.

[41] *Ibid.*, III, 1541.

In 1890, Butte's total population was only slightly in excess of ten thousand. Yet, there were forty-three *boccie* alleys in its Meaderville district alone.[42] By 1920, as its immigrant population died or moved elsewhere, that Italian center ceased to be homogeneous. Formerly good restaurants became little more than roadhouses, like the "Italian" Rocky Mountain Cafe, sporting gaudy fronts which the residents of Butte today enter primarily for drinking and dancing. The children of Meaderville's immigrants seem to have moved into Butte proper.

In eastern Montana relatively few immigrants were attracted to agriculture, despite the fact that railroad land could be obtained in the 1880's for as little as $2.60 per acre. By the nineties one could buy a round-trip Northern Pacific "excursion ticket," from Chicago to Bozeman for only $49.50 to view such agriculture lands. The Great Northern Railroad also possessed vast landholdings, and it sought, by every possible means, to encourage settlement along its tracks. As in the Dakotas, Italians generally refused to be taken in by descriptions of the Great Plains as a fertile paradise. The treeless landscape, harsh winters, grasshoppers, and the brutal risks of dry farming, with its recurring cycles of drought years, all combined to discourage settlers, especially garden-oriented Italians. The risks were simply too great. Deserted farm buildings now stand where settlers thought they could make a living out of an agricultural system that called for huge outlays of capital for farm machinery.

Young immigrants, especially, yielded to the attractions of America's new western towns. Homesick wives forced their husbands to move into these centers, following an urban migration pattern characteristic of the late nineteenth and early twentieth centuries. Italians became truck farmers outside Billings, Missoula, Anaconda, and Great Falls. Of the 2,499 foreigners naturalized in the state during 1898, some 127 were Italians. A report of the Montana Bureau of Agriculture stated that arid land conditions were keeping immigrants from settling there in greater numbers.[43]

[42] Work Progress Administration, *Copper Camp*, 240.

200

As in Colorado, Montana's immigrants on occasion felt the pressures of prejudice. The local press seemed to thirst for articles that featured violence among foreigners. A 1907 Montana headline read: "Italian Section Hand Held Up and Badly Cut." There followed a gruesome story in which violence and race were coupled with a description of "a murderous assault with pistols, knives, and a razor" inside a boxcar located "on a portion of an Italian section gang." The account went on to note how "the boxcar was literally covered with blood and resembled a slaughter house." The same issue of the newspaper printed a black-bordered boxed headline which proclaimed: "Finns Resist Arrest. Three Drunken Men Cause Riot and Are Bound Over by Justice."[44]

In 1908 a public debate on immigration held at Red Lodge was won by a person who took the affirmative on the question: "Should There Be No Immigration of Foreigners?" The town's newspaper reported that he did a thorough job of showing the importance of "prohibiting foreign immigration into our Country."[45] One must, however, take into account other evidences of pro-immigrant sentiment. Adverse newspaper accounts need to be balanced with dozens of testimonials—by civic officials and by the press—to the worth in a community of individual immigrants. Then, evidences of violence toward them tend to fade in significance. Yet, it would be incorrect wholly to discount the existence of antiforeign feeling.

The Italians in Montana, even by 1910, numbered only 6,600. This first-generation figure does not, however, tell their story. Compared to other nationalities (for example, the Dutch, who numbered only 1,054 in 1910), the Italians formed a sizable share of the foreign population. In staffing the earliest Jesuit missions, in mining activities, and in helping to build cities, they—like such other nationalities in Montana as the Finns and the Basques—played their part in shaping frontier life.[46]

[43] Cited in Industrial Commission, *Reports*, XV, 576.

[44] Red Lodge (Montana) *Republican Picket* (July 26, 1907).

[45] *Ibid.* (February 21, 1908).

[46] Statistics for Montana are in *Butte City Directory* (Butte, 1895) and *Thir-*

Wyoming

The population of Wyoming rose very slowly from the 1870's to the turn of the century. The state's major historian records that in the 1890's only "a few rather pathetic efforts were being made to attract farmers," be they Europeans or from other states.[47] A smaller number of Italians reached Wyoming than settled in Montana. Here some took up sheep raising or established sheep-feeding pens. Some were track workers who had followed the railroads into the state. Others worked as miners, and the rest settled in Cheyenne or Laramie and became truck farmers. The majority of these came from the northern provinces of Lombardy, Veneto, Piedmont, and the Trentino. By the first quarter of the twentieth century they had secured a virtual monopoly over vegetable production near Wyoming's two largest cities. Except for this, there is less to be said about the Italians in Wyoming than in any other western state. By 1920 they numbered just under two thousand persons, remaining virtually static throughout the next decade.

The Road to Salt Lake

Throughout much of the nineteenth century the Mormon Zion, with its Salt Lake City base, aroused great curiosity abroad. Few foreign travelers to the American West failed to include Deseret Territory in their itineraries, or to feature it in books of travel. Although the Mormons did not coax large numbers of Italian adherents to remote Deseret, they actively recruited converts. In 1849, Lorenzo Snow, but recently ordained as one of "Mormonia's" Twelve Apostles, left for Italy with Joseph Taranto (sometimes Toronto). Taranto was a native of Sicily who had given Brigham Young personal savings of twenty-five hundred dollars to help build the Mormon temple at Nauvoo, Illinois.[48]

---

teenth Census of the United States, I (1910), 836–38. In contrast to their countrymen elsewhere, however, the Italians of Montana never established their own newspaper.

[47] T. A. Larson, *History of Wyoming* (Omaha, 1965), 306.

[48] Lamont Toronto, a descendant of Joseph Toronto, was secretary of state in Utah in 1957.

Traveling via New York, Liverpool, Paris, Le Havre, and Marseilles, Snow and Taranto arrived at Genoa, Italy, on June 25, 1850, accompanied by Elder Thomas B. H. Stenhouse. Later in 1850, Elder Jabez Woodard also arrived there. These missionaries were to focus their attention on the northwestern areas of Italy, Liguria, and Piedmont. The four elders, on October 19, 1850, ascended a high mountain outside Genoa where they offered prayer and, as if to turn the tables on the American West, formally pronounced the benighted peninsula of Italy a missionary field. On that solemn occasion they named the mountain where they prayed "Mount Brigham" and the rock upon which they stood, the "Rock of Prophesy."[49]

Among the first fruits of the Mormon labors in Italy, Elder Snow conducted various baptisms of converts in the icy waters of the Angrogne River at La Tour. He then established three branches of the church: one at Angrogne, another at St. Germain, and another at Bartholomew—all in the province of Piedmont. Numerous converts from the Prarostino District had French names, among them Bertoch, Pons, Rochon, and Gaudin. As these communities spoke French, Snow wrote a tract for their instruction entitled *The Voice of Joseph*. This was translated into French and printed in England. Elder Stenhouse also printed at Genoa a publication known as *Le Reflecteur*.

Snow departed from Italy in 1852 and left Elder Woodard in charge there.[50] Elder Stenhouse also left to open up a missionary field in Switzerland. To Elder Snow belongs the honor of publishing the book of Mormon in Italian during 1852. Three years later Woodard's work in Italy was taken over by Elder Stenhouse, who combined the Italian[51] and Swiss Mormon missions. By 1855 the

[49] Kate B. Carter (comp. and ed.), *Heart Throbs of the West*, IV (Salt Lake City, 1943), 282. (Published by Daughters of Utah Pioneers.)

[50] The *Millenial Star*, a journal published by the Church of Latter Day Saints, contains mention of Lorenzo Snow's letters from Italy in the following issues: XIII (1851), 25–26, 89–90, 107–108, 186, 252–53, 301–302; XIV (1852), 107–108; XV (1853), 4, 61–62, 127–28, 202, 282, 555–58, 670–71, 752–53; XVI (1854), 9, 61, 62, 110–11, 204–206, 350–51, 457–58; XVII (1855), 46, 454–56.

[51] Two other Elders, Thomas Margetts and George D. Keaton, joined Elder Woodard in Italy before his return to the United States in 1854.

three branches of the church in Italy had sent fifty converts to America, and sixty-four others made up the membership in their homeland. Most of these converts were Protestant Vaudois of the Waldensian persuasion from the high Alpine valleys along Italy's western frontiers.

In 1866, seventeen of these Vaudois families reached Salt Lake City. Later, more of them settled there and at Ogden. For these people the hardships of pioneer life in Utah were real ones. Immigrants sorely missed both the greenery of their Alpine homeland and its fresh milk, cheeses, wines, chestnuts, and fruits. In a frequently dry and arid climate, they were reduced at times to eating weeds, roseberries, and bran. Grasshoppers consumed their crops, and the dust clogged their nostrils.

Italian women joined other foreign zealots of Mormonism in pushing handcarts across the plains to a new Zion. The clothes they wore were ripped to shreds as they collected buffalo chips or dipped precious water out of buffalo tracks after a rainstorm. Abandoned as useless were the beautiful silks brought from their homeland. One of the women described her depressing arrival at Salt Lake City in 1855 after a journey of eight months: "The little log and adobe dwellings appeared as boulders over the surface of the ground." Settling ultimately at Ogden, she called the place "a comparative desert." With "patient industry, perseverance and Heaven's blessings" she was to witness its gradual transformation, however, "to a beautiful and desirable land in which to dwell."

The Mormons, eager to attract converts, were frequently kind to foreigners. Leonetto Cipriani, the Italian aristocrat who traveled through Salt Lake City in 1853, found various talented Italians there and was touched by the friendship shown him by a Neapolitan music teacher named Gennaro Capone. Another musician, Captain Domenico Ballo, headed an instrumental band there which had blown its way across the plains to Salt Lake City's first bandmaster, long before the Mormons became renowned for their musical activities.[52]

Other foreign sightseers would follow Cipriani to Salt Lake

[52] Schiavo, *Four Centuries,* 171.

City; among these were the French botanist Jules Remy and the British naturalist Julius Brenchley. They visited the city in 1855 and later wrote a skillful book together on Mormon society. Richard Burton, the English adventurer, came to the Great Basin in 1860, gathering notes for his *The City of the Saints* (London, 1861). By 1875, Burton's book was translated into Italian, an indication that Mormon recruiting in Italy had been relatively successful, although less so than in Scandinavia and England. Entitled *I Mormoni e la Città dei Santi*, this work encouraged persons in Italy who were already thinking about emigrating to do so.

All such foreigners were fascinated by polygamy and commented upon it. Italians did not easily understand the religious requirements of Mormonism. Foreign-born Mormons were excommunicated for such offences as rebellion, negligence, and "general immorality." Polygamy, however, appealed to certain Italian males. In 1874 one of these wrote, in a letter to the editor of New York's *L'Eco d'Italia*: "What would your readers say if I were to boast an offspring of 62 children? And remember that I am only 50 years old so that I can expect a still greater number of children from my 22 wives, all of them healthy and able to procreate."[53]

Mormon society achieved early renown because of the way in which it provided employment for foreigners. Immigrants were absorbed in the annual harvest, in private employment at Salt Lake City or in the "Public Works" activities of the Church of Latter Day Saints. Mormonia's Italian converts also went into Utah's remote mining towns. Southwest of Salt Lake, at Bingham Canyon, from the mid-1870's into the 1920's, seventeen different nationalities clustered around its mines. At its peak the area supported 9,000 inhabitants. The Irish were among the first to appear. They were followed by the Chinese around 1875, who came in to run its restaurants and laundries. Then Serbs, Croats, and Slavs arrived, as well as Italians, Russians, Finns, Swedes, Armenians,

---

[53] Quote repr. from Schiavo, *Four Centuries*, 171. Individual histories of Mormons appear in Carter (ed.), *Heart Throbs*, 282–89.

Montenegrans, and the inevitable Cornish pickmen, or "Cousin Jacks." Bingham Canyon's Piedmontese Italians, proficient at hammer work and leverage, were nicknamed "Short Towns" because of their stocky builds.

Each nationality organized its own labor gangs, with a foreman in charge who could speak English. They formed colonies around individual boardinghouses—the Austrians and Slavs at Highland Bay and Phoenix, the Greeks at Copperfield, the Finns and Swedes at Carr Fork. There were other subcommunities at Yampa, Frogtown, Dinkeyville, and Jap Town. All these settlements were connected to a typically lengthy main street, with Bingham's houses crowded along it down a narrow canyon. Dance halls, boardinghouses, and thirty saloons lined this seven-mile-long, forty-foot-wide thoroughfare.

Each foreign group maintained its own stores, bakeries, and restaurants. The Greeks alone had five candy shops and ten coffeehouses, which operated into the mid-1920's. The Italians were second only to the Greeks (who numbered 1,210 persons in 1912) in Bingham's foreign population pattern. That year a report submitted to the United States Department of Commerce and Labor listed 402 North Italians and 237 South Italians in Bingham Canyon. By 1965 the town was to have a total population of only 37 persons, its valuable land having been absorbed by mechanized mining operations.

Feuds between Bingham's various nationalities were not uncommon. They, however, usually united in opposition to "the Company"—that is, the Utah Copper Company, which was to be replaced by the Kennecott Copper Corporation. Yet strikebreakers among them, especially Greeks imported from Crete, helped to end what came to be known as the great Bingham strike of 1912. Mine authorities were vigilant for any sign of labor agitators among immigrants and were usually successful in putting them down, basing criminal indictments upon sedition charges and, at the very least, jailing labor organizers on vagrancy charges. Because of distrust, apathy, and excess emotionality among Bingham's immigrant laborers, union leaders had little success in organizing members of the first generation. The leading authority on this small but bursting community believes that "in the main it was economics and not ideology that guided the immigrants."[54]

Several Utah counties were strongholds of foreigners. One of these was Sanpete County which, by the 1860's, had an unusually high percentage of foreign-born residents (42.68 per cent). The history of the Italian miners in the coal mining area of Carbon County, southeast of Provo, featured foreign rivalry, especially with the Greeks. Yet, without the co-operation of these two national groups Carbon County's thirty-two coal mines would probably never have become unionized. This occurred in the 1920's only after many years of effort. Alongside the Greeks, the Italians also led an ideological fight in 1924 against Utah's Ku Klux Klan.[55]

The state's Italian immigrants achieved eventual prominence within the Mormon Church. Like Taranto earlier, some entered its innermost circle. One of these was Philip Cardon (Cardone) who introduced the culture of silkworms into Utah and who became a respected elder.[56] Through both church and state, thus, Utah's Italians expressed their individuality. As elsewhere, they established their own newspapers. Among these was *The Cactus*, an early Salt Lake City journal printed by the firm of Sangiovanni Company, and later *La Gazetta* and *Il Corriere d'America*, both weeklies also published there.[57]

A writer of prominence came out of the Utah Italian community. Bernard Augustine DeVoto was for twenty years editor of *Harper's* "Easy Chair" and a popular specialist on the history of

[54] H. Z. Papanikolas, "Life and Labor Among the Immigrants of Bingham Canyon," *Utah Historical Quarterly*, Vol. XXXIII (Fall, 1965), 289. All the data on Bingham is based on that excellent study.

[55] P.A.M. Taylor, *Expectations Westward, the Mormons and the Emigration of Their British Converts in the Nineteenth Century* (Ithaca, 1966), 245; H. Z. Papanikolas to author, a.l.s., December 30, 1957.

[56] *Guida*, 116. Paul Cardon of Logan, Utah, a descendant, became prominent in the U.S. Department of Agriculture and in the 1950's was head of the international agency known as the Food and Agricultural Organization.

[57] Common Council for American Unity, *Foreign Language Publications in the United States*, 8; Douglas C. McMurtrie, "Early Printing in Utah Outside of Salt Lake City," *Utah Historical Quarterly*, Vol. V (July, 1932), 84.

the American West. DeVoto was the son of Florian Bernard De-Voto, whose father had been an Italian cavalry officer. Bernard's mother, a Mormon, gave birth to him in 1897 at Ogden. Among the best known of DeVoto's books were *The Year of Decision* (Boston, 1943) and *Across the Wide Missouri* (Boston, 1947). Of his life in Utah, DeVoto wrote: "I was the child of an apostate Catholic and an apostate Mormon." He described his childhood as "oscillating between the poles of Rome and Deseret," a life that "found its own stability in adhering to neither." DeVoto's father read Greek and Latin for entertainment, and Bernard, remembering how he once chanted couplets from Pope's *Iliad* to his playmates, thought of himself as "a laboratory specimen of frontier relationship which no literary or academic formula could express." There can be little doubt that much of DeVoto's flinty resilience, recalcitrance, and independence of mind, for which he became well known, stemmed from his western youth.[58]

Great numbers of Italians did not go to Utah, but by 1920 they constituted 3,225 foreign-born inhabitants (and possibly another 4,000 of the second generation) out of a total foreign population of 59,200. While the Italians did not come to the Intermountain West in large numbers, they found there more of the rusticity of life typical of rural Italy than did their compatriots who settled in the cramped cities of the eastern seaboard. As in Italy, they helped to refine the countryside. Yet, they could never establish permanent enclaves there. Immigrant colonies in the West simply failed to preserve their identity. The Meadervilles, Binghams, Tontitowns, and Italian-Swiss colonies were temporary congregations of immigrant workers. People stayed together in such places only long enough to acquire use of the English language and experience with American customs. When more attractive opportunities arose, they migrated elsewhere, commingling with the mainstreams of American life. This was especially evident in Montana and Utah.

[58] *Current Biography*, September, 1943; Catherine Drinker Bowen, "The Historian," in *Four Portraits and One Subject; Bernard DeVoto* (Boston, 1963), 10, 21.

X

INTO THE NORTHWEST

FROM THE 1880's ONWARD the westward push of the transcontinental railroads encouraged migration into the Pacific Northwest. The rich farm valleys of Oregon, Washington, and northern Idaho proved to be undeniably attractive to persons weary of the summer dust and winter cold of the Great Plains. City dwellers too saw the crisp beauty of America's Northwest as more than usually appealing. With a few dollars one could buy a ticket at Chicago and board the Great Northern Railroad or the Chicago, Milwaukee and St. Paul to Seattle, Tacoma, or Portland. The advantages of so verdant a countryside were regularly featured in the major Italian immigrant journal *L'Eco d'Italia* of New York City. This paper described a land of orchards, forests, and abundant running water. Immigration agencies also pointed out that one could find ready employment in sawmills and fish canneries, at logging camps and in the mines of the Northwest.

To the immigrant the lure of its unfilled stretches of fertile land and inland waterways augured the best imaginable future. The Italian was especially attracted by the possibility of small-scale, diversified farming—primarily fruit, vegetables, and grass crops. He heard of "wheelbarrow farming" in the Northwest conducted by Scandinavians and Germans who, like himself, could not have afforded California's inflated land prices and the expensive irrigation facilities necessary in an arid climate. In the Northwest, the Italians learned, big trees were sometimes far enough apart so that one could plow around them. And, for some operators at least, tree-cutting and mixed farming paid well. People spoke of "Oregon fever," by which they meant the optimism and expansive attractiveness of the entire Northwest. Whether one went to Oregon, Washington, or Idaho, the air was clear, the weather was invigorating but reasonably mild, and a spirit of adventure was everywhere apparent. So, immigrants flocked there in droves.

Idaho

Geographically, historically, and economically, Idaho is a part of the West Coast and yet is linked to the Rocky Mountain states. As a natural "spilling over" of population from Montana occurred, the people who formed this influx found numerous pursuits open to them in the farthest northwest. In studying Idaho's history, it is easy to lose sight of the importance of mining because there is so much lumbering activity there. Nevertheless, a group of remote coal mining towns in Idaho's northern area—Rathdrum, Mullan, Wallace, and Kellogg—became early centers of foreign activity. Finns as well as Italians went there in the late 1870's. According to the Lewiston *North Idaho Teller* for May 12, 1877, "a full one-half of our adult population are foreign born." That foreigners were sought was indicated by the *Teller* for November 11, 1876. In an article entitled "Immigration Coming," the newspaper welcomed them: "We have the land and we want people to occupy and to cultivate it. We can promise them good returns. . . . Then let the immigrants come and be welcome, and let more follow them till our hills and valleys are lively with an industrious and thriving population."

Italians and other foreigners in northern Idaho operated farms, restaurants, hotels, and a variety of small businesses. There was a De Borgia Mining District, a Torino Mining Company, and an Italian Mining Association. Although a few immigrants went to Pocatello, Idaho Falls, and Boise, the northern mines absorbed them in considerable numbers. During 1910 the federal census recorded 2,067 Italians in Idaho out of a total foreign-born population of 94,713. Native-born Italians in Idaho never grew beyond this figure.

Washington

The first Italian influence in present-day Washington was actually an extension of Jesuit missionary activities in Montana. Mengarini, Ravalli, Giorda, and their fellow priests labored, at one time or another, in what is today the state of Washington. The major Jesuit figure in Washington was Father Cataldo. As previously noted, Cataldo's first post in 1865 was among the Indians of Idaho. Later the church recognized his executive abilities and made him for many years the superior-general of all Jesuit missions in the Northwest. These were years during which he founded churches, convents, and academies from Wyoming to Alaska, including, as we have seen, Gonzaga University.[1]

Other Jesuits besides Father Cataldo labored among the Washington Indians from their Montana missions. In 1869, Father Grassi combined St. Paul's Mission with Immaculate Conception Mission and called it St. Regis. In 1888 he also resuscitated St. Andrew's on the Umatilla Indian Reservation in Oregon.[2] Father Griva labored among the Skoielpis until about 1925. As early as 1866, Fathers Cataldo and Tosi ministered to the Spokanes at Mission St. Michael near Peone Prairie. In 1870, already known as the apostle of the Nez Percés, Cataldo visited the Yakimas. In 1885 he erected a school among the Blackfeet. Similarly, Father Barcelo worked among the Crows after 1880. Following Barcelo's death, Father Prando was sent in 1887 to found St. Xavier Mission. And, in eastern Oregon, among the Umatilla, Father Grassi labored from the early 1880's onward. Spurred by the appeal of Father Cataldo, Miss Catherine Drexel of Philadelphia gave Father Grassi four thousand dollars with which to build a school for Umatilla children. Grassi was succeeded by Father Caruana. In 1892 sickness forced Caruana to give way to Father Joseph

[1] Schiavo, *Four Centuries*, 251; Bischoff, *Jesuits*, 218–19.

[2] After his death in 1892, Father Morvillo succeeded him. See Wilfred Schoenberg, *Jesuits in Oregon*, 15.

Chianale. Ultimately, Brother Gaspar Ochiena and Fathers Grassi and Parodi had all labored among the Okinagan Indians of Washington. As late as 1925, Fathers Celestine Caldi and Griva still ministered to the Okinagans.[3]

The major migration of Washington's Italian settlers occurred after 1881. In the decade of the eighties, Washington's total population more than quadrupled; its farms increased nearly five times in value; the value of its farm products trebled; and the output of its fisheries increased six times. Manufacturing employment grew even more dramatically. Many immigrants were railroad workers who followed their jobs into the state. By 1900 there were several thousand Italians there. They farmed the rich pasture lands of the Northwest, fished along the Columbia River and Puget Sound, and worked in the orchards of the interior. In the Pacific Northwest they found nature as bountiful as had been predicted. A generous rainfall produced fine harvests of fruit, vegetables, and field crops. At Seattle, Tacoma, Aberdeen, Bellingham, and Everett they shipped in salmon, halibut, and cod caught in northern waters. Neapolitan, Genoese, and Sicilian fishermen sailed as far north as Alaska in search of some of the best quality fish in the world. Many came to own their own boats; others managed canneries and packing companies, shipping their catch all over the United States.[4] Many foreigners worked in the western lumber camps. In 1890, 40 per cent of the sawmill employees in Washington and Oregon were foreign-born, and, by 1900, some 60 per cent of the loggers were. As in the mining industry, the I.W.W. sought to organize foreign lumber workers in Washington, involving them in strike actions at Grays Harbor in 1912 and in 1916 at the formerly open-shop mill town of Everett.[5]

The ratio of Italians to other persons engaged in mining is suggested in the statistics concerning an accident that occurred on November 7, 1910, at the Lawson Mine in Black Diamond, Wash-

[3] A. M. Jung, *Sketch of the Jesuit Missions Among the American Tribes of the Rocky Mountain Indians, passim.*

[4] Industrial Commission, *Reports,* XXIV, 499.

[5] Vernon H. Jensen, *Lumber and Labor,* 104, 121–23.

ington. There, in one of the deepest shafts in the United States, an underground explosion killed or maimed eighteen miners. Thirteen of these were Italians.[6]

In several books Angelo Pellegrini tells what it felt like to be an immigrant in the Northwest after the turn of the century. In *Americans by Choice* he writes cogently of the primitive woodsy environment, and of the virginal countryside to which Italian eyes were unaccustomed: "The forest at the back door, the ugly frame shacks, the grass-covered streets and unstable board walks were such a sharp contrast to the humanized Italian landscape that they gave an initial impression of poverty rather than wealth. . . . The new environment was [however] an invitation to work."[7]

Easily the best account of an Italian family in the sawmill and lumber towns of the Northwest is another Pellegrini book, *Immigrant's Return* (New York, 1951). He recalls such details of his boyhood as his astonishment over the richness of the countryside, his horror over the prodigality and waste of natural resources, and his appreciation of the democracy and toleration practiced toward foreigners out west.

The majestic ruggedness and wealth of the land never failed to impress immigrants. In 1906 one of these, Guido Sella, about whom Pellegrini writes, went to work on a construction project in the lower Columbia River basin. Through Pellegrini's perceptive eyes Sella remembered being awed by its surrounding wilderness: "In less than a month after we had left the civilized landscape of Castenuovo, we were in a prehistoric land. Mountains lost in the clouds. Endless deserts. Forests impenetrable. Rivers as big as the ocean. Snakes and wolves and bears and mountain lions everywhere. . . . Not even a cottage—anywhere. There in that wilderness infested with wild animals we slept in tents."[8]

As in Montana some foreigners were drawn toward Washington's small towns. It is striking that among Washington's many Italian truck farmers, a fair number lived in Douglas County, an

[6] Orofino (Idaho) *Tribune*, November 11, 1910.
[7] *Americans by Choice*, 12.
[8] *Ibid.*, 82.

apple growing center, yet did not become fruit orchardists. In a state where apple growing would have been a natural outlet for their talents, immigrants frequently remained contented with raising more familiar crops. In this and other instances they hardly proved to be experimental or ingenious. They were, however, attracted toward dairying and flower growing, and they formed a large cut-flower co-operative at Tacoma. Sometimes Italians bought acreage together; some families held as many as five hundred acres in 1900.[9] One finds relatively little antiforeign sentiment over this extensive landholding in the Northwest except for some hostility toward the Japanese prior to World War II.

By 1910 there were over 13,000 Italians in Washington State. They established two newspapers, *La Gazzetta Italiana* and *La Rivista del Ouest*, in Seattle. They also founded the customary lodges and societies toward which foreigners were drawn.[10] In the Northwest no person of Italian background achieved more prominence than Henry Suzzallo, whose family came from Ragusa (now Dubrovnik) on the Dalmatian coast. In 1915 he rose to the presidency of the University of Washington. After quarreling with the state governor, however, he resigned in 1926, only to earn further national distinction four years later when he became chairman of the board of trustees and president of the Carnegie Foundation for the Advancement of Teaching. This position he occupied until his death in 1933. Suzzallo once publicly avowed that there was not a drop of Anglo-Saxon blood in his veins.[11]

The governor of Washington during much of the 1950's was Albert Rosellini, whose career was honored at Seattle in 1957 during an "Italian Week." Upon being given the keys to the city that year, Italian Ambassador to the United States Manlio Brosio complimented the state of Washington on its cosmopolitanism in which foreigners had participated: "Seattle has truly proved itself an international city."[12]

[9] Industrial Commission, *Reports*, XXIV, 498, 642; *Guida*, 118.

[10] *Ibid.*, Ayer, *Directory*, 1236–38.

[11] Dumas Malone, "Biography and History," in Joseph R. Strayer, *The Interpretation of History* (Princeton, 1943), 146.

214

Oregon

As one travels up the Pacific coast into central Oregon, the landscape is broken by a highway marker which abruptly announces to the motorist the location of the town of Garibaldi. This community of several thousand persons lies some fifty miles west of Portland, the capital of Oregon. According to one story it was founded by an Italian seaman who jumped ship and remained behind to name a town after the great Italian leader Garibaldi.[13] The spot is a reminder that although the Italians have not created a large number of the place names in the West, they have originated their share.

From the time of the early Malaspina expedition to the northwest coast until 1827 there is no record of an Italian in all of Oregon; nor, for that matter, did many other whites inhabit the region. But in 1827 the brig *Owyhee*, under the command of Captain Giovanni Dominis, entered the Columbia River, being one of a handful of ships to reach that coast in such an early day. Dominis spent two weeks carefully navigating the treacherous river, sounding its bottom as he collected a precious cargo of furs for the China trade.[14] In 1829, Dominis returned to the Columbia in search of a new cargo of furs. On this trip, in fact, he conceived the notion of curing quantities of river salmon to be sold in the East. On April 15, 1831, he returned to Boston with fifty-three barrels of this precious fish.[15] Although the fish had cost him little, Dominis' cargo did not reap the rewards that he had expected, because the United States government taxed the shipment as a foreign import. The significant factor about this first attempt to market such fish was that the *Owyhee's* cargo began a large trade

[12] "Proud Seattle Celebration: The Citizens Pay Tribute to Their Italian Heritage," *Life*, Vol. 43 (December 9, 1957), 169–71.

[13] The most common version of its naming, cited in L. A. McArthur, *Oregon Geographic Names* (Portland, 1944), is that an early pioneer who admired Garibaldi named the town.

[14] Samuel Eliot Morison, "New England and the Opening of the Columbia River Salmon Trade, 1830," *Oregon Historical Quarterly*, Vol. XXVIII (June, 1927), 113–20.

[15] Schiavo, *Civil War*, 224–25.

in salted salmon between the East and West coasts of the United States. Dominis was also the first man to plant peach trees in Oregon, and from California he brought sheep there too. Throughout the 1830's, according to the historian Hubert Howe Bancroft, he hunted for sea otter furs on the northwest coast. Also exchanging rum for furs, he was one of the pioneer traders in "Old Oregon." It is of incidental interest, too, that his son married Queen Lilioukalani of Hawaii.[16]

Another Italian of some importance in early-day Oregon was S.N. Arrigoni. He was a Milanese who, in 1856, thirty years after Dominis, landed in Portland while wandering around the world with a new Irish wife. Along the banks of the Willamette, Arrigoni founded a hostelry which he named "The Pioneer." As Portland's first hotel of note, it became extremely popular, and before long Arrigoni operated a three-hundred–bed establishment and apocryphally claimed on his guest list the name of Italian patriot Giuseppe Garibaldi. Arrigoni had a passion for inviting famous people to his hotel, and Generals Ulysses S. Grant and William Tecumseh Sherman actually did stay there. His exceptionally fine service caused this hotel and yet another, called Arrigoni's, to become known up and down the coast. Their owner became one of the organizers of Portland's Arlington Club and of its first Masonic Lodge; in his home were to be found the first sewing machine and piano in the state. Arrigoni's hotels boasted the first telegraph office and express service in Oregon, and he gave Portland its first street light, a small oil lamp which stood outside his Pioneer Hotel. Upon his death in 1869, Arrigoni was rated as one of Oregon's most appreciated pioneers.[17]

As elsewhere in the West, Jesuits were among the earliest immigrants in Oregon. Three of the six Italians listed in the first state census of 1850 were priests.[18] The best known of Oregon's Jesuits

[16] *Ibid.*, 225–26; Horace S. Lyman's *History of Oregon*, III (4 vols., New York, 1903), 201–202; Frances Fuller Victor, "Flotsom and Jetsom of the Pacific," *Oregon Historical Quarterly*, Vol. II (March, 1901), 41.

[17] *Guida*, 108–10; H. W. Scott (ed.), *History of Portland* (Portland, 1890), 146; Joseph Gaston, *Portland, Oregon* (Chicago, 1911), II, 753–54.

was Father John Nobili, a Roman who arrived at Fort Vancouver in 1844. For five years he worked among Indians and trappers of the Hudson's Bay Company in what was then called the Oregon country. Of his missionary activities he wrote:

> I was there alone among 8 or 9 thousand Indians of different languages and manners. In all, I think I baptized and gave the other sacraments to nearly one thousand three or four hundred Indians, many of whom had the happiness to die soon afterward, including about five hundred children carried off by the measles. In May, 1847, I founded the first residence of St. Joseph among the Okinagans, two days journey from Thompson's River. . . . I was with deep sorrow snatched away from my dear Indians, in the midst of whom I had hoped to die, and called South to the residence of the Flatheads. Here I passed the winter in a very precarious state of health and would undoubtedly have died were it not the will of God that the good and charitable Father Mengarini and Father Ravalli restored me with their fostering care.[19]

Nobili won the admiration of Hudson's Bay Company trappers by the courage and devotion to duty he displayed during a virulent epidemic that broke out among them. He, like the other Jesuit priests on that frontier, not only lived with the Indians but studied their customs and learned their language. As a result of his influence the Indians of the Nesqually River region renounced the primitive custom of burning their dead and of torturing surviving wives and husbands. Similarly, the Chilcotins abolished polygamy.

Nobili often lived on herbs and roots alone. If he was lucky, he supplemented this fare with horse, dog, or wolf meat. As a result his health became greatly impaired. In order that he might recuperate, he simply had to be ordered out of the Northwest. Summoned by his superiors in 1849 to return to civilization, Father Nobili left for California, where he began a new life as an educator.

[18] Jesse S. Douglas, "Origins of the Population of Oregon in 1850," *Pacific Northwest Quarterly*, Vol. XLI (April, 1950), 104.

[19] Quoted in John B. McGloin, "John B. Nobili, S.J., Founder of California's Santa Clara College," *British Columbia Historical Quarterly*, Vol. XVII (July–October, 1953), 215–22.

With Father Michael Accolti, formerly of St. Francis Xavier Mission on the Willamette, he founded Santa Clara College two years later.[20]

Still later, one of the Italian priests who went to Oregon became almost a living legend in a quite different way from Father Nobili. This was the Jesuit Michael Balestra. After 1910 he made St. Michael's parish in Portland a center for Italian-Americans. Balestra lived frugally, begged clothing and food for the poor, and helped educate wayward waifs. For more than fifty years he ministered to Portland's Italians, generating widespread loyalty. There have, of course, been other Italian priests in Oregon (among them Fathers Bolla, Cestelli, and Villa). Some were perhaps more significant than Father Balestra, but none outlasted him in terms of service rendered and adaptation to the environment of an emerging state.

As in Washington the railroads and the lumber industry accounted for many of the new arrivals. Italian day laborers in those industries mostly came from Sicily, whereas the farmers among the newcomers were from northern Italy. These were tenants or truck-vegetable raisers until they could buy their own land, usually in the vicinity of Portland. By 1910 there were over 5,500 Italians in Oregon. This population was served by three foreign-language newspapers—*Il Lavoro Progresso* (established at Portland in 1895), *La Stella,* and *La Tribuna Italiana.*[21]

After the turn of the century immigrants were attracted to the fishing villages of British Columbia and Alaska. From the West Coast ports of San Francisco, Portland, and Seattle they migrated annually toward fishing grounds off the Alaskan coast. They fished for halibut and salmon, and they prospered, though they found the climate north of Puget Sound brisk. Only a few chose to remain in the North throughout the year. Even today such fishermen winter annually in California. A system of net fishing, called

20 Goggio, *Italians,* 9.

21 *Guida,* 110; Immigration Commission, *Reports,* XXIV, 528; Rowell, *Newspaper Directory,* 1262; Ayer, *Directory,* 1236–38.

218

Paranzella, was perfected by these Italians, who literally dragged the floor of the ocean for bottom fish, or *frutti di mare.*[22]

Western Canada

In the late nineteenth century the vast prairies of western Canada attracted attention as one of the last agricultural frontiers in the westward migration of North America. After the turn of the century thousands of new immigrants traveled into that region in response to attractive immigration literature. The Canadian West acted as a magnet for divergent people, including Icelanders, German Mennonites, Doukhobors from Russia, and, of course, Italians. These nationalities participated in the rapid expansion of railroads, agriculture, and dozens of mining and lumber camps.[23]

In contrast to the number of Italian travel accounts concerning the western United States, there are relatively few such books regarding immigrants in western Canada. An exception is Vincenzo Ruggieri's *Du transvaal a l'Alaska* (Paris, 1901). Ruggieri, who originally wrote his narrative in Italian, made his way from Vancouver to Juneau, Alaska. Then he went on to Skagway, the Yukon River, and Klondike Territory. He reported in detail upon the Eskimos, the flora, the fauna, and the insects of western North America above the Canadian boundary.

By the 1890's, Canada's four western provinces had been opened to foreign colonization. European agents vigorously advertised the attractions of life in British Columbia, Manitoba, Alberta, and Saskatchewan. As in the Dakotas, the winters in Saskatchewan were rigorous, and the combination of alternate freezing and drought, poor crops, and low farm income led some immigrants to move westward to the milder climate of Vancouver in British Columbia. The southern Alberta prairie is much like northeastern Montana—a semiarid region suited to raising oats, flax, wheat, barley, and sugar beets. It registers temperatures as low as forty-

[22] See N. B. Scofield, "Paranzella, or Trawl Net Fishing, in California," *Transactions of the Pacific Fisheries Society . . . 1915,* 45–51.

[23] Carl Wittke, *A History of Canada* (New York, 1928), 255–56.

five degrees below zero Fahrenheit. Farther northward the frontier was even rawer—with neither railroad nor medical facilities available.

Although the population of Canada remained relatively sparse, it increased almost 35 per cent in the first decade of the present century, due primarily to the influx of immigrants. Some of the greatest percentages of regional increase in Canada were recorded in its western provinces. From 1900 to 1910, Manitoba increased 78 per cent and Saskatchewan 439 per cent. More than sixty thousand Italians were among the foreigners who entered Canada in this era. Although some drifted into Calgary, Edmonton, and Vancouver, most labored on railroads, construction projects, and wheat farms.[24]

In the Provincial Library of British Columbia at Victoria there is a printed prospectus depicting the activities of an Italian agricultural community of the 1920's. Called the North Italy Farmers' Colony Ltd., this group settled at Loretta in the province of Manitoba. Its brochure was entitled: *Opportunities That Manitoba Offers to the Italians* (1926). These attractions appeared in bucolic, peaceful photographs of logging operations, farm life, and community living. The promotion of such colonies attracted migrants who otherwise would never have ventured into such a harsh climate.

Despite an exodus of foreigners to the United States and homeward, several thousand Italians entered Canada each year during the 1920's. These continued to find fresh opportunities for employment on the cutting edge of a new frontier. Harsh weather and poor harvests were braved by persons who loved the freedom of land ownership. The Canadian Pacific Railroad was especially active in providing farm acreage, housing, and loans to such immigrants as wished to settle on its western lands.[25]

While the record of the Italians in western Canada is fragmentary and hard to recapture, a sampling of newspaper headlines

24 *Ibid.*, 279–80.

25 Canadian immigration statistics are in the *Canada Yearbook*, an annual publication which lists by nationality the number of immigrants entering Canada.

as World War II approached reminds one of their presence: "Italians Celebrated Columbus Day," Vancouver *Sun,* October 13, 1936; "120,000 Italians Live in Canada," Vancouver *Province,* June 11, 1940; "Vancouver Italians Pledge Loyalty to Canada As War Declared," Vancouver *Province,* June 10, 1940. Although subjected in time of war to much the same momentary suspicion as enemy aliens in the United States, the Italians in western Canada were few in number and fared reasonably well during the war. At Lethbridge, in Alberta Province, an Italian mayor, for example, was able to retain his office without interruption, despite the war. When the conflict ended, interest in the Italians was again reflected in the headlines of Canadian newspapers: "Vancouver Italian Colony Celebrated Columbus Day," Vancouver *Province,* October 13, 1952; "Station Group to Aid Newcomers," Victoria *Colonist,* May 8, 1955, and "Making Canadians," Victoria *Times,* May 10, 1955. The Italians established their own newspaper in western Canada. As late as 1957, Vancouver's *L'Eco d'Italia* called itself *"L'unico settimanale Italiano nell'Ouest Canadese"* ("the only Italian weekly in the Canadian West"). That year its masthead announced that it served over 100,000 readers in Canada's western provinces.[26]

A few Italian names have been left on the Canadian landscape, among them Garibaldi National Park in British Columbia, Malaspina Peak, and Malaspina Glacier. Other than Alessandro Malaspina, however, few Italian explorers ever visited western Canada. The best known of these was the Duke of Abruzzi who, in the summer of 1897, ascended 18,090-foot Mount Elias, second-highest peak in North America, but he did not leave his name on any part of the Alaskan Chain north of Puget Sound.

Although it cannot be claimed that the few thousand of Italy's immigrants who went to western Canada left a substantial influence, not all foreign influences need be immigrant inspired. Some grow out of the cultural or artistic background of Europe itself. One of the most popular tourist sites in Victoria is "Mrs. Butchart's Gardens." Daily bus loads of tourists are taken to this 130-

[26] *L'Eco d'Italia,* July 24, 1957.

acre estate outside the capital city of British Columbia. There formal Italianate gardens flank a large Pompeiian residence known as Benevento. A lily pool, banked with colorful flower beds, is surrounded by statues, where an environment of Lebanon cedars and sculptured hedges exists that is similar to that found on California estates like the Henry E. Huntington Library and Art Gallery in San Marino, or Villa Montalvo at Saratoga. This type of residence, combining the concept of Italian villas and English country manors, represented an ideal to their builders. Though not directly transplanted to the New World by immigrants, this ideal formed a subconscious part of their Mediterranean heritage.

XI

SUCCESS IN THE SUN: *Islands of Southwestern Settlement*

THE "SOUTHWEST" is one of America's most amorphous geographical regions. A weird world of sand, its boundaries remain in dispute primarily because this is an area of "sub-conscious regionalism." The historian, the geographer, the novelist, and the economist all have their own definitions of what constitutes the figurative metes and bounds of this dry and intriguing land. The inhabitants of each part of the widespread Southwest have also defined its boundaries locally. Some consider the entire region drained by the Colorado River as "Southwest." Some speak of Oklahoma and Texas as "Southwest." Others think of Arizona, New Mexico, and Nevada as "Southwest."[1] In this book California is excluded from the "Southwest" because immigrants there underwent a markedly different acculturation from those in other parts of the region. Every other state west of, and including, Texas (as well as south of Utah) is discussed in this chapter.

Whatever its boundaries, the Southwest had less appeal for the Italian than did non-arid regions. They found there few moist woodlands like those on the American East Coast. Immigrants of farm background were unaccustomed to dry farming. Descriptions filtered back to Italy of the vast distances, great heat, and

[1] In 1944 the Henry E. Huntington Library at San Marino and the Rockefeller Foundation sponsored a conference designed to identify the boundaries of the Southwest. The general conclusion, an unspectacular one, was that the region did not lend itself readily to definition. Merrill Jensen (ed.), *Regionalism in America*, describes the Southwest as an area of essentially unfixed boundaries.

223

scorched southwestern plains. This produced confusion among immigrants. Prospective migrants heard that water was so scarce that it cost five cents per glass. Added to such fears were stereotyped myths about Indians and western bad men. These factors discouraged immigrants from going into the Southwest, unless they were tuberculars or asthmatics seeking a cure.

Texas

Of all the states in the Southwest, Texas was the best known to the immigrants. For newcomers, however, the Lone Star State conjured up a vision that ranged from the well-watered bayou country of its eastern Louisiana border to a wind-swept, dusty Panhandle district that was bleak and uninviting. There was confusion as to whether Texas was one place or many. Here was a land of cattle, oil derricks, arid plains, a humid coastline, and miles of cotton fields. In short, Texas was a region of such fabled contrasts that it was bound to attract curious and challengeable settlers. But Texas required that they be resolute and flexible. How did the Italians measure up?

Only a handful of them reached Texas in the first half of the nineteenth century. Except for the Spanish element and some Germans, few foreigners of any nationality, in fact, made up its early population. Among the earliest Italians was Angelo Navarro. He was a native of Corsica who became, in 1777, one of the founders of San Antonio. The city of Corsicana may have been named in Navarro's honor. One of the first land commissioners in Texas (1834–35) was his son, José Antonio Navarro. He was also a member of the convention which declared Texas independent of Mexico.[2] Other Italians participated in the Texas Revolution. As noted earlier, the Marchese di Santangel was one of Sam Houston's most loyal adherents, operating a press at New Orleans which lashed out fiercely at the Mexicans.

A curiously named Italian, Decimus et Ultimus Barziza (named "Tenth and Last" by his father), went to Texas prior to the Civil

[2] A. W. Williams and E. C. Barker (eds.): *The Writings of Sam Houston* VII, (8 vols., 1938–43) 396, cited in Schiavo, *Four Centuries*, 310.

War and rose to prominence there. His father was the Viscount Filippo Ignacio Barziza, a Venetian who had settled at Williamsburg, Virginia. The younger Barziza was well traveled and sophisticated. A graduate of William and Mary College, he fought with Hood's Fourth Texas Infantry during the Civil War. Barziza, a Confederate captain, was taken prisoner at the Battle of Gettysburg. He was the only known Texan to publish an account of his experiences as a prisoner of war. Afterwards Barziza became a highly effective criminal lawyer and was elected to the Texas House of Representatives from Harris County.[3]

Barziza's story was, of course, not typical of the mass of Italians in Texas. After it became a state, the Italians joined the large-scale migration into Texas, usually as railroad and farm workers or as storekeepers and restaurateurs. By 1890 several thousand Italians were in Texas. Among them was a wealthy nobleman, Count Giuseppe Telfener, like Barziza also atypical. A native of Foggia, this Italian with a German name became interested in Texas after marrying, in the spirit of the times, the daughter of an American millionaire, herself the child of Irish immigrants. In the early 1880's, Telfener originated a plan to send five thousand Italians to Texas. He bought several thousand acres of land near El Paso and built ninety-two miles of track for a prospective railroad, to be called the New York, Texas, and Mexican Railway. Unable to continue financing so expensive an undertaking, the count abandoned the project in 1884 and returned to Italy. About 1,000 Italians nevertheless reached Texas under Telfener's sponsorship. But, finding themselves stranded in the middle of a wilderness, most returned east. In 1887 his creditors sued Telfener for breach of contract over land purchases. They were awarded a judgment of almost four hundred thousand dollars. The railroad he began ultimately became a part of the Southern Pacific system.[4]

As elsewhere, the Italians in Texas participated in a wide variety

[3] Decimus et Ultimus Barziza, *The Adventures of a Prisoner of War*, 1863–64, 3–18.

[4] Schiavo, *Four Centuries*, 310, has reconstructed this episode from a variety of unusual sources.

of construction jobs. In the early 1890's, they helped to build the Colorado River Dam near Austin; they also deepened the harbor at Galveston, and were part of the labor force that laid the Texas Pacific Railroad and Southern Pacific tracks across the largest of all the United States.[5]

At the town of Bryan, in Brazos County, 2,400 Sicilians who had worked as section hands on the Houston and Texas Railroad established a colony after their labor was no longer needed by that road. In a remote area on the banks of the Brazos, eighty miles from Houston, they bought bottom land at a very low price because the area was regularly flooded. After preparing land for cultivation, they planted cotton, corn, and other crops. The cost of maintaining themselves proved cheap. They could buy meat for five cents a pound, and land was so abundant that its use was given free for two years to those who promised to clear it of timber. This wood the Italians sold at two dollars for each eight board feet.

By 1900 some five hundred Italian families had settled at Bryan. Most of these became property owners, their individual landholdings sometimes reaching four hundred acres. In southeastern Texas other Italians grew rice. Near Dickinson they truck-farmed vegetables for the Galveston market and became vineyardists in the neighborhood of Gunnison. As at Sunnyside in Arkansas, or at Verdella in Missouri, or at Ogden in Utah, the Italians of Texas showed a high respect for property. Land ownership meant not only an induplicable form of security; it also signified status, or the fact that they had "arrived."[6]

Although the Texas climate was sometimes uncomfortable, the Italians seemed better suited to heat there than other foreigners, especially the Scandinavians. Norwegians and Swedes were never attracted in large numbers into the Southwest but, as is well known, centered their activity in the more bracing upper midwestern regions of Minnesota, Wisconsin, and Michigan.[7]

[5] Foerster, *Italian Immigration*, 354–55.

[6] Lord, *Italian in America*, 89, 145–47; Pecorini, "The Italian as an Agricultural Laborer," *Annals*, American Academy of Political and Social Science, Vol. XXXIII (January–June, 1909), 384.

[7] Carleton C. Qualey, *Norwegian Settlement in the United States*, 199–200.

Surprisingly, the *Eco d'Italia*, the major nineteenth-century Italian-language newspaper in America, considered Texas "the state best suited for Italians." By 1900 there was in operation a "Società di Colonizzazione Italiana del Texas." At Perla and Keechie this organization bought over 25,000 acres of land which it divided into 50-acre lots. Each of these tracts it allocated to immigrant families. This society spent almost a million dollars in a farm development program that featured the purchase of land and later acquisition of farm machinery and building materials.[8]

If one samples the manuscript population schedules of the census of 1900, he sees statistical scatterings of Italians throughout Texas. These lived at least temporarily in what might be called ethnic "islands," none of which were large communities. Each of these specialized in the production of certain staples. At Bryan immigrants raised corn and cotton; near Dickinson they grew berries and vegetables; at Houston and San Antonio they engaged in fruit growing. Immigrant truck-farming colonies were also located on the outskirts of Galveston and Dallas. Except for a small colony of northern Italians at Montague, immigrants were not attracted to northern Texas, where water was scarcer.[9]

In 1912, when their ambassador to the United States made an inspection trip in Texas, he found his former countrymen spread all over the state. At "Diggenson" [*sic*] he noted about a hundred Sicilian families, mostly from Palermo. "Each one possesses from four to ten acres of excellent land, well cultivated, worth $100 to $200 per acre. They raise strawberries to be sold throughout the great American market." The ambassador found similar colonies at Hitchcock, Goliad, Greenville, Paris, and Texarkana. Of the thirty thousand residents then in Galveston, about fifteen hundred were Italians. At Bryan the percentage of foreigners was startling. Three thousand Sicilians lived there at a time when its entire population was only five thousand. At Houston more than

---

[8] Preziosi, *Gli Italiani*, 110–12.

[9] Pecorini, "The Italian as an Agricultural Laborer," *Annals*, American Academy of Political and Social Science, Vol. XXXIII (January–June, 1909), 164; Lord, *Italian in America*, 125.

one thousand Italians turned out to meet the ambassador, bearing fraternal flags, some of them mounted on horseback. At Beeville he met several persons who had arrived from Italy only a few years before and who, having invested a total of three hundred dollars in the rental of twenty acres of land, already owned eighty acres and reported that they had six thousand dollars in the bank. A man named Beretta owned more than one hundred thousand acres of land at Laredo along the Río Grande River.[10]

The ambassador noted, however, that the Italians had encountered their share of misfortune in Texas. At Rockport, on the Gulf of Mexico, dry, shifting sands had over a three-year period cost Italian farmers some sixty thousand dollars in losses, leading to the abandonment of certain ranches. At Del Rio, two hundred miles northwest of Laredo on the Río Grande, an attempt to cultivate grapes had ended in disaster. The ambassador cautioned newcomers to select the area in which they wished to settle with the greatest care.[11]

Throughout the Southwest, Italians were also active as miners. By 1900, five hundred Venetians, Piedmontese, and Modenese had settled at Thurber, Texas, where they worked in the Texas and Pacific Coal Company's mines. Elsewhere in Texas, immigrants mined not only coal, but copper, zinc, and lead.[12]

One ought not to attempt portrayal of the regional role of any nationality without searching for its means of expression. In Texas, as elsewhere, newspapers formed the most common media by which people kept in touch with one another. From 1906 onward *Il Messagiero Italiano* was published at Galveston and San Antonio while, from 1914 to 1935, *La Tribuna Italiana* was printed at Dallas. In 1931 the latter had reached a circulation of 6,835. More recently *La Tribuna* has been published as the *Texas Tribuna*.[13]

The career of one individual of Italian background who settled

---

[10] Des Planches, *Attraverso*, 164–68, 179, 181, 189.

[11] *Ibid.*, 188, 190.

[12] Lord, *Italian in America*, 111.

[13] *Texas Newspapers*, 1813–1939 (Houston, 1941), 63, 181.

in Texas is wholly unique. This was Charles (Angelo) Siringo. True to that state's tradition of self-glorification, he became a writer of prominence who consistently wrote in a western vein. J. Frank Dobie, dean of southwestern literary lore, called Siringo's *A Texas Cowboy, or Fifteen Years on the Hurricane Deck of a Spanish Pony* (Chicago, 1885) "the cowboy's Bible." Dobie wrote that "Siringo was not only the first authentic cowboy to publish an autobiography; of all cowboys, both spurious and authentic, who have recollected in print he was the most prolific in autobiographic variations."[14] Siringo was born in Texas in 1855, the son of an Italian father and an Irish mother. More than a million copies of his first book, *A Texas Cowboy*, were printed. Among his other works were *A Cowboy Detective* (Chicago, 1912); *A Lone Star Cowboy* (Santa Fe, 1919); *History of Billy the Kid* (Santa Fe, 1920); *Riata and Spurs* (Boston, 1927). Dobie believes Siringo's value as a writer was that "His cowboys and gunmen were not of Hollywood and folklore. He was an honest reporter." Although Siringo was an unusual individual (also a Pinkerton detective), his career illustrates how rapidly the second generation of foreigners in the West adjusted to its wide open spaces.

The majority of immigrants were not, however, similarly talented, and continued to be common workmen. Into the twentieth century many remained employed in railroad track laying and repair. Occasionally these construction jobs were a source of genuine anxiety for foreigners. In 1916, Dominic Ciolli wrote an article, "The Wop in the Track Gang," that rendered a perceptive view of immigrant labor conditions in Texas on a railroad section gang.[15] Ciolli described the Italian community of Bryan along the Brazos River where, when only twelve years old, he was sent to work for a ranchman down in Texas. He stayed on that job three years. "I had to work pretty hard," he reported, "cooking for the cowboys, washing their shirts and cleaning their boots" as well as feeding stock:

[14] J. Frank Dobie, in the introduction to C.J. Siringo, *A Texas Cowboy* (New York, 1950), x.

[15] Cited in Mangano, *Sons of Italy*, 10–11.

One day I learned there were lots of Italians at a place twenty miles away, called Bryan, and, as the cotton picking season was coming on, I could probably get work. A week later, I skipped off, following the Brazos River, until I reached a settlement of about 350 Sicilian families. The first of them came there thirty years ago to work on the railroad, and, finding that the Americans didn't want the cheap land along the river because it was flooded every spring, they were persuaded to buy it. As soon as they made a little money, they sent for their families and more of their townsfolk, until now there are over 3,000 of them. Half of them own from thirty to one hundred acres each. They raise corn and cotton. Their property extends along the river for eighteen square miles. They have drained it and have made it quite a nice little town with fifteen stores and one church. There isn't any school, so they send the children mule-back or in donkey carts ten miles to school. They do work mighty hard. The women and children help too. . . . I was taken on to pick cotton, but as soon as the season was over, there was nothing for me to do there, so I had to move on.

At this point the writer started to work as a section hand on the railroad:

There were nine dilapidated box cars, six for the half hundred men, one for the hand cars, one for the tools, and the last for the padrone and timekeepers. . . . Ours was the only car with windows. On both sides of the cars on the ground were rusty tin boxes, propped up by stones. These were stoves. Heaps of rubbish covered the ground and there was an awful stench. . . . As I entered one car for the first time, the odor choked me. I saw eight beds of boards placed across two boxes. On these lay bags of straw, and for a covering the men used old tan coats or horse blankets. The blankets were covered with vermin. Dirt of two years covered the mattresses. Roaches and bed-bugs livened the walls, the beds, and their surroundings. The tables were covered with oil-cloth or newspapers as dirty as the floor. Under the tables were a few large dishes with the garbage of many a meal. I opened the cupboard. There was a can of tomato paste covered with a film of vermin and green mold, a loaf of soggy bread, a few rusty forks and spoons, and three or four tin dishes. In all the other cars it was the same. All doors were closed at night, no windows, no air. . . . When it rained the men's clothing was drenched. No one undressed before going to bed. The cars . . . were good for nothing but human beings.[16]

Ciolli and his fellow workers would ride out to their jobs with a section gang on a hand car each morning. They worked on the rails, "amid cursing and swearing," and sweat rolled off in streams as they lifted heavy rails for ten hours, eating bread and sausages at noon. It was such workers who were attracted to the anarchistic promises of I.W.W. organizers.

This "pick and shovel era" was, however, supplanted by one in which laborers settled down to home ownership, to a city life, to greater stability and to increased material satisfactions. By 1920 there were more than eight thousand foreign-born Italians in Texas and twice or three times that number who belonged to the second generation.

Oklahoma

As elsewhere in the Southwest, frontier conditions in Oklahoma, the presence of the unfamiliar Indian, and the mysteries of ranch life kept immigrants from going there in large numbers. The first Italians in the Oklahoma of the 1890's went into the southeastern portion of the state's "Indian Territory." In the boom camps of Coalgate, Philips, Alderson, and Hartshorne they mined coal. At McAlester, another mining center, hundreds of Piedmontese labored at the turn of the century for what were then good wages: $2.56 per eight-hour day of work. At Krebs, several thousand more were employed in the mines. Foreign miners voiced only one complaint—the prohibition against alcoholic beverages in "Indian Territory." One miner argued that he had a special need for a bracing drink after coming out of nauseating and gaseous underground tunnels, and complained: "I worked for years in Asia Minor; notwithstanding that the Koran strictly forbids to Mohammedans the use of spirituous drinks, the Turks allowed us Christians to drink wine, beer, and other liquors at our pleasure."[17] Not so in "Indian Territory." As a substitute, Okla-

16 *Ibid.,* 11–12.
17 Lord, *Italian in America,* 109.

"Indians in search of a home," as seen by an Italian artist. About 1880.

This item is reproduced by permission of the Huntington Library,
San Marino, Calif. From Egisto Rossi, *Gli Stati Uniti*

homa's thirsty Italians consumed quantities of a well-known
"medicinal tonic," or Febrifuge, "Fernet," the best brand of which
was manufactured in Italy under the Italian "Branca" trade name.
It is still widely marketed in Oklahoma and elsewhere in the
United States.

The behavior pattern of immigrants was remarkably similar
wherever they settled. The Italians in the Oklahoma mines cultivated the usual garden vegetables in small patches near their
wooden houses. Frugality was general. Not trusting hard-earned
savings to local bankers, they preferred to bury money beneath
the ground. "I will wager," said one observer, "that here at Krebs
there are at least fifty thousand dollars buried underground."[18]

In the twentieth century, Italians were to be employed in Oklahoma's oil fields; still others settled in its largest cities, Tulsa and
Oklahoma City. They reached their greatest number about 1910,
when there were some 2,600 native-born Italians in Oklahoma.

[18] *Ibid.*, 110.

New Mexico

That high and colorful mesa land of the piñon tree, New Mexico, has never forsaken its Latin heritage. Although the dominant characteristic of its tradition has been Spanish, some part of it has been Italian. Centuries, however, elapsed between the explorations of Friar Marcos (Fra Marco da Nizza), the Jesuits Eusebio Kino and Giuseppe Salvatierra, and later clerics who continued a long Italian record of ministering to the Indians of that region. The Sisters of Charity, a teaching and nursing order that contained many young Italian novitiates, arrived at Santa Fe in 1865. This was an early date for women to appear on the edge of a dangerous frontier. A world of crude realities, therefore, faced these sisters. Some notion of the problems they confronted appears in the narrative of a Ligurian nun, Sister Blandina Segale. Buried in her fascinating reminiscences, entitled *At the End of the Santa Fe Trail*, is an account of meeting Billy the Kid while traveling by stage in 1877 from Trinidad to Santa Fe. "The Kid's" armed band was terrorizing the area, and therefore most stagecoaches traveled heavily armed. When the stage on which Sister Blandina traveled into New Mexico was suddenly attacked by outlaws, she took her own brand of action:

> "Please put your revolvers away," I said in a voice which was neither begging nor aggressive. . . . Spontaneously the weapons went under cover. The light patter of hoofs could be heard as they drew near the carriage opening. As the rider came from the rear of the vehicle, he first caught sight of the two gentlemen in the front seat, which gave me a chance to look at him before he saw us. I shifted my big bonnet so that when he did look, he could see the Sisters [riding in the stage]. Our eyes met; he raised his large-brimmed hat with a wave and a bow, looked his recognition, fairly flew a distance of about three rods, and then stopped to give us some of his wonderful antics on broncho maneuvers. The rider was the famous "Billy the Kid."

The good sister extracted from "the Kid" a promise that she and her associates would be protected from further attacks by his gang.[19]

Sister Blandina's co-workers ultimately built a hospital for railroad laborers in New Mexico, a trade school for Indians, and various places of worship. In order to construct these buildings, they had to open a quarry, burn their own lime, run a brickyard, and operate saw and lumber planing mills. These sisters entered into activities as diverse as ministering to Apaches or trying to end lynch law. Theirs was a life with few compensations to it outside the spiritual realm.

Among the most talented and highly educated priests and nuns on the American frontier occasional strong nostalgia for their homeland was unpreventable. As they faced the rawness of the primitive, one sees its grip in the most personal accounts of Jesuits, whether in Montana or Lower California, and among the Sisters of Charity in New Mexico. Something of the eternal fascination of Italy was characterized by the immigrant writer Constantine Panunzio in his *The Soul of an Immigrant*. He quotes Donizetti's famous lines:

> Oh, Italia, Italia beloved
> Land of beauty and sunlight and song!
> Tho' afar from thy bright skies removed
> Still our fond hearts for thee ever long!

The sunlight of the Southwest was also bright, but the members of Italy's religious orders, lonely and isolated from their compatriots, were there only because of a missionary impulse, a way of life not easily understood by others.

In 1867 the New Mexico sisters were joined in southern Colorado by a group of Neapolitan Jesuits. Because of Italy's revolutionary mood in the 1860's, some of these Jesuits had been expelled from the country by Giuseppe Garibaldi. Anticlericalism

---

[19] Sister Blandina Segale, *At the End of the Santa Fe Trail*, 98–99. Ramon Adams' *Burs Under the Saddle* (Norman, 1964), 453, casts doubt upon the accuracy of the Segale account of her meeting with Billy the Kid. Adams' *A Fitting Death For Billy the Kid* (Norman, 1960), 239, charges the nun with inaccurate dating.

in Italy, as well as fear and resentment of Jesuit political activity, suddenly made these Jesuits available for service in the American Southwest. After the Civil War came to an end, the bishop of Santa Fe, John Lamy, had gone to Rome to explain his pressing missionary needs. As a result, Father Donato M. Gasparri was assigned to New Mexico with a small group of priests and brothers. Born near Naples in 1834, he had served in Zaragosa and Valencia, Spain, and, fortunately, could speak Spanish. With Gasparri came Fathers Rafael Bianchi and Livio Vigilante, as well as Brothers Rafael La Vezza and Prisco Caso. On May 27, 1867, their *piccolo treno* headed west from New York, most of them never to return there. By wagon and carriage they made their way to St. Louis and then to Fort Leavenworth. The party, during its 7,340-mile trip, included as many as twenty persons. It was led by Bishop Lamy himself, the man about whom Willa Cather wrote *Death Comes for the Archbishop* (New York, 1927).

Gasparri's narrative faithfully traces this party's arrival in the wilderness. Like Sister Blandina's account, it is full of exciting moments. The group of clerics traveled by pack animal from Fort Leavenworth southwestward. Along the Arkansas River, whose banks Gasparri describes as "infested with Indians," they suddenly came across many "signs of destruction, such as houses in ruins, earth piled up over dead bodies, parts of corpses, arms, clothes, and abandoned wagons." One morning they "saw a band of twelve Indians, well armed and well provided." The priests were horror-stricken. But they were surprised when the Indians "asked us for coffee and tobacco, and they in turn offered us buffalo meat." They gave thanks to God that they were not among those overland parties attacked by these very Indians. Yet, they lost several drovers and a nun because of cholera. Each was buried on the plains. The party reached Santa Fe on August 15, 1867, without further losses.[20]

Gasparri and his associates, the fathers and brothers Persone, Gentile, Paoli, Mandalari, Leone, and Tomassini, were to minis-

[20] D. M. Gasparri, "Account of the First Jesuit Missionary Journey Across the Plains to Santa Fe," *Mid-America*, Vol. XX (January, 1938), 57–58.

ter for years to the Navajos and other tribes as well as to whites. They built schools, churches, and missions in the valleys of the Río Grande, the Pecos, the Arkansas, and the Purgatorio rivers. In Colorado these Italians were active at Pueblo, Trinidad, and throughout the San Luis Valley, as far away as Denver. Father Bianchi died in 1868, the year after he arrived in New Mexico. With the parish of Bernalillo as their headquarters, these priests founded the *Revista Católica*, a journal published from 1875 until quite recently. Its first printer was Father Enrico Ferrari, and its staff consisted of the Italian fathers Lorenzo Fide, Raphael Tummolo, Giuseppe Marra, and Alfonso Rossi. Gasparri was the superior of the New Mexico Jesuit mission band until 1880, and was followed by Father Aloysius Gentile, another Italian. Gasparri died in 1882.

At times Jesuit influence in New Mexico's courts and legislature was resented, because of the priests' broad powers and exemption from government supervision. A recent history of New Mexico summarizes the matter: "Unfortunately, many of the Catholic educational leaders were Italian Jesuits, only recently expelled from their homeland. These men like Father Finotti and Father Gasparri, were dynamic and competent exponents of their point of view and vigorously assailed the advocates of public schools in the harshest language."[21] There were also moments when the Italian Jesuit efficiency even aroused the enmity of non-foreign secular priests.

Despite considerable anti-Catholicism in New Mexico, by 1877 the Italian Jesuits had founded a college in Las Vegas. In 1884 they began another at Morrison.[22] Four years later the staffs of both institutions were transferred to Denver. New Mexico's Neapolitan Jesuit mission was officially disbanded in 1919, as secular religious facilities necessary to care for the state's population re-

[21] Warren A. Beck, *New Mexico, a History of Four Centuries* (Norman, 1962), 209.

[22] See William G. Ritch, *Jesuitism in New Mexico, an Answer to Father Finotti*.

placed their efforts. Fifty-two consecutive years of Italian missionary activity in New Mexico, thus, came to an end.[23]

After 1880 increasing numbers of foreigners reached the coal mines of northern and western New Mexico, its sheep ranches to the south, as well as Santa Fe and Albuquerque. Montague Stevens, a cultivated Englishman who in the 1880's brought his bride to settle on a ranch near New Mexico's San Augustine Plains, wrote a book, *Meet Mr. Grizzly. A Saga on the Passing of the Grizzly* (London, 1950), in which he recorded the presence of many foreigners. In fact, he was surprised that so many overland travelers who camped on his lands could not speak English. A study of New Mexico's foreign inhabitants points out that "as early as the middle of the nineteenth century, the population of New Mexico was surprisingly cosmopolitan as to origin, if not as to culture." Its author observes: "Italy is the country to watch, however, for her representation trebled in the decade between 1870 and 1880." The number of first-generation Italians in New Mexico nearly doubled between 1890 and 1900. By the decade 1900 to 1910, while half the foreign-born in New Mexico were Mexicans, "Italy finally came into her own, carrying off second place with 1,959 persons in the latter year out of a population of 327,301 persons." The study concludes: "From no other nation did immigration proceed in such a constantly and rapidly increasing stream, for from 1860 to 1910 there was not a decade in which the Italian representation was not tripled. In conclusion, it should be noticed that during the entire territorial era the foreign-born

[23] Sources on Father Gasparri include: A. M. Mandalari, *Missione del Nuovo Messico e Colorado, lettere edificanti . . .* ; and Donato M. Gasparri, S.J., "An Account of the Voyage of . . ." in *Lettere edificanti della Provincia Napoletana della compagnia di Gesù*, a diary dated April 19, 1867, in Archives of San Felipe di Neri Rectory, Albuquerque. An effective history in Italian is Giuseppe M. Sorrentino, *Dalle montagne rocciose al Rio Bravo*; see also E. R. Vollmer, "Donato Gasparri, New Mexico–Colorado Mission Founder," *Mid-America*, Vol. XX (April, 1938), 96–106. On *Revista Catolica* see Ralph E. Twitchell, *The Leading Facts of New Mexico History* (Cedar Rapids, 1911), II, 343. See also M. Lilliana Owens, *Jesuit Beginnings in New Mexico, 1867–1882.*

population of New Mexico exhibited a satisfying, and rather surprising, degree of cosmopolitanism."[24]

Arizona

As in New Mexico, there was little Italian activity from the sixteenth century onward, when Friar Marcos first entered Arizona, until the second half of the nineteenth century. In the later period, however, the foreign-born population was, until the 1890's, actually greater than the American-born population. In the 1860 federal census reports, Arizona is listed as a county of New Mexico. Almost none of its non-Indian residents were born in the West. Three-fourths of the soldiers stationed there were immigrants from Europe, mostly Ireland and Germany. The census for 1870 lists 3,849 native-born Americans in Arizona versus 5,809 foreign-born; that of 1880 lists 24,391 native-born versus 16,049 foreign-born. Only a small proportion of these foreign-born were, however, Italians. The coming to Arizona of the Southern Railroad increased their number. A few of these immigrants merit individual mention, if only to establish their occupations. There was a Charles Salari who operated the Phoenix Hotel as early as 1884; an Alex Rossi, saloonkeeper at Tucson; an E. F. Sanguinetti, a merchandiser at Yuma; and a Donofrio family who operated a confectionery at Phoenix. The Corella family, in Arizona as early as the 1840's, was also prominent in the new territory.

The most renowned of the Italians to come to Arizona was the future mayor of New York City, that crusading progressive, Fiorello La Guardia. He was the son of an army bandmaster, who had originally come to America as accompanist to the opera diva Adelina Patti. La Guardia's father was born at Foggia, his mother at Trieste. Young Fiorello lived at Fort Huachuca from 1890 to

[24] Richard A. Greer, "Origins of the Foreign-Born Population of New Mexico During the Territorial Period," *New Mexico Historical Review*, Vol. XVII (October, 1942), 281–87; the best overall source on the Italians in New Mexico is the judicious doctoral dissertation by Frederick G. Bohme, "A History of the Italians in New Mexico." Regarding Montague Stevens see Erna Fergusson, *New Mexico a Pageant* . . . (New York, 1951), 284; Agnes Morley Cleaveland, *No Life for a Lady* (Boston, 1941).

1892. His family then moved to Prescott for the next six years. La Guardia considered Prescott the town in which he put down his first American roots: "He lived at the fort and went to school in the town, which lay a mile away over a rough and winding dirt road. His playground was the great outdoors where he hunted and rode 'the wildest broncos of the range.' He saw what Indians looked like, spoke to miners and cowboys, went camping in the hills with soldiers, tended the chickens and cow that his father kept, and enjoyed his share of schoolboy pranks and fights." La Guardia and his biographers have attributed some of his most individualistic, as well as reformist, characteristics to the almost ideal boyhood he spent in the fresh air of Arizona.[25]

"All my boyhood memories are of those Arizona days," he wrote. He remembered Fort Huachuca as "miles and miles from urban civilization," and although located in barren and bleak surroundings, it was, in his words, "a paradise for a little boy." La Guardia "learned to shoot when we were so small the gun had to be held for us by an elder." He remembered his family's "two room 'dobe house, with a detached kitchen" that "had a canvas roof, and the house had plank sides and flooring."[26]

La Guardia grew to think of Prescott as "the greatest and most wonderful city in the whole world," a place where people were more than kindly, among whom his father—as leader of the 11th U.S. Infantry Band—became very popular. He participated in concerts, blowing the cornet, while his sister, Gemma, played the violin and their father accompanied them on the piano. Although there was a rigid distinction between officers and enlisted men, extending even to their children, this did not bother young Fiorello, who, throughout his life, recognized no such barriers. As he put it: "I would just as soon fight with an officer's kid as I would with anyone else." Later, La Guardia remembered with the greatest affection his public school teachers in Prescott and his early training on the frontier.[27]

[25] Arthur Mann, *La Guardia, a Fighter Against His Times*, 26ff.
[26] Fiorello H. La Guardia, *The Making of an Insurgent*, 19.
[27] *Ibid.*, 20.

The educational value of those days on the future mayor, congressman, and judge was incalculable, as he himself insisted:

> What I saw and heard and learned in my boyhood days in Arizona made lasting impressions on me. . . . For instance, I loathe the professional politician. . . . This attitude had its origin in the badly dressed, slick and sly Indian agents, political appointees, I saw come into Arizona . . . robbing the Indians of the food the government provided for them.

La Guardia remembered being ashamed of eating apples and cookies in front of hungry Indian children. In later life he was to do something about the welfare of needy children.[28]

On the Arizona frontier he also developed a lifelong distaste for professional, "tinhorn" gamblers. "Nearly every saloon in Prescott had its gambling department, mainly for crap, faro and some Chinese game," he recalled. "The guns were laid on the table at easy reach, and of course the games were on the level." That is, until the game called "policy" came to town. "I remember Mother telling me that it was the same as Lotto, which was sponsored in her native Trieste by the city or state. Mother would play a ten cent policy slip every week. If she had an exceptional dream, she would risk a quarter. She never won. No one else I knew ever won." When the operators of the game quickly left town, young Fiorello "figured it out then as nothing but petty larceny from the pockets of the poor," and showed his mother "how she couldn't win." He was to move strongly against such deception and fraud later in his life.[29]

"Another early impression that made its mark on my mind," La Guardia recalled, "was gained from watching the railroad being built between Ashfork, Prescott and Phoenix." There was little machinery employed during this construction job. "It was all manpower and draft animals. The laborers were all Mexicans and Italians." Even then he was shocked by the fact that there were no social security laws, employer liability regulations, or workmen's

[28] *Ibid.*, 22.
[29] *Ibid.*, 25.

compensation provisions to protect immigrants or non-immigrants. The memory of this spurred him on later to fight for such measures. La Guardia was only twelve years old when, in 1894, federal troops in Arizona were called out to guard the property of the Atlantic and Pacific Railroad during the nationwide Pullman strike. He could not "quite understand why it was unlawful for employees to inform other employees of grievances, or why they should be kept away from one another by a court mandate, enforced by bayonets of United States soldiers." Such memories were later "very helpful," La Guardia wrote in his *Autobiography*. "It was nearly half a lifetime later, as a member of Congress, that I had an opportunity of taking part in preparing the Railways Labor Act and in passage of the Norris–La Guardia Anti-Injunction Act."[30]

A final amusing, yet poignant, memory was to have its effect when La Guardia assumed power in New York. This concerned an organ-grinder who came to town when he was a boy in Prescott:

> He, and particularly the monkey, attracted a great deal of attention. I can hear the cries of the kids: "Dago with a monkey! Hey, Fiorello, you're a dago too. Where's your monkey?" It hurt. And what made it worse, along came Dad, and he started to chatter in Neapolitan with the organ grinder. He hadn't spoken Italian in many years, and he seemed to enjoy it. Perhaps, too, he considered the organ grinder a fellow musician. At any rate, he promptly invited him to our house for a macaroni dinner. The kids taunted me for a long time after that. I couldn't understand it. What difference was there between us? Some of their families hadn't been in the country any longer than mine.[31]

As Mayor of New York, La Guardia received a report one day from its police department. It complained that roaming organ-grinders posed both a traffic menace and a hazard to small children, who rushed out onto the city streets in pursuit of them. Despite the criticism he received, the mayor banned all organ-grinders from New York's public streets. He used as an excuse "the advent of the

[30] *Ibid.*, 26–27.
[31] *Ibid.*, 27–28.

phonograph and the radio" as well as "free public concerts in parks, libraries, museums and other public places." Organ-grinders and their monkeys no longer fitted the times, he said. Did not the cause of his action, however, cut deeper? Did it not go back to that humiliation and ridicule which La Guardia, proud son of an army bandmaster, once experienced on the frontier when he was likened to an illiterate, begging, organ-grinder?

La Guardia's courage, integrity, faith in the future of democracy, and inflexible belief in reform probably stemmed from his childhood influences in Arizona. This affection for the West is expressed in the words of the man himself. "To me," he wrote shortly before his death, "that is truly God's country—I love everything about it. Perhaps my memories of Arizona are so pleasant because I had a happy, wholesome boyhood." La Guardia, one of the shrewdest men produced by the American melting pot, underwent formative experiences in the West that resembled those of another statesman, Theodore Roosevelt. It is legendary how strongly Roosevelt's days as a youthful rancher in the Dakota Badlands influenced the later man and president. Both La Guardia and Roosevelt came in contact with western attitudes that seemed to kindle an enthusiasm for government service, unhampered by urban prejudices.

No other Arizona Italian ever reached the prominence of a La Guardia; they generally worked for the railroads or for such large mining concerns as the Phelps-Dodge Corporation, or for the New Cornelia Copper Company. After 1879 foreigners headed for the Tombstone silver mines. But not all Italians were railroad workers or miners. For example, at Charleston, a sort of bedroom for Tombstone, Antonio Fleres, born in Italy in 1820, was listed in *The Great Register of the County of Cochise* in 1882 as owner of the Occidental Hotel. The Tucson *Citizen* spoke of the Occidental as having "first-class accommodations for both ladies and gents." On October 16, 1881, that newspaper, however, reported that during a party at the hotel someone had ignited firecrackers and several giant powder kegs in front of the Occidental, which seriously damaged the hotel and adjoining structures. Its owner,

Fleres, seems to have had a son, age thirty-two, who listed himself as a Charleston merchant. Charleston is today a ghost town. A sizable number of Italian miners settled at Morenci. By 1910, after Arizona's Italians reached a peak of about fifteen hundred, their total numbers declined. Few native-born Italians went to live in Arizona thereafter, because of the state's remoteness and the restrictive federal immigration law of 1924.[32]

IN 1927 THE PRIDE OF ARIZONA'S ITALIANS in their old country was quickened by the unexpected arrival on the waters of the state's Lake Roosevelt of a seaplane manned by Commander Francesco de Pinedo and his crew. De Pinedo, an Italian naval officer, was an aerial pioneer on his way around the world, who had traversed the Atlantic and flown over the length of South America into the United States and then westward via New Orleans, Galveston, San Antonio, and Albuquerque. At that early date a trip of this magnitude had not yet been undertaken. But while De Pinedo's airship was refueling on Lake Roosevelt, a bystander tossed a lighted cigarette onto its gasoline-strewn waters and flames destroyed De Pinedo's airplane. Because of this tragedy a spirit of national sympathy went out to De Pinedo's party. He and his fellow aviators were feted at the White House by President Coolidge and throughout America. This accident, in the middle of a unique world-wide flight, focused national attention upon the convergence of Italians and Americans in the remote West.[33]

To close the story of the Italians in Arizona one should call attention to a contemporary artist, Ted Ettore De Grazia. He is best known for a painting, "Los Niños," used on UNICEF's 1964 Christmas cards. Born at Morenci in 1909, he is the son of a copper miner who took him back to Italy at the age of eleven. After

---

[32] Mention of early Italians in Arizona is in *Guida,* 79; and Richard E. Sloan, *Memories of an Arizona Judge* (Stanford, 1932), 8–9; and his *History of Arizona* (4 vols., Phoenix, 1930), V, 306; R. W. Fulton and C. J. Bahre, "Charleston, Arizona, a Documentary Reconstruction," *Arizona and the West,* Vol. IX (Spring, 1967), 55, 62.

[33] Francesco de Pinedo, *Il mio volo attraverso l'Atlantico e le due Americhe,* 174–225.

five years there he returned to the Southwest to become one of its leading artists. About De Grazia a renowned colleague, the painter Thomas Hart Benton, writes: "De Grazia's art stands out and takes on distinction in the welter of abstractions now thrust upon us. It is full of a delicate and very human poetry which everybody feels and everybody can understand. We are much in need of art like this. De Grazia has shown up at the right time."[34] Called "a master of fantasy," De Grazia utilizes the barren southwestern landscape to highlight drawings of Indians, horses, and, in particular, children of all races. How much his talent stems from the immigrant past is, of course, virtually unknowable.

Nevada

After the Comstock mining strike of 1859, a sprinkling of Italians moved eastward into Nevada from California. For more than twenty years they were to help carve out a 190-mile labyrinth of mining shafts and tunnels in the Comstock Lode. Again, the names of individual Italians in Nevada are useful to establish occupations: Signor M. Crosetta, as early as 1861, operated the Virginia Saloon at Virginia City. In that community a Molinelli Hotel still stands which dates from the same year. To care for their spiritual needs, the Nevada Italians as early as 1865 engaged a Catholic priest, Father Dominic Monteverdi of the Passionist Order. For eighteen years he labored among them with zeal.[35]

An astonishing number of foreigners were in Virginia City from an early date. In October, 1870, its Italian residents held a dinner to celebrate the unification of Italy. That year the city's Germans organized a "Jollification" to mark the fall of Paris during the Franco-Prussian War. In 1872, Virginia City had also become sufficiently cosmopolitan to see its Swiss population observe their country's independence anniversary with a twenty-two–gun salute, a dinner, and an evening of dancing and speeches.[36]

[34] *"Ted Ettore De Grazia," The Masterkey,* Vol. XXXVI (October–December, 1962), 124–26; Ted Ettore De Grazia, *Padre Kino, a Portfolio* . . . .

[35] Schiavo, *Four Centuries,* 175 .

[36] Virginia City *Territorial Enterprise,* Oct. 18, Feb. 10, Sept. 10, 1870; Feb. 1, 1871; Sept. 22, 1874.

The New York newspaper *Eco d'Italia*, in its April 16, 1869, issue, pointed out that many Italians had located at Treasure City, Nevada. Some of these, who had intended to become grocers or restaurateurs, decided instead to work in the mines, where the rewards were more promising.[37] The federal manuscript census of 1870 confirms the presence of these Italians at Treasure City—a remarkably cosmopolitan mining camp made up of Austrians, Hungarians, Frenchmen, and other European nationalities. The Italians listed occupations predominantly connected with mining. Except for one butcher, the rest became mule packers, charcoal burners, ore smelters, or quartz millers. They did not become financially opulent, but, compared to other miners, they declared substantial personal savings to the census taker, running usually from two to three hundred dollars.[38]

The naming of the mining town of Verdi indicates that Nevada's Italians remembered the homeland, there as elsewhere. A number of charcoal burners kept a smelter operating in the 1870's at Eureka. After the turn of the century more such foreigners appeared. At the copper mining camps of Ely and McGill they were separated from other inhabitants. As at Bingham Canyon, Utah, this provided an excellent means of controlling antagonisms between immigrant nationalities at these company towns. Also, it insured separation along economic lines, another tenet of company housing policy. More permanent and skilled employees received the best housing and were thereby encouraged to be more loyal to "the company."[39]

The effects of such procedures on immigrant miners were diverse, according to one authority:

Although company housing policy fostered segregation, company employment policies, particularly after World War I, did just the

[37] Schiavo, *Four Centuries*, 175.

[38] MS Census of 1870, Treasure City, White Pine County, Nevada, Microfilm Roll 211, 1870 Census Population Schedules, National Archives, Washington, D.C.

[39] Russell R. Elliott, *Nevada's Twentieth Century Mining Boom* (Reno, 1966), 228–31.

opposite. Increased educational opportunities combined with the increased demand for skilled laborers to give these individuals the opportunity to move upward in the economic scale. By the 1930's, numerous second-generation Greeks, Serbs, and others, with grade and perhaps high school educations were being apprenticed as carpenters, plumbers, electricians, and bricklayers. Once the economic barrier was breached, and after years of common participation in the public schools, the barriers to intermarriage were broken.[40]

A considerable number of immigrants from southern Europe were attracted to the company towns of Ruth and Kimberly in White Pine County. They came in answer to a demand for a cheap, stable labor supply. At Ely their growing number led to antiforeign feeling. Opposition to the foreigner was mainly along economic lines, as the *Ely Mining Record* for April 18, 1908, stated: "His mission here is to cut wages to a point where an American cannot live, to save a few dollars and return home. . . . No community can prosper on this cheap class of labor."[41] As immigrants, however, became assimilated into such local unions as "Lane City Miner's No. 251," opposition to these workers diminished. Indeed, immigrants were among the strikers during the July, 1909, strike against the Cumberland-Ely Company. They demanded $3.50 per day for all men working underground. Of the three hundred strikers who closed down that company's Veteran Mine for over two years, most were immigrants, specifically Greeks and Serbians. Whenever foreigners were loyal to "the company," rather than to unions, they, of course, risked renewed worker-hostility.[42]

In addition to mining, some Italians raised vegetables on the outskirts of Reno. Still others, much later, became interested in restaurant and cabaret properties at Nevada's capital, Carson City. In 1892 they organized there a lodge and fraternal organization, the "Società di Benificenza Italiana." In 1902, Italians founded the "Ordine Internazionale dei Druidi" in Nevada; upon

[40] *Ibid.*, 231.
[41] *Ibid.*, 256.
[42] *Ibid.*, 259.

celebration of its twentieth anniversary, there were over one hundred members on its rolls. By 1922 the "Lamp Bearers," an Italian women's organization at Reno, had a substantial membership. The remoteness of Nevada's population from large urban centers lent solidarity to these groups. Contact with the outside world was mainly via Sacramento and San Francisco.[43] From a Nevada population of over fifteen hundred in 1880, its native-born Italians increased to over twenty-eight hundred in 1910 and to more than twenty-six hundred as late as 1930. By the latter year this population supported a weekly newspaper, the *Bollettino del Nevada*.

After the turn of the century a small group of Italians who had settled near Pyramid Lake in western Nevada became involved in a long-term dispute with the federal government. In the 1860's their forebears, of Genoese origin, had come into the region from California to raise fodder and vegetables for the boom towns of Virginia City and Austin. When the Central Pacific Railroad built various repair shops at Wadsworth, some of these Italians had started farming near by, to supply its workers. After the shops were disbanded early in the twentieth century, they and their families stayed on as ranchers. Unfortunately, the lands on which they located were technically upon the reservation of Nevada's Paiute Indians. In 1924, Congress made possible the purchase of these lands by whites. By 1929, except for a first payment, the Italians had, however, defaulted in their land payments. In 1936 the federal government (specifically the Department of the Interior's Bureau of Indian Affairs) in effect "called time" on the settlers, seeking thereby to invalidate their claims to the area. But the Italians had a powerful political friend. Beginning in 1937, Nevada's Senator Pat McCarran annually introduced a series of Congressional bills to award these lands to the Italians who had squatted upon them. At one time, the Italians claimed $350,000 damages.

Seeking to have some twenty-one hundred acres (of which only seven hundred were irrigated) awarded to the Italians, Senator McCarran declared that the Italians' supremacy over the Nevada

[43] *La Capitale, edizione di Pasque* (Sacramento, 1922), n.p.

Indians was obvious: "These people came in there as early as 1864.
. . . They are in the desert country where no Indian ever constructed a ditch before a ditch was constructed by these white
people. . . . So you are taking nothing whatever from the Indians."[44] McCarran was, nevertheless, unsuccessful in his defense
of the Italian claims, and, in 1948, the federal government repos-
sessed part of their lands. Just before McCarran's death in 1953,
his bill to buy out their remaining claims was, however, passed by
the Congress and signed by President Dwight D. Eisenhower.

Actually, the Paiute Indians and the Italians were friendly, as
one local resident noted: "When an Indian gets into trouble over
to Fallon or Fernley, and gets thrown into jail, he sends for old
Bill Ceresola, the head squatter, to come and bail him out." There
were, however, instances when the Italians sold the Indians water,
by the gallon, or perhaps more appropriately by the demijohn. In
the desert, this did not represent the height of friendship.[45]

The story of the Italians in Nevada might well be ended by recounting the experiences of one of their most successful families,
the Saturnos. At age twenty, Leopoldo Saturno, an immigrant
ranch hand, settled on an irrigated farm along Reno's Truckee
River. He was a native of San Marco d'Urri, a tiny village that
still clings to the Appenine foothills southeast of Genoa. In Nevada, Leopoldo and his wife, Teresa, raised five children. By the
time he died in 1919, they had laid the foundation of a fortune in
Reno's real estate market. By a series of shrewd investments, two
of Leopoldo's sons, Joseph and Victor, further increased the family
wealth to an estimated two million dollars.

The Saturno children not only lived without ostentation. They
also retained an unusual sense of conscience about the homeland
whence their forebears came. In 1959, when Joseph had reached
the age of seventy-one and Victor was sixty-four, they decided to
give each of the inhabitants of the village of San Marco twenty-

[44] A. J. Liebling, "The Lake of the CuiUi Eaters," *New Yorkers*, Vol. XXX
(January 8, 1955), 46.

[45] *Ibid.*, (January 1, 1955), 37.

five shares of Bank of America stock. The gift totaled about $350,000, each inhabitant's bloc of securities amounting to $1,250. The dividends from this benefaction (some $100 per year) alone represented half the per capita income of their father's native village.

The Saturno gift came as a shock to the inhabitants of San Marco's half-deserted huddle of decaying slate-roofed houses. The San Marcoans, who were without cars, telephones, or a police force, could scarcely believe what had occurred. Few remembered old Leopoldo Saturno. In fact, the villagers were so embarrassed by his children's gift that they hardly knew how to react. In a burst of gratitude, the village had a bronze bust made of Leopoldo, inviting the brothers to attend its unveiling. The brothers made a three-month trip throughout Italy which, however, led to so much publicity that their own privacy was forever altered. So many photographs of them were printed in European newspapers that the brothers were recognized everywhere they went. In desperation, they fled back to Reno. Even in Nevada, they could no longer maintain their anonymity. "We're hiding out here," Joseph told an inquirer in 1961. "We don't want people to know we're here. As soon as they find out, we'll move again." Letters asking for handouts poured in on the Saturnos. They tried to answer each of these by hand. Finally, in desperation, they gave up. One such inquiry from France was addressed: "Saturno Bros., Angels of Reno, Nevada."

Reports came back to the Saturno brothers that their gift had caused unhappiness among certain inhabitants of San Marco. The old village's life was disrupted by the publicity it now received. Villagers were, furthermore, no longer content with their lot, the homes in which they lived, or with their future. Others wanted to go to America but found that the Italian emigration quota of about five thousand persons per year was oversubscribed for decades to come. "We felt that giving them stock," said Joseph, "would put joy in everyone's heart." While this tribute to their father brought some happiness, it also emphasized the gap between the village he had left and the New World in which he had found his fortune in far-off Nevada.[46]

IN THE SOUTHWESTERN STATES Italians like the Saturnos had grown up with the country and with the times. They had leavened its youthful energy with Old World customs and traditions—until these foreign values were themselves overcome by the vitality of the American scene.

[46] All quotations from *Time*, November 23, 1959, 31, and *Los Angeles Times*, May 7, 1961, 2.

XII

ITALY IN CALIFORNIA: *A Mediterranean America*

In California the Italian westward migration flowered best.[1] To that American Acadia went the largest number; there they found themselves and made a unique contribution to its progress. The similarities between Italy and California were obvious. Once raw and youthful, long stretches of its coastal belt resembled ancient Tuscany or Campania. Its terraced bluffs near Santa Barbara and also at Carmel reminded one of the Riviera's Santa Margherita, San Remo, and Rapallo. Blue skies, olive trees, and craggy cliffs took one back mentally to Posilippo on the Bay of Naples. Even California's rainfall was much like Italy's—with the heaviest in the north. Scenery, and the mildness of the Golden State's seasons, proved a powerful attraction. In this "Italy of America," later immigrants found that almost anything grown back home could be raised. Some believed that a classical civilization beside the western sea might well result from California's colonization.

Italian contact with California was by no means as early as that of the Portuguese Cabrillo or the Englishman Drake. In fact, Italy's first missionaries, Giuseppe Salvatierra and Francesco Clavigero, operated in Lower rather than Upper California. The

---

[1] Parts of this chapter were presented in Madison, Wisconsin, on April 24, 1954, at the annual meeting of the Mississippi Valley Historical Association and appeared in abbreviated format as "Italy in California," *The Pacific Spectator,* Vol. IX (Autumn, 1955), 408–19. See also my "Success in the Sun: The Italians in California," in Henry Clifford (ed.), *Westerners Brand Book.*

already mentioned Malaspina expedition of 1791 was more clearly Californian. Such early visitors were, however, not immigrants.

Who were a few of California's first Italians? Not until the end of the province's Spanish period does the name of an Italian colonist come into view. This was Juan B. Bonifacio; with the governor's permission he landed at Monterey in 1822 off the ship *John Begg*. A resident English trader, W.E.P. Hartnell, employed Bonifacio as a hide and tallow stevedore. He proceeded to raise a sizable family (though not as large as Hartnell's of twenty-nine children). Bonifacio died a naturalized Mexican citizen.[2] Similar to Bonifacio's is the story of Battisto Leandri, known locally as Juan Bautista. He arrived in southern California in 1823, kept a store at Los Angeles, and married María Francisca Uribe at San Gabriel Mission. Leandri became a judge, or *juez de paz*, also holding other local offices as an adopted *Angeleno*. At his death in 1843 he was the respected owner of part of Rancho San Pedro and the grantee of Rancho Los Coyotes.

Richard Henry Dana, author of *Two Years Before the Mast* (1840), that classic account of pastoral California, mentioned encountering various Italian seamen in its southern coastal waters. He described seeing a large boat near San Pedro filled with Italians "in blue jackets, scarlet caps, and various-colored underclothes, bound ashore on liberty . . . singing beautiful Italian boat songs all the way in fine, full chorus." Among the songs Dana recognized "the favorite 'O pescator dell'onda.' " Still later he ran across "three or four Italian sailors mounted and riding up and down the beach on the hard sand at a furious rate," as well as dancing in the near-by town. Almost every time an Italian shore boat went ashore, it was, Dana said, "filled with men gaily dressed singing their *barcarollas*."[3]

[2] H. H. Bancroft, *History of California*, II (7 vols., San Francisco, 1885), 723.

[3] Regarding Leandri, see Fray Felipe Arroyo to Fray José Joaquín Jimeno, February 11, 1839; Anna María Leandri to J. B. Leandri, March 10, 1837; J. B. Leandri to Fray Tomás Eleuterio de Estenaga, February 5, 1839, and Testimony of Hugo Reid, A. M. Zabaleta, and M. F. Uribe during 1839, all in Stearns Manuscripts, Huntington Library, San Marino, California; Bancroft, *History of California*, IV,

The earliest full description of California and its inhabitants by an Italian was written by Paolo Emilio Botta, son of historian Carlo Botta. The younger Botta was the ship's doctor aboard the *Héros*, a French vessel commanded by Auguste Duhaut-Cilly. His fresh and vivid account of the province was printed in French in the latter's *Nouvelles Annales de Voyages*. The Italian version was translated by Botta's father and entitled *Viaggio Intorno al Globo, principalmente alla California ed alle isole Sandwich* (1841). Young Botta was in California during 1827, very early in the history of the province. He described its sleepy, pastoral characteristics under Mexican rule with real fidelity. Concerned with its animal and aboriginal life, trade, society, and government, Botta's book is a generally overlooked source. He visited the coastal area from San Diego to the Russian establishment at Fort Ross, his account forming an important part of Duhaut-Cilly's narrative. Botta later became an archaeologist of note.[4]

Unlike Botta, most of the earliest Italians in California left no records, and their letters to relatives and friends back home have been lost. Were it not for the surviving paintings which an artist, Leonardo Barbieri, painted, it would not be known that this skillful craftsman came to California in 1847 and that he painted portraits of members of the state constitutional convention of 1849. His portraits of Prudenciana Vallejo, sister of General Mariano Guadalupe Vallejo and wife of Don José Amesti of Monterey, hang in the Monterey Customs House and show the man's unusual talent. At the Santa Barbara Historical Museum, Barbieri's portrait of José de la Guerra—head of a famous California colonial family—is especially fine. There must have been other artists like Barbieri, now unknown, who wandered about the West seeking to use their artistic talents.[5]

709; S. B. Dakin, *A Scotch Paisano* (Berkeley, 1939), 73, 75, 76; Dana's quotes are from *Two Years Before the West* (New York, 1959), 127-32.

[4] P. E. Botta, *Observations on the Inhabitants of California, 1827-1828*, is but a fragment of his work. See Appendix B.

[5] A reproduction of Barbieri's portrait of Prudenciana Vallejo appears in R. G. Cleland, "California: The Spanish Mexican Period," *Antiques Magazine*, Vol. LXIV, (November, 1953), 373. Later another Italian painter carried on the

Some Italian vessels arrived in California weighed down with huge blocks of Carrara marble which their captains sold to defray the expenses of their voyage.[6] Among the early ships to arrive were the *Flaminio Agazini* (1825), the *Rosa* (1834), the *City of Genoa* (1837), and *La Democrazia* (1850). So many Italians arrived that the prime minister of the Kingdom of Sardinia, Massimo d'Azeglio, ordered a consulate opened at San Francisco. In 1850, King Victor Emmanuel II appointed the already mentioned Leonetto Cipriani the first Sardinian consul there, ostensibly because of services as a Tuscan volunteer in the Italian liberation movement the year before. In addition to caring for the large numbers of his countrymen attracted by the Gold Rush, the unpaid Cipriani imported into San Francisco a house of some twelve hundred separate parts, assembled by seven hundred hooks and twenty-six thousand screws. Unfortunately for him, Cipriani was dissuaded by Italians already there from buying San Francisco land for twelve thousand dollars and sixteen thousand dollars which later sold for two hundred thousand dollars and three hundred thousand dollars, respectively. Some years before, if one can believe his writings, he had missed an opportunity to buy a dozen acres in the heart of New York City near Union Square for twenty thousand dollars because his banker had gone bankrupt.

After two years of service Cipriani found the position of consul so expensive and in such conflict with his financial operations that in 1853, he resigned. After he sold his San Francisco property, including his Italian-made house on Sutter Street, he returned east via Panama. While in the East he apparently organized his

---

Barbieri tradition. See Theodore W. Lilienthal, "A Note on Gottardo Piazzoni, 1872–1945," California Historical Society *Quarterly*, Vol. XXXVIII (March, 1959), 7–10.

[6] Bancroft, *History of California*, V, 687; Schiavo, *Four Centuries*, 172; T. O. Larkin to J. C. Calhoun, January 1, 1845, a.l.s., Larkin Papers, Bancroft Library, University of California, mentions a Genoese brig-of-war putting in at Monterey; William Heath Davis, *Sixty Years in California* (San Francisco, 1889), 626, states that the *City of Genoa* flew the Chilean flag; Camillo Branchi, "*Gli Italiani nella storia della California*," repr. from *L'Universo*, Vol. XXXV (May–June, 1956), 8.

already mentioned 1853 wagon-train expedition westward. On subsequent voyages to America (of which he made seven), Cipriani engaged in mining and stock raising, buying and selling several ranches. During the Civil War he is also supposed to have offered President Lincoln a plan to kidnap Confederate General Pierre Beauregard.

Cipriani's successor as consular secretary (but never consul) was Federico Biesta, a lawyer who in 1859 probably started *L'Eco della Patria*, the first Italian newspaper west of the Mississippi. The titular head of the consulate was Patrice Guillaume Dillon, San Francisco's French consul who, because he did not understand Italian, relied heavily upon Biesta. One of Biesta's consular dispatches, today in the state archives of Turin, Italy, is a substantial report on the Italians of California, which he estimated as 6,000 in number by the 1850's. Biesta's remarks about California's early Italians merit quotation:

> The Italian population is one of the best, most active and hardworking in California. Strong, industrious, and accustomed to suffering and toil, our nationals tend to their own affairs without taking part in those regrettable disorders that the heterogeneous people of the state give vent to from time to time. Generally, whether in San Francisco or in the interior, the Italians thrive and prosper in their businesses, and there is probably not a village in all California in which Italian business is not well represented, just as there is not a mining district where companies of Italian miners are not noted for their good conduct, their fraternal harmony, and for the energy which they bring to their work.[7]

One of the most successful of the Gold Rush arrivals was Domenico Ghirardelli. He became prosperous primarily because he did *not* seek the legendary gold of the Sierra. Instead, as a supplier of sweets, he traveled through the Mother Lode mining towns of Columbia, Clear Valley, and Hornitos selling chocolate and

[7] Schiavo, *Four Centuries*, cites Bulferetti, "*Leonetto Cipriano, Console Sardo in California*," *Archivio Storico di Corsica* (1939), 94–102. Ernest S. Falbo, "State of California in 1856," *California Historical Society Quarterly*, Vol. XLII (December, 1963), 311–33 is based upon consular dispatches, Archivio di Stato, Turin.

hard candies called *caramele*. Whenever business lagged, he left a town behind for more promising places. After the Gold Rush, he settled at San Francisco. In 1859, with Biesta, Cipriani, and Nicola Larco, he founded the Italian hospital association. A San Francisco factory, which he began in 1851, manufactured both liqueurs and chocolates. After his death in Rapallo, Italy, in 1894, his heirs long continued to operate the Ghirardelli Chocolate Company.[8]

The Gold Rush had acted as a lodestone, attracting immigrants of many nationalities to California. On April 26, 1851, *L'Eco d'Italia*, the New York Italian newspaper, stated that there were more than six hundred Italians in San Francisco alone. Several hundred of these were Ligurians who had arrived on ships carrying coal from England. Others were gold seekers from South American countries, to which they had earlier migrated. In California's "Mother Lode" country they named one river mining area "Italian Bar" just as the Mormons had called their particular haunt "Mormon Bar." Though their names were not to be associated with large gold strikes, a few Italians found instant wealth. Like Ghirardelli, others became food suppliers and merchants. Biesta speaks of one Italian who began a steam-powered imitation marble works at San Francisco and of another who founded a vermicelli and macaroni factory. A storekeeper, Mastro Gagliardo, did business at the rate of five thousand dollars per day at Mariposa. The ruins of stores and hotels run by Italians named Bruschi, Trabucco, Brunetti, Vignoli, Noce, Marre, and Ginocchio still dot the Mother Lode countryside. In 1858 some three hundred lonesome miners, loaded with gifts, walked nine miles to welcome the first Italian woman ever to travel into the California mines. We shall never know who the lady was or whose gifts she accepted. Those who resisted the lure of gold remained at San Francisco to earn more substantial if less spectacular wealth as gardeners or fishermen. Still others followed new pursuits. A

[8] Robert O'Brien, "The Story of Domenico Ghirardelli," San Francisco *Chronicle*, July 4, 1947, October 18, 1948; Ruth Teiser, *An Account of Domingo Ghirardelli and the Early Years of the Ghirardelli Company*; San Francisco *Call*, January 18, November 29, 1894.

man named Tresconi raised forty thousand cattle on a quarter million acres near Monterey.[9]

Near Los Angeles, farther to the south, Alessandro Repetto, a Genoese, purchased a five-thousand-acre rancho after the Civil War. It became the future site of the city of Montebello. He lived there with an Indian woman, raising sheep and cattle for almost twenty years. In 1885 he died, leaving the rancho to an heir, his brother Antonio, who lived in Liguria. Antonio, however, preferred to live in Italy. He came to California only long enough to collect his inheritance, sell the rancho for almost one hundred thousand dollars, and return home.

The predominant religion of Italians followed them wherever they went. Probably the first description of California and Oregon by an Italian was the missionary Louis Rossi's *Six ans en Amérique, Californie, et Oregon*, published in Paris in 1863. During 1851, Fathers John Nobili and Michael Accolti established Santa Clara College—later Santa Clara University—with only $150 in hand. Nobili had served a missionary apostolate in the Oregon country after 1844, having been recruited by Father De Smet, as recounted earlier. Accolti lived on until 1878.

Other Jesuits associated with De Smet in missionizing the Northwest ended their ministries in California. Among these were the already mentioned Anthony Ravalli, physician and missionary to the Flatheads and Kalispels; Joseph Caruana, who had lived among the Coeur d'Alenes; Camillus Imoda, Jerome d'Aste, Joseph Giorda—all founders of missions; Peter Rappagliosi, apostle to the Blackfeet; Joseph Cataldo (founder of Gonzaga University), who had celebrated his golden jubilee as a nonagenarian priest among the Indians; then Philip Canestrelli, Joseph Joset, and Lawrence Palladino, missionary and historian. In addition, there were Fathers Bertolio and Grassi. Mengarini, indefatigable apostle to the northwestern Indians, died in 1886, having spent most of his life since 1851 at Santa Clara College, where he became vice president and treasurer.

[9] *Eco d'Italia*, July 29, December 9, 1865, cited in Schiavo, *Four Centuries*, 174–75; Idwal Jones, *Vines in the Sun*, 113; Gardini, *Gli Stati Uniti*, *passim*.

To this hardy band must be added the name of Dominic Giacobbi, who worked with Fathers Michael Accolti and Aloysius Masnata in the California mission fields. After September, 1872, Giacobbi joined young Jesuits there at a time when enthusiasm characterized California's clerical scene, and new churches and colleges expanded their staffs. Giacobbi spent the rest of his life under the supervision of Fathers Aloysius Varsi and Nicholas Congiato, both presidents of Santa Clara College and St. Ignatius College in San Francisco, as well as at the Novitiate of the Sacred Heart in Los Gatos. He taught, ministered to the sick and lonely, trained young priests for the Jesuit order, and, with Father Congiato, a Sicilian, began growing vines at Los Gatos. This led to the production of some of the finest wines of California (still renowned is the Jesuits' Black Muscat). Into his eightieth year Father Giacobbi literally labored in the vineyard of the Lord.[10]

Others sent by the Jesuit Torinese Province included the Piedmontese Father Anthony Maraschi. After teaching at Holy Cross and Loyola colleges in Baltimore, in 1855 he founded St. Ignatius College, later the University of San Francisco. One of its earliest professors was Father Joseph M. Neri, a Jesuit priest-inventor who made some remarkable contributions to the advancement of research in electricity. In 1874 he devised a lighting system for exhibition and lecture purposes that utilized carbon electric lights. Neri's experiments occurred about ten years before Thomas Alva Edison's invention of the incandescent lamp. In 1874, Father Neri installed a searchlight in the tower of the college; its rays could be seen at a distance of two hundred miles. Neri employed large batteries, then magnetic machines, and finally dynamos. He utilized California's first Brush machine, first storage battery, and first magnetic electric machine. In 1876, Neri illuminated San Francisco's Market Street for the first time by using three arc lamps of his own invention. Many such versatile Italian Jesuits died in their adopted California; by 1879 only 113 of them were alive there.[11]

[10] Richard A. Gleeson, *Dominic Giacobbi, a Noble Corsican*, passim.
[11] *P.G. & E. Progress*, XXXII (September, 1955), 12; Branchi, "*Gli Italiani*

California's Italians experienced little discrimination. Indeed, some seemed to blend so well with the countryside that these came to look upon the state as their own Italy. They worked successfully with other nationalities and only rarely does one encounter mention of their own intolerance. Italian discrimination practiced against the Chinese is, however, evident from an account in the San Francisco *Chronicle* for February 22, 1880:

A "Swiss-Italian Anti-Chinese Company of Dragoons" has been formed, numbering forty members. E. Caspani has been chosen Captain, with P. Pozzi, First Lieutenant, and A. Varunia, Second Lieutenant. A resolution to notify the city authorities that the company is prepared to render them any assistance in removing the Chinese was adopted.

By thus attempting to keep in step with the mood of the day, California Italians cannot be said to have contributed to racial tolerance.

They, however, did make unusual contributions to music. As early as 1851 the Pellegrini Opera Company Troupe presented Bellini's *La Sonnambula* at San Francisco's Adelphi Theater. By 1854 that city, where about half of California's Italian population was to cluster, boasted several opera companies, which featured everything from *Fedora to Giosuè il Guardacoste,* staged by the Italian Opera Troupe, with Madam Clotilda Barili as its prima donna. In the 1850's, under the management of the renowned P.T. Barnum, Eliza Biscaccianti (known as "The American Thrush") was enthusiastically received at San Francisco. In 1854 alone eleven separate opera seasons were staged there. During California's early mining years a particular favorite was Gaetano Donizetti's *Daughter of the Regiment,* which received more per-

nella storia della California," repr. from *L'Universo,* Vol. XXXV (May–June, 1956), 10, 11n.; Schiavo, *Four Centuries,* 172–73, 249–50; John B. McGloin, *Eloquent Indian,* 19, 25–26, 114; *Notizie storiche e descrittive delle missioni della Provincia Torinese della Compagnia di Gesù nell'America del Nord,* 1–52: An Italian account of California's Franciscan missions is P. Ladislao Dragoni, *Il mio pellegrinaggio attraverso l'alta California Francescana.* In the same vein, see Lodovico Preta, *Storia delle missioni Francescane in California.*

formances than any other opera. In 1861, Madam Biscaccianti came back to the scene of her earlier triumphs and tried to establish a local opera company. When she met with scant success, she took to drink, and was reduced to singing, eventually, in the Bella Union Saloon, "where the customers did not mind if she leaned unsteadily against a wall or table." In the 1860's the Bianchi Opera Company presented the California premieres of Gounod's *Faust* and Verdi's *Un Ballo in Maschera.* Among the divas popular in those years were a Signora Brambilla and the soprano Euphrosyne Parepa-Rosa, imported by the impresario Thomas Maguire, known as "the Napoleon of the San Francisco Stage."[12] The Golden Gate also attracted the composer Pietro Mascagni, as well as the divas Luisa Tetrazzini and the already mentioned Adelina Patti.

Madam Patti touched off what came to be known as the "Patti Epidemic." Born in 1843, she was the daughter of Salvatore Patti, a Sicilian singer and impresario. Her mother was a Roman. Her first appearance at the Golden Gate in 1884 was preceded by an elaborate press build-up. Mobs followed her everywhere. When she sang a Bellini, Verdi, or Rossini opera, San Francisco "went mad over her, a happy insanity that sent crowds following her carriage—or besieging the stage door to cheer when she appeared." Photographs of her and of Madam Scalchi, a contralto, adorned shop-window displays of opera cloaks for the Patti season and Patti-style painted fans, lace handkerchiefs, pearl opera glasses, and opera bags.

The year before, in 1883, La Patti had received Brigham Young for lunch aboard her private railway car in Salt Lake City. He asked her to sing at the Mormon Tabernacle, a rare occurrence. "Still," writes her biographer, "nothing in the course of the whole tour could compare with the scenes enacted at San Francisco. There," he records, "the Adelina Patti epidemic . . . developed from a fever into a condition of delirium. . . . The crowds stood in line during the whole of the night, and many sold their places next morning at from ten to twenty dollars apiece. Speculators

[12] Davis, *History of Opera,* 86–88.

obtained fabulous prices for seats. Thousands of people were unable to gain admission at the opening performance." Because of the crowds and a line that extended for blocks outside the ticket office, Madam Patti's impresario was fined seventy-five dollars for violating a city ordinance that forbade obstruction of passageways in theaters. The judge in whose courtroom the impresario appeared offered, however, to take the fine out in opera tickets. These cost from seven dollars to thirty dollars each. The Sherman & Clay Music Company experienced three thousand dollars in damages as ticket seekers knocked out windows and even stood on the tops of new pianos with hobnailed boots, demanding the last unsold tickets. Every inch of standing room was bought. The rush to hear Patti was so great that her company was persuaded to stay on an extra week. She demanded what few other divas could—including an aggravating delay before the curtain went up, during which she meticulously counted her fee of five thousand dollars, paid in full preceding each performance. These ended with the traditional singing of "Home Sweet Home." Her "farewell tours" were repeated annually for years.[13]

Italians were avid theatergoers in pre–world War I San Francisco, as a stage-shifter at Maguire's Opera House recalled:

> Whenever we wanted singers for the chorus and hadn't time to train them, we used to go down to the wharf and get the Eyetalian fishermen. You'd find every one of 'em knowing their score and singing *Ernani* and *Traviata*. You could only use a limited number, but every evening they'd crowd in at the stage door. "I'm in the chorus! I'm in the chorus!" they'd say. We'd know they wasn't but we'd let them in when nobody was looking.[14]

Madam Patti's fame was followed by that of a young soprano who was also to captivate San Francisco. In 1905, two years after Mascagni conducted performances of his *Cavalleria Rusticana* and *Zanetto* there, Luisa Tetrazzini, fresh from being stranded in an opera troupe in Mexico, was discovered by the city aficiona-

---

[13] Hermann Klein, *The Reign of Patti*, 209; Davis, 88–89.

[14] San Francisco *Bulletin*, August 18, 1917.

dos. She made many appearances there after going on to sing at New York's Metropolitan Opera House and at Covent Garden in London. On Christmas Eve of 1909 she sang outdoors to a crowd of two hundred and fifty thousand at Lotta's Fountain without using a cicrophone. As the years passed Tetrazzini gained so much weight (presumably from eating the chicken dish named in her honor) that wags said it was hard to differentiate her from the bull whenever she sang Bizet's opera *Carmen*.

In those years the Metropolitan Opera began to travel to San Francisco. During one of the Met's tours, in 1906, the renowned Enrico Caruso participated uniquely in a great event of San Francisco's history. On the evening of April 17 the tenor performed the role of Don José in the opera *Carmen* at the city's Grand Opera House. While Caruso sang marvelously, his leading lady, Olive Fremstad, "seemed somewhat pale and restrained, singing only with considerable effort, and complaining of a strange premonition." It was the night of the unforgettable earthquake and fire. Only on that crucial evening was Caruso ever relegated insignificantly to the background. During the early morning hours of April 18 he was awakened by a loud crash in his suite at the Palace Hotel. The entire building trembled and shook as he ran downstairs to the lobby. There, in a state of terror and disarray, he excitedly embraced Alfred Hertz, conductor of the Metropolitan Opera. Caruso wore (among other things) a towel around his neck, and clutched a framed and inscribed portrait of Theodore Roosevelt. In the lobby Caruso also met the baritone Antonio Scotti, who was staying in the same hotel, and who had been awakened by a feeling of seasickness. The two Italians joined the throngs of people running toward Union Square in order to escape the danger of buildings collapsing on all sides along Market Street. Once the aftershocks of the quake ended, the confused musicians hired a wagon and driver for three hundred dollars, loaded their luggage aboard, and made their way to the country estate of Arthur Bachman. The still distrustful Caruso, however, spent the next night under a tree in Bachman's backyard. Then he took the train from Oakland eastward; when asked about his experiences at San Francisco, Caruso shouted: "Give me Vesuvius!"[15]

The long succession of Italian artists and composers that traveled to San Francisco did not end with Caruso. In 1913, Ruggiero Leoncavallo conducted various performances of his *Pagliacci* at the new Tivoli Theater. He was followed by the Chicago Opera, with Muratore, Ruffo, Muzio, and Schipa among its singers. In the 1920's the Scotti Opera Company kept the Italian operatic tradition alive. Finally, in 1921, Naples' San Carlo Opera Company arrived. One of its principal conductors was Gaetano Merola, an energetic young man who had first visited the city in 1906 as a pianist. In 1923, Merola organized the San Francisco Opera Association in the Italian Ballroom of the St. Francis Hotel. He obtained donations of fifty dollars each from twenty-seven hundred founding members. That year the new company's opening performance with the impresario's nephew, Armando Agnini, as stage director, took place on the night of September 23. Merola conducted Puccini's *La Bohème*, the tenor Giovanni Martinelli singing Rudolfo, and Queena Mario the role of Mimi. This performance launched the second-oldest continuous opera group in the nation. Merola was to be its director for some thirty years.[16]

Music was not the only art supported by California Italians. At San Francisco, after the turn of the century, "Salvini," an actor of many talents, was long the rage of its theater, although he played exclusively in the Italian language. Giuseppe (Papa) Coppa coaxed operatic and literary artists, among them Jack London, George Sterling, and Mary Austin, inside his Torinese restaurant, renowned for its murals, its thirty-five-cent meals, and its free Napa claret. In its interior, singers, artists, writers, and actors talked, made love, reminisced, and boasted. Gelett Burgess published a novel about Coppa's artistic coterie entitled *The Heart Line* (New York, 1907).[17]

[15] Oscar Lewis and Carroll D. Hall, *Bonanza Inn, America's First Luxury Hotel* (New York, 1939), 324–25, 332–35; Davis, *History of Opera*, 92–93.

[16] *Ibid.*, 92–97.

[17] A. R. Neville, *The Fantastic City* (Boston, 1932), 231–32; Franklin Walker, *Ambrose Bierce, the Wickedest Man in San Francisco* (San Francisco, 1941), 18;

Italian performers at the Bay City felt completely at home in its many cafes, which still serve *cappucinos* and *branda,* as they did in Caruso's day. A large enough Italian colony existed to support everything from daily opera to a daily Italian press. Newspapers at San Francisco were filled with advertisements of such representative businesses as a Hotel Verdi, a Piemonte Saloon, a Trentino Hotel, restaurants named Buon Gusto and Il Trovatore, and no less than three Hotel Romas.

San Francisco has boasted a succession of seventeen Italian newspapers. The first of these was *La Voce del Popolo,* established in 1859 as a daily, which became *L'Italia.* In 1966, after almost a century of publication, *L'Italia* ceased to be printed. Pierino Mari, publisher of a new journal, *L'Eco d'Italia,* succeeded to all its rights as well as to those of *La Voce del Popolo.* At times five Italian newspapers were published simultaneously in San Francisco. A startling amount of the news in these concerned Genoa, Turin, and other cities of northern Italy, as well as the Italian-speaking part of Switzerland. As late as 1931 there were also Italian newspapers at Dunsmuir, Martinez, Sacramento, Stockton, and Weed. Only at San Francisco and Los Angeles are Italian newspapers still published. As of 1968, *L'Italo-Americano,* at the latter city, had not missed publication of even one of its issues over a period of sixty years. Its owner, Cleto Baroni, then seventy-three years of age, had been its editor since World War I, the paper having been founded by his uncle. Both men had turned down numerous opportunities to sell out the paper as their readers were absorbed by the floodtide of English-language journalism. They never did so.[18]

Idwal Jones, "San Francisco," in *The Taming of the Frontier* (New York, 1925), 99–124; Warren Unna, *The Coppa Murals.*

[18] Aside from *La Voce del Popolo,* a few Italian newspapers published at San Francisco were *L'Indipendente, L'Unione, L'Unione Nazionale, Il Proletario, La Tribuna, Il Lavoratore Industriale, L'Eco della Patria, L'Elvezia, L'Eco della Razza Latina, La Colonia Svizzera, L'Imparziale, La Critica, Il Corriere del Popolo.* At Los Angeles *L'Eco della Colonia,* established in 1894, was supplanted in 1908 by *L'Italo-Americano.* In 1966, *L'Italo-Americano* was still being published by Cleto Baroni. See A. Frangini, *Italiani di San Francisco ed Oakland, California, Cenni biografici;* Ayer, *Directory,* 1236–38.

A hospital and several mutual benefit societies at San Francisco also date from an early period. In this environment no one needed to be lonesome for Italy. One could hear the Royal Italian Band at the Mechanic's Pavilion or *Tosca* at the Tivoli almost any Sunday afternoon. Italians there developed an active community life, even assembling a social register, or "Blue Book," called *Attività Italiane in California* (1902).

An annual Columbus Day pageant has been held in San Francisco for many years.[19] This pageant is staged in part by fishermen, among them the grandsons of Italians who established themselves on San Francisco Bay in the 1850's. The first of these fishermen were Genoese, many of whom later sold their gear to Sicilians. Generally uneducated, they had one great goal in life—to own their own boats. Because other Italians found it hard to understand the dialect of the Sicilians, they banded closely together, preserving old customs and folkways. Some older Sicilians still speak no English. Although a few northern Italians continue to fish for a living, most have gone into other trades.

California's Italian fishermen used a type of vessel known as a felucca, traditionally fishing the deep waters outside the Golden Gate. They also employed "San Francisco Bay Cats" as crab boats. While Sicilians haunted the sloughs at the confluence of the San Joaquin and Sacramento rivers, the Chinese for a time monopolized the shrimping trade. These Orientals, with their square-sailed junks, appeared on the scene about 1865. The Italians, with their colorful lateen-rigged feluccas, roamed farther afield, going out for two or three days at a time to crab and fish. Strong anti-Chinese sentiment cut down the number of Orientals allowed to fish in the bay, much to the advantage of the Italians. In the late nineteenth century dozens of feluccas could be seen moored at their favorite haunt on both sides of the slip along the foot of Union Street. By 1910, San Francisco's Fisherman's Wharf had a fleet of seven hundred fishing vessels manned by twenty-five hun-

[19] Charles Speroni, "The Development of the Columbus Day Pageant of San Francisco," *Western Folklore*, Vol. VII (October, 1948), 325–35; Paul Radin, *The Italians of San Francisco*, 38.

dred fishermen. Resting there from wearying hours at sea, the Italians mended their nets, sang, and told each other stories about the home country.[20]

The Genoese and other North Italians who eventually surrendered their fishing rigs to the Sicilians demonstrated occupational flexibility. A large number went into the refuse and scavenger business. Today one of San Francisco's strongest, and oldest, unions is its Scavenger's Protective Association. It is dominated by Italians, who collect a large part of the city's garbage.

It was in agriculture, however, that the talents of California's Italians flowered. In viniculture and viticulture especially they applied Old World care and New World methods. From the 1880's onward, North Italians from Genoa, Turin, and the Lombard vineyard towns began to appear in the California vineyards in sizable numbers. These tall, fair-haired people were not so often the *pescivendoli* or *lustrascarpe* associated with the eastern cities of America. They were pastoral, farming folk who neither sold fish nor shined shoes. Theirs was a passion for the culture of the grape.

In 1881, Andrea Sbarboro, a Genoese banker born in Acero, interested some of these still rootless *contadini* in settling co-operatively on fifteen hundred acres of land at Asti, near Cloverdale. Sbarboro had been in California since 1852 and had opened an Italo-American night school, writing his own textbook for the courses he offered. He had also organized the California Promotion Board. As founder of six of the earliest building and loan associations in the state, he became a lender of money to small home builders in San Francisco. Later, in 1899, he started the Italian-American Bank. Sbarboro envisioned a semi-Utopian colony of about a thousand persons. A student of the writings of John Ruskin and Robert Owen, and of the co-operative theories of the Rochdale weavers, he hoped to settle unemployed farmer-immigrants on fertile land. A secondary interest of his was the produc-

---

[20] See the excellent photographs in John H. Kemble, *San Francisco Bay, a Pictorial Maritime History* (Cambridge, Maryland, 1957), 100–102. Cf. Raymond F. Dondero, "The Italian Settlement of San Francisco," M.A. thesis in Geography, iii.

tion of fine wines ("not to be excelled") in an ideal climate. In company with chemist Pietro C. Rossi, who became his head winemaker, Sbarboro founded the Italian-Swiss Agricultural Colony in the Sonoma Valley. Fighting first that dreaded enemy of the vine, phylloxera, and then the usual succession of flood years near the Russian River, Sbarboro's Italian workers were magnificent. He gave them all the wine they could drink in addition to good wages (which they preferred to stock in the colony). Unfortunately, these laborers refused to buy a single share of the company's 2,250 shares of stock. Originally worth only $135,000, this stock soared to $3,000,000 in value by 1910. In later years it was to be worth many more times that price.

After a few lean years, the new Italian Colony, located on five thousand acres of land, prospered. Its 1897 vintage was so large that there was not enough barrel cooperage in all California to hold it. Sbarboro, therefore, ordered a reservoir built in solid rock which became the largest wine tank in the world. It was eighty-four feet long, thirty-four feet wide, and twenty-five feet high; its highly glazed surfaces held five hundred thousand gallons of wine. In May, 1898, when the tank was first emptied, a dance was held inside it for two hundred persons. There was no crowding, though an orchestra occupied the center of the novel ballroom. The colony also had its own general store, schoolhouse, bakery, smithy, cooperage shop, post office, telephone and telegraph outlet, and railroad depot.

By 1911 the Italian-Swiss Colony won the highest award ever given American champagne—the Grand Prix of the Turin International Exposition for its "Golden State Extra Dry." By shipping railroad tank cars full of wine eastward, the colony came to control much of the United States wine market. In 1942 eastern distillers purchased "The Colony" as a hedge against wartime whisky-making restrictions. In 1953 the Angelo Petri family, who also owned a Tennessee cigar factory, in addition to the Petri Wine Company, bought the company from the National Distillers Product Corporation, for a reported sixteen million dollars. This purchase included branch wineries at Lodi, Asti, and Clovis,

California, and bottling plants in Chicago and Fairview, New Jersey, as well as the New York distributing organization of Gambarelli and Davito. The purchase increased Petri's production to forty-six million gallons per year, the largest wine-producing capacity in the United States. The Italian-Swiss Colony still transports wine eastward, now by ships equipped with stainless steel tanks rather than in the traditional wicker-raffia Tipo Chianti flasks of its founders. Only a few of the founders' sons still work the rich soil of Asti.[21]

The president of "The Colony," Louis Petri, is the grandson of Raffaello Petri, who began a small San Joaquin Valley winery in 1886; it grew to manufacture a locally popular brand of wine. In 1949 the Petri interests bought the Mission Bell Winery in the San Joaquin Valley for $3,250,000, thereby doubling total capacity to twenty million gallons. In 1951 the Petris organized three hundred small and medium-sized growers into the Allied Grape Growers Inc., a co-operative to which the Petri interests sold all their various wineries in the central valley of California. In return, Petri assumed sales rights to the Allied Grape Growers's total output. Still later the Petri interests bought the Inglenook winery at Rutherford, the possessors of one of California's finest prestige labels.[22]

In a smaller way, but producing wines of higher quality, other Italians also prospered as vintners. The Mondavi family achieved unusual success in the Napa Valley, where they operated the former winery of Charles Krug and Company. The Mondavis, by the mid-1940's, were producing some of the best white wines in California, while another vintner, Louis M. Martini at St. Helena,

[21] Andrea Sbarbaro, "Wines and Vineyards of California," *Overland Monthly*, Vol. XXV (January, 1900), 65–76; 95–96; Jones, *Vines*, 110–16; Lord, *Italian in America*, 134–44; *Sixth Annual Report. The Italian-Swiss Agricultural Colony* (San Francisco, 1887); M. B. Levick, "A Man With Three Thousand Monuments," *Sunset*, Vol. XXX (January, 1913), 93–94; C. Dondero, "Asti, Sonoma County, an Italian-Swiss Agricultural Colony," *Out West*, Vol. XVII (July–December, 1902), 253–66.

[22] *Time*, LXI (April 27, 1953), 102, 104; Philip Ferry, "California Wine Goes to Sea," *Westways*, Vol. L (March, 1958), 32–33.

distinguished himself because of his meticulousness in producing Cabernet Sauvignon and Pinot Noir red wines. Angelo Pellegrini has pointed out that Martini's career demonstrates elements of quiet greatness: "I sought him out because I had reason to believe he had brought some of the more admirable qualities of his people to the American community." Pellegrini saw individuals like Martini as unique: "In truck gardening, in the construction trades, on the railroad, where men worked with pick and shovel, I had seen the gradual disappearance of the peasant immigrants of Martini's generation; men who were unafraid to work, who gloried in it, and who had made an art of manual labor. . . . Every employer of such men despaired of replacing them as one by one they put away their tools." Men like Martini had never needed protection, but others did. As early as 1913, when concern for the working man rightfully came to feature protection of former *braccianti*, public attention came to be focused upon their welfare. That year California's legislature established a Commission of Immigration and Housing to protect the large numbers of Mexicans, Portuguese, and Italians in the state's labor camps and lodging houses. California's agricultural pattern, therefore, slowly changed from the applauding of primitive entrepreneurship to reform of working conditions.[23]

Such concern for laborers in the fields was slow to develop. Southern California, in particular, was to lag behind the northern part of the state for decades. Dozens of small wineries, even smaller than Martini's, employed Italians; the history of these enterprises will never be written. They have simply dropped out of sight. Some were near failures. Others flourished for a time, then disappeared. In 1869, Justinian Caire tried to establish a "wine-community" of forty-five Italian-French vintners on Santa Cruz Island. Isolated from the mainland by the Santa Barbara Channel, the island is twenty-five miles long and three to nine miles wide. Caire, a San Francisco silver and gold broker, wanted to build an

[23] Pelligrini, *Americans by Choice*, 48, 54; Spencer C. Olin, Jr., "European Immigrant and Oriental Alien . . . ," *Pacific Historical Review*, Vol. XXXV (August, 1966), 303–15.

Old World colony in its central valley. Like such other Utopian-inspired projects as the German Agricultural Colony established at Anaheim eight years before, Caire's dream withered on the vine. We know too little of its story today.

Near Los Angeles in the 1880's the peasant tenacity of a hardy Piedmontese, Secondo Guasti, led him to establish what came to be called "the globe's largest vineyard," the Italian Vineyard Company. Guasti had arrived in the United States during 1881 at the age of twenty-two. In the sands of Cucamonga, where other vintners refused to invest capital, Guasti planted to grape thousands of acres of semi-arid land. From these he produced millions of gallons of dessert wine—sun-drenched and high in sugar as well as in alcoholic content. Guasti's favorite was a little-known reddish Grignolino. His successors remain among the largest producers in the United States of such fortified wines as sherry, port, and angelica. Guasti's pioneer work at Cucamonga was followed by the founding of half a dozen wineries or more, which took over the vines which he had planted.[24]

California's tradition for both production and high quality stems from the founders of its wine industry. In 1886 its leaders called in Guido Rossati, of the Italian Ministry of Agriculture, who advised them to highlight skill over quantity. This the vintners of California have never forgotten. Indeed, Italy's patient techniques of wine making have generally become California's.[25]

The major crisis faced by the California wine industry was Prohibition. As early as 1908 old timers like Sbarboro, who had become president of California's Manufacturers and Producers Association, had seen it coming. That year he published, under the title *Temperance Versus Prohibition* (San Francisco, 1908), a series of letters from United States consuls in wine-drinking countries stating that alcoholism was practically unknown abroad. Sbarboro became California's foremost advocate of the use of wine

[24] Jones, *Vines*, 217–19.

[25] G. Rossati, *Relazione di un viaggio di istruzione negli Stati Uniti d'America*; Edmondo Mayor des Planches, *Gli Italiani in California*, 18–19; V. P. Carosso, *The California Wine Industry*, 134; Arthur Inkersley, "The Vintage in California and Italy," *Overland Monthly*, Vol. LIV (October, 1909), 406–11.

as both an art and a temperance measure. In 1908 also he founded the California Grape Protective Association to foster these views. But the Anti-Saloon League stepped up its effective prohibition campaign. Although the wine industry defeated various state prohibition proposals from 1914 onward, the wartime hysteria on behalf of temperance made federal enforcement of prohibition a seeming inevitability. In 1919 the United States Congress passed the Eighteenth Amendment, enforced by the Volstead Act. Non-Italian vintners, like California's Wente brothers, were, of course, equally affected by this disastrous legislation, and they fought vigorously against it, alongside the Sbarboros.

During the confining 1920's, Italians were restricted to the vinting of sacramental wine, the growing of table grapes, and the marketing of various substitute products, from grape bricks to grape-flavored sherbet. During the Prohibition era the Vai brothers, southern California competitors of Guasti, marketed a "California Padre Wine Elixir," advertised as a "system builder," or tonic. Established wineries could not afford to jeopardize their legal standing, and therefore produced such by-products. Many immigrants, however, produced wine at home. Bootlegging too was rampant. No one will ever know how many persons were enriched by a law which was impossible to enforce. In northern California one observer reported: "Every family sells wine and every cabin has its vat. The result is that an American laborer is always without money, and the Italian is always increasing his savings account."[26]

When the Prohibition period came to an end, professional vintners returned to the making of fine wines. California Italians ultimately helped to produce approximately 90 per cent of the nation's wine requirements. Out of the valleys of California each fall they also shipped thousands of boxes of grapes to all parts of

[26] Regarding Prohibition in California, see Horatio F. Stoll, "The Founding of the Grape Protective Association," *California Grape Grower*, Vol. I (December, 1919), 2; Marquis and Bessie R. James, *Biography of a Bank, the Story of Bank of America*, 213; Cleto Baroni (ed.), *Gente Italiana di California*, 49–52; John R. Meers, "The California Wine and Grape Industry and Prohibition," California Historical Society *Quarterly*, Vol. XLVI (March, 1967), 19–32.

the United States—not only for eating but for wine making by Italians in their basements.

Not all of California's Italian agriculturists have been wine makers. Large numbers of Swiss-Italians from Switzerland's Canton Ticino have gone into dairying. These people, who came from the Italian-speaking area of Switzerland, resembled the North Italian Piedmontese and Lombards, both in appearance and outlook. They brought to America virtually none of the folkways of less literate South Italians. From 1870 onward hundreds of them began to buy rich meadowlands from Santa Barbara northward, especially along California's coastline. They built a network of farm roads from their barns to coastal wharves at San Simeon, Cambria, Cayucos, and Morro Bay, from which they supplied northern and southern California. These butter and cheese makers settled throughout the Coast Ranges, the largest number clustered around San Luis Obispo.[27]

As early as 1866, Italian-Swiss came to work at El Rancho Corral de Piedra, the Marin County dairy ranch of George and E. W. Steele. With a herd of fourteen hundred cows, this dairy was the second largest in the state. The Steeles employed milkers from the Val Maggia, an Italian district of Switzerland which ultimately lost 40 per cent of its population from 1850 to 1930. The Swiss-Italians also settled at dairies in San Luis Obispo, Marin, and Sonoma counties. All-year grazing and a mild climate made dairying so profitable that these newcomers were encouraged to import wives from Switzerland's Italian-speaking Canton Ticino District. Some immigrants returned briefly to Europe in order to marry. The Italian-Swiss not only went into dairying; they also became chicken growers at places like Petaluma, the egg capital of California.[28]

By 1911, California's Italians annually put on the market thirty-five million pounds of fish. They produced that year nearly nine

[27] E. Hore Patrizi, "The Italians in California," San Francisco *Star*, June 14, 1913.

[28] Claghorn, "Agricultural Distribution," in Industrial Commission, *Reports*, XV, 503.

From *Out West* (1902)

Founders and builders of the Italian-Swiss Colony.

From *Out West* (1902)

Italian-Swiss Colony workmen in their dining room about the turn of the
century. Note the cook at the end of the table, with apron tied around
his middle. One man reads a newspaper. Others appear to be drinking
coffee, rather than wine. This must have been the midday meal on a
working day.

From *World's Work* (September, 1904)

Picking grapes after 1900 in a vineyard of the Italian-Swiss
Colony, Asti, Sonoma County, California.

Louis M. Martini Winery

Stone-aging cellar for sherry located in the Villa del Rey vineyard, St. Helena, Napa County, California, 1960.

From *World's Work* (September, 1904)

Making hay in California. The immigrants and their wine were inseparable, but intoxication was very rare.

From *World's Work* (September, 1904)

An Italian vegetable gardener's Sunday amusements with his family—Italian-Swiss Colony, California, after 1900.

From *World's Work* (September, 1904)

The home of an immigrant family at Landis, New Jersey,
after the turn of the century.

 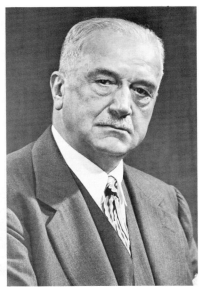

Louis M. Martini, founder of the Martini Winery, St. Helena, Napa County, California, one of the great producers of Cabernet Sauvignon, Pinot Noir, and other red table wines.

A. P. Giannini, founder of the Bank of America.

million dollars worth of fresh and dried fruit, three million dollars in cereals, seven million dollars in potatoes and beans, and over five million dollars in other foodstuffs. In 1911 their total agricultural production exceeded sixty-five million dollars, and they owned two hundred million dollars in real estate, ten million dollars in stocks and bonds, and thirty million dollars in bank deposits. Their affluence attracted special commendation from President William Howard Taft.[29]

In contrast to California's Orientals and Mexicans, her Italians, like her French and German population, did not remain migrant workers. They moved into outlying ranches and farms vacated by earlier occupants and there they stayed, determined to operate their own properties.

The story of the Italian-Swiss Colony and of the Petri fortunes was matched by the Gallo and Di Giorgio families. Born in Italy in 1874, Joseph Di Giorgio, as early as 1893, became an importer and then a grower in the southern San Joaquin Valley. He was also president of the Atlantic Fruit Company and with his brother, Rosario, founded the Di Giorgio Fruit Corporation. In 1910 the Di Giorgios bought the marketing and shipping interests of the Earl Fruit Company. They developed agricultural holdings throughout Kern, Fresno, and San Diego counties as well as in other states and countries. The canned goods produced by the Di Giorgios were packed under the S & W label. Joseph died in 1951 and Rosario in 1955.

The Di Giorgios became the largest shippers of fresh fruit in the world. The corporation they founded came to control more than forty thousand acres of land—principally in California, but with some acreage in South America, Central America, and Mexico. By 1944 the estimated net worth of the corporation reached thirty million dollars, and its common stock was listed daily on an

[29] H. F. Raup, "The Italian-Swiss Dairymen of San Luis Obispo County," *Yearbook*, Assoc. of Pacific Coast Geographers, Vol. I (1935), 3–8; H. F. Raup, "The Italian-Swiss in California," California Historical Society *Quarterly*, Vol. XXX (December, 1951), 305–14; M. E. Perrett, *Les Colonies Tessinoises en California*; Clay Pedrazzini, "The Italian-Swiss of California," in *The Swiss in the United States*, 93–101.

open securities exchange. Following well-established Italian agricultural tradition, several thousand of the company's employees lived in a company-town environment on its various ranch sites. In the early 1960's, when labor-management disputes broke out with the Di Giorgio Corporation, critics paid too little attention to this limiting factor in the company's background.

In addition to agriculture, Italians like the Di Giorgios were involved in food preservation. The name of Marco J. Fontana is also well known in that field. Indeed, the Fontana and Di Giorgio families co-operated closely. But Fontana arrived in the United States much earlier, in 1859. By 1889 he founded the California Fruit Packing Corporation. Calpac, as it is known, became the largest fruit and vegetable canning organization in the world. In the early days of the Italian-Swiss Colony, Fontana had worked at Asti for a fellow Ligurian, the banker Andrea Sbarboro. With another Ligurian, Antonio Cerruti, Fontana originated the brand name Marca del Monte, later shortened to the well-known Del Monte label. His son, Mark Edmund, came to operate packing plants and farms in Oregon, Washington, Utah, Idaho, Illinois, Alaska, and Hawaii. By 1965, long after Fontana's death, Calpac owned twenty-four thousand acres of cultivated land and leased another seventy-four thousand. It also contracted annually for the crops of hundreds of farms and owned forty-four canneries and fifty warehouses throughout the United States. Calpac's annual sales that year were almost four hundred million dollars.[30]

Italians entered a variety of agricultural enterprises. From an early date California's artichoke crop, centered in Castroville, was largely controlled by Italian truck farmers. Meanwhile, Cristoforo Colombo Brevidero founded the southern California lilac industry. Another Italian, John Lagomarsino of Ventura, became president of the state association of lima bean growers. Italians were among the first to experiment in raising silkworms in the West. The introduction of bell peppers, artichokes, eggplants and broccoli to California is also traceable to Italians. The western tomato

[30] Sketches of both Fontana and Sbarboro are in Cassignoli and Chiariglione, *Libro d'Oro,* 23–30.

industry began with Camillo Pregno, who, in 1900, taught Merced farmers how to grow tomato vines on stakes, as was the custom in his native country. He and other Italians became tomato puree packers, their product being in demand for pasta sauces.[31]

During 1940, Joseph Maggio, "Carrot King" of California, started marketing that vegetable in the Imperial Valley and built a "million dollar operation" there, near Holtville. At harvest time Maggio employed as many as two thousand employees in one field. He eventually ran an "assembly-line organization" that dug, selected, tied, washed, iced, crated, and loaded up to forty-two railroad carloads of carrots per day.[32]

The story of the California Italians should not be separated from the state's total population pattern. In 1860, 38.6 per cent of California's population was foreign, a large influx having occurred in the preceding decade. During the 1870's nearly two-thirds of the migrants to California were foreigners. In the 1880's the foreign-born still represented nearly half of the state's net annual migration. From 1860 to 1870 close to 40 per cent of California's population was foreign-born. About 55 per cent of such persons came from western Europe. After 1900 the foreign-born population of California, previously composed mostly of northwest Europeans and Asiatics, changed its character. A heavy immigration from eastern and southern Europe developed, and an inflow of agricultural laborers from Mexico also increased.

At San Francisco 68 per cent of its 1910 population was made up of the foreign-born or of children of the foreign-born. Los Angeles County, however, listed only 35 per cent of its population that year as of foreign background. A separate, Protestant, rural

[31] Carey McWilliams, *California: The Great Exception* (New York, 1949), 115, and his *Factories in the Field* (Boston, 1944), 122–24; Winfield Scott, "Old Wine in New Bottles: When Italy Comes to California Through the Panama Canal," *Sunset*, Vol. XXX (May, 1913), 519–26; Claghorn, "Agricultural Distribution," in Industrial Commission, *Reports*, XV, (1901), 495–507; "Marco J. Fontana," *La Capitale* (Sacramento, 1922), 33; "Italians in California," *California Mail Bag* (August, 1871), xxii–xxv; Dondero, Raymond F. "The Italian Settlement of San Francisco," 67.

[32] Mason Sutherland, "Californians Escape to the Desert," *National Geographic Magazine*, Vol. CXII (November, 1957), 706–707.

culture existed in the southern part of the state, largely created after its land boom of 1887, abetted by cheap transcontinental passenger rates. The religious difference between northern and southern California was real. In 1906 the population of Los Angeles was 56 per cent Protestant; that of San Francisco was less than 15 per cent Protestant. Mexicans made up a large portion of southern California's Catholicism. Into its American era California remained Catholic at least for a time. Throughout the state the 1906 Catholic population (of those reporting church membership) was 58 per cent. Cosmopolitan San Francisco, especially its Italian and Irish residents, helped to swell this percentage.[33]

It was inevitable that California would attract such a babel of foreign tongues. Its vivid contrasts in climate and topography as well as in flora and fauna all contributed to the state's magnetic appeal. Because it offered much wider opportunities than almost any other place, there came to California hundreds of times as many persons of whom we have no knowledge than those who left behind a record. They were of every nationality. From 1860 to 1890 the Irish had competed with the Chinese for numerical supremacy. After the turn of the century the Italians outnumbered both these nationalities, exceeded only by the Mexicans. Whereas there had been fewer than three thousand Italians in California in 1860, and no more than five thousand in 1870, by 1905 there were some sixty thousand, half of them engaged in agriculture—contrary to a national tendency of Italians to forsake agriculture for industry. The largest influx had occurred in the 1880's, when steerage accommodations from Italy to New York dropped to only forty dollars. By the 1920's, Italians comprised 11.7 per cent of the foreign population, the largest foreign stock in the state. During the "new immigration" period when they had arrived, 90 per cent of the Italian-Swiss in the United States went to California. From the 1930's to the 1950's, California had somewhere between one hundred thousand and one hundred and fifty thousand Italian-born residents, the largest for-

[33] Bureau of the Census, *Special Reports of Religious Bodies: 1906*, I, 33; Carey McWilliams, *Southern California Country* (New York, 1946), 159.

276

eign element except for Mexicans. Of these, the biggest settlement of Italians, some twenty-seven thousand at its peak in 1935, clustered about San Francisco.[34]

The prestige of Italians increased as they made their mark professionally and in California's public life. The name of Angelo Rossi, mayor of San Francisco from 1931 to 1944, made them proud that two Italians presided over America's eastern and western portals—Rossi at the Golden Gate and Fiorello La Guardia at the Statue of Liberty. (In New York, Mayor Vincent Impellitieri later continued what for a time seemed almost a tradition.) Rossi (1878–1948), born at Volcano in Amador County, was, like La Guardia, the son of immigrant parents. A product of grammar and night schools, he traveled the road from errand boy to florist. As a supervisor of the city and county of San Francisco, he ultimately emerged as a forceful Republican mayor.

In 1967, San Francisco was to have yet another mayor of Italian descent. This was Joseph L. Alioto, son of an immigrant Italian fisherman who had founded a restaurant on Fisherman's Wharf. Alioto, an attorney, entered the mayor's office after giving up the presidency of the California Rice Growers Association, at a salary of one hundred thousand dollars per year. By that time Alioto's Restaurant, like Di Maggio's and other prominent Italian waterfront restaurants, had passed into the hands of second-generation persons, including San Francisco's new mayor. By then most of

[34] Since 1930 the Mexicans have had the largest foreign population in California. See Warren S. Thompson, *Growth and Changes in California's Population*, 69, 72; M. J. Spinello, "Italians of California," *Sunset*, Vol. XIV (1904–1905), 256; Doris M. Wright, "The Making of Cosmopolitan California," California Historical Society *Quarterly*, Vol. XIX (December, 1940), 340, and Vol. XX (March, 1941), 65–79; Davis McEntire, *The Population of California* (San Francisco, 1946), 67–72, 76, 80; Pecorini, "The Italian as an Agricultural Laborer," *Annals*, American Academy of Political and Social Science, Vol. XXXIII (January–June, 1909), 380–90; G. V. Panattoni, *Professionisti Italiani e funzionari pubblici Italo-Americani in California*, 1, gives various estimates of California's Italian population, native-born and derivative, running from 167,760 to 236,622, in 1930. See also Dondero, "The Italian Settlement of San Francisco," iii; Bureau of the Census, *Sixteenth Census: Characteristics of the Population*, Vol. II, Part I (Washington, 1943), 564, estimates California's Italian-born population in 1940 as 100,911.

the first generation lay in the Italian cemetery in near-by Colma.

An indefinable strength of manner and purpose characterized the second-generation immigrant. One sees this immediately in an Angelo Rossi as well as in an Amadeo Pietro Giannini. Both were born on American soil but under economic and social conditions far different from those of, say, Joseph Alioto or Edmund Fontana—whose parents had assured their families financial success. Rossi and Giannini were chronologically much closer to the immigrant experience.

In the financial history of the American West no name is writ larger than Giannini's. He was not, however, the first Italian banker in California. Giannini was preceded by Felix Argenti, a San Francisco banker of the 1850's, whose prominence antedated even Sbarboro's. But Giannini's record was to overshadow that of all other western bankers, immigrant and non-immigrant. And it was closely entwined with the story of his fellow Italians. By 1902, San Francisco Italians were served by two of their own financial institutions, the Colombo and the Italian-American Bank. These two banks had a subscribed capital of three hundred thousand dollars and seven hundred and fifty thousand dollars, respectively.[35] They were primarily city-centered, with limited lending resources. The bank that Giannini was to found would be linked not only with the history of immigrants in San Francisco but also with that of an expanding rural California.

In fact, Giannini's great initial success was directly linked to the role of the immigrant on the land. Before World War I, California was primarily an agricultural state. Italian farmers who had settled along the slopes of the coast ranges frequently sought to buy the land on which they cultivated vines, peas, beans, and other crops, but they ran into trouble. The price of land at the turn of the century was exorbitant. In addition to land prices as high as five hundred dollars per acre a small ranch that cost five or ten thousand dollars required half again that much money for equipment with which to develop the soil. Irrigation and earth-filling operations cost farmers as much as twenty thousand dollars before they

[35] Des Planches, *California,* 73.

278

could actually begin farming. The operating of orchards and vine-yards, harvesting of field crops, and raising of poultry and live-stock were beyond the means even of many native farmers. Refused loans by large banks because they had little collateral, farmers looked to local merchants. Out of this circumstance, these merchants evolved into bankers. If a storekeeper owned an iron safe, he was one step away from becoming a merchant-banker, who not only provided customers with a secure place to keep money, but frequently acted as real estate broker, business adviser, travel agent, and tax consultant. Giannini became such a merchant. Popular, and trusted by his clients, he was to found the largest bank in the world. This son of Luigi Giannini, who had emigrated from Genoa to San Jose to become a hotelkeeper, started as a push cart peddler, but was eventually to be called "Giant of the West," by his biographer, and "Big Bull of the West," by the *Saturday Evening Post*.

"A.P." Giannini has been referred to as the greatest banking innovator of modern times. Just as J. P. Morgan was the banker for men of great wealth, Giannini became the banker to a genera-tion of immigrant fishermen, fruit peddlers, small ranchers, and workmen. He first organized the Bank of Italy to aid fellow Ital-ians at North Beach, San Francisco's Italian colony. To keep them from going to loan sharks for money at ferocious rates of interest, Giannini preached the advantages of interest-bearing sav-ings accounts. He proudly announced that he would loan a worker as much as twenty-five dollars "with no better security than the callouses on the borrower's hands."

San Francisco's earthquake and fire of 1906 gave Giannini an unusual opportunity. In later years it was laughingly said that Italians had fanned out the fire with wine-soaked blankets, this because of low water pressure. Actually an atmosphere of panic had prevailed. With all other banks closed, and while the ashes of the fire still swirled about his feet, Giannini transacted business on Washington Street Wharf. His counter consisted of a plank supported by two barrels. During the fire Giannini had safeguarded his bank's assets by secreting cash, gold, and bank records under a load of oranges aboard two wagons. These he pulled to the water front with teams of horses borrowed from his stepfather, Lorenzo Scatena. Whereas the great San Francisco banks, their vaults gutted by fire, were unable quickly to reopen due to the demands of depositors for ready cash, Giannini began to dole out loans and advances to distressed clients, each of whom he knew personally.

Giannini's conduct during the earthquake and fire determined his whole future. His example gave heart to discouraged immigrants, impressed by the enthusiasm and roaring voice of this tall, confident man. Italians who had never before trusted bankers brought him gold hoarded in stockings, tin boxes, and mattresses, gold which helped rebuild San Francisco. Giannini also garnered new accounts for his bank, accounts containing the savings of bakers, cooks, marble-cutters, and fishermen. As Giannini's reputation for honesty spread, the Bank of Italy doubled its business volume within one year after the fire. It extended its operations beyond North Beach to San Francisco's Mission District and then successively became the largest bank in the state, then the largest in the nation, and finally the largest bank in the world—under a new name, the Bank of America. This was done despite fierce competition from other banks.

Until his death in 1949, Giannini kept an iron grip on his bank's operations. He saw to it that immigrant families had a voice in the management of the bank. Local branch managers, cashiers, lesser as well as major personnel, were Italians. Giannini disregarded obsolete but conventional banking practices as he established a system of branch banks throughout the West and virtually revolutionized American banking practice in favor of the small depositor—the "little fellow" at North Beach whom he had started out to benefit. Such was his stamina and personal interest in people that he saw as many as fifty persons per day throughout much of his life.

Giannini did not expect visitors to discuss money matters exclusively, or even mainly. He listened just as attentively to domestic news: of sickness or death; of an engagement, a wedding, a confirmation, a new baby. As Giannini looked at it, almost anything that concerned people also concerned the bank. If the father of a new baby was a poor man, Giannini might fish a five-dollar gold piece from his pocket. For the little fellow; and remember that a savings account in his name can be started for a dollar. In ninety-nine cases out of a hundred the parent would cross the marble floor to a savings window.[36]

Of such "tender shrewdness" was the Bank of America built by the son of an immigrant. By 1930, Giannini controlled 35 per cent of the banks in California.

Giannini's wide success helped the status of his countrymen. During World War II, when the governor of California proposed that all unnaturalized aliens, including Italians, forfeit their businesses and professional licenses, the state attorney general, Earl Warren (later Chief Justice of the United States) ruled that they should not be deprived of their status. This decision, behind which lay the prestige of Giannini, contributed greatly to the loyalty which these persons demonstrated toward California and the nation.[37]

The versatile Giannini was a kind of Renaissance man who filled a vacuum in the lives of the Italians out west. He was not only versatile but he was a man big enough for the bigness of the West. For the Italians his symbol was almost spectacular, for he had placed himself at the center of the most respectable of all businesses—banking. That an Italian, rather than a Yankee type, or a German, or a Jew, should have achieved this seems remarkable; but Giannini's achievement was unusual only in the American environment where the immigrant needed special insight and imagination. Giannini's scale of vision and sense of bigness was unique. One Giannini took the place of countless immigrant politicians, so sorely lacking on the West Coast.

[36] James, *Biography*, 45.

[37] In at least two instances, the elections of 1926 and 1934, Giannini's power was felt politically in California. See Russell M. Posner, "The Bank of Italy and the 1926 Campaign in California," California Historical Society *Quarterly*, Vol. XXXVII (September, 1958), 267–75; (December, 1958), 347–58; also Posner's "A. P. Giannini and the 1934 Campaign in California," Historical Society of Southern California *Quarterly*, Vol. XXXIX (June, 1957), 190–201.

One California Italian politician did for a time become almost as prominent as Giannini. This was Anthony Caminetti. All but forgotten today, he rose quickly on the political scene and was appointed commissioner of immigration by President Wilson. Caminetti was born at Jackson Gate in Amador County on July 30, 1854. His father had arrived in Boston in 1839, joining a band of Argonauts who sailed around the Horn during the California Gold Rush. The senior Caminetti found a rich placer claim and later took up farming successfully. Anthony worked his way through the state university and was admitted to the bar in 1877. He was district attorney of Jackson County for several years before becoming a member of the state legislature and senate. He served in these two bodies for eight years after 1882. From 1890 to 1895 he was the first native-born Californian elected to the United States House of Representatives, and probably the first Italian-American so elected. As a Protestant his acceptability in political circles was enhanced. Caminetti ran for state senator in 1899 on the Democratic ticket but, in an age of California Republican supremacy, was defeated. He was, however, in the state senate from 1907 to 1913.

As state assemblyman and senator, Caminetti secured changes in California's educational system which affected both the curriculum and the establishment of new schools. In 1889 he introduced a bill making Admission Day a legal holiday, and obtained passage of the Caminetti Mining Law of 1893, which secured navigational changes on the Sacramento and San Joaquin rivers. This bill also reintroduced hydraulic mining, formerly banned, into California. Caminetti acquired considerable mining property in Amador and Calaveras County and much farm land. He was most loyal to that section of the state, arranging for the Alpine Highway to be constructed through the area, for an Indian reservation to be established there, and for the selling of thousands of dollars of school bonds to the state. Before he left the state capital, he helped pass a Chinese exclusion bill, which was indicative of his future attitude on matters of race.

Despite his foreign parentage, Caminetti believed in strict im-

282

migration control. In a technical sense, his appointment as commissioner of immigration in 1913 met President Wilson's need to placate immigrant public opinion and for West Coast representation in the Cabinet. In the words of Professor John Higham, Caminetti "had the instincts of a 100 per center; it was he who had directed the roundup of the Wobblies during the war and who had initiated action for the new deportation law of 1918." During the nativist-inspired anti-Red era that followed World War I, Caminetti exercised great repressive influence in support of Attorney General A. Mitchell Palmer's severe deportation measures. As commissioner, Caminetti, caught up in the Red Scare of that era, clamped down on immigrants. He also became identified with anti-Orientalism. His record on deportations was that of a prosperous but insecure middle-class citizen. The author of a history of the Department of Labor writes: "Of all the commissioners-general up to that time Caminetti was the most unfortunate. A student of administrative organization observed that his inexpert administration of his office was nerveless to the point almost of paralysis." Yet another source on Caminetti reported that personal "consciousness of his inexperience led him to refuse to take any action at all. His table was piled high with undispatched business, with records of men and women held in immigration stations awaiting his decisions. He argued by pounding the table, swinging his arms and evading the issue. In this way he refused to face a problem."[38] Yet Caminetti's influence upon immigrants, albeit negative, cannot be denied. When President Wilson left office in 1920, Caminetti did likewise, retiring to California, where he died on November 17, 1923. Here was an Italian who, though he never renounced his immigrant background, used it in a manner totally at variance with the spirit of non-restrictive immigration that had allowed his very parents to come to America.[39]

[38] John Lombardi, *Labor's Voice in the Cabinet*, 128–29.

[39] Regarding Caminetti, see *Who's Who* (Chicago, 1922), 601; Higham, *Strangers*, 228, 231; *Amador County History* (Jackson, 1927), 21, 26, 61, 92–93. There is also material on him in the James D. Phelan Papers, Bancroft Library, University of California, Berkeley. A dull but useful book that relates antiradicalism to antiforeignism is William Preston, Jr., *Aliens and Dissenters, Federal Sup-*

California's Italians seem to have lacked both time and training to tell their story. An exception is an obscure and anonymous early narrative by one of them entitled *Da Biella a San Francisco di California: Ossia storia di tre Valligiani Andornini in America* (Turin, 1882). It has remained unknown even to American bibliographers. Though few western Italians turned toward writing, they had a sense of history. California's pioneer historian, Hubert Howe Bancroft, glowingly described the services of a principal assistant in compiling the largest multivolume history of western America. Bancroft's associate was "General" Enrico Cerruti, a native of Turin who fled his homeland at an early age to become a "Latin American Consul General." After a tempestuous Italian revolutionary career, Cerruti ended up in Bancroft's employ, and the historian became "strongly attached to him." As a Latin, Cerruti was instrumental in obtaining the family archives of the Vallejos of Sonoma and other California Hispanic families, later deposited in what became the Bancroft Library of the University of California at Berkeley. Cerruti killed himself at Sonoma in 1876, and Bancroft lamented: "If I had him back with me alive, I would not give him up for all Nevada's mines."[40]

The exodus to western America occasionally produced eccentrics. A virtually unknown part of the immigration record was made by persons who became hermits or penurious hoarders of earthly goods. There was a California counterpart to Umberto Gabello, the miner in Colorado who had dug a strange cave house in which to live. Called "The Human Mole," he was Baldasare Forestiere from Messina. In 1904, Forestiere settled at Fresno, a city with an excessively warm summer climate. He had worked in the Boston subways and knew how cool a life underground could be; he bored a series of tunnels that eventually covered twenty acres. In these caverns he built kitchens, sleeping quarters, even a ballroom—all with pick and shovel. Forestiere's grey world, ten to fifteen feet below the surface, was as much as twenty degrees

pression of Radicals, 1903–1933. Caminetti appears throughout. See also Stanley Cobben, *A. Mitchell Palmer: Politician* (New York, 1963), 218–19, 223–25, 233.
[40] H. H. Bancroft, *Literary Industries* (San Francisco, 1890), 365–76, 383–445.

cooler than aboveground. After thirty-one years of digging, he constructed some sixty tunnels, grottoes, and niches. Some rooms Forestiere walled in with brick or concrete; others he covered over with glass. In a few tunnels left open to the sky he even planted citrus trees. The prodigious "Human Mole" died in 1946, after which his caves, complete with furniture, were closed. Eight years later, the labyrinth was reopened, and the secret world of Baldasare Forestiere is now called "The Fresno Underground Gardens." His realm—created by a yearning to dig and dig—holds a curious fascination for tourists.

More widely known is the story of Simon Rodia, builder of the Watts Towers in southern California. These bizarre artistic creations, ninety-nine, ninety-seven, and fifty-five feet high, were fashioned out of bits of glass, tile, artifacts (such as corncobs), and old boots garnered from near-by junk heaps. Rodia had come to America from his native Italy at about the age of ten. He had virtually no education and was reputedly a widower when he showed up in southern California. Without scaffolding, Rodia built the first of the towers in 1921 on a piece of property he had purchased along East 107th Street. Five years later, when Los Angeles annexed the town of Watts, Rodia became involved in a conflict with the city's Department of Building and Safety. Because he had no building permit, and because the towers were considered unsafe, demolition and condemnation hearings dragged on for years. Meanwhile, Rodia, who said he wanted to build something really big, went on with thirty-three years of erecting and defending a "gigantic fantasy of concrete, steel and rubble." The tallest tower is almost ten stories high.

Sam Rodia, as he came to be called, was a persistent, indeed obstinate, laborer. He fought off anything that interrupted construction of his towers. For years neighbors heard him singing Italian arias at the top of his voice while he worked. Fastened to a scaffolding by a window-washer's belt, he gripped a pail of cement and a burlap pouch filled with broken tile and sea shells. Sam paid local children a penny or more for bits of tile, bottles, or castoff crockery. What he could not use he buried in his back yard, as he did his 1927 Hudson touring car. "I'm worried to death to get this work done before I leave," he once confided to a by-stander, "but I'm a happy man." Another observer recalled that "everyone thought he was crazy" as he sang away in his beloved towers.

During the World War II blackouts, Rodia was ordered to take down the gay lights with which he had decorated his towers. As the war years passed, he grew more tense and quarreled increasingly with some of his neighbors. Children tormented the aging eccentric, throwing rubble over his seven-foot-high property walls. They also stole apricots from his precious tree, although he was generous in giving them its fruit as well as cookies. There was recurring trouble with city authorities who questioned the safety of the towers. Rodia proudly reassured critics that his filigreed lacework of chicken wire, steel rods and cemented bathroom tiles would withstand any earthquake. Sam was also plagued by curiosity seekers who asked him the same questions over and over and who resented his refusal to allow them to take his photograph. He no longer seemed pleased to see friends from the Temple Bethel Pentecostal Church on Washington Avenue or to provide them with bed sheets to cover newly baptized converts. The days of drinking "Dago Red" in the gazebo of his garden lay behind.

In 1954, at the age of eighty-one, Rodia tired of his project, deeded the towers to Louis Sauceda, gave away his furniture and household effects, and left Los Angeles for the northern California town of Martinez. Publicity and public bickering over whether the towers were structurally sound left him so embittered that he never returned to Los Angeles. Rodia, who died in 1965, apparently felt misunderstood and rejected by the society for which he had performed a labor of love. For four years, during which time the towers were left unattended, the white sea shells that ringed Rodia's "boat of Marco Polo" were smashed by vandals. Many of the plates that the old man had imbedded in his structures were broken in a ridiculous search to find rumored hidden treasure.

These mosaic-covered structures proved so strong that they could not easily be pulled down, even by steel cables attached to tractors. Called by art appreciators a "paramount achievement of twentieth century folk art in the United States," Rodia's towers were ultimately declared a monument to be protected by the Los Angeles Cultural Heritage Board.

Why had Simon Rodia built his towers? They may have been a monument to his adopted country; perhaps they also symbolized his own heroic view of himself. He was once asked why he had built the towers so strong? He replied: "If a man no have feet, he no stand."[41]

Italian artistry came out in ways that were other than eccentric. In the field of drama, for example, there was, by the turn of the century, an Italian troupe in residence at San Francisco called Il Circolo Famigliare Pisanelli. This group performed in the Teatro Bersaglieri, a rented hall. Nightly, the Italian quarter's opera lovers assembled at the Circolo: "One night it is 'La Traviata,' the next 'Rigoletto'." There was also a Thespian aspect to performances at the Circolo. Characteristic among them were plays staged as dialect comedy, then considered "very humorous." The effect of such drama depended upon the locality where the scenes were laid and the type of people whom it depicted. An effervescent vaudeville atmosphere prevailed at the Circolo. As many as 600 persons would crowd two half circles that made up its theater. Tragedy, love songs between the acts, solos, duets, and pantomime were featured in a spontaneous and gay environment.[42]

San Francisco's Italian theater flourished in an animated and gossipy atmosphere. Audiences attended as much to meet old friends as to see the performance. Clannishness too prevailed. Amateur groups called *compagnie filodrammatiche* put on well-attended performances; by 1905 the Teatro Apollo was a center for these performances. In a typical evening one could view a play of Giovanni Verga's *Cavalleria Rusticana*, with music from Mascagni's opera of the same name; this might be followed by a

---

[41] Regarding Forestiere, see "Realm of the Human Mole," *Westways*, Vol. XLVIII (July, 1956), 8–9. Rodia's story is told in Robert S. Bryan, "Sam Rodia and the Children of Watts," *Westways*, Vol. LIX (August, 1967), 3–6.

[42] J. M. Scanland, "An Italian Quarter Mosaic," *Overland Monthly*, Vol. XLVII (April, 1906), 327–34.

farce entitled *Prestami la Tua Moglie per Dieci Minuti* (*Lend Me Your Wife for Ten Minutes*), which, in turn, would be followed by a Grand Ball. Tickets for the entire evening cost twenty-five cents. Between the acts there were operatic selections. Well into the 1930's the Teatro Italiano in San Francisco continued to perform a repertoire that included the plays of Goldoni, D'Annunzio, and Pirandello. The actress Mimi Aguglia, well known also in Europe, was a centralizing theatrical personality for several decades at San Francisco. Today, although its tradition is remembered there, the city's Italian theater is no more.[43]

California's great visual resemblance to Italy helped make Italians feel at home whether they dug caves underground, or built towers, or produced operas and plays. Along the Santa Barbara coastline these colorful similarities are especially apparent. Thus an Italian like José Lobero, who gave that city's civic theater its name, settled there. This gold-seeker opened a tavern and saloon, funds from which allowed him to build what Howard Swan, in his book *Music in the Southwest,* calls "the most elaborate and magnificent theater yet to be erected in southern California," a building that seated thirteen hundred people. The botanist Dr. Francesco Francheschi attempted to transform Santa Barbara into a Latin oasis. By introducing such plants as the Pineapple Guava, the Lippia Repens, and Pittosporums, Francheschi tried to create a botanical Riviera in miniature, a wish that has partly come true.

Santa Barbara also attracted members of Italy's titled nobility. There and elsewhere prior to the turn of the century Italian noblemen were sought after by American heiresses. Eva Mackay, a daughter of John W. Mackay of San Francisco society, one of the "kings of the Comstock Lode," married the Prince of Galarto, Ferdinand Julian Colonna, of the Neapolitan branch of that family. This international marriage was an obvious alliance of California silver and a European title, a bargain that ended in divorce a few years after its celebration.[44]

[43] A superb study is in the series of monographs "San Francisco Theater Research," prepared by the Works Progress Administration; it is entitled *The Italian Theater in San Francisco* (San Francisco, 1939, mimeographed), *passim.*

Far removed from the wealthy scions of royalty at Santa Barbara, California's interior towns, with Italian names like Asti and Lodi, reminded one of dusty Piedmont or flat Lombardy. The Barolo, Barbera, San Gioveto, and Chianti produced by Italians in these inland areas tasted like the wines of Italy. Festivals during vintage seasons recalled festivities in the old country. *Contadini* cultivated patches of *basilico* to put in their *pasta* or *minestra*. Immigrant farm folk had transplanted their herbs as well as themselves. As they played *boccie* on the hard, dusty courts of country residences, immigrants relived life in their native Italy.

California's cities also reflected the transplanting of Italy to the new environment. "Little Italy" in San Francisco was a world in itself. Its presses ground out miles of doughy *tortellini* and *lasagne* as well as reams of *La Voce del Popolo*. Fernet Branca and Florio's Marsala bottles lay resplendent in the showcases of Italian grocery stores. Countless bakeries off Columbus Avenue featured *grissini* and hard breads *al'Italiana*. At a restaurant like the Fior d'Italia one could buy Milanese cutlets or *zabaglione*. A merchant could join the Camera di Commercio Italiana or, in the years before the Second World War, put his money in the Banca Populare. One could read *La Colonia Svizzera* if he came from the Italian-speaking Swiss Canton of Ticino. In fact immigrants did not need to learn English at all. Italian physicians, lawyers, and bankers took care of basic needs.

San Francisco's Washington Square, like its New York counterpart, was crowded with yelling Italian children. Tomatoes and garlic dried in back yards. On Fisherman's Wharf mariners mended their nets as they had done for generations at Leghorn or Genoa, propping up sagging spirits after an unsuccessful catch by tapping straw-covered demijohns of red wine. But, whereas the homeland water front had encouraged immigrants to leave Italy's overcrowded shores, San Francisco's wharf area produced DiMaggios—Joe, Vince, and Dom—as well as Ernie Lombardi. San Francisco's Italians also contributed Frank Crossetti and Tony

[44] Oscar Lewis, *Silver Kings, the Lives and Times of MacKay, Fair, Flood, and O'Brien* (New York, 1947), 91–92, 102.

Lazzeri to major league baseball. They played the game in an environment bereft of slums in the usual sense. Los Angeles' North Broadway and San Francisco's mission districts seemed less cluttered, depressing, and confining than the Columbus squares of eastern metropoli.

Today only the remnants of Italian influence remain, especially at Los Angeles. Left behind there is a smattering of ethnic grocery stores and restaurants as well as St. Peter's Church, since 1919 the Italian national church for a community which was once more than 90 per cent baptized Catholics. By 1968 less than ten Italian families were left in this parish, headed by Father Luigi Donazan. Former parishioners from the Los Angeles suburbs, however, still come in from afar to celebrate the traditional feast days of their home town. Most regular communicants at St. Peter's came from the province of Bari.

Few California Italians got their air on a fire escape. The sun shone regularly and its rays warmed both their bodies and spirits.

Immigrants were not the only persons to note the Arcadian similarity of Italian scenery to California's. Charles Dudley Warner's *Our Italy* (New York, 1891) and Peter C. Remondino's health-stressing *Mediterranean Shores of America* (Philadelphia, 1892) also exploited resemblances that went beyond the pages of books. A California county emblazoned its 1905 *Sunset* magazine advertisement with the masthead: "The Italy of California, Glenn County." Chambers of commerce at both San Diego and Riverside issued brochures concerning "their" *Italy of America.* Land boom advertising referred to California as the "American Italy." Grace Ellery Channing and Ernest Peixotto published articles on "What We Can Learn from Rome" and "Italy's Message to California" in *Sunset* (March, 1903). The connection between the two areas seemed inescapable. More recently, literary historian Franklin Walker has pointed out that Oscar Wilde's reference to Los Angeles as "a sort of Naples" was consonant with that city's hyperconsciousness of a "sub-tropical" climate and its hoped-for rebirth of classical Mediterranean civilization.

In 1875 the Los Angeles Immigration and Land Cooperative Association published a newspaper entitled *The New Italy*. Described as "the immigrant's guide to homes in southern California," it was the forerunner of a later barrage of booster propaganda for which California and its many chambers of commerce have become famous. *The New Italy's* January issue advertised three thousand head of sheep for $2.50 each, with one thousand lambs thrown in free, as well as beef tenderloin at 10 cents per pound, potatoes at 1 cent and flour at $5.00 per barrel.[45]

In all the competition for residents who sought an outdoor life, there was even a rivalry over which locality merited the mantle "Vesuvius of the West," as indicated by an illustration in California's *Golden Era* of May, 1888, captioned "San Diego—Naples of America." This same illustration exaggerated the similarities between the Neapolitan coastline and San Diego Bay by enlarging San Miguel to make it look like an inactive Vesuvius. Long Beach also claimed to be a new Naples. There was not quite so much debate over the future site of the West's Venice, for the real estate boom of the eighties in southern California saw promoter Abbot Kinney building elaborate imitation lagoons and terraced piazzas there along the Pacific.[46]

Near Los Angeles lived the most vigorous Victorian Italophiles as well as clever land speculators who wished customers to savor the taste of Roman holidays. These hucksters well recognized the appeal of publicity based on romantic similarities between an ancient culture and California's. The Southern Pacific Railroad Company, which stood to benefit enormously, also encouraged the creation of a full-blown Mediterranean America out west. An attempt to match the appeal of earlier Spanish place names like Santa Monica, Santa Barbara, or Santa Clara doubtless motivated the choice of such Latin boom names as Arcadia, Hesperia, Rialto,

[45] Los Angeles *Times*, July 20, 1947.

[46] Franklin Walker, *A Literary History of Southern California* (Berkeley, 1950), 118–19; see J. H. Tigner, *The Italy of America . . . Riverside County, California*; San Diego Chamber of Commerce, *The Italy of America*, and *Our Italy*.

Tarragona, Terracina, Verona, and Venice. The majority of these Latin-named townsites were, however, casualties of the California land bust of 1887.

Have such other Latin aspects of the California scene as the noonday siesta, viniculture, floriculture, sausage-making, art craftsmanship, the opera, and a cosmopolitan cuisine lost ground? Rooted in its Hispanic past, southern California, in the years before smog, preserved a rural coloration that stemmed from Mediterranean origins as well as a mild climate. There, Italian stone masons laid out winding roads through prosperous estates, the Italian influence of which was obvious. One of these became the Henry E. Huntington Library and Art Gallery at San Marino. On the campuses of Scripps and Occidental colleges one saw lingering evidences of Italian-inspired rococo porticoes, manicured cypress gardens, and decaying classical status. Farther to the north Senator James Phelan's Villa Montalvo at Saratoga resembled Pompeii's Casa dei Vetti, complete with atriums, Janus-headed vases, and bursting fountains. The facade of Stanford University's Chapel is an example of mosaic work similar to Rome's Church of St. Paul Outside the Walls. The Romanesque red-brick architectural styles of the University of California campus at Los Angeles and St. Andrew's Church in Pasadena indicate the popularity of these architectural forms.[47]

California's original mission-rancho and vineyard pattern of life did not entirely give way to a "vertical skyscraper culture." For some years after the Second World War, foreign influence upon the state's culture continued, admittedly as a side light to the main drama of urbanization. The vitality of immigrants thus had helped to buttress the foundations of a verdant Mediterranean America—this in an age of brutalization of the environment by the megalopoli of the future.

[47] Regarding California's Italianate influence see Ernest C. Peixotto, *Romantic California*, 3–23; his "Italy's Message to California," *Sunset*, Vol. X (March, 1903), 367–78; and his "Italy in California," *Scribners*, Vol. XLVIII (July, 1910), 75–84.

Conclusions

XIII
OLD CUSTOMS IN A NEW LAND

"Now therefore ye are no more strangers and foreigners . . . ."
—EPHESIANS, 2:19.

By 1900 the Italian immigrants had sown their prosperity in the West. They had found success in the sun. During summer months, immigrant seasonal workers might be shop laborers, home tailors, barbers, or railroad trackmen, but increasingly they planned to stay on in the new land. As the population of western cities grew, harvesters of tomatoes, cucumbers, and strawberries were needed in large numbers. While immigrants worked in the fields, they often lived in granaries or abandoned farm buildings. Such seasonal work also kept the immigrants busy in remote canning centers, cranberry marshes, hop fields, orchards, and vineyards. Some of these found a forgotten acre or two on which to build a small dwelling, draining a swamp or fertilizing a sandhill. Many a farm too rocky for its original owners was made to yield a paying crop. Growing cotton, sugar cane, watermelons, and rice in the southwestern states, apples and peaches on the western slopes of the Ozarks, and grapes, almonds, and asparagus in California, Italians wedded themselves to the rich soil of America. They traded migratory status for ownership of the land they were once hired to till. From shanty houses crowded with in-laws, babies, and lodgers, and Italians moved out of the vegetable fields, orchards, and railroad sidings toward a new respectability.

For those who chose life on the soil over that on city pavements, the emergence from itinerancy was rapid. As we have seen, foreigners from a country where land hunger was acute would do almost anything to acquire a plot of their own. They would work nights in a near-by town or in a mine or for the local cement plant, in addition to holding down jobs as field hands. This outside income made it easier for immigrants to become small western farmers.

EVERY WRITER comes to that portion of his work where he should attempt a summary. At such a point he must ask. What conclusions can logically be reached? In what respects has Americanization *not* eradicated racial background? What of the "inner feelings" of immigrants both about their own status and about the society they adopted? What remnants of the culture they left behind did these people bring with them to the New World? What traits, folkways, beliefs, superstitions, or habits of thinking stemmed from the culture of the old country? Beyond assimiliation into a *new* society, what contributions did they, perhaps unconsciously, make to American life? Some of these questions having to do with transplanting an old culture to a new land must remain unanswered. The generalizations that follow are partly applicable to immigrants who lived in the East, but they mostly concern those who moved West and virtually lost contact with the large eastern colonies of their countrymen.

There was a real contrast between the living conditions of those attracted to the West and those who remained—even in farming —in the East. There agricultural colonies, never far from large urban centers, frequently duplicated the environment of the tenement districts of eastern cities. Hence the living quarters of itinerant berry pickers at Hammonton or Vineland, New Jersey, resembled the slovenly hovels which Italian farmers had but recently vacated. Such migrants often had little incentive to tidy up their places of work, which they felt would never belong to them. Thus they often sent their money home, rather than invest it in another man's property. In 1903, despite low wages, a small group of Italian berry pickers at Hammonton mailed home 408 money orders amounting to $8,744.39. Farther west, where land was easier to obtain, more money seems to have been invested in homes or household improvements, or used to launch small businesses.[1]

In California the Di Giorgios, Maggios, Martinis, and Gallos became enormously successful. At first these "vegetable eaters," as detractors might have called them in earlier days, aroused the envy of competitors. Foerster has commented on the Italian sense of realism, which helped these immigrants to overcome prejudice and to strive for actual, instead of imagined, success. Because they were expedient in coming to grips with the competitive American environment, pervasively enthusiastic, and determined to the very limits of their strength, the Italians could not but be admired by so practical a society.

In the American West there was, however, a wide disparity between the financial opportunities open to Italians and those available to certain other foreigners. In his book *British Investments and the American Mining Frontier*, Clark C. Spence has made clear how extensively the English invested capital in the West from 1860 to 1901. Large quantities of north European money flowed into the mines of Colorado and Arizona, into the ranches of Wyoming and Texas, and into the lumber camps of the Pacific Northwest. The French, Belgians, and Dutch all actively sought out investment opportunities at a time when the natural resources of the western United States were thrown open to world exploitation. Yet, virtually no Italian capitalists participated in what Vernon Parrington satirized as "the Great Barbecue" of United States resources in the late nineteenth century. Unlike the English, the Italians had little surplus capital with which to speculate.

Furthermore, some factors discouraged immigrant migration westward. In the old Southwest, although European farmers were needed, southerners never quite accepted foreigners without a measure of prejudice, a problem which still exists. Prejudice helps to explain the lack of cosmopolitanism down South, especially in

[1] Meade, "The Italian on the Land," in *Labor Reports*, 524.

contrast to its pre-Civil War era, when the French and Spanish actively colonized the lower Mississippi Valley. As has been seen, one course of action, attractive to relatively few immigrants, was to migrate to southwestern agricultural colonies like Austin Corbin's Sunnyside. Not many American businessmen, however, were willing to risk staking such immigrants unacquainted with new farming problems, climate conditions, and a different system of marketing crops. Once the Italian-Swiss colonies in California, or Tontitown, were established by Italians themselves, they did, however, attract workers.

On the Pacific slope, where immigrants seemed to prosper best, the percentage of foreign-born was high. Not only was there a thick European resident population but, of course, there were many Japanese and Chinese. In 1870 nearly three out of ten Westerners were foreign-born. That year California's Irish constituted one in four of that state's immigrant residents. After 1920 a decrease occurred in the number of immigrants in the twenty-two states beyond the Mississippi. Except for California, where foreign-born Italians increased from 88,504 in 1920 to 107,249 in 1930, their numbers generally decreased. The percentage of the foreign-born in the West dropped by nearly half between the two World Wars. This could be ascribed to the elimination of available high-quality public lands, to the decline in the mountain states of mining enterprise, to the great economic depression after 1929, and to the westward migration of native American stock. By 1940 less than one out of nine Westerners was foreign-born. Great numbers, of course, lived in the East. In 1920, when the first-generation Italians in California numbered over 80,000, and that of a state like Texas only about 8,000, over half a million Italians were living in New York, over 200,000 in Pennsylvania, and over 300,000 in Rhode Island. Perhaps the most important negative factor was the decline in the quota of immigrants allowed into the United States by the Immigration Acts of 1917 and 1924. The latter law reduced the annual Italian quota to only 5,500 persons. Yet the restriction of immigration sometimes helped to increase social homogeneity.[2]

It should be repeated that numbers or percentages alone do not adequately tell the story of western foreigners.[3] Their record is, rather, based upon the variety of experiences they encountered:

> The immigrants who went directly to the frontier made many important contributions, but they did so in large part within the pattern which had already been set by the earlier settlers. There were [only a few] small isolated communities that attempted to provide a replica of the old world on the frontier.[4]

East or west, immigrants did not simply transfer to America the society, habits, and dress they had known abroad. Local customs dictated change. The fluidity of a western frontier broke down past attitudes, as the son of an immigrant recalled:

> Not even Italy, where my parents had been born, was real, in the way that America, and more particularly Salt Lake, was real. The actual world was the world which I had seen, felt, tasted from the day of my birth, and which, each day, I was growing into with an ever greater awareness.[5]

The farm-dwelling immigrant exhibited characteristics similar and yet different than the city-dweller. He seemed less dependent upon the institution of the church, at least after the first few years of his arrival. For older persons the Latin Mass, however, frequently represented a form of security that would not be available to them in today's English spoken service during this age of ecumenical worship. On occasion younger, "fallen away" Catholic immigrants helped to found new foreign-speaking congregations generally affiliated with one of the Protestant evangelical faiths. Such a person rather quickly forgot the celebration of ecclesiastical holidays popular in the old country and the singing of folk songs

---

2 See Allan McLaughlin, "Italian and Other Latin Immigrants," *Popular Science Monthly*, Vol. LXV (August, 1904), 341; also "Italians in the United States," *Literary Digest*, Vol. XCIII (April 23, 1927), 31; Earl Pomeroy, *The Pacific Slope* (New York, 1965), 262, 284.

3 Taeuber, *Changing Population*, 63, 310, and Haskett, "Problems and Prospects," in *World Population, Migrations*, 58–60, also stress this point.

4 Taeuber, *Changing Population*, 64.

5 Pagano, *Golden Wedding*, 175.

with friends, except perhaps at weddings. What he forgot the quickest was the very language spoken for generations by his fore-fathers. In his *Culture on the Moving Frontier*, Louis B. Wright has pointed out the importance of English literature in the rapid assimilation of immigrants. As their children went to common schools, whether the parents were Yugoslav miners in the Mesabi Range or Italian fruit pickers at San Jose, they read the same books as other schoolmates. Only in certain cities, one of which was San Francisco, could immigrant children attend a parochial school where they could hear their parents' tongue spoken. And, follow-ing the passage of a relatively few years, after-school classes in Italian became harder to find. In the public schools the national-istic McGuffey *Readers*, Portia's "Speech on Mercy," or Scott's *Ivanhoe*—assigned reading for all—had a part in making immi-grants look upon English, and not Italian, as their literary inherit-ance. In some cases, because the first generation spoke only a local dialect, English was the first *common* language immigrants had yet spoken.[6]

Perhaps the best example of the adult immigrant's gradual movement away from his own heritage was the way in which he regarded his daily reading. Members of the first generation were understandably loyal to their own newspapers. While they were still learning to speak English, a colorful Italian-American press flourished. From the 1850's onward the number of Italian journals published in the West grew. Whereas in 1859 there were only a few such papers—the most notable being *L'Eco della Patria* and *La Voce del Popolo* at San Francisco—by 1931 there were at least thirty Italian newspapers west of the Mississippi. That year San Francisco alone boasted five of these; one had a circulation of 20,000. Denver had two Italian papers, Pueblo two, Portland two, Seattle two, and Los Angeles, Salt Lake City, Omaha, Dallas, and Des Moines one each.

The enthusiasm with which the residents of a midwestern town greeted the appearance of an Italian newspaper is shown by the following account: "The first issue of the new Italian paper, *La*

[6] Wright, *Culture on the Moving Frontier*, 222–23.

Tribuna Italiana, appeared Saturday, and was received with much joy among the Italian residents of this city and vicinity, where it was distributed gratis. The Italians had been anxiously awaiting its appearance for several weeks."[7]

Despite the gradual decline in the number of first-generation readers of the foreign-language press, a few of these newspapers showed a remarkable persistence. Most became four-to-eight-page weeklies; the dailies came to be confined chiefly to a handful of large cities. Increasingly, editors stopped filling their front pages with material cribbed from Italian periodicals. Instead they began to focus attention on local births, marriages, deaths, and folksy neighborhood doings not always reported by "American newspapers." The editorial page might continue to feature viewpoints tailored to the foreign taste. But eventually immigrant communities became as interested in their own events as in "canned" dispatches from Genoa, Rome, or Florence. Whereas immigrant papers had originally been started because of the dearth of news from home in the American press, reader interest eventually shifted. Those papers that survived achieved a new identity and became neither wholly Italian nor wholly American but, rather, Italian-American. The limited number of first-generation immigrants located in widely scattered communities precluded the possibility of creating a great foreign press. Also, divergent religious, political, and social views aroused animosities among subscribers.

Once American-born children formed new households, they wanted to patronize American stores and journals. After their parents died, they cancelled subscriptions to Italian-language newspapers. Inserting columns of English material to attract the younger generation could not save most of these journals. Immigrant newspapers usually folded when readers did not feel the need to look back to the old country for reassurance. At that point the immigrant was no longer an immigrant. He had become an Ameri-

[7] Herrin *News,* October 6, 1905, quoted in Manfredini, "The Italians Come to Herrin," *Journal of the Illinois State Historical Society,* Vol. XXXVII (December, 1944), 317–28.

can. Mutual aid societies and patriotic organizations that had also served to demarcate the immigrant's alienism from American society suffered a similar fate. When psychological props were no longer required, an unspoken revolt occurred against these vestiges of the immigrant past.

For some older persons only slowly did the breakdown in *Italianità* occur; these clung to the symbol of Columbus and his discovery of 1492, just as French immigrants basked in the memory of Lafayette's participation in the American Revolution. For such persons, unlike those who had become Protestants, the Catholic heritage also kept old memories alive. The southern Italians, especially, celebrated the feast days of San Rocco, San Gennaro, and St. Anthony in a personally meaningful way. Some immigrant communities held more than thirty religious celebrations per year. St. Anthony's Day might begin with the firing of salutes early in the morning, followed by a procession to the local church, High Mass, a community dinner, games, and a parade, with bands, floats, and fireworks, at night. Parishioners spared no expense to make these celebrations memorable. Contributions from local firms and voluntary individual offerings helped to defray their costs. A description of the preparations made for a 1905 Columbus Day celebration in a small midwestern town illustrates the importance some immigrants attached to these events:

Guido Spagnolina, a veteran balloon maker from Italy, is preparing to build one of the largest and most gorgeously illuminated paper balloons ever sent up in this country. He is planning one twenty-five feet high and decorated with 500 candles. As the balloon ascends and gets up four or five hundred feet, the candles that festoon it become detached and drop to the earth like shooting meteors. . . . His large balloon made for Columbus Day will be a duplicate of the one with which he won the first prize at the Florence festival. . . . Louis Oldani was instructed to go to St. Louis and purchase regalia and a paraphemalia that will be used for the parade. It will be a brilliant historical pageant. The streets of Herrin will resemble a festival day of the 16th century. There will be men in armour, mounted horsemen, courtiers, cavaliers, fifteenth century sailors, floats resembling the old sailing vessels in which Columbus and his men crossed the Atlantic.[8]

Despite the colorfulness of his activities, the Italian generally expended less effort to retain his folkways than did other nationalities. The Germans, for example, fought vigorously in many states for permission to organize German-language public schools. No such enthusiasm was shown by most Italians for their native language. Coming to the West in smaller numbers than the Germans or the Irish, the Italians felt in no position to push for the dubious benefits of foreign identification. In copying the ways of native Americans, the sons and daughters of foreigners became more orthodox Americans.

Public schools usually helped to ameliorate generational conflicts. This because of the greatly underestimated immigrant respect for schooling, in addition to the enthusiasm of the children. At the social level, if not at the educational, the public school was part of the immigrant's salvation. Compulsory attendance laws were strongly backed by immigrant leaders anxious to overcome the stigma of ignorance. In Minnesota "the offspring of immigrants uniformly outranked the others, even in the populous Middle Atlantic and north central states."[9] The immigrant zeal for schooling in the West refutes the cliché that Americanization was primarily sponsored by Anglo-Saxon nativists. Schooling became the key to future success, and it offered the solution to the many problems the immigrant needed to overcome in order to compete in a new society.

Some immigrants, of course, continued to send their *bambini* to parochial schools and colleges. As has been noted, however, a minority of Italians abandoned their Roman Catholic faith to embrace evangelical and Lutheran churches, as well as such denominations as the Baptists, Congregationalists, and Presbyterians. Americanization for such folk also meant Protestantization, despite Catholic efforts to keep immigrants in churches of their

[8] Herrin *News*, October 5, 1911, quoted in *ibid.*

[9] Smith, "New Approaches to the History of Immigration in Twentieth Century America," *American Historical Review*, Vol. LXXI (July, 1966), 1273.

own faith. Even among Catholics, however, the young were absorbed into English-speaking parishes, further loosening ethnic affiliations. As for older Italians, they were loyal to native priests and disdainful of those Irish clerics who staffed Italian dioceses. For these older, more pious Italians it seemed regrettable that the number of priests produced by the Italian-American environment was small, especially when compared to the Irish.

Ultimately the number of Italians in America was about one-third of the Irish population. Of the thirty million Catholic communicants in the United States about half were of Irish descent and one-sixth were of Italian background. Individual Italians nursed a strong grievance against these Irish immigrants. By mid-twentieth century not one Italian bishop of the more than one-hundred Catholic bishops in the United States was of Italian background. Among that church's twenty-one archbishops there was no cleric of Italian descent. Italian culture may have undermined the priestly vocation in the Italian subconscious. Celibacy, particularly in southern Italy, was widely deprecated. Sexual expression was there seen as irrepressible, and proof of manhood. Conversely, because many Irish men never married, celibacy posed no such problem for them. This helps to account for the large number of priests the Irish sent to America. The greater total wealth created by the American Irish community also contributed to their near monopoly in the American Catholic hierarchy.

Religiously and socially, the Italians, as compared to the Germans in the West, adopted a way of life suited not to their European past but to their American future. In contrast, the Germans, seemingly more brittle, sought to withstand the tug of Americanization, but they were unsuccessful. In Kansas, German Mennonites settled in closed communities and attempted to maintain their own schools, customs, and religious system. Texas Germans also doggedly resisted change. Whenever social or cultural patterns they could not respect were thrust upon them "by aggressive means, through legislation or intimidation or boycott, they resented the suitation very strongly." The Germans even spurned ideas "in no way objectionable, and, in fact, more suited to their new life in America than were the continental ways to which they adhered."[10] Only infrequently were Italians critical, aloof, or superior in attitude. What they wanted was acceptance.

As latecomers, Italians had to bow to customs already imposed upon society by others. They felt bound to adopt existing systems until they had achieved enough success to follow their own way of life. In doing so, however, they frequently abandoned the old way of life forever. The Italian community achieved wealth and political influence later than the Germans, Irish, Scots, or Jews. The need to catch up encouraged Americanization.

There were few great fortunes, such as those of the Carnegies, Guggenheims, and, later, the Kennedys, among the Italians. And unlike the Irish, those Italians who did become prosperous did not generally achieve political power. The "new money" of the Italian community came from restaurants and taverns, construction, trucking, the marketing of produce, and such unfashionable businesses as cesspool contracting, roofing, and rock masonry. Furthermore, Italian immigrant wealth never quite matched that of America's earlier and more stable immigrant fortunes. A small number of first-generation Italian congressmen and senators reached public office. Lacking political experience, they would have to wait for prestige until the second generation could earn it in the professions and the business community.

Although Italians respected the entrenched American system sufficiently to abandon the old, there were parts of it that they abhorred. America's strait-laced moral code set the price of community respectability at rigid temperance, an impossible demand to make of most Italians. Some immigrants swallowed their pride and temporarily abandoned drinking wine. But others refused to conform, and kept on swallowing zinfandel, California's alternative to Chianti. Yet, as Merle Curti has pointed out in his study of a Wisconsin county during the late nineteenth century, "there

[10] John A. Hawgood, *The Tragedy of German-America. The Germans in the United States of America During the Nineteenth Century—And After*, 40. More recent scholarship is Terry G. Jordan, *German Seed in Texas Soil: Immigrant Farmers in Nineteenth Century Texas* (Austin, 1966).

was a strong sentiment for temperance," and "the immigrant was expected to do things the way the old stock specified." When Prohibition darkened the land in the 1920's, Italians found the era incomprehensible. In his *The Paesanos*, Jo Pagano has one of his characters say: " 'By God, what a country! Make a goddam criminal out of you joost to take a glass of healthy wine!' "[11]

Few Italians participated in temperance societies, as did Scandinavian and English immigrants. Yet, in contrast to the reckless imbibing of whisky by native Americans, the Italian could nurse a bottle of red wine by the hour. Most Italians kept wine in their cellars throughout the bleak Prohibition era. While feasting beneath the shade of a grape arbor, they enjoyed the simple conviviality that accompanied washing down *pasta* with what Americans called "Dago Red." This type of relaxed drinking of the most harmless sort seldom led to drunkenness. Alcoholism was, indeed, unusual among most immigrants. They enjoyed food fully as much as wine. Italians hounded neighborhood stores that carried Genoese *baccalà*, *torrone* from Cremona, hard-crusted breads, tuna packed in olive oil from Lucca, Eureka lemons raised from Sicilian seeds, and various other regional delicacies. In such establishments one could also find imported Florentine Chianti and Milanese *boccie* balls for Saturday afternoon games.

Immigrants held these *boccie* matches on any level plot of ground available. *Boccie* players vociferously wagered money, a shot of *grappa*, or a bottle of wine on the outcome of a match. The intricacies of the game fascinated their American neighbors. Each player was allowed two wooden or steel balls, known as *boccies*. The lead-off player rolled a smaller ball, the jack, down the smoothed, dirt-floored alley. Noisy contestants tried to hit this moving target and to knock their opponents' balls away from the jack. The proud winner was the person who came the closest to the jack ball. San Francisco's Bocce Ball Restaurant still caters to customers who play the game and to opera buffs who come to hear "*La donna è mobile*" or "*Un bel dì*" and to sip *poncino*, or coffee laced with brandy.

[11] Curti, *Making*, 138; Jo Pagano, *The Paesanos* (Boston, 1940), 3.

The *boccie* game was both a symbol of the past and an indication that the immigrant could afford time to relax. Similarly, rich meat courses on Sundays supplanted the polenta (corn meal), *pasta*, and chestnut bread of earlier days. Old style or new, there was an integrity about immigrant cooking that was unforgettable, as the son of a native Italian family that lived in Salt Lake City recalled:

> The feast was nearly ready. The side dishes had already been heaped upon the kitchen table—platters of tuna and anchovies and pickled olives and mushrooms surrounded by sliced salami and cheese. There were bowls of dried olives, swimming in olive oil and flavored with garlic and orange peel; there was celery, and sweetly aromatic *finnochio*, and wafer thin Italian ham. . . . The roasts and chickens were finishing at the same time; the pastries, heaped on the side table, were flaky and crumbling; the chicken soup was clear yet full-bodied in flavor, the spaghetti sauce was rich and thick.[12]

The whole tenor of immigrant life steadily improved. At week's end a worker who had worn rough laboring clothes was anxious to change into a white shirt with collar, new necktie, and patent leather shoes. He invested in upholstered parlor furniture, carpets, electric lights, and flush toilets—all evidences of new-found wealth. Yet, the more he indulged in such amenities, the more the immigrant grew to be like his American neighbors.

A study of the social atmosphere in Minnesota's mining towns suggests that more immigrants were assimilated than were alienated. Rural urbanization helped many foreigners achieve acceptance. Although immigrants who settled in the Mesabi and Vermilion ranges encountered small-town "cultural islands" grounded in sentiments of nationality, these islands could not withstand "the assimilating effects of shared experience." The small western town encouraged unity. Traditionally, foreign women were more sheltered than their men. But immigrant wives in western towns quickly made friends with persons of different nationality. There occurred an "astonishingly rapid adjustment of all groups to prevailing American folkways" that extended to

12 Pagano, *Golden Wedding*, 84.

school children, civic activities, and recreation. A growing number of immigrants married outside their national group, further exercising "a mediating role among newcomers of the father's nationality." In the small towns of Minnesota, religious life too became markedly interethnic, even in Roman Catholic congregations. Business and commerce played their part in encouraging Americanization, with immigrant businessmen, especially those who formed partnerships with native Americans, acting as "links between two worlds." Whereas eastern stores operated by immigrants listed their products in both English and Italian, western tradesmen generally used only English in their advertising.[13]

Although it is distortive to assert that discrimination was absent from the immigrant story, east or west,[14] the prejudice once practiced against the immigrant has been overstressed. What is often forgotten is that ultimately antiforeign nativist leadership in the American West came to be, according to one historian, "conspicuously immigrant in background." One thinks first of Caminetti's use of public office to persecute immigrants, of Haakon Langoe and Olaf Tveitmoe, two Norwegian leaders, after World War I, of the Americanization movement in the Northwest; earlier California's anti-Chinese movement of the 1870's was fanned by Irish labor leader Denis Kearney and, as has been seen, by Italians still earlier. It seems ironical that anti-immigrant activity should have, even occasionally, been spearheaded by immigrants themselves.[15]

Except for the West's treatment of Orientals, however, rank nativism was relatively rare. The California of 1849 had produced a foreign miner's tax reflective of frontier prejudices, yet racial tension failed to develop throughout large areas of the Far West.

[13] This paragraph draws heavily upon the findings of Timothy L. Smith, Clarke Chambers, and Hyman Berman, as reported in Smith, "New Approaches to the History of Immigration in Twentieth Century America," *American Historical Review*, Vol. LXXI (July, 1966), 1267-70.

[14] Hawgood, *Tragedy*, 192, in speaking of German embarrassment at the hands of Texas nativists, states, "the welcome accorded to the German immigrants and settlers during the forties had turned by the fifties into scornful intolerance."

[15] Pomeroy, *Pacific Slope*, 285.

Just as charges of racism were used to improve the working conditions of native Americans, some immigrants employed "race" to achieve economic betterment. In 1894 an angry outburst appeared in a Butte, Montana, newspaper under the title "An Italian Speaks." The writer decried the fact that the Anaconda Copper Mining Company did not employ more of "his people." This letter, an obvious attempt to embarrass that company, asked: "How many Italians work for the company? I think I can count them on the fingers of one hand, and I say to you all, that if it were not for the Butte & Boston, the Boston & Montana, W. A. Clark and other companies, the Italian colony would have to pack its blankets and walk out of town." At this time there was as yet virtually no "Italian colony" in Butte. The writer himself obviously wanted a job; his way of gaining one was to create an incident by using the local press.[16]

Antiforeign sentiment afflicted mining especially, where the large number of people employed might suddenly be put out of work if the operations shut down. A surplus of immigrants could lead to tension when unemployment was severe. Several states, including, in 1889, Illinois, Wyoming, and Idaho, prohibited corporations from hiring any alien who had not declared his intention to become a citizen.

There were also, as has been pointed out, petty but complicated labor disputes in the western mining camps. Mine operators were ruthless with labor, whether in Pennsylvania or in Montana. And the Italians, like any other nationality, were caught up in such tensions. The Red Lodge (Montana) *Republican Picket* on November 15, 1907, devoted a sizable descriptive story to a hassle in which an Italian miner struck a mine operator over the head with a cigar clipper. The emphasis in this sort of reporting was on the dramatic aspects of labor violence. Press accounts frequently stressed such weapons as "foreign implements," "Italian razors," or "Montenegran stilettos."

Neglected unskilled workers were drawn toward the Industrial

---

[16] J. B. Bosckis in *Butte Miner*, republished in Helena *Daily Record*, November 3, 1894.

Workers of the World (I.W.W.), which sought to force the adoption of working reforms but which had a reputation for violence. In 1907, an Italian "Wobbly," Joseph Ettor, organized and directed a stormy lumber mill strike at Portland, Oregon, which ultimately swept the entire Pacific Northwest. In punishing foreigners convicted of "violence" during such outbreaks, judges frequently penalized them to the full extent of the law. An act of violence involving immigrants drew extraordinary attention. Whenever conflicts occurred between immigrants themselves, criticism was magnified even further. However keen the competition between the Irish and Italians, it never became as acute as the earlier rivalry between Irish "paddies" and Chinese "coolies" who built the transcontinental railroad. Yet, it was frequently noticed, especially by the press.[17]

If one reads old newspapers indiscriminately, it is possible to reach the conclusion that there were unceasing attacks upon foreigners. The United States has indeed passed through prolonged phases of intolerance. During such periods news of racial matters made exciting headlines. As one historian writes in a book on American nativism: "Every time a simple Italian laborer resorted to his knife, the newspapers stressed the fact of his nationality; the most trivial fracas on Mulberry Street caused a headline on Italian Vendetta."[18] Were individual instances of xenophobia, however, typical of what westerners thought of immigrants? Was the intolerance shown by California's Native Sons of the Golden West seriously comparable to the good will of the majority of that state's population toward these newcomers? Except in times of depression, immigrant labor was very much in demand in the West. Even in 1893, when a national panic made the importation of cheap labor especially unpopular, stringent immigration restriction did not occur, partly because of the resistance to it of the West.[19]

[17] Robert L. Tyler, "The I.W.W. and the West," *American Quarterly*, Vol. XII (Summer, 1960), 182, cites Portland *Oregonian*, March 10, 1907; Wittke, *Irish in America*, 188–91, 225.

[18] Higham, *Strangers*, 90.

[19] *Ibid.*, 73.

Antiforeign feeling rose again nationally about 1905, as racists felt threatened. By then the changed nationality of immigration affected reactions to it. Neither the South nor the West "had been a favorite destination for New Immigrants; both together had only half as many as New York City."[20] Yet, in the Far West the number of "New Immigrants" more than tripled, to reach 5.6 per cent of the white national population. As a result, a certain amount of nativism was bound to occur. By 1914 antiforeign tension again grew strong, partly because of international problems and an economic slump the year before.

What made immigrants unpopular were economic and social beliefs far removed from the new soil they tilled. For example, anarchism—a terrifying word to nineteenth-century Americans— had been rooted in the Italian political scene for decades. In an age when European anarchists were considered the principal instigators of labor unrest, clandestine groups of conspirators regularly organized themselves for insurrections in Italy. The immigrant took the brunt of American abuse directed against similarly minded anarchists who had come to the United States. Calls for deportations of undesirables and for immigration restriction were partly based on a nebulous association of the immigrant with political assassination and Machiavellian poisonings—concepts quite beyond the reach of the average Italian vineyardist or dairy worker.[21]

The immigrant's association with the radical fringe of the labor movement also brought disfavor upon him. The American public could never quite make up its mind about immigrant involvement in unionism. Some writers averred that immigrants shied away from union membership. Quite the opposite was true. Trade unions had existed in Italy since the 1840's, but not many workers had been able to join them.[22] As has been seen, socialistically

[20] Ray Ginger, *Age of Excess, the United States from 1877 to 1914* (New York, 1965), 241–43.

[21] Recent scholarship on the subject of foreign anarchists in the United States is extensive. See Sidney Fine, "Anarchism and the Assassination of McKinley," *American Historical Review*, Vol. LX (July, 1955), 777–99.

[22] Horowitz, *Italian Labor*, 37.

minded immigrants were especially attracted by industrial union-ism. Low-paid, unskilled workers shut out of the American Fed-eration of Labor (which applied a literacy test in 1897) sorely needed protection. A worker's sheer physical strength was no guarantee of security. A man needed a union behind him, or so it seemed to some. According to a government report published after the turn of the century, trade unionism among North Italians (supposedly more enlightened than southerners) was nearly three times as high as among native Americans, some of whom con-sidered themselves "free men," and consequently would not join unions.[23]

The immigrant's historical reputation is riven with stereotyped images of alleged racial or ethnic "characteristics." One immigra-tion historian has pointed out how inaccurate it is to make such generalizations as that English and Irish immigrants are auto-matically "imbued with sympathy for our ideals and our democrat-ic institutions," or that Serbo-Croatians have "savage manners," that Poles are "high-strung," and that Italians are "non-farmers" disposed toward brigandage and poverty. Before the first World War, supposedly objective government reports frequently made similar generalizations.[24] The immigration restriction move-ment of the 1920's—carefully examined by John Higham and Barbara Solomon—was supported by pseudo-scientific findings, sometimes developed from government hearings. Generalizations repeated about Italians concerned their supposed low rate of literacy, tendency toward crime, disturbed emotional tempera-ment, and laziness.[25] Both Italians and Jews were subject to accu-sations of radicalism. The Sacco and Vanzetti case was to drag on from 1920 to 1927, through the post–World War I red scare and deportation delirium. However unfair, this *cause célèbre* would cast further doubt on the loyalty and dependability of suspected foreign anarchists. As organizers and agitators attracted immi-

[23] Hourwich, *Immigration and Labor*, 328, 452.
[24] Oscar Handlin, *Race and Nationality in American Life*, 107–108.
[25] *Ibid.*, 125–30.

grants and non-immigrants into extreme wings of the labor movement, "Italian workers in times of crisis often found no one willing
to speak their case but the ultra-radicals."[26]

It is, however, a correlative of our melting-pot culture that we
think of people as having the same kind of background, outlook,
and experience. The immigrant record in the West suggests quite
the opposite. In dealing with the immigrant theme, historians tend
to overlook, or even to deny, that acculturative patterns are different. Behavioral experiences in the American environment were
never constant. Some immigrants arrived with values already very
similar to those of the American middle class. In Europe there
was, furthermore, much regional, as well as rural-urban variation.
To avoid cultural stereotyping this should be remembered. It
should also be recalled that some immigrants "got stuck" in the
process of shifting from one society's set of values to those of
another.

Helping to alter the stigma attached to being an immigrant was
an alternate tide, or spirit, that grew up in America by the early
twentieth century. This was "hyphenated Americanism," deplored by President Theodore Roosevelt. Speaking of non-dis-
crimination against all Americans, irrespective of ethnic descent
or religious faith, he once stated:

> When I refer to hyphenated Americans, I do not refer to naturalized
> Americans. Some of the very best Americans I have ever known were
> naturalized Americans, Americans born abroad. But a hyphenated
> American is not an American at all. The one absolutely certain way
> of bringing this nation to ruin . . . would be to permit it to become a
> tangle of squabbling nationalities, an intricate knot of Ger-
> man-Americans, Irish-Americans, French-Americans, Scandinavian-
> Americans, or Italian-Americans, each preserving its separate na-
> tionality, each at heart feeling more sympathy with Europeans of
> that nationality than with other citizens of the American Republic.[27]

[26] Oscar Handlin, *The American People in the Twentieth Century* (Cambridge,
1954), 60.

[27] "Speech Before the Knights of Columbus," New York City, October 12,
1915, in *The Works of Theodore Roosevelt, Memorial Edition*, XX, 456.

To claim that all immigrants were in harmony with the American environment at every step of their stay in the New World would, of course, be inaccurate. Meaningful frustrations occasionally marred their vision of life in America. There was a callous hardness in American life that some Italians did not like. Pasquale d'Angelo once remarked that he sometimes could not "understand these people in America and their cold ways. They will go to the funeral of their best friend and keep a straight face. I believe they feel ashamed if in a moment of forthrightness they've turned to look at a flower or beautiful sunset." D'Angelo once wrote of passing a flower store where he saw a glorious display of color: "It seemed as if these cold people made it a silly point of honor not to stop or glance."[28]

The Italian novelist Cesare Pavese, writing of immigration in his novel *La luna e i falò*, has an immigrant who had returned from California say: "At Fresno where I lived I went to bed with many women, one of them I almost married, and I never found out where they had their father and mother and their land." This character speaks of American women "who came from who knows where." Obviously there were plenty of Americans, in Pavese's mind, who were themselves "uprooted." Pavese's returned immigrant had doubted whether he should settle down with a woman in such a culture as America's: "I often thought what race of children would have come out of us two—out of those smooth hard flanks, out of that blond belly nourished on milk and orange juice, and out of me, out of my thick blood."[29]

D'Angelo, however, could not bring himself to be permanently downhearted. "Something had grown in me during my stay in America. Something was keeping me," he wrote, "in this wonderful perilous land where I had suffered so much and where I had so much more to suffer . . . somewhere I would strike the light." D'Angelo continued, "Without realizing it, I had learned the great lesson of America: I had learned to have faith in the future.

[28] D'Angelo, *Son of Italy*, 80, 83.

[29] Pavese quoted in Donald Heiney, *America in Modern Italian Literature*, 178–79.

No matter how bad things were, a turn would inevitably come—as long as I did not give up."[30]

Foreigners who refused to be buried in America's industrial centers lost themselves in the vastness of its West. As has been seen, there were some who did not relish going back to the soil and who sought to forget the monotony of European peasant life. By the turn of the century less than 7 per cent of Italian immigrants worked as farmers, although more than two-thirds of these had once lived off the countryside. In a new farm environment many immigrants, nevertheless, found social acceptance and commingling with the "better people" relatively easy. Merle Curti's study of late nineteenth-century Trempeleau County, Wisconsin, stresses the unity of races in a rural environment: "Whether foreign-born or native Americans," this extended to such social gatherings as outdoor picnics which "brought most elements of the population together on an equal and entirely democratic basis." Individual immigrants might deviate from the Puritan norm, but "proper deportment" encouraged the native-born to extend a welcome.[31]

Despite increased acceptance, immigrants often wished to return to the homeland for a visit or permanently. If an immigrant remained unmarried, he felt freer to go back to Italy. During economic crises thousands did so. In the panic year 1907 and in other years of depression potential immigrants back in the home country were warned not to leave during "bad times" abroad. And there were always those immigrants who returned, to report that America's stars were not their own.

The heaviest return to Europe occurred during the years 1907 to 1914, at a ratio of about four arrivals to every departure—a process halted only by the travel restrictions of World War I. Immigrants returned home because of dissatisfaction with life in the United States, poor health, a desire to rejoin relatives in the homeland, the ups and downs of the business cycle (including unemployment), and the inability of some to adjust to a new society.

[30] D'Angelo, *Son of Italy*, 115, 171.
[31] Curti, *Making*, 98–99.

A few were always ready to forsake a high standard of life and, by repatriation, to seek out the traces of their childhood and their spiritual origins. This return does not refute the notion that immigrants were uplifted rather than downtrodden. The majority (especially those who had been economically successful) never returned to the old country. Returnees tended to be the ones who had succeeded only moderately well. Those who had really become enriched frequently stayed on in the United States. If the immigrant's new roots had taken hold, there was not much point in going back to Europe permanently. These resolved to make even more money and to bring up their children as Americans.[32]

A subtle, overlooked cause for the return of "birds of passage" was what some foreigners construed as disrespect shown them by Americans. Even relatively friendly phrases like "Hey buddy!" or "Come here, Mac!" were not always taken in a kindly way. Whether such touchiness was less keenly felt in the West is conjectural; whether fewer immigrants, therefore, returned home from there is also a speculative matter. But other factors did keep "western foreigners" from going back in large numbers. Distance, in an age before the airplane, was one of these factors. Still another was heavy investment in farm machinery, vineyards, and orchards. A western immigrant who had become deeply engrossed in ranching usually had a good deal to give up. Family responsibilities also grew apace as the yearning to repatriate usually diminished.[33]

An emotional experience generally awaited those who returned, even temporarily. One returnee found Naples "the most kaleidoscopically animated city in the world," a place where "commotion is king and tumult is queen," a city in motion:

[32] Theodore Saloutos, *They Remember America* (Berkeley, 1956), and Wilbur S. Shepperson, *Emigration and Disenchantment*, discuss the reasons why Greeks and Englishmen returned home.

[33] Of the 3,174 Italians who landed in New York during April, 1896, 27.17 per cent had been in the country before. There is evidence, however, that a lower percentage out west engaged in remigration. See Industrial Commission, *Reports*, XV, lxxviii. Carr, "The Coming of the Italian," *Outlook*, Vol. LXXXII (February 24, 1906), 422, points out that more than 104,000 Italians returned to their homeland in the year 1904.

People, horses, wagons, carriages, bicycles, donkeys, autos, hearses, wheelbarrows, flower carts, fruit carts, vegetable carts, pass as if on a revolving stage. Everybody is talking, gesticulating, singing, laughing, as though there was just so much action to be gotten out of life, and this was the last day. It is all contagious, electrifying.[34]

Thornton Wilder, in his novelette *The Cabala* (New York, 1926), reflects upon the changes that overtook returning immigrants: "They had invested their savings in the diamonds on their fingers, and their eyes were not less bright with anticipation of a family reunion. One foresaw their parents staring at them, unable to understand the change whereby their sons had lost the charm the Italian soil bestows upon the humblest of its children, noting only that they have come back with bulbous features, employing barbarous idioms and bereft forever of the witty psychological intuition of their race. Ahead of them lay sleepless nights above their mothers' soil floors and muttering poultry."

Returnees, lugging along imitation leather suitcases, became familiar figures in the Italian villages. They usually dressed expensively but in poor taste. The men wore coats that were too long, ties that were gaudy and wide, Panama hats, and the inevitable heavy gold watch chain. Along with costly Havana cigars, gold objects were *de riguer*. Returnee immigrants were a study in gold—gold cigarette cases, gold pins stuck into ties, and showy imitation gold rings adorning one or more fingers. Above all, one's front teeth had to be faced with gold. Women who had left their native villages with black scarves on their heads returned wearing ridiculous-looking bulky hats, their patent leather black purses stuffed with dollar bills. In short, the returning immigrant's display of prosperity was considered amusing back home—or their vulgar materialism aroused violent envy. Yet good-hearted returnees, like the Saturno family, were eager to help their native village by building a new water fountain or buying the church a new clock.[35]

Some who had come back only for a short time to show off

[34] Michael A. Musmanno, *The Story of the Italians in America*, 158.
[35] Based on Pola, *Stars*, 281.

wealth, became enamored of their local village. A few became peasants again and re-established intimacy with their local countryside. The great United States depression of 1929 and Fascist promises of jobs in the homeland encouraged these folk. Relatives too urged them to stay on. Unmarried returnees met local women, settled down, forgot their broken English. Often they became the only village residents able to afford two-story houses with balconies and brass doorknobs as well as prestigious Fiat autos. During the Abyssinian War of 1935 and World War II, persons who let their United States re-entry permits expire ended up being drafted for military service by the Fascist regime. These lived to curse the day they left the states.

An historian of immigration has suggested that the return European migration should receive greater attention.[36] Returnees tried to introduce American ideas, techniques, and methods into their homeland, and, sometimes, the industry, thrift, and cleanliness of "model immigrants" was admired there. Looked upon as successes, Yankeefied Italians were eager to recount the wonders of the New World to all who would listen, to confirm the content of past letters home. Those who had remained behind still stood in awe of that fabled land where Indians had yielded up gold so that immigrants could fill their teeth with it. Their relatives also described western America as a place of equality and opportunity. A new familiarity with the Far West made some emigrants after 1924 no longer content to stop at New York, the eastern gateway. These moved across the country by rail or auto, or via the Panama Canal, toward the western gate, San Francisco.

Undiminished tension remained between the first and second generation. Immigrant parents had taught their children skepticism about the world and the people in it, in part to protect them against disappointments. Back in the homeland, where families were beset by premature death, lingering illness, and unpredictable tragedy, it was an unspoken rule not to take on burdens outside one's family. Once security increased in America, however, harsh-

[36] Marcus Lee Hansen, *The Immigrant in American History* (Cambridge, 1942), 196.

ness toward others softened. The second generation no longer misinterpreted the competition of neighbors as a threat to existence. As the less hostile American environment seemed to highlight co-operation, endemic fear of the outside world, like respect for authority, underwent inevitable generational changes.

As the sons of immigrant farmers came of age, their offspring, born on American soil, grew to love that soil. They, furthermore, were more progressive than their parents in wresting from it the riches of the earth. Replacing the sweat and grime of their fathers, came experimentation with new farm machinery and equipment, new varieties of seed and fertilizer, and new crops. Just as the Toscano cigar smoke of the older generation no longer swathed Italian ranch houses so did old ways of agriculture disappear. The sons of immigrants, by joining the same farm co-operatives as their American neighbors, achieved social acceptance. As cultural inhibitions weakened, those immigrant children who became professional folk (in part because they could now afford to be educated) cast off their parents' reliance upon foreign values, the very reliance that had given those parents security.

In a "reversal of the generations," impatient young people taught their elders new concepts. About this a sociologist has written: "Rather than the parent teaching the child the old culture patterns, the child often interpreted the new culture to the parent."[37] This phenomenon was, of course, the opposite of the European experience. There the older generation remained firmly in command. As the homeland formed a steadily less significant part of the immigrant experience, one immigrant child recalled his parents' loyal concept of "Italia," that:

> ancient soil which they, aliens in a foreign land, could neither deny nor yet forget completely—the Italy of their childhood, motherland, home, source of all their deepest memories and deepest desires—and mine too? Mine, who had never smelled the ground my father had trod, who had never known the fields and the grass, the hum of the crickets and the odor of the vineyards at night; who had never lain and looked at the clouds floating across the blue Italian sky? No, for

[37] Pisani, *Italian in America*, 161.

this land which was to my father's generation the source . . . there remained in my veins no more than a distant echo, as of a story dimly told and dimly remembered; and this too was fitting.[38]

About the alienation of the second generation from the Italy of their fathers the writer of these same lines observed:

Myself, for example, born in America, brought up in the schools and the streets of the New World, creating a life and being created by it—what knew I of Italy? A country built like a deformed shoe depending from maps of Europe pored over in musty schoolrooms; a name, a flavor, a language, which my people spoke; what reality was there in all this, what remembrance?[39]

Immigrant parents, by their example, never allowed children to minimize the relationship of success to long hours of work. Success meant maintaining *onore di famiglia*, cohesive family pride and honor. Not to labor for one's family was to risk a *brutta figura*, or loss of dignity. By the work of all members of a family, and through self-sacrificing perseverance, the immigrant could prevail, even over more experienced American neighbors. Whether in the San Joaquin Valley of California or in the berry fields of Independence, Texas, the immigrant code tolerated few human parasites. Whether picking cotton or cultivating peach trees, everyone was supposed to work. Only through frugality and work could the Italian achieve his greatest ideal—land ownership and its corollary, independence. To make their children independent and fully competitive, immigrant parents, therefore, taught a disguised brand of materialism.[40]

With material success, however, came those internal negative changes in attitude that caused tension between young and old as well as the erosion of family feeling. The teachings of parents were increasingly rebuffed or covertly disobeyed. As individualism grew, opposing traditional family values waned. Children came

[38] Pagano, *Golden Wedding*, 86.

[39] Pagano, *The Paesanos*, 194.

[40] Leonard W. Moss and Walter H. Thompson, "The South Italian Family, Literature and Observations," *Human Organization*, Vol. XVIII (Spring, 1959), 35–41.

320

to resent established patterns of authority. The dictates of parents seemed unreasonable in the new environment. Immigrant women and children demanded more contact with the outside world. Pagano describes the mounting tension between the generations after one of his prodigal brothers returned home to Colorado:

> Lou told us of the places he had been. New York and St. Louis and New Orleans. He had been to San Francisco, too, where the ships came from China; and he told us about the Grand Canyon and Yosemite, and the great trees that grew in Oregon. We listened with all our ears—all except my father who . . . sat silently. Lou paid no attention to him. It was almost as though he was boasting about his travels to irritate my father. And you could feel the breach widening between them. It was like a wall that each passing moment built higher. But none of the rest of us cared. For the first time in our memory my father had been pushed into the background. Lou was the important person in the house now, and he dominated every-thing that went on in it. And all of us shivered in secret delight. It was as though Lou were paying off the grievances which each of us, through the years of parental authority, had accumulated against my father, and to which we had never, until now, had any recourse.[41]

By the time members of the first generation had reached old age they lamented the fact that the second could not also find its pleasures among the simple things of life, as in "the good old days." It was difficult for these two generations to communicate. When the son of a California vineyardist tried to explain *why* his generation was different, words did not come easily:

> Dad, when you first came west, you had very little money and almost no means by which you could leave your land, even for a short trip. Most of your friends had come to America from 1907 to 1913. You were all broke together; you all had troubles in common, and you shared your happiness, success and sorrows in common. And those days, sitting under your grape arbor drinking wine and playing *boccie* was, naturally, a great relaxation. Why expect the same from us? Today even your own generation—what is left of it—has lost its early unity. Many of your old friends are jealous of the success of

41 Pagano, *Golden Wedding*, 107.

their former fellow immigrants. With riches came a falling apart of those close-knit afternoons under our grape arbor.[42]

As the years the immigrant spent in America increased, he could virtually feel prosperity in the air. Pagano describes his parents' growing security, first at Salt Lake City, then at Los Angeles. He points out that his father's saloon gave him a prosperous living and how his family became "solid members of the community, sober, industrious and well-established." The immigrant's growing self-respect came to be the very heart of his community life:

> Now there was this house in Lincoln Heights, overlooking the city, now there was the street car line into town, to the market, with its clamoring, busily shopping crowds; now there were Saturday nights, with the money sack dumped onto the kitchen table, and the ledger book where my father kept his accounts (the ham with hot peppers and eggs sizzling on the stove, meanwhile, and the jug of illicit red wine waiting); now there was talk of investing in property with the money they were accumulating, and, perhaps, a trip to Italy before they died. Then Rose with her second baby, and Marguerite about to get married, and Vincent promoted to teller in the bank. Ever-surging, ever-replenishing future.[43]

Looking back over the past, however, Pagano could not help but think of his parents' early difficulties:

> I thought of Coalville and their struggles there. I thought of them as their wedding picture showed them—the stalwart, red-cheeked youth who had been my father, with his swirling black mustache and great barrel chest; the timid, big-eyed girl who was my mother— and I thought of all the promise life had held for them in those days, the promised glory which America, the promised land, had held forth to their eager and hopeful hearts.[44]

Pagano, a writer, joined the Hollywood movie industry as had Rudolph Valentino—who, in such films as *The Sheik*, inspired

---

[42] Quotation is based upon the recollections of Chris Manna of Acampo, California, a friend of the author.

[43] Pagano, *Golden Wedding*, 81, 224.

[44] *Ibid.*, 251.

pardonable pride in Italian men as the most successful lover of the silver screen.

Each year brought increased affluence to both first and second generations. This did not, however, draw the two groups closer together. Each sat under the family grape arbor; but, unbelievable as it may seem, some oldsters resented the successes of their younger folk. These members of the first generation nursed regrets that *they* had not had the opportunity to receive an American education. This attitude flawed the relationship even between fathers and sons, as the suspicion welled up in the minds of the former that they could have bested their offspring had they been given similar opportunities. Such perverse thoughts made for uneasy tension between two age levels. Deep respect for education (which the former had never received) made elders intolerant of those who wasted it.

A study of minority attitudes toward learning in United States cities indicates that American Jews showed a greater respect for education than did Italian immigrants. Jews tended to view learning as a vital stepping stone toward upward mobility. A contrary South Italian peasant notion that man is subject to a destiny (*destino*), or a fate beyond his control, impeded the assimilation of second-generation children in urban environments. The South Italian stress on family, as an alternative to education, also surely interfered with the immigrant's upward mobility. Furthermore, overly strong family ties irritated the second generation's revolt against the established power structure.[45]

A serious Italian immigrant problem was this overstrong family structure. Mother-centered and father-dominated, it remained rigid and deeply ingrained. Immigrants from the villages of southern Italy and Sicily, especially, brought inflexible provincial mannerisms with them. One of these was that family welfare came before personal ambition. Although *most* immigrant parents wanted as much education as possible for their children, in some families a "bad" child might be one who left home for an educa-

[45] Fred L. Strodtbeck, "Family Interaction, Values, and Achievements," in David C. McClelland, *et al, Talent and Society* (New York, 1958), 135–91.

tion. The "good" child stayed home to help. The "ideal" child might be someone like Perry Como or Joe DiMaggio; although they became non-intellectual "celebrities," they remained big-hearted, generous, and relatively unchanged boys.

Other differences divided the generations. Some immigrant elders felt that their youngsters, after mingling with prominent persons, deprecated that proud reserve and dignity (*dignità*) within which peasants were expected to behave. In provincial Italy, not to keep one's place in society was, indeed, an impertinence. To "make time" at the expense of this personal dignity was not understood by the first generation. An unconscious sense of guilt was thereby generated.

Pagano recalled that his mother and father and their *paesani* friends "seemed oblivious of the passing of the time." They were, in essence, "lost in the past, lost in their youth." As he listened to them he remembered "the thousand and one tales" they told:

> that reached back to a poverty-stricken childhood in the Old Country and that swept forward into the America of another and vanished day, an America which was, to their eager eyes and hopeful hearts, a truly Promised Land: I saw the barren wooden shacks, the deep shafts striking into the heart of the ground, the coal-dust-blackened men coming home at sunset from the mines. . . . I had not transformed it by my young blood and young desire into the fruitful life which for them it had been.[46]

It was natural that immigrant offspring, who had seen mothers and fathers travel the road from poverty to riches, as well as the replacement of horse and buggy by the airplane, no longer fully shared the same values. They had outgrown the environment of their elders. Immigrant children aped the mores and customs of less rigidly ruled friends. Why continue to live together in a rural community? Why should daughters not select future husbands without parental sanction? In the new environment it became unspeakably old-fashioned to turn one's unopened pay envelope over to parents.

[46] Pagano, *The Paesanos*, 18–19.

324

Unlike their parents, members of the second generation reached out for social status, moved into better neighborhoods, and stressed a new identity. A psychological study of second-generation Italians distinguishes three "reaction-types"—rebels who gravitated increasingly toward the "American way of life"; the "in-group" which adhered to the values of the Italian community; and the "apathetic," who retired from ethnic conflict and who thereby minimized nationality groupings.[47]

Erik Erikson's book *Young Man Luther* (New York, 1958) describes a split in ancestral images that is apt to occur in the second generation of migrating families. Second-generation peasants, like Luther, are frequently highly ambivalent about their ancestry. What psychiatrists call a "negative identity fragment" sometimes follows. A family may wish to live down part of its past identity—even though it may sentimentalize the "family romance" at times. This creates considerable emotional conflict.

Second-generation ethnic liberation came about on both economic and social grounds. Between the wars the Italian out west was not kept out of particular neighborhoods or clubs, so long as he could afford them financially. The second generation did not personally feel throbs and pangs of shame. The new social strata in which its members moved severed connection with past irritations. America's racist misconceptions faded, and third and fourth generations came to maturity and forgot their origins altogether, to become lost in the security of a plural society.

Slowly even naturalized citizens attained government positions. As city commissioners, judges, town clerks, or county supervisors, they prepared themselves for responsibilities at all levels of government, even the national political scene. This process, which involved the wooing of immigrants by politicians at vote-getting time, helped improve their status. Further loss of ethnic identity and adaptation to the western environment by dissolution of old ties, traditions, folkways, and prejudices resulted.

By the 1920's the Italian immigrants had achieved new status.

[47] Irvin L. Child, *Italian or American? The Second Generation in Conflict*, *passim*.

Some had grown more conservative. These voted for the Republican Party, disassociated themselves from strikes and socialism, embraced nationalist views, and, as has been seen, even became nativists, of sorts. An authoritarian past, derived from a Catholic heritage and from respect for stability, made them preservers of order, rather than radical innovators. Such persons emphasized law-abiding, "proper," public behavior. With most Italians the American melting pot came to mean respect for institutions that represented authority—banks, churches, and the army. Under the umbrella of citizenship, family, and newly acquired business connections, the supercitizens among them paraded loyalty to the established order. If they were not overt flag-wavers, these at least wanted to be more than worthy of the New World in which they lived. Their mottoes lauded "deeper roots and loyalties" than they had given to Italy itself. Some anglicized both first and last names; Lombardi became Lombard, and Tomassini was changed to Thomas. Newspaper tributes to individuals who had "made good" now appeared regularly. As immigrant success became newsworthy, journalistic accounts lauded the most prosperous immigrants in "jubilee" or "anniversary" numbers of newspapers, or in connection with foreign folk festivals, patriotic demonstrations, and feast days.

Italians sought to overcome the stigma fastened upon them by the Al Capones and Chicago-style criminal gang members. No one was harsher in condemning gangsters than the immigrant himself. Western Italians of the first generation were quick to point out that a higher percentage of the second than of the native-born, "old" immigrants lived in cities. There, social dependency and criminality were more prevalent than in "cleaner" rural neighborhoods. Indeed, as the 1920's burst upon America with jazz and bootleg booze, the immigrant was wont to blame the very environment for "causing" the emergence of a Capone:

> In place of the 'Festa Campestre,' (the village dance) the 'Festa Patronale,' (the feast of the patron saint) America offers to the Italian man the curse of the saloon, the poisonous atmosphere of cheap moving pictures, and the dangers of the slum dance hall. In

Italy we know the difference between a peasant who has lived there always and one who has spent a few years in America and then gone back. The former is poorer but the latter is quite rotten.[48]

Doubtless an overstatement of the culpability of the environment, this particular passage concerned the eastern United States, which stood in contrast to the western states, where crime among second-generation Italians was then less well known.

By 1930, America's "Great Immigration" was virtually at an end. Except for a few refugees or displaced persons, immigration, under the rigid control of the Immigration Act of 1924, had practically ceased. Between the two world wars the problems that faced all Americans confronted its foreign population as well. Prohibition, the rise of the dictators, the urbanization of the country, and the great depression all confused the social pattern. Prohibition continued to seem bizarre to Italians. In quiet defiance they went on brewing both beer and wine. Their youngsters skipped many a Saturday evening bath when the family tub was filled with mysterious fermenting alcoholic beverages. As to the depression, it increased the competition for jobs, in which foreigners were at some disadvantage. Fortunately the mid-1930's brought a higher standard of living for them, as well as for the nation as a whole. With the return to prosperity came a reduction of competition with non-immigrant workers. Immigrant unionization by the American labor movement helped take the ethnic tension off competition with other "cheap laborers." Employer and employee discrimination was subsequently reduced.

The problem of the dictators, however, created continuing embarrassment, particularly as one of these was a countryman of theirs. During the Mussolini era, immigrant nostalgic nationalism grew more responsive, however, to Italophilism than to Fascist ideology. Twenty-one years of fascism from 1922 to 1943, indeed, convinced immigrants that their patriotism could not ultimately be given to a Fascist homeland. Most, therefore, refused to modernize their *Italianità* to fit the Duce's brand of politics. Among these was Arturo Toscanini, in whom all Italians took exceptional

[48] Sartorio, *Social and Religious Life,* 22.

pride as the greatest musical conductor of modern times; he, too, permanently immigrated to America, after having begun formal retirement in the homeland. A 1928 booklet about the Italians, published in California, called fascism "the shame of the homeland." Despite what a Luigi Villari might write, back in that homeland, about the immigrant attitude, the chasm between Italy and her progeny in America grew virtually unbridgeable. Immigrants who originally approved of fascism later admitted they had been blinded to the evils of Mussolini's regime by his dramatic Ethiopian imperialistic adventure, as well as by his impressive programs of draining swamps, building bridges, roads, and hospitals, and making other public improvements. When the United States finally went to war against Italy in 1941, its immigrants, almost to a man, repudiated the political regime in Italy.[49]

In World War II the sons of the immigrants brought them a renown never before possible. After the war the Italians of America again showed their loyalty in another special way. This was during Italy's desperate anti-Communist struggle of 1948. In the Italian elections that year, with the United States trying to rebuild Europe, Communists seemed on the verge of coming to power. Spontaneously, immigrants wrote their relatives thousands of letters urging them to back Italy's newly won democracy.

Some six million persons of Italian origin ultimately lived in the United States. They formed one of the lesser strains of America's culture. North America's literary nourishment, after all, had come by way of England. Countless more travel accounts and journals about the United States had been published by other foreigners than by Italians. Although contact between the two countries had been constant, there was only a slight intellectual substratum to support it. Actually "American sympathy with Italian republicanism faded away in a fascination with Italy as a jewel in the Old World Museum."[50]

The Italian conception of America and the American appraisal

[49] Villari, *Gli Italiani*, 24, erroneously makes it appear to his Italian audience that most Italo-Americans approved of fascism.

[50] Strout, *Image*, 110.

of Italy remained indistinct until after World War II. Whereas Italian immigrants had given their allegiance to America, its materialism had disgusted visiting intellectuals like Ugo Ojetti and Giuseppe Giacosa. Conversely, the sentimentality of Italians repelled those Americans who admired practicality. As a result, each people tended to minimize the achievements of the other. While America, for the illiterate peasant, might be the land of deliverance, for Italy's intellectuals it held less appeal. But World War II, following upon Italy's escape from fascism's corrupting provinciality, caused an American rediscovery of Italy.

Thousands of Americans, who had traveled abroad during and after the war, had encouraged this mutual reconfrontation. By the 1950's the emergence of a democratic post-war Italy and a fad for things Italian—Necchi sewing machines, the movies of Sophia Loren, Italian sports cars, and women's knits—suddenly made "Italianity" fashionable.

After World War II, Italians were, nevertheless, avid to learn more about America. Conversely, for second-generation children, who now sought to rediscover the land of their forebears, the disorder of the Italian political scene did not inspire admiration. Italy's antiquity and mellow countryside, however, as well as lingering family associations, did attract them. The return to the place of their parents' birth had become a spiritual hegira for members of the second generation. Once there, they usually did not want to stay for long. Novelist Jo Pagano has one such returnee say: "I longed with a fierce, almost panic-stricken desire for the familiar noise of America, the clang of streetcars, the hum of machines, all the raucous clatter that was for me associated with home."[51] The materialistic children of America's immigrants yearned for breakfast ham and eggs with buttered toast and jam. Hamburgers, milk shakes, and filtered cigarettes suddenly seemed important. Clothes that needed dry-cleaning were impractical in primitive villages, and flush toilets non-existent. Nostalgia be damned; it was the plumbing they missed.

Elderly immigrants, too, could no longer understand the old

[51] Pagano, *The Paesanos,* 204.

329

country. Angelo Pellegrini's *Immigrant's Return* (1951) tells the story of an immigrant who had risen to become a university professor in Washington State. When, years after his arrival, he revisited his homeland, he was startled to learn how thoroughly Americanized he had become. The limitations of the Old World no longer revived old loyalties. A lifetime of fulfillment had occurred not in Europe but on the other side of the Atlantic. The average immigrant, upon revisiting the scenes of his youth, became aware of the changes that had come over him. When he returned to America, he had a new sympathy for it, especially after his "pick and shovel days" of brawn and sweat were over.

One of the mysteries of the Italian record in America is that so talented a people contributed so little to literature. As they moved into the middle class, they produced few historians, novelists, or poets, compared to the Irish or the Jews. No great novel has yet been written by an Italian emigrant. There is no such book to compare with Ole Rölvaag's *Giants in the Earth*, about Scandinavian emigration. As opposed to other nationalities, their cultural deprivation can be explained only in part by their non-literate peasant origins. The older generation, occupied initially with biting economic problems, could not find the time, nor had they the education, to contribute much culturally to their new homeland.

The very cohesiveness of family life may have militated against personal creativity. Only with the erosion of that introverted family structure did new generations of Italian origin attempt to write books. They wrote practically nothing that could be called history. Ideally the first generation should have written its own story, with all its legendry and folklore. Italy's major writers, among them Ignazio Silone, Carlo Levi, and Cesare Pavese, ultimately did write about the emigrant, but they were intellectuals with a word of mouth, detached view of America. The immigrant experience was inadequately written about or distorted. The Italian in the Far West founded no historical journal or historical society. His story remained untold.[52]

[52] The *Italian Quarterly*, founded at U.C.L.A. in the 1950's, was perhaps the only journal of any lasting significance begun by Italian immigrants.

Surprisingly, the Italian immigrant record has been described best by second-generation novelists, rather than by historians. Disguised as fiction, the novels of Jo Pagano and John Fante treat realistically the impact of the first generation upon its children. Fante tells what it meant to be an Italian by emotion and an American by conviction. Born in Denver, Colorado, in 1911, he spent his life in the West. As a Hollywood scenario writer he wrote about his experiences in *Full of Life* (Boston, 1952). Fante's best-known book, *Dago Red* (New York, 1940), is about a character who is ashamed of his nationality. He detests being called a "Dago" or a "Wop" and develops a brutality to compensate for his alienation. As he thinks of the past, he remembers a drunken lout of a father and a long-suffering mother who lived out her life in the family kitchen. Only tardily does Fante's principal character realize how foolish he has been to hide his past. Fante treated the same theme in his book, *Wait Until Spring, Bandini* (New York, 1938), which reflects the sense of shame caused by the broken English and Old World mannerisms of the viewpoint character's immigrant parents. His embarrassment extends even to the way in which school lunches were prepared:

> At the lunch hour I huddle over my lunch pail, for my mother doesn't wrap my sandwiches in wax paper, and she makes them too large, and the lettuce leaves protrude. Worse, the bread is home-made; not bakery bread, not "American" bread. I made a great fuss because I can't have mayonnaise and other "American" things.[53]

Fante's *Full of Life* was written as comedy, but it is as sad as comedy can be and still remain comedy. The book was produced as a film, its morbidity excised, starring Judy Holliday.

Pagano, another second-generation movie writer, in a strongly autobiographical book, *Golden Wedding*, captured the mood of foreign miners in Colorado and of fruit sellers in California. *Golden Wedding* portrays the strains of immigrant family life, with all its volatile, subsurface characteristics. Pagano's family wan-

[53] Quote is from Fante's "The Odyssey of a Wop," *American Mercury*, Vol. XXX (September, 1933), 89–97.

dered from Coalville to Denver, then to Salt Lake City, Fresno, and Los Angeles. His book treats the courage that inspired immigrants to seek their fortune so far from Italy's shores, and it pictures their lot in the West of their adoption. Pagano's novels, *The Paesanos* (1940) and *The Condemned* (New York, 1947), are likewise set in California. As an impecunious teenager, he wrote his first prose behind the counter of his father's vegetable concession in Los Angeles's Grand Central Market. Pagano published his first story in *Scribner's Magazine* at the age of nineteen and went on to become a friend of William Faulkner during the latter's stint in Hollywood.

The artist-writer Valenti Angelo describes his early years in Tuscany in *Nino* (New York, 1938) and later California years in his *Golden Gate* (New York, 1939). Each of these books he sensitively illustrated. Angelo's *Paradise Valley* (New York, 1940) keeps the same motif. In *Little Leo* (New York, 1951), Leo Politi —also a delicate illustrator—tells the charming children's story of how he revisited Italy in his Indian suit, thereby beginning a fad among the youngsters of his father's native village. Other writers of Italian origin, however, have ignored the immigrant theme. Among these was the gifted Bernard DeVoto and the Italo-American authors John Ciardi, Hamilton Basso, and Frances Winwar (Francesca Vinciguerra).[54]

The western immigrant theme has been treated by occasional non-Italian writers. Idwal Jones made California's northern Swiss-Italian wine growing country the literary backdrop of the portrait he paints in *The Vineyard* (New York, 1946). Alice Tisdale Hobart's piece of western fiction, *The Cup and the Sword* (New York, 1942), set in California's San Joaquin and Napa valleys, includes an account of the Griffanti family, Italians who people its pages, as do Frenchmen and Armenians. Sidney Howard's Pulitzer Prize–winning play *They Knew What They Wanted* (1928) drew national interest to the Italianate vineyards of the Napa Valley. In 1956, Frank Loesser converted Howard's play into a popular

[54] Other examples are in Olga Peragallo (ed.), *Italian-American Authors and Their Contribution to American Literature.*

Broadway musical entitled *The Most Happy Fella,* a high-spirited show with colorful Verdi-like motifs, among them "Abbondanza" and "Sposalizio." A similar excursion into drama was the 1957–58 film *Wild Is the Wind,* starring Anna Magnani and Anthony Quinn, a portrayal of nationalistic conflicts posed by life on a western sheep ranch.[55]

In addition to drama, other influences, such as the effect of Italian cooking upon American cuisine, deserve to be examined. The freer immigrant attitude toward drink and food seemed to fit in with life in the American West. As its cities matured, major restaurant chefs, among them Alex Perino at Los Angeles, earned real prestige in their field. The activities of western foreigners in the arts, and the influence of the West upon their work, are among other obscure topics untouched as non-fiction or fiction. As a field for literary exploitation, the role of foreign fishermen netting their catch has been only hinted at by John Steinbeck. And no one has really written about the western immigrant miner, logger, or rancher.

Scattered throughout the West, the Italians were too few in numbers to change its culture radically. Yet, their assimilation into its life stream subtly influenced America in one more way. This was an ideational influence—the "American Italy" theme originally employed effectively during the nineteenth century in tourist promotion. This popular way of looking at the West as a "Garden of the World" was related to the myth of California as a "Garden of Italy." This symbolism stressed Mediterranean similarities between Old World and New. The "Garden of Italy" concept, however, developed independently of immigrants in the West. Its inspirers were actually "Anglos." Although indifferent to most foreigners, they admired Mediterranean antiquity in architecture and literature, and made a bid for the prestige which American tourists associated with the European "grand tour." Foreign artisans in California helped the cause along by creating the Italianate physical atmosphere so popular with the Victorian

---

[55] Ideally, such a film might have been directed by either of two Italo-American Western producers, Frank Capra or Vincente Minnelli.

333

"better class." Except for seekers after this sort of "culture," other Americans more frequently thought of the Italian language (if they thought of it at all) as that of their vegetable man instead of Dante. However inattentive to foreigners the snobbish custodians of pioneer historical societies may have been, it was clear that immigrants had come to live among their neighbors for all time.[56]

Although it is difficult to isolate the contributions of any ethnic group to a new culture, what did the Italians bring to America that lingers on today? One can speak of characteristics: For the Italians these included an authoritarian tradition of family unity; a village or "town square" background; cosmopolitanism in food and living habits; the almost unconscious Greco-Roman folk tradition of Mediterranean civilization plus the Medieval, authoritative heritage of the Roman Catholic Church. A warm people, the Italians tended to enrich the emotional life of the places in which they settled. They frequently introduced color, vitality, and artistry into the sometimes bleak, even austere, American scene. Though they conformed in their own dress and appearance, there was little repression of beauty in Italians, especially in language and art. In almost every major American city there were parks and private grounds where terrazzo-layers, stonemasons, landscapers, and nurserymen left behind evidence of their inventiveness.

Whenever applause for their efforts flagged, the immigrants themselves developed and fanned a self-congratulatory environment and mystique. Supported on Columbus Day and on the Fourth of July by politicians with an eye cocked toward the foreign vote, immigrant newspapers, lodges, and fraternal organizations reveled in repeating all those uncritical clichés about how well the "foreign element" had blended into "the spirit of America." Extollers of the immigrants produced statistics about how many of them had become federal and state officials, professors,

---

[56] Regarding the "Garden of Italy" concept, see Rolle, "Italy in California," *The Pacific Spectator* (Autumn, 1955), 408–19; and Rolle's "Success in the Sun: The Italians in California," in Clifford (ed.), *Westerners Brand Book*, 13–31; as well as Rolle's *California: A History*, 368–69. The "Garden of the World" concept is discussed in Henry Nash Smith's *Virgin Land* (Cambridge, Mass., 1950).

judges, artists, scientists, and backers. All sorts of evidence could be totted up to prove resounding success.

Little was said, however, about the ethnic price of all this "success." Some historians are bound to feel that the melting-pot experience was more epochal than was the loss of national identity. Others point out that the price of the immigrant's adjustment to American society has meant no less than the tragic loss of his own identity. Immigrants who adjusted, in essence, melted into invisibility, ethnically speaking.[57] This view, however penetrating, has been rejected by the vast majority of immigrants themselves. They chose to trade their original identity for the Horatio Alger image of success. To be more American than the Americans has been the goal of most immigrants.

The foreign record in the West challenges the cliché that the history of immigrants in America is basically the "history of alienation." The rapidity with which most nationalities were assimilated suggests, instead, accommodation and acquiescence to the environment. About this phenomenon Eric Hoffer writes:

> It is doubtful whether without the vast action involved in the conquest of a continent, our nation of immigrants could have attained its amazing homogeneity in so short a time. Those who came to this country to act (to make money) were more quickly and thoroughly Americanized than those who came to realize some lofty ideal. The former felt an immediate kinship with the millions absorbed in the same pursuit. It was as if they were joining a brotherhood. They recognized early that in order to succeed they had to blend with their fellow men, do as others do, learn the lingo and play the game.[58]

Although provocative studies of the alien's loneliness have been written, these leave one with the impression that in nineteenth-century America the term "immigrant" meant a foreign-born individual living in some large and hostile eastern city. Too much has been made of the "inner struggle" of the immigrant for security and status in an unfriendly New World. For most immigrants

[57] See *Annual Report of the American Historical Association* (Washington, 1964), 12.
[58] Hoffer, *True Believer*, 111.

who went west, life was not a disappointment but, rather, a challenge, even an adventure. Their reactions to America were enthusiastic and fresh—in short, the opposite of disillusioned. They generally escaped ethnic crowding, slums, ghettoes, and a large measure of prejudice, partly because of the western outlook. Western attitudes were often generous and easy going, especially in small communities, where immigrants were less concentrated than in a purely urban setting. Studies of other nationalities than the Italians bear out these generalizations.[59]

Despite their initial sufferings, the immigrants found freedom in America's West rather than rigidity, openness rather than closed privilege. A few were too old or dour to change, but most sensed the expansiveness. In both horizon and spirit, they became anything but refugees. If they seemed disloyal to their original homeland, they also cast off traditional prejudices and were liberated from past uncertainties. As expectant capitalists, immigrants accepted the middle-class American belief that men were masters of their environment. For Italians the West remained the place of hope they had heard about across the seas. In California or Texas they could go as far as their talents would take them, or so they believed. If discrimination occurred, they could wear it down—just as they had withstood climate, economics, life itself. Although that life had its grubby and dull side, all men, immigrants included, seemed perfectible in the new environment. People who knew their goals and who worked hard could create in this

[59] In fairness to Handlin's *The Uprooted*, perhaps he never meant his theme to be more than a poetic statement inapplicable to the immigrant experience in the entire United States. But his view of the immigrant is undeniably sentimental, stereotyped, and maudlin, told in such phrases as "the hot tenement room," "the pinned-up sleeve where the crushed arm had been" and "the muffled sobs through the wall where the weary mother could not rest." Professor Donald T. Hata, Jr., is completing a study of Japanese immigrants that will criticize the Handlin approach, adding to the refutations of Rudolph Vecoli and Norman Pollack, as described in notes of the introduction. Other forthcoming articles bordering upon my book are: Moses Rischin, "Beyond the Great Divide: Immigration and the Last Frontier," *Journal of American History* (1968); and Joseph Giovinco, "Democracy and Banking: The Bank of Italy and California's Italians," *California Historical Society Quarterly*. As the history of western immigration is still fragmentary, many other articles in this field are bound to appear.

New World the universe they deserved. Armed with this discovery, those who had so longed for it were rewarded by a better day than they had known before. These became not "the Uprooted" but the Upraised.

Appendices

APPENDIX A: *Italian Clerics in the Spanish Southwest*

ITALIAN PRIESTS were long excluded from missionary work in the Americas because the *Patronato Real* of Spain and the Portuguese *Padroado* dictated a virtual national monopoly over such activity; further, Italy, unlike France, was for centuries neither a nation nor a colonizing force. Hence, if Italian priests wished to be missionaries, they had to incorporate themselves into Spanish or Portuguese missionary contingents. About 1660 the Spanish King allowed a fourth of the missionaries to overseas dominions to come from three geographical localities: Milan, the Two Sicilies, and his "Imperial Lands."

Thereafter the Roman church recruited much of its missionary strength from the Italian peninsula. In Spanish America during the seventeenth and eighteenth centuries a sizable number of Italian clerics arrived. In both New Spain and New France, Jesuit "Black Robes," as well as the members of other religious orders, made imposing contributions to the taming of the wilderness.

In North America, whether in the Spanish Southwest or in the French Mississippi region, the basic pattern of colonization was, however, established by Spaniards and Frenchmen rather than by Italians. Yet it is surprising how much freedom to Christianize the wilderness Spain gave to foreign clerics. The remoteness of its frontiers, of course, helped to dictate this freedom. And, in the earlier explorative tradition of Columbus, Verrazano, and the

Cabots, many Italian clerics went to work under the flag of Castile, to subdue savage aborigines whose souls were in need of salvation.

A full century before the first Englishmen landed at either Jamestown or Plymouth Rock, soldiers and priests of the King of Spain had gone into the Caribbean and then on to Mexico. Northward from there they enlarged Spain's sphere of influence. An almost legendary belief that her conquistadores sought only gold has obscured Spain's genuine interest in colonizing the new lands in which her colonists found themselves. Although in small bands and sometimes individually the King's men relentlessly pursued gold, they, with equal zealousness, worked to save souls and to bring order to a wilderness. One finds a variety of nationalities involved in the process by which Spain asserted its sovereignty over southwestern North America.

One of the most controversial, enigmatic, and colorful figures ever to appear in Spain's new American empire was the Italian priest Fray Marcos de Niza, or Fra Marco da Nizza (1495–1558), who led a controversial foray into present-day Arizona and New Mexico. In 1539, after erecting a cross on a heap of stones in the middle of a wilderness, he took possession of the entire region to the north of the Santa Cruz Valley of today's Arizona for the Spanish Crown. This accomplishment, in the company of a Negro companion, Estebanico, served to fortify the legend of the fabled Seven Cities of Cibola, first brought back to Mexico City by the Spanish castaway Cabeza de Vaca. Fray Marco's inaccurate description of the gleaming golden walls of several Indian "cities" (which later proved to be white-washed adobes) helped lead to the mounting of the large Coronado expedition of 1540. Coronado's *entrada* would penetrate the mainland as far distant as Kansas for Spain. Although Fray Marcos misled his superiors as to wealth in the distant north, he became, for a time, Father Provincial of the Franciscan Order in Mexico.

Fray Marcos was to be followed by a monumental Italian, Eusebio Francesco Kino. In the settlement of that arid, windswept, and dusty Southwest, the most prominent of various Italian Jesuits to be sent to Spain's outpost of empire was the German-educated Father Kino (sometimes Chino or Chini). Born in 1645 at Segno, near Trento, in 1678, he left Genoa via Seville and Cádiz, for the New World, not reaching Mexico until 1681. Kino's activities were many and diverse. The cattle industry of the Southwest dates in large measure from the ranchos established by him throughout a belt 250 miles in width. At the missions he founded, Kino not only introduced many varieties of livestock, but European grains and such fruits as grapes and pomegranates. Kino has also been credited with making the first astronomical observations in western America.[1]

Kino's study of cartography implemented the Spanish advance northward. He explored the Altar, Sonora, Santa Cruz, and San Pedro rivers, in addition to the lower Gila and Colorado. In 1683 he was appointed royal cosmographer of an expedition commanded by Admiral Isidro de Atondo y Antillon which unsuccessfully tried to colonize Baja California. During the period 1698–1701, Kino prepared maps, ultimately printed in Paris, proving for the first time that California was not an island. He also made major improvements in mapping Spain's North American empire from the Colorado River to the Gulf of Mexico.[2]

Kino's explorations, made over a period of twenty-five years, on horseback and afoot, put Pimería Baja (in northern Mexico) and Pimería Alta (in southern Arizona) on the map. He made some fifty journeys of 100 to 1,000 miles in length, including six trips to the Gila River, two to the land of the Yumas on the Colorado, and one into what was then called "California." Kino, who covered from 25 to 75 miles per day, was indeed the "Padre on Horseback" that his biographer, Herbert Eugene Bolton, once called him. He has been described as "merciful to others but cruel to himself." At least twenty southwestern cities owe their origins to this indefatigable traveler.

[1] See Ellen Shaffer, "The Comet of 1680–1681," *Quarterly*, Historical Society of Southern California, Vol. XXXIV (March, 1952), 57–70; and Kino's own *Esposición astronómica de el cometa* (Mexico, 1681).

[2] See Ernesto J. Burrus, *Kino Reports to Headquarters* . . . (Rome, 1954); and the same author's *Kino's Plan for the Development of Pimería Alta, Arizona, and Upper California* (Tucson, 1961).

During the years 1687 to 1711, Kino established some twenty missions in "Greater Sonora." After founding Nuestra Señora de Los Dolores on the San Miguel, he built an important mission system on the Magdalena and Altar rivers. In the present-day United States the most important of these was San Xavier del Bac, now a national monument near Tucson. As the first person to attempt colonization of Lower California, Kino was, according to Bolton, an explorer, astronomer, cartographer, mission builder, ranch man, cattle king, dispatcher of pack trains to mines he helped open, and defender of the frontier. Kino died in 1711 in the mission village of Santa Magdalena, which he had founded.[3]

As if to enhance the Kino legacy during the long period from 1687 to 1767 other Italian priests worked under Spanish supervision. One of these was inspector of Jesuit missions in Sonora and Sinaloa, Juan María de Salvatierra, or Salvaterra, a Milanese whose mother was of noble Visconti blood. In a position of such importance within his order, Salvatierra's activities in Lower California did much to further the work of Kino. In 1697 he founded the first of the peninsula's missions at Loreto following upon the earlier work there of Kino himself. He also established the celebrated "Pious Fund" to support continual missionary activity. In 1704, Salvatierra became provincial of the Society of Jesus in New Spain and ultimately started some seven missions.[4]

Associated with Salvatierra were the Sicilian fathers Francesco María Piccolo and Francesco Saverio Saetta. The latter was slain by the Pima Indians of Pimería Alta in 1605. Piccolo founded three more missions in Lower California.[5] In working among the

[3] See E. J. Burrus and F. Zubillaga (eds.), *Francisco J. Alegre, Historia de la Provincia de la Compañía de Jesús de Nueva Espana.*

[4] On Salvatierra, see Miguel Venegas, *Juan Maria de Salvatierra,* trans. and ed. by Margaret Eyer Wilbur (Cleveland, 1929); and Schiavo, *Four Centuries,* 80.

[5] Regarding Piccolo see E. J. Burrus, "Francesco María Piccolo (1654–1729), Pioneer of Lower California in the Light of Roman Archives," *Hispanic American Historical Review,* Vol. XXXV (February, 1955), 61–76; and Burrus, *Padre Francisco María Piccolo* . . . (Madrid, 1962); as well as Piccolo's own *Informe del Estado de la nueva Christiandad en California* (1701). See Ernest J. Burrus, *Vida del P. Francisco J. Saeta, S.J., Sangre Misionera en Sonora* (Mexico, D.F., 1961).

savage Indian tribes of the Southwest, such men sometimes met death either at the hands of natives or by starvation and exposure. During a great Indian rebellion of 1680 twenty-one missionaries and several hundred Spaniards were killed. One of the Italians to be martyred in that rebellion was Father Jesus Lombardi. Father Antonio Carbonelli also was killed in this region in 1696.[6]

It would be difficult to compile a complete list of Italian clerics in the Spanish Southwest during the seventeenth and eighteenth centuries.[7] What would seem more valuable is to establish the *relative* degree of Italian influence. Although engaged in saving souls under the flag of another nation, these priests were dressed in the robes of a church which claimed to be universal. After King Charles III of Spain expelled the Jesuits from the Mexican provinces in 1767, they fled to Italy as exiles. One of the most learned men in the order there, the Mexican-born Francisco Clavigero, went to the city of Cesena. There he published his most famous work, the four-volume Italian-language *Storia Antica del Messico,* in 1780. Likewise, his *Storia della California* was first published at Venice in 1789.[8] Such pioneer works did much to publicize and to describe the New World to Italians, and were of value in recruiting Franciscan friars who ultimately helped replace the Jesuits in the Southwest. There can be no doubt that these Italians, always working with other Europeans, tamed a vast wilderness.

[6] Theodosius Meyer, *St. Francis and the Franciscans in New Mexico* (Santa Fe, 1926), 40; Schiavo, *Civil War,* 289.

[7] According to Schiavo, *Four Centuries,* 80, there were the following other Italian clerics in Lower California from 1697 to 1767: Gerónomo Minutili of Sardinia, Benito Guisi, drowned while crossing the Gulf of California, Ignazio Maria Napoli, and Sigismondo Taraval of Lodi, as well as Giacomo Druet of Turin, and Pietro Nascimben of Venice. Branchi, "Gli Italiani nella storia della California," reproduced from *L'Universo,* Vol. XXXV (May–June, 1956), 4, mentions Fathers Minutili and Domenico Crescoli, J. J. Baegert, *Observations in Lower California,* trans. by M. M. Brandenburg and Carl L. Baumann (Berkeley, 1952), 206, names Father Miguel del Barco. Other early Italian clerics in Mexico are mentioned in F. G. Bohme, "The Italians in Mexico: A Minority's Contribution," *Pacific Historical Review,* Vol. XXVIII (February, 1959), 2.

[8] A translation is Sara E. Lake and A. A. Gray (eds.), *The History of California by Don Francisco Javier Clavigero* (Stanford, 1937).

APPENDIX B: *Pioneer Italians and the Pacific Slope*

NOT ALL THE ITALIANS to come to the New World were men of the cloth. In the earliest phases of the exploration of the Pacific coast, many were civilians in the service of Spain as historically nameless members of ship crews sailing to America. Until late in the eighteenth century, Spain claimed most of the Pacific region up to what is now the Canadian border. Italians also visited the interior of New Spain. One of these was Girolamo Benzoni, a Milanese, who as early as 1541 wandered throughout what is now greater Mexico and wrote a history and description of the region entitled *Historia del Mondo Nuovo* (Venice, 1565). Benzoni's book was later reprinted in various languages and it acquainted Italians with the geography of North America. Of similar effect in adding to Europe's knowledge of Mexico was the book, *Idea de una nueva historia general de la America Septentrional*, by the Italian chronicler Lorenzo Benaducci Boturini, published at Madrid in 1746. These works and the personal accounts of other Italians motivated south Europeans to come to America.

Peripheral to the coverage of such books, but nevertheless important, were the activities of yet another Italian traveler, Dr. Giovanni Francesco Gemelli Careri (1651–1718). This Calabrese undertook a round-the-world voyage from 1693 to 1697, the last phase of which occurred aboard a Manila galleon, plying between Manila in the Philippines and Acapulco, Mexico. The closest that Careri came to what is today the continental United States was probably the island group which he called St. Catherine's in his six-volume *Giro del Mondo* (Venice, 1719). He erroneously located an island at 36°, 4 minutes latitude that was probably Santa Catalina Island in the Santa Barbara Channel group, off southern California. The outstanding authority on the Manila galleon voyages writes: "When the galleons followed the upper California coast, they kept no nearer to it than was necessary to guide their course. . . . after the long and perilous crossing from the Philippines, pilots and commanders were averse to taking the further risks involved in the close reconnaissance of a rugged and forbidding coast." Fear of Indians (guns were handed out even to passengers) also kept the galleons out to sea.[1]

Because Careri's computation of latitude (the captain of his ship had died) is as much as two and a half degrees in error, one modern cartographer has questioned the accuracy of his observations. But it must be remembered that Careri was a doctor of civil law and not a mariner. He was, however, a keen and educated observer, and he left one of the best accounts in existence of a voyage on the Manila galleon. That portion of his trip lasted 204 days, or seven months. His book, published in 1699, the year after he returned to Italy, aroused much interest concerning Spain's New World empire. Translated into English by 1704, the book cannot be overlooked as a major cartographic source.[2]

The first Italian actually to anchor on the California coast was Captain Alejandro Malaspina, who made a voyage around the world in the years 1786 to 1788. Later, from 1789 to 1794, this mariner was placed in command of an international exploratory expedition of more than five years duration. He sailed up the west coast of Mexico from Acapulco as far as Alaska. Born in 1754, Malaspina had entered the Spanish maritime service early in life and distinguished himself sufficiently by his middle thirties to head this important scientific venture in command of the ships *Descubierta* and *Atrevida*. Seeking the fabled straits of Anián, he was disappointed not to find that passage for which mariners had searched for decades. As Malaspina sailed along the coasts of British Columbia, he, however, noted the insularity of Nootka Island, sounded the Strait of Juan de Fuca, and named various landmarks. There exist today a Malaspina Glacier, a Malaspina Strait, and a Malaspina Peak. After making various explorations, Captain Malaspina sailed back down the northwest coast to California.

---

[1] Schurz, *Manila Galleon*, 239–40.

[2] Wagner, *Cartography of the Northwest Coast*, 139; Schurz, *Manila Galleon*, 29, 253, 267, 384; see also William H. Wallace, "Journal of the Great Voyage from the Philippines to America," *Journal of American History*, Vol. II (4th Quarter, 1908), 585–86; Edward Gaylord Bourne, *Discovery, Conquest and Early History of the Philippine Islands* (Cleveland, 1907), 65. A translation of Careri's narrative is in Churchill, *Folio Collection*, IV, 1–606.

His expedition landed at Monterey on September 16, 1791. Malaspina also put ashore a corpse (one John Green who had shipped as a gunner at Cádiz), probably the first American in California.[3] A description of Malaspina's activities in California appears in *La vuelta al mundo por las corbetas* Descubierta *y* Atrevida *al mando del capitán de navio D. Alejandro Malaspina desde* 1789 *á* 1794 (Madrid, 1885). In this book, printed long after the captain's death, is to be found Malaspina's observations on the status of California. He praised Fray Fermín Francisco de Lasuén, the Franciscan father-president of the California Missions who treated him kindly during a twelve-day stay in California. Malaspina was likewise entertained by the Spanish governor, Pedro Fages. Malaspina marveled at the province's unusually fine climate and subtropical vegetation, writing:

> eran los dias suauamente serenos, por manera que las observaciones astronómicas no tuviesan la menor interrupcion; la caza, la pesca, la actividad de los soldados del presidio y los ganados excelentes que pastaban en acquellas immediaciones, suministraban ya una comida bien sabrosa, ya varios objetos tan nuevo como instructivos para la zoologia.

Upon his return to Spain, Malaspina was honored and promoted to the rank of *brigadier de escuadra,* or rear admiral, for his explorations. As a foreigner, however, he incurred the displeasure of the crown and was arrested and imprisoned from 1795 to 1805, supposedly for an intrigue concerning criticism of injustices in the Spanish colonies. Enfeebled by his long imprisonment, he died in 1809 at Mulazzo, Lunigiana, his ancestral home. Like Columbus, another Italian mariner before him in the service of Spain, he died disappointed that he had not received a just reward. Malaspina may have run afoul of Manuel Godoy, Spanish chief-of-state. Dr. Henry Raup Wagner in 1949 told this writer that in Spain he had once seen the set of treatises criticizing government in the Spanish colonies that caused Malaspina to be imprisoned.[4]

[3] See Donald C. Cutter, *Malaspina in California* (San Francisco, 1960); and Charles E. Chapman, *A History of California, the Spanish Period* (New York, 1921), 404.

In addition to those Italians like Malaspina and Botta who went to the remotest reaches of New Spain, several of her viceroys, Antonio María de Bucareli and Miguel de la Grua y Talamanca, Marques de Branciforte, seem to have been originally of Italian lineage. One should, however, exercise caution in "reading into" their life pattern attributes which are particularly Italian. More important to the record of the Italians in western North America were the actual deeds of a race of sturdy missionaries, explorers, and travelers noted for their knowledge of the world outside their Mediterranean homeland. Their talents were without doubt of great benefit to a unified and expanding Spanish empire.

APPENDIX C: *De Tonty in Mid-America*

WHILE CERTAIN ITALIANS helped Spain to plant its flag upon the remote frontiers of the King of Castile, some of their countrymen found themselves in the service of another foreign power. Thousands of miles to the east of New Spain, these Italians, like their compatriots in the Spanish Southwest, comprised a significant part of another vanguard of population—a French vanguard. By the seventeenth century the fur trade had placed France's North American frontier of settlement hundreds of miles inland from her colonization bases on the St. Lawrence River. By 1679, Robert Cavelier de la Salle had reached the Illinois country and, subsequently, he claimed the major waterways of the Mississippi basin for Louis XIV.

[4] On Malaspina's trial see Marcos Jiménez de la Espada, *Una Causa de Estado* (1881). See also Francisco Javier de Viana, *Diario del viaje explorador de las corbetas españoles* Descubierta y Atrevida (1849); William I. Morse, *Letters of Alexandro Malaspina, 1790–1791* (Boston, 1944); Galbraith, "Malaspina's Voyage Around the World," California Historical Society *Quarterly*, Vol. III (October, 1924), 215–37; Augusto Leri, "*L'influenza italiana nella grandezza di Spagna, Alessandro Malaspina e la relazione del suo viaggio*," *Rivista Marittima*, anno 38, 271–305; see also the two biographies by Carlo Caselli, *Alessandro Malaspina* (Milan, 1929), and E. Bona, *Malaspina* (Rome, 1935). See also Branchi, "*Gli Italiani nella storia della California*," reproduced from *L'Universo*, Vol. XXXV (May–June, 1956), 6.

Accompanying La Salle was the unpretentious soldier of fortune Henri de Tonty (or Tonti). Born an Italian,[1] he came from a family with a record of service to the King of France. A brother, Alfonso, also became a French Army officer in America, operating as a captain of Cadillac's at Detroit. For some years Alfonso was the civilian and military governor of Detroit. Alfonso's son, Henry, was governor at Fort St. Louis. Still another cousin commanded posts at Fort Illinois. During a French expedition to Sicily, Henri de Tonty lost his hand in combat and came to be known among the Indians as "the man with the iron hand," this because he covered his fearsome metal hand with a glove.

With La Salle, Tonty reached the Illinois region in the winter of 1679–80, and at Lake Peoria they built Fort Crevecoeur. As La Salle soon had to go back eastward toward Lakes Erie and Ontario, Tonty remained in command of the Illinois country. When La Salle rejoined Tonty he found that his subaltern had been through a mutiny and that an Iroquois invasion had forced him northward in the dead of winter. In the Wisconsin woods Tonty had lived for weeks upon roots, wild garlic buried beneath the snow, and wild game. After being seriously wounded, he finally reached safety at Green Bay at the end of 1680.

Together with La Salle he returned, after a quick recovery, to the Illinois country. At Starved Rock, a natural fortification on the Illinois, they built Fort St. Louis. Still together, they reached the broad banks of the Mississippi on February 6, 1682, but did not arrive at its mouth until the following April. Then they took formal possession of the great valley for the King of France, in whose honor they named the area Louisiana. Tonty is also credited with building Fort Niagara and constructing the *Griffin*, reputedly the first vessel to cross the Great Lakes.[2]

For a quarter of a century Tonty, despite many hardships, was faithful to the flag he carried into the wilderness for France. In

[1] On this, see the statement in Edmund R. Murphy, *Henry de Tonty* (Baltimore, 1941), 3.

[2] Goggio, *Italians*, 3.

1683 he saw his chief, La Salle, for the last time before La Salle returned to France to recruit an expedition of four hundred colonists for a new colony on the Texas coast. This colony, to be located near the mouth of the Mississippi, was to be a depot for the collection of furs and a base for protecting the Gulf Coast from enemy buccaneers. Tonty, wishing to co-operate in this venture, traveled overland to meet La Salle in 1686. On the way he built a small post on the Arkansas (once called Tonty's River), thereafter known as Tonty's Fort. But in 1687 his old chief and comrade-in-arms, La Salle, was murdered by his own companions near the Brazos River. Tonty was, for a decade and a half thereafter, in command of much of the Mississippi region for France until his death in 1703. Tonty's cousin, incidentally, was the noted fur trader Daniel Duluth.

APPENDIX D: *Numerical Distribution of Italians in Twenty-Two Western States*

WHILE THIS IS NOT basically a compilative study, it is desirable to glance statistically at the population record set by the Italians. The following table summarizes their numerical distribution in the twenty-two states covered by this book. In general, the Italian-born population in these states reached its peak about 1910. With some exceptions—as in California, Missouri, and Nevada—the Italian population in these states began to decline thereafter. If one were to include the figures for second-generation residents, the picture would be quite different. But by 1920, the first generation had begun to pass from the scene, a fact recorded in the census figures mentioned above. Soon thereafter the quota restrictions of the United States Immigration Act of 1924 had become operative, freezing an immigration pattern in the United States of only 5,500 Italians per year. As there was no serious thought of repealing this highly restrictive law, for decades its effects upon the flow of immigrants into the United States were most confining.

349

Twenty-Two States Treated in This Study

| | Foreign-Born Italians Resident There | | | | | | | (By Birth) |
	1870[1]	1880[2]	1890[3]	1900[4]	1910[5]	1920[6]	1930[7]	1940[8]
Louisiana	1,889	2,527	7,767	17,431	20,233	16,264	13,526	9,849
Arkansas	30	132	187	576	1,699	1,314	952	791
Oklahoma	*	*	11	601	2,564	2,122	1,157	893
Missouri	936	1,074	2,416	4,345	12,984	14,609	15,204	13,168
Iowa	54	122	399	1,198	5,846	4,956	3,834	3,461
Minnesota	40	124	828	2,222	9,669	7,432	6,401	5,638
N. Dakota	**	**	21	700	1,262	176	102	80
S. Dakota	4	71	269	360	1,158	413	305	238
Texas	186	539	2,107	3,942	7,190	8,024	6,550	5,451
Utah	74	138	347	1,062	3,117	3,225	2,814	2,189
New Mexico	25	73	355	661	1,959	1,678	1,259	1,148
Colorado	16	335	3,882	6,818	14,375	12,580	10,670	8,352
Arizona	12	104	207	699	1,531	1,261	822	715
Montana	34	64	734	2,199	6,592	3,842	2,840	2,265
Idaho	11	35	509	779	2,067	1,323	1,153	893
Washington	24	71	1,408	2,124	13,121	10,813	10,274	8,853
Wyoming	9	15	259	781	1,961	1,948	1,653	1,215
Oregon	31	167	589	1,014	5,538	4,324	4,728	4,083
California	4,660	7,537	15,495	22,777	63,615	88,504	107,249	100,911
Kansas	55	167	616	987	3,520	3,355	2,165	1,654
Nebraska	44	62	717	752	3,799	3,547	3,642	3,201
Nevada	199	1,560	1,129	1,296	2,831	2,641	2,563	2,258

* Not listed.

** Dakota Territory.

[1] *Compendium of the Ninth Census of the United States* (Washington, 1872), 392–93.

[2] *Compendium of the Tenth Census of the United States* (Washington, 1883), Part I, 486–87.

[3] *Abstract of the Eleventh Census of the United States* (Washington, 1894), 38–39.

[4] *United States Census Reports*, Volume I (Twelfth Census) (Washington, 1901), clxxiv.

[5] *Abstract of the Thirteenth Census of the United States* (Washington, 1914), 204–207.

[6] *Abstract of the Fourteenth Census of the United States* (Washington, 1920), 308–309.

[7] *Abstract of the Fifteenth Census of the United States* (Washington, 1930), 134–35.

[8] *Sixteenth Census of the United States* (Washington, 1943), Volume II, Parts I–VII.

Bibliography

The footnotes of this volume refer to numerous sources that do not appear in the following selected bibliography. In order to conserve space, only references that bear directly upon the experience of these particular immigrants are listed. State and national histories, directories, and guides, therefore, do not appear here although mentioned in the footnotes. Foreign-language newspapers, unless extensively used, are not cited here, although they are mentioned in the text.

Manuscripts

Gasparri, Donato M., S.J. "An Account of the Voyage of . . . ," a diary (April 19, 1867, in Archives of San Felipe di Neri Rectory, Albuquerque, New Mexico).

Kimpton, Lawrence, to author, November 29, 1955.

Larkin Papers, Bancroft Library, University of California (Berkeley).

Loria, Archille, to Frederick Jackson Turner, February 17, 1894, Huntington Library, San Marino, California.

MS Census of 1870, Treasure City, White Pine County, Nevada, Microfilm Roll 211, 1870 Census Population Schedules, National Archives, Washington, D.C.

Papanikolas, H.Z., to author, December 30, 1957.

Ravalli, Anthony, to Narcissa Caldwell, June 16, 1884, Montana Historical Society, Helena, Montana.

Record Book of the Montana Immigration Society, MS at Montana Historical Society, Helena, Montana, March 22 to April 7, 1872.

Stearns Manuscripts, Huntington Library, San Marino, California.

Via, Anthony, S.J., to author, November 30, 1955, in Jesuit Historical Archives, Oregon Province, Mount St. Michaels, Spokane, Washington.

GOVERNMENT DOCUMENTS

Abstract of the Eleventh Census of the United States, Washington, 1894. Pages 38–39.

Abstract of the Fifteenth Census of the United States. Washington, 1930. Pages 134–35.

Abstract of the Fourteenth Census of the United States. Washington, 1920. Pages 308–309.

Abstract of the Thirteenth Census of the United States. Washington, 1914. Pages 204–207.

Abstracts of the Reports of the Immigration Commission, 64 Cong., 3 sess., *Sen. Doc. 747*. Vol. I (Washington, 1911), 97.

Bureau of the Census. *Compendium of the Ninth Census of the United States*. Washington, 1872. Pages 392–93.

———. *Compendium of the Seventh Census*. Washington, 1854.

———. *Compendium of the Tenth Census of the United States*. Washington, 1883. Part I, pages 486–87.

———. *Special Reports of Religious Bodies: 1906*. Vol. I. Washington, 1910.

Bureau of Labor. *A Report on Labor Disturbances in Colorado from 1880 to 1904*. Washington, 1904.

Claghorn, Kate H. "Agricultural Distribution of Immigrants," reprinted from United States Industrial Commission *Reports*. Washington, 1901.

Edwards, Alba M., ed. "Appendix B of Hitherto Unpublished Thirteenth Census Occupation Statistics," in *Sixteenth Census of the United States (1940). Comparative Occupation Statistics, 1870–1940*. Washington, 1943.

House Journal, 2nd Session, Montana Legislature for 1866. Helena, 1867.

Meade, Emily F. "The Italian on the Land," *United States Bureau of Labor Reports*, No. 70, Vol. XIV (Washington, 1907), 475–530.

Sixteenth Census of the United States. Washington, 1943. Vol. II, Parts I–VII.

United States Census Reports. Vol. I (Twelfth Census). Washington, 1901. Page clxxiv.

United States Industrial Commission. *Reports of the Immigration Commission.* 41 vols. Washington, 1900–11.

NEWSPAPERS

Butte (Montana), *Anaconda Standard,* 1895.
Butte (Montana), *Miner,* 1894.
Carbon County News (Montana), 1955.
Denver (Colorado), *Labor Enquirer,* 1884.
Denver (Colorado), *La Parola del Popolo,* 1958.
Denver (Colorado), *Post,* 1955.
Helena (Montana), *Daily Record,* 1894.
Helena (Montana), *Daily Rocky Mountain Gazette,* 1870.
Helena (Montana), *Weekly Herald,* 1872.
Herrin (Iowa), *News,* 1905, 1911.
Lewiston *North Idaho Teller,* 1876–77.
Los Angeles *L'Italo-Americano,* 1953–66.
Los Angeles *Times,* 1947, 1961.
Missoula (Montana), *Daily Missoulian,* 1904.
New York, *L'Eco d'Italia,* 1865–1957.
New York *Tribune,* 1884.
New Orleans *Daily Picayune,* 1890–91.
New Orleans *Times-Democrat,* 1890–91.
Orofino (Idaho), *Tribune,* 1910.
Red Lodge (Montana), *Republican Picket,* 1907, 1908.
Sacramento *La Capitale,* 1922.
Salt Lake City (Utah), *The Millenial Star,* 1851–55.
San Francisco *Bulletin,* 1917.
San Francisco *Call,* 1894.
San Francisco *Chronicle,* 1880, 1947, 1948.
San Francisco *La Voce del Popolo,* 1910.
San Francisco *Star,* 1913.
Vancouver *L'Eco d'Italia,* 1957.
Vancouver *Province,* 1940, 1952.
Vancouver *Sun,* 1936.
Victoria (British Columbia) *Colonist,* 1955.
Victoria *Times,* 1955.

Virginia City (Montana), *Montana Post*, 1865.
Virginia City (Nevada), *Territorial Enterprise*, 1870–74.

THESES AND DISSERTATIONS

Bohme, Frederick G. "A History of the Italians in New Mexico," Ph.D. Dissertation in History, University of New Mexico, 1958.
Dondero, Raymond. "The Italian Settlement of San Francisco," M.A. Thesis in Geography. University of California, Berkeley, 1950.
Palmer, Hans C. "Italian Immigration and the Development of California Agriculture," Ph.D. Dissertation. University of California, Berkeley, 1965.
Waldron, Gladys H. "Antiforeign Movements in California, 1919–1929," Ph.D. Dissertation. University of California, Berkeley, 1945.

BOOKS

Arese, Francesco. *A Trip to the Prairies and in the Interior of North America, 1837–1838*. Trans. and ed. by Andrew Evans. New York, 1934.
Baker, Paul R. *The Fortunate Pilgrims: Americans in Italy*. Cambridge, 1964.
Baroni, Cleto, ed. *Gente Italiana di California*. Los Angeles, 1928.
Barziza, Decimus et Ultimus. *The Adventures of a Prisoner of War, 1863–1864*. Austin, 1965.
Beltrami, J.C. *Down the Great River*. Philadelphia, 1891.
———. *La découverte des sources du Mississippi et de la Rivière Sanglante*. New Orleans, 1824.
———. *Notizie e lettere pubblicate per cura del Municipio de Bergamo e dedicate alla Società Storica del Minnesota*. Bergamo, 1865.
———. *A Pilgrimage in Europe and America* . . . . 2 vols. London, 1828.
Beltrami, Luca. *Padre Samuele Mazzuchelli, missionario domenicano nell'America del Nord dal 1829 al 1864*. Milan, 1928.
Benzoni, G. *Historia del Mondo Nuovo*. Venice, 1565. Republished in English by Hakluyt Society, London, 1857.
Bercovici, Konrad. *On New Shores*. New York, 1925.
Berthoff, Rowland T. *British Immigrants in Industrial America, 1790–1850*. Cambridge, 1950.
Billington, Ray Allen. *America's Frontier Heritage*. New York, 1966.
———. *The Protestant Crusade, 1800–1860*. New York, 1938.

Bischoff, William N. *The Jesuits in Old Oregon, 1840–1940*. Caldwell, Idaho, 1945.

Bjork, Kenneth O. *West of the Great Divide: Norwegian Migration to the Pacific Coast, 1847–1893*. Northfield, Minnesota, 1958.

Bogue, Allan. *From Prairie to Corn Belt, Farming on the Illinois and Iowa Prairies in the Nineteenth Century*. Chicago, 1963.

Bolton, Herbert Eugene. *The Padre on Horseback*. San Francisco, 1932.

———. *Rim of Christendom*. New York, 1936.

Bonfadini, R. *Vita di Francesco Arese*. Turin, 1894.

Botta, P.E. *Observations on the Inhabitants of California, 1827–1828*. Trans. and ed. by J. F. Bricca. Los Angeles, 1952.

———. *Viaggio intorno al globo, principalmente alla California ed alle isole Sandwich*. Rome, 1841.

Boturini, Benaducci. *Idea de una nueva historia general de la America Septentrionale*. Madrid, 1746.

Brooks, Van Wyck. *The Dream of Arcadia: American Artists in Italy, 1760–1915*. New York, 1958.

Brown, Francis James, ed. *One America*. New York, 1952.

Brunner, Edmund de S. *Immigrant Farmers and Their Children*. New York, 1929.

Burns, Robert I. *The Jesuits and the Indian Wars of the Northwest*. New Haven, 1966.

Burrus, E.J. and F. Zubillaga, eds. *Francisco J. Alegre, Historia de la Provincia de la Campañía de Jesús de Nueva España*. 4 vols. Rome, 1956–60.

Caccia, Antonio. *Europa ed America, scene della vita dal 1848 al 1850*. Monaco, 1850.

Canestrelli, Philip. *A Kootenai Grammar*. Reprinted in Spokane, 1959.

Capellini, Giovanni. *Ricordi di un viaggio scientifico fatto nell'America settentrionale nel MDCCCLXIII*. Bologna, 1867.

Carosso, Vincent. *The California Wine Industry*. Berkeley, 1951.

Cassignoli, G.B., and H. Chiariglione. *Libro d'oro degli Italiani in America*. Pueblo, 1904.

Castelli, Carlo. *Il viaggio aereo dell'illustre Cavalier Don Paolo Andreani*. Milan, 1783.

Castiglioni, L. *Viaggio negli Stati Uniti dell'America Settentrionale fatto negli anni 1785, 1786 e 1787*. 2 vols. Milan, 1790.

Child, Irvin L. *Italian or American? The Second Generation in Conflict*. New Haven, 1943.

Chittenden, H.M., and A.T. Richardson, eds. *Life, Letters and Travels of Father Pierre-Jean De Smet, S.J., 1801–1873.* II. New York, 1905.

Cipolla, Arnaldo, *Nell'America del Nord, Impressioni di Viaggio in Alaska, Stati Uniti e Canada.* Turin, 1925.

Cipolla, C. M. *Verso il Far West. Le esplorazioni dell'Occidente Nord-Americano e la ricerca dei passaggi verso il Pacifico.* Turin, 1952.

Cipriani, Leonetto, *Avventure della mia vita.* 2 vols. Bologna, 1934.

Commager, Henry Steele, ed. *Immigration and American History, Essays in Honor of Theodore C. Blegen.* Minneapolis, 1961.

Common Council for American Unity. *Foreign Language Publications in the United States.* New York, 1952.

Confederazione Generale dell'Industria Italiana. *Annuario di statistiche del Lavoro.* Rome, 1949.

Corsi, Edward. *In the Shadow of Liberty.* New York, 1935.

Cortese, N. *Le aventure Italiane ed Americane di un Giacobino molisano.* Messina, 1935.

Crepeau, Rosemary. *Un Apôtre Dominicain aux Etats-Unis. Le Père Samuel Charles-Gaeten Mazzuchelli.* Paris, 1932.

D'Angelo, Pasquale. *Pascal d'Angelo, Son of Italy.* New York, 1924.

Danhof, Clarence H. "Farm-Making Costs and the 'Safety-Valve': 1850–1860," in *The Public Lands, Studies in the History of the Public Domain.* Ed. by Vernon Carstensen. Madison, 1963.

Davie, M.R. *World Immigration, With Special Reference to the United States.* New York, 1936.

Davis, William L. *A History of St. Ignatius Mission.* Spokane, 1954.

De Grazia, Ted Ettore. *Padre Kino, a Portfolio . . .* Tucson, 1962.

De Pinedo, Francesco, *Il mio volo attraverso l'Atlantico e le due Americhe.* Milan, 1928.

De Smet, P.J., *Voyages aux Montagnes Rocheuses chez les tribus indiennes du vaste territoire de l'Orégon . . . par le R.P. De Smet, 1801–1873.* Liege, 1913.

———. *Western Missions and Missionaries.* New York, 1852.

Des Planches, Edmondo Mayor. *Attraverso gli Stati Uniti per l'emigrazione Italiana.* Turin, 1913.

———. *Gli Italiani in California.* Rome, 1904.

De Vecchi, Paolo. *Due lettere al Prof. Angelo Mosso a proposito dell'ultimo suo libro "La Democrazia nella religione e nella scienza."* Florence, 1901.

Diomedi, Alexander. *Sketches of Modern Indian Life*. Woodstock, Maryland, 1894.

Dragoni, P. Ladislao. *Il mio pellegrinaggio attraverso l'alta California Francescana*. Arezzo, 1930.

Dunne, Peter M. *Early Jesuit Missions of Tarahumara*. Berkeley, 1948.

———. *Pioneer Black Robes on the West Coast*. Berkeley, 1940.

Erickson, Charlotte. *American Industry and the European Immigrant, 1860–1885*. Cambridge, 1957.

Falbo, Ernest, trans. and ed. *The California and Overland Diaries of Count Leonetto Cipriani . . . from 1853 Through 1871*. Portland, 1962.

Ferri-Pisani, Camille. *Lettres sur les Etats-Unis*. Paris, 1862.

———. *Prince Napoleon in America, 1861*. Bloomington, Indiana, 1959.

Foerster, Robert F. *The Italian Emigration of Our Times*. Cambridge, 1919.

Frangini, A. *Italiani di San Francisco ed Oakland, California. Cenni biografici*. San Francisco, 1914.

Gallenga, Antonio. *Episodes of My Second Life; English and American Experiences*. Philadelphia, 1885.

Gans, Herbert J. *The Urban Villagers, Group and Class in the Life of Italian-Americans*. New York, 1962.

Gardini, Carlo. *Gli Stati Uniti, ricordi di Carlo Gardini*. 2 vols. Bologna. 1887.

Garlick, Richard C. *Italy and the Italians in Washington's Time*. New York, 1933.

Garraghan, Gilbert J. *Chapters in Frontier History*. Milwaukee, 1934.

———. *The Jesuits of the Middle United States*. 3 vols. New York, 1938.

Garretto, Vito. *Storia degli Stati Uniti nell'America del Nord, 1492–1914*. Milan, 1916.

Gates, Paul W. *The Illinois Central Railroad and Its Colonization Work*. Cambridge, 1934.

Giles, Pearce. *The True Source of the Mississippi*. Buffalo, 1881.

Ginzberg, Eli, and Hyman Berman, eds. *The American Worker in the Twentieth Century*. New York, 1963.

Glazer, Nathan, and Daniel P. Moynihan. *Beyond the Melting Pot, the Negroes, Puerto Ricans, Jews, Italians and Irish of New York City*. Cambridge, 1963.

Glazier, Willard. *Down the Great River*. Philadelphia, 1891.

Gleeson, Richard A. *Dominic Giacobbi, a Noble Corsican.* New York, 1938.

Goggio, Emilio. *Italians in American History.* New York, 1930.

Gordon, Milton M. *Assimilation in American Life.* New York, 1964.

Govorchin, Gerald Gilbert. *Americans from Yugoslavia.* University of Florida, 1961.

Grindrod, Muriel. *The Rebuilding of Italy: Politics and Economics, 1945–1955.* London, 1955.

Guida degli Stati Uniti con particolare riferimento alla opera svoltavi degli Italiani. New York, 1937.

Handlin, Oscar. *Race and Nationality in American Life.* Boston, 1956.

———. *The Uprooted.* Boston, 1952.

Haskett, Richard C. "Problems and Prospects in the History of American Immigration," in *A Report on World Population Migrations as Related to the United States of America.* Washington, 1956.

Hawgood, John A. *The Tragedy of German-America. The Germans in the United States of America During the Nineteenth Century— And After.* New York, 1940.

Heiney, Donald. *America in Modern Italian Literature.* New Brunswick, 1964.

Higham, John. *Strangers in the Land.* New Brunswick, 1955.

Hofstadter, Richard. *Social Darwinism in American Thought.* New York, 1962.

Horowitz, Daniel L. *The Italian Labor Movement.* Cambridge, 1963.

Hourwich, Isaac. *Immigration and Labor.* New York, 1912.

Hutchinson, E.P. *Immigrants and Their Children, 1850–1950.* New York, 1956.

Italian-Swiss Colony. *Sixth Annual Report.* San Francisco, 1887.

The Italian Theatre in San Francisco. San Francisco, 1939.

James, Marquis, and Bessie R. *Biography of a Bank, the Story of Bank of America.* New York, 1954.

Jensen, Merrill, ed. *Regionalism in America.* Madison, 1951.

Jensen, Vernon H. *Heritage of Conflict: Labor Relations in the Nonferrous Metals Industry up to 1930.* Ithaca, 1950.

———. *Lumber and Labor.* New York, 1945.

Jones, Idwal. *Vines in the Sun.* New York, 1949.

Jung, A.M. *Sketch of the Jesuit Missions Among the American Tribes of the Rocky Mountain Indians.* Spokane, 1925.

Keating, William H. *Narrative of an Expedition to the Source of St.*

Peter's River, Lake Winnepeek, Lake of the Woods, etc., Performed in the Year 1823 by Order of the Hon. J.C. Calhoun, Secretary of War, Under the Command of Stephen H. Long, U.S.T.E. 2 vols. Philadelphia, 1824.

Kellogg, Louise P. *The French Regime in Wisconsin and the Northwest.* Madison, 1925.

Kino, Eusebio F. *Kino, Historical Memoir of Primería Alta.* Trans. and ed. by Herbert Eugene Bolton. 2 vols. Cleveland, 1919.

Klein, Hermann. *The Reign of Patti.* London, 1920.

La Guardia, Fiorello H. *The Making of an Insurgent. An Autobiography, 1882–1919.* Philadelphia, 1948.

Lami, A. C. *Beltrami e la scoperta delle sorgenti del Mississippi.* Rome, 1921.

La Rochefoucauld-Liancourt, François de. *Travels through the United States. 1747–1827.* 4 vols. London, 1799.

Laveille, R. P. *Le P. De Smet, 1801–1873.* Liege, 1913.

Levi, Carlo. *Christ Stopped at Eboli.* New York, 1950.

Lockwood, Frank C. *With Padre Kino on the Trail.* Tucson, 1934.

Lombardi, John. *Labor's Voice in the Cabinet.* New York, 1942.

Lonn, Ella. *Foreigners in the Confederacy.* Chapel Hill, 1940.

Lord, Eliot, ed. *The Italian in America.* New York, 1905.

Lucas, Henry S. *Netherlanders in America, Dutch Immigrants to the United States and Canada, 1789–1950.* Ann Arbor, 1955.

McGloin, John B. *Eloquent Indian.* Stanford, 1949.

Malaspina, Alejandro. *La vuelta al mundo por las corbetas Descubierta y Atrevida al mando del capitán de navio D. Alejandro Malaspina desde 1789 á 1794.* Madrid, 1885.

Mandalari, A. M. *Missione del Nuovo Messico e Colorado, lettere edificanti . . . .* Naples, 1911.

Mangano, Antonio. *Sons of Italy, a Social and Religious Study of the Italians in America.* New York, 1917.

Mann, Arthur. *La Guardia, a Fighter Against His Times, 1882–1933.* Philadelphia, 1959.

Masi, Eugenia. *G.C. Beltrami e le sue esplorazione in America.* Florence, 1902.

———. *"Notizie di G.C. Beltrami sugli indigeni Americani,"* in *Atti del XXII Congressodegli Americanisti.* Rome, 1926.

Maynard, Theodore. *Too Small a World; the Life of Francesca Cabrini.* Milwaukee, 1945.

Mazzuchelli, Samuel. *Memorie storiche ed edificanti di un missionario apostolico dell'ordine dei predicatori fra varie tribù de selvaggi e fra cattolici e protestanti degli Stati Uniti.* Milan, 1844.

Mengarini, Gregorio. *Narrative of the Rockies* . . . . Missoula, 1938.

———. *A Selish or Flat-Head Grammar: Grammatico Linguae Selicae.* New York, 1861.

Metelli, Fratelli. *Guida Manuale.* New York, 1882.

Mulder, William. *Homeward to Zion, the Mormon Migration to Scandinavia.* Minneapolis, 1957.

Musmanno, Michael A. *The Story of the Italians in America.* New York, 1965.

Neufeld, Maurice F. *Italy: School for Awakening Countries.* Ithaca, 1961.

Notizie storiche e descrittive delle missioni della Provincia Torinese della Compagnia di Gesù nell'America del Nord. Turin, 1898.

Overton, Richard C. *Burlington West: A Colonization History of the Burlington Road.* Cambridge, 1941.

Owens, M. Lilliana. *Jesuit Beginnings in New Mexico, 1867–1882.* El Paso, 1950.

Pagano, Jo. *Golden Wedding.* New York, 1943.

———. *The Paesanos.* Boston, 1940.

Palladino, L. B. *Indian and White in the Northwest; or a History of Catholicity in Montana.* Baltimore, 1894.

Panattoni, Giovacchino V. *Professionisti Italiani e funzionari pubblici Italo-Americani in California.* Sacramento, 1935.

Panunzio, Constantine. *The Soul of an Immigrant.* New York, 1921.

Parish, John Carl. *The Man with the Iron Hand.* Boston, 1913.

Partoll, Albert J., ed. *Mengarini's Narrative of the Rockies* . . . . "Sources of Northwest History, Number 25." Missoula, 1938.

Pedrazzini, Clay. "The Italian-Swiss of California," in *The Swiss in the United States.* Madison, 1940.

Peixotto, Ernest C. *Romantic California.* New York, 1910.

Pellegrini, Angelo. *Americans by Choice.* New York, 1956.

Peragallo, Olga, ed. *Italian-American Authors and Their Contribution to American Literature.* New York, 1949.

Perilli, Giovanni. *Colorado and the Italians in Colorado.* Denver, 1922.

Perrett, M. E. *Les Colonies Tessinoises en Californie.* Lausanne, 1950.

Pinedo, Francesco de. *Il mio volo attraverso l'Atlantico e le due Americhe.* Milan, 1928.

Pisani, Lawrence. *The Italian in America, a Social Study and History.* New York, 1957.

Pola, Antonia. *Who Can Buy the Stars?* New York, 1957.

Porter, Robert P. *The West from the Census of 1880, a History of the Industrial, Commercial, Social, and Political Development of the West from 1800 to 1880.* Chicago, 1882.

Preston, William Jr. *Aliens and Dissenters, Federal Suppression of Radicals, 1903–1933.* Cambridge, 1963.

Preta, Lodovico. *Storia delle missioni Francescane in California.* San Francisco, 1915.

Preziosi, Giovanni. *Gli Italiani negli Stati Uniti del Nord.* Milan, 1909.

Qualey, Carleton C. *Norwegian Settlement in the United States.* Northfield, 1938.

Radin, Paul. *The Italians of San Francisco.* San Francisco, 1935.

Ratti, Anna Maria. "Italian Migration Movements, 1876 to 1926," in National Bureau of Economic Research, *International Migrations.* II. New York, 1929–31.

Ricci, Eugenia. *Il Padre Eusebio Chini, esploratore missionario della California e dell'Arizona.* Milan, 1930.

Ritch, William G. *Jesuitism in New Mexico, an Answer to Father Finotti.* Santa Fe, 1878.

Robilant, Irene Contessa di. "*Gli Stati Lontani, e la costa del Pacifico,*" in *Vita Americana.* Turin, 1929.

Rolle, Andrew F. *California: A History.* New York, 1963.

———, ed. *The Road to Virginia City.* Norman, 1960.

———. "Success in the Sun: The Italians in California," in *Westerners Brand Book.* Ed. by Henry Clifford. Los Angeles, 1962.

Roosevelt, Theodore. "Speech Before the Knights of Columbus," New York City, October 12, 1915, in *The Works of Theodore Roosevelt, Memorial Edition.* 24 vols. New York, 1923–26.

Roselli, Bruno. *Francesco Vigo, una grande figura storica fra gli Italiani degli Stati Uniti.* Rome, 1932.

———. *Vigo, a Forgotten Builder of the American Republic.* Boston, 1933.

Roselli, Nello. *Mazzini e Bakounine, 12 anni di movimento operaio in Italia, 1860–1872.* Turin, 1927.

Rossati, G. *Relazione di un viaggio di istruzione negli Stati Uniti d'America.* Rome, 1900.

Rossi, Adolfo. *Un Italiano in America.* Milan, 1899.

Rossi, Egisto. *Gli Stati Uniti e la concorrenza Americana.* Florence, 1884.

Rossi, Joseph. *The Image of America in Mazzini's Writings.* Madison, 1955.

Rossi, Louis. *Six ans en Amérique, Californie et Oregon.* Paris, 1863.

Ruggieri, Vincent. *Du Transvaal a l'Alaska.* Paris, 1901.

Rundell, Walter, Jr. "The West as an Operatic Setting," in *Probing the American West.* Santa Fe, 1962.

San Diego Chamber of Commerce. *The Italy of America.* San Diego, 1892.

——. *Our Italy.* San Diego, 1892.

Sarti, Telesforo. *Il parlamento subalpino e nazionale.* Rome, 1896.

Sartorio, Enrico C. *Social and Religious Life of Italians in America.* Boston, 1918.

Schermerhorn, R. A. *These Our People: Minorities in American Culture.* Boston, 1949.

Schiavo, Giovanni. *Four Centuries of Italian-American History.* New York, 1952.

——. *Italians in America Before the Civil War.* New York, 1934.

——. *The Italians in Missouri.* Chicago, 1929.

Schoenberg, Wilfred. *Jesuit Mission Presses in the Pacific Northwest.* Portland, 1957.

——. *Jesuits in Montana, 1840–1960.* Portland, 1960.

——. *Jesuits in Oregon, 1844–1959.* Portland, 1959.

Schoolcraft, Henry Rowe. *Narrative of an Expedition Through the Upper Mississippi to Itasca Lake, the Actual Source of This River.* New York, 1834.

Schofield, N.B. "Paranzella, or Trawl Net Fishing in California," in *Transactions of the Pacific Fisheries Society . . . 1915.* Seattle, 1916.

Segale, Blandina. *At the End of the Santa Fe Trail.* Milwaukee, 1948.

Sforza, Carlo. *The Real Italians.* New York, 1942.

Shannon, James P. *Catholic Colonization on the Western Frontier.* New Haven, 1957.

Shepperson, Wilbur S. *Emigration and Disenchantment . . . .* Norman, 1965.

Shevky, Eshref. *Social Areas of Los Angeles.* Berkeley, 1949.

Simonin, Louis L. *Il Far-West degli Stati Uniti: I pionieri e i pelli rossi.* Milan, 1876.

Smith, William Carlson. *Americans in the Making: The Natural History of the Assimilation of Immigrants.* New York, 1939.

Solomon, Barbara Miller. *Ancestors and Immigrants* . . . . Boston, 1956.

Sondern, Frederic, Jr. *Brotherhood of Evil, the Mafia.* New York, 1959.

Sorrentino, Giuseppe M. *Dalle montagne rocciose al Rio Bravo.* Naples, 1949.

Spence, Clark C. *British Investments and the American Mining Frontier, 1860–1901.* Ithaca, 1958.

Stella, Antonio. *Some Aspects of Italian Immigration to the United States.* New York, 1924.

Stone, Alfred H. *Studies in the American Race Problem.* New York, 1908.

Strafforello, Gustavo. *Il nuovo monte Cristo.* Florence, 1856.

Strout, Cushing. *The American Image of the Old World.* New York, 1963.

Taeuber, Conrad, and Irene B. *The Changing Population of the United States.* New York, 1958.

Teiser, Ruth. *An Account of Domingo Ghirardelli and the Early Years of the Ghirardelli Company.* San Francisco, 1945.

Thompson, Fred. *The I.W.W., Its First Fifty Years, 1905–1955.* Chicago, 1955.

Thompson, Warren S. *Growth and Changes in California's Population.* Los Angeles, 1955.

Tigner, J. H. *The Italy of America . . . Riverside County, California.* Los Angeles, 1908.

Tonty, Henri de. *Dernieres découvertes en l'Amérique Septentrionale de M. de la Salle* . . . . Paris, 1697.

Torrielli, Andrew J. *Italian Opinion on America.* Cambridge, 1941.

Tremelloni, Roberto. *Storia dell'industria Italiana contemporanea.* Turin, 1947.

Trisco, Robert F. *The Holy See and the Nascent Church in the Middle Western States, 1826–1850.* Rome, 1964.

Unna, Warren. *The Coppa Murals.* San Francisco, 1952.

Varvaro Pojero, Francesco. *Una corsa nel nuovo mondo.* 2 vols. Milan, 1876.

Vigna del Ferro, Giovanni. *Un viaggio nel Far West Americano.* Bologna, 1881.

Villari, Luigi. *Gli Italiani negli Stati Uniti.* Rome, 1939.

Weibel, George F. *Rev. Joseph M. Cataldo, S.J., a Short Sketch of a Wonderful Career.* Spokane, 1928.

The West from the Census of 1880. Chicago, 1882.

Whyte, William Foote. *Street Corner Society, the Social Structure of an Italian Slum.* Chicago, 1943.

Wittke, Carl. *The Irish in America.* Baton Rouge, 1956.

Work Progress Administration. *Copper Camp, Stories of the World's Greatest Mining Town, Butte, Montana.* New York, 1943.

———. *The Italian Theater in San Francisco.* San Francisco, 1939.

———. *The Italians of Omaha.* Omaha, 1941.

Wright, Louis B. *Culture on the Moving Frontier.* Bloomington, 1955.

Wyllys, Rufus Kay. *Pioneer Padre, the Life and Times of Eusebio Kino.* Dallas, 1935.

ARTICLES

Adamic, Louis. "The Land of Promise," *Harper's Magazine,* Vol. CLXIII (October, 1931), 618–28.

Adamoli, Giulio. "Letters from America," *The Living Age,* Vol. XXV (April 1, 1922), 32–38.

"America and Italy," *Spectator,* Vol. LXVI (April 4, 1891), 466–67.

Barzini, Luigi Jr. "The Real Mafia," *Harper's Magazine,* Vol. CCVIII (June, 1954), 38–46.

Beltrami, J. C. "To the Public of New York and of the United States," reproduced in *The Magazine of History,* Vol. XL (1930), 173–202.

Benson, Lee. "Achille Loria's Influence on American Economic Thought: Including his Contribution to the Frontier Hypothesis," *Agricultural History,* Vol. XXIV (October, 1950), 182–99.

Branchi, Camillo. *"Gli Italiani nella storia della California,"* reproduced from *L'Universo,* Vol. XXXV (May–June, 1956).

Brandfon, Robert L. "The End of Immigration to the Cotton Fields," *Mississippi Valley Historical Review,* Vol. L (March, 1964), 591–611.

Cance, A. E. "Immigrant Rural Communities," *The Survey,* Vol. XXV (January 7, 1911), 587–95.

———. "Piedmontese on the Mississippi," *The Survey,* Vol. XXVI (September 2, 1911), 779–85.

Capsoni, G. *"Constantino Beltrami e la scoperta delle sorgenti del Mississippi,"* *Annali Universale di Statistica* (July, 1869).

Carr, John F. "The Coming of the Italian," *Outlook*, Vol. LXXXII (February 24, 1906), 419–31.

———. "The Italian in the United States," *World's Work*, Vol. VIII (October, 1904), 5393–404.

Case, Lynn M. "The Middle West in 1837, Translations from the Notes of an Italian Count, Francesco Arese," *Mississippi Valley Historical Review*, Vol. XX (December, 1933), 381–99.

Casson, Herbert N. "The Italians in America," *Munsey's Magazine*, Vol. XXXVI (October, 1906), 122–26.

Castiglione, G. E. di Palma. "Italian Immigration into the United States," *American Journal of Sociology*, Vol. XI (September, 1905), 196.

Christianson, Theodore. "The Long and Beltrami Explorations in Minnesota . . . ," Minnesota History *Bulletin*, Vol. V (November, 1923), 249–64.

Claghorn, Kate Holladay. "The Changing Character of Immigration," *Public Opinion*, Vol. XXX (February 14, 1901), 205.

Colojanni, Napoleone. "Homicide and the Italians," *The Forum*, Vol. XXXI (March, 1901), 63–68.

Cook, Pauline. "Iowa Place Names of Foreign Origin," *Modern Language Journal*, Vol. XXIX (November, 1945), 617–28.

Corsi, Edward. "Italian-Americans and Their Children," *Annals*, American Academy of Political and Social Science, Vol. CCXXIII (September, 1942), 100–106.

Coulter, J. L. "The Influence of Immigration on Agricultural Development," *Annals*, American Academy of Political and Social Science, Vol. XXXIII (January–June, 1909), 149–55.

Coxe, John E. "The New Orleans Mafia Incident," *Louisiana Historical Quarterly*, Vol. XX (October, 1937), 1067–1110.

Cunningham, George E. "The Italian, a Hindrance to White Solidarity in Louisiana, 1890–1898," *Journal of Negro History*, Vol. L (January, 1965), 22–36.

Davenport, William E. "The Italian Immigrant in America," *Outlook*, Vol. LXXIII (January 3, 1903), 29–37.

———. "Italian Immigration," *Outlook*, Vol. LXXVI (February 27, 1904), 527.

Dondero, C. "Asti, Sonoma County, an Italian-Swiss Agricultural Colony and What It Has Grown To," *Out West*, Vol. XVII (July–December, 1902), 253–66.

365

Douglas, Jesse S. "Origins of the Population of Oregon in 1850," *Pacific Northwest Quarterly*, Vol. XLI (April, 1950), 95–108.

Drayer, Allen. "Italians in Knobview," *The Interpreter*, Vol. II (April, 1923), 15–16.

———. "Italy in the Ozarks," *American Fruit Grower*, Vol. XLIII (September, 1923), 14.

Espinosa, J. M. "The Neapolitan Jesuits on the Colorado Frontier, 1868–1919," *Colorado Magazine*, Vol. XV (March, 1938), 64–73.

Falbo, Ernest S. "State of California in 1856," California Historical Society *Quarterly*, Vol. XLII (December, 1963), 311–33.

Fante, John. "The Odyssey of a Wop," *American Mercury*, Vol. XXX (September, 1933), 89–97.

Ferrero, Felice. "A New St. Helena," *The Survey*, Vol. XXIII (November 6, 1909), 171–80.

Ferry, Philip. "California Wine Goes to Sea," *Westways*, Vol. L (March, 1958), 32–33.

Fine, Sidney. "Anarchism and the Assassination of McKinley," *American Historical Review*, Vol. LX (July, 1955), 777–79.

Firkins, Ina Ten Eyck. "Italians in the United States," *Bulletin of Bibliography*, Vol. VIII (January, 1915), 129–32.

Foulke, William D. "A Word on Italian Immigration," *Outlook*, Vol. LXXVI (February 20, 1904), 459–61.

Galbraith, Edith C. "Malaspina's Voyage Around the World," California Historical Society *Quarterly*, Vol. III (October, 1924), 215–37.

Gale, E. C. "A Newly Discovered Work on Beltrami," *Minnesota History*, Vol. X (September, 1929), 261–71.

Gasparri, D. M. "Account of the First Jesuit Missionary Journey Across the Plains to Santa Fe," *Mid-America*, Vol. XX (January, 1938), 57–58.

Greer, Richard A. "Origins of the Foreign-Born Population of New Mexico During the Territorial Period," *New Mexico Historical Review*, Vol. XVII (October, 1942), 281–87.

Hedges, James B. "The Colonization Work of the Northern Pacific Railroad," *Mississippi Valley Historical Review*, Vol. XIII (December, 1926), 311–42.

Higham, John. "From Immigrants to Minorities: Some Recent Literature," *American Quarterly*, Vol. X (Spring, 1958), 83–88.

Hill, A. J. "Constantine Beltrami," Minnesota Historical Society *Collections*, Vol. II (1860), 183–96.

Howard, Helen A. "Padre Ravalli: Versatile Missionary," *The Historical Bulletin* (January, 1940), 33–35.

Inkersley, Arthur. "The Vintage in California and Italy," *Overland Monthly*, Vol. LIV (October, 1909), 406–11.

"Italians in California," *California Mail Bag* (August, 1871), xxii–xxv.

"Italians in the United States," *Literary Digest*, Vol. XCIII (April 23, 1927).

Karlin, Jules A. "The Italo-American Incident of 1891 and the Road to Reunion," *Journal of Southern History*, Vol. VIII (May, 1942), 242–46.

Kendall, J. S. "Who Killa de Chief?" *Louisiana Historical Quarterly*, Vol. XXII (January, 1939), 492–530.

Kollmorgen, Walter M. "Immigrant Settlements in Southern Agriculture: A Commentary on the Significance of Cultural Islands," *Agricultural History*, Vol. XIX (April, 1945), 69–78.

Kuppens, F. X. "Christmas Day, 1865 in Virginia City, Montana," *Illinois Catholic Historical Review*, Vol. X (July, 1927), 48–53.

Lee, Everett S. "The Turner Thesis Reexamined," *American Quarterly*, Vol. XIII (Spring, 1961), 77–83.

Levi, Carlo. "Italy's Myth of America," *Life*, Vol. XXIII (July, 1947), 84–90.

Levick, M. B. "A Man With Three Thousand Monuments," *Sunset*, Vol. XXX (January, 1913), 37–46, 93–94.

Liebling, A. J. "The Lake of the CuiUi Eaters," *New Yorker*, Vol. XXX (January 1 and 8, 1955), 37, 44.

Lilienthal, Theodore W. "A Note on Gottardo Piazzoni, 1872–1945," *California Historical Society Quarterly*, Vol. XXXVIII (March, 1959), 7–10.

McGloin, John B. "John B. Nobili, S.J., Founder of California's Santa Clara College," *British Columbia Historical Quarterly*, Vol. XVII (July–October, 1953), 215–22.

McLaughlin, Allan. "Italian and Other Latin Immigrants," *Popular Science Monthly*, Vol. LXV (August, 1904), 341.

McMurtrie, Douglas C. "Early Printing in Utah Outside of Salt Lake City," *Utah Historical Quarterly*, Vol. V (July, 1932), 84.

Maisel, Albert Q. "The Italians Among Us," *Reader's Digest*, Vol. LXVI (January, 1955), 1–6.

"The Making of Americans," *Outlook*, Vol. LXXIV (August 22, 1903), 969–71.

Manfredini, Dolores M. "The Italians Come to Herrin," *Journal of the Illinois State Historical Society*, Vol. XXXVII (December, 1944), 317–28.

Marraro, Howard R. "Count Luigi Castiglioni, an Early Italian Traveller to Virginia (1785–1786)," *Virginia Magazine of History and Biography*, Vol. LVIII (October, 1950), 473–91.

———. "Pioneer Italian Teachers of Italian in the United States," *Modern Language Journal*, Vol. XXVIII (November, 1944), 555–82.

Meade, Emily Fogg. "Italian Immigration into the South," *South Atlantic Quarterly*, Vol. IV (July, 1905), 217–23.

Merlino, S. "Italian Immigrants and Their Enslavement," *The Forum*, Vol. XV (April, 1893), 183–90.

Moore, Anita. "Safe Way to Get on the Soil: The Work of Father Bandini at Tontitown," *World's Work*, Vol. XXIV (June, 1912), 215–19.

Morison, Samuel Eliot. "New England and the Opening of the Columbia River Salmon Trade, 1830," *Oregon Historical Quarterly*, Vol. XXVIII (June, 1927), 113–20.

Moss, Leonard W., and Walter H. Thompson. "The South Italian Family, Literature and Observations," *Human Organization*, Vol. XVIII (Spring, 1959), 35–41.

Mulder, William. "Through Immigrant Eyes: History at the Grass Roots," *Utah Historical Quarterly*, Vol. XXII (1950), 34–49.

Olin, Spencer C., Jr. "European Immigrant and Oriental Alien: Acceptance and Rejection by the California Legislature of 1913," *Pacific Historical Review*, Vol. XXXV (August, 1966), 303–15.

Ostrander, Gilman M. "Turner and the Germ Theory," *Agricultural History*, Vol. XXXII (October, 1958), 258–61.

"Our Italian Immigration," *Nation*, Vol. LXXX (April 20, 1905), 304.

Owens, M. L. "Frances Xavier Cabrini," *Colorado Magazine*, Vol. XXII (July, 1945), 171–78.

Papanikolas, Helen Zeese. "Life and Labor Among the Immigrants of Bingham Canyon," *Utah Historical Quarterly*, Vol. XXXIII (Fall, 1965), 289–325.

Pecorini, Alberto. "The Italian as an Agricultural Laborer," *Annals, American Academy of Political and Social Science,* Vol. XXXIII (January–June, 1909), *passim.*

Peixotto, Earnest. "Italy in California," *Scribner's,* Vol. XLVIII (July, 1910), 75–84.

———. "Italy's Message to California," *Sunset,* Vol. X (March, 1903), 367–78.

Perrigo, Lynn I. "The Cornish Miners of Early Gilpin County," *Colorado Magazine,* Vol. XIV (May, 1937), 92–101.

Pollack, Norman. "Handlin on Anti-Semitism: A Critique of American Views of the Jew," *Journal of American History,* Vol. LI (December, 1964), 391–403.

Posner, Russell M. "A. P. Giannini and the 1934 Campaign in California," Historical Society of Southern California *Quarterly,* Vol. XXXIX (June, 1957), 190–201.

———. "The Bank of Italy and the 1926 Campaign in California," California Historical Society *Quarterly,* Vol. XXXVII (September, 1958), 267–75; (December, 1958), 347–58.

Preziosi, Giovanni. "Settlers in Tontitown," *Interpreter,* Vol. VIII (January, 1929), 55–58.

"Proud Seattle Celebration: The Citizens Pay Tribute to Their Italian Heritage," *Life* (December 9, 1957), 169–71.

Raup, H. F. "The Italian-Swiss Dairymen of San Luis Obispo County," *Yearbook,* Association of Pacific Coast Geographers, Vol. I (1935), 3–8.

———. "The Italian-Swiss in California," California Historical Society *Quarterly,* Vol. XXX (December, 1951), 305–14.

"Realm of the Human Mole," *Westways,* Vol. XLVIII (July, 1956), 8–9.

Rischin, Moses. "The Jewish Labor Movement in America," *Labor History,* Vol. IV (Fall, 1963), 227–47.

Robbins, Jane E. "Italian Today, American Tomorrow," *Outlook,* Vol. LXXX (June 10, 1905), 382–84.

Rolle, Andrew F. "America Through Foreign Eyes," *Western Humanities Review,* Vol. IX (Summer, 1955), 261–64.

———. "The Italian Moves Westward," *Montana, the Magazine of Western History,* Vol. XVI (January, 1966), 13–24.

———. "Italy in California," *The Pacific Spectator,* Vol. IX (Autumn, 1955), 408–19.

Root, George A. "Gunnison in the Early 'Eighties,'" *Colorado Magazine*, Vol. IX (November, 1932), 204–205.

Roselli, B. "Arkansas Epic," *Century*, Vol. XCIX (January, 1920), 377–86.

Rossi, Joseph. "The American Myth in the Italian Risorgimento: The Letters from America of Carlo Vidua," *Italica*, Vol. XXXVIII (1961), 163–66.

Sbarbaro, Andrea. "Wines and Vineyards of California," *Overland Monthly*, Vol. XXV (January, 1900), 65–76; 95–96.

Scanland, J. M. "An Italian Quarter Mosaic," *Overland Monthly*, Vol. XLVII (April, 1906), 327–34.

Schuyler, Eugene. "Italian Immigration into the United States," *Political Science Quarterly*, Vol. IV (September, 1889), 480–95.

Scott, Winfield. "Old Wine in New Bottles: When Italy Comes to California Through the Panama Canal," *Sunset*, Vol. XXX (May, 1913), 519–26.

———. "The Italian-Swiss in California," California Historical Society *Quarterly*, Vol. XXX (December, 1951) 305–14.

Senner, J. H. "Immigration from Italy," *North American Review*, Vol. CLXII (May, 1896), 649–57.

"Settlers in Tontitown," *Interpreter*, Vol. VIII (January, 1929), 55–58.

Shannon, Fred A. "Culture and Agriculture in America," *Mississippi Valley Historical Review*, Vol. XLI (June, 1954), 3–20.

Sharp, Paul F. "The Northern Great Plains: A Study in Canadian-American Regionalism," *Mississippi Valley Historical Review*, Vol. XXXIX (June, 1952), 61–76.

Smith, G. H. "Count Andreani, a Forgotten Traveler," *Minnesota History*, Vol. XIX (March, 1938), 34–42.

Smith, Timothy L. "New Approaches to the History of Immigration in Twentieth Century America," *American Historical Review*, Vol. LXXI (July, 1966), 1265–79.

Speroni, Charles. "The Development of the Columbus Day Pageant of San Francisco," *Western Folklore*, Vol. VII (October, 1948), 325–35.

Spinello, Mario J. "Italians of California," *Sunset*, Vol. XIV (1904–1905), 256–58.

Stevenson, Frederick Boyd. "Italian Colonies in the United States: A New Solution of the Immigration Problem," *Public Opinion*, Vol. XXXIX (October 7, 1905), 453–56.

Stone, Alfred H. "The Italian Cotton Grower: The Negro's Problem," *South Atlantic Quarterly*, Vol. IV (January, 1905), 42–47.

————. "Italian Cotton Growers in Arkansas," *Review of Reviews*, Vol. XXXV (February, 1907), 209–13.

Sutherland, Mason. "Californians Escape to the Desert," *National Geographic Magazine*, Vol. CXII (November, 1957), 706–707.

Taliaferro, Major Lawrence. "Autobiography of Major Taliaferro," Minnesota Historical Society *Collections*, Vol. VI (1894), 240–42.

"Ted Ettore De Grazia," *The Masterkey*, Vol. XXXVI (October–December, 1962), 124–26.

Tosti, Gustavo. "Agricultural Possibilities of Italian Immigration," *Charities*, Vol. XII (May, 1904), 474.

Tyler, Robert L. "The I.W.W. and the West," *American Quarterly*, Vol. XII (Summer, 1960), 175–87.

U.S. Commissioner of Labor. "Class Conflict in Colorado," *Wayland's Monthly* (April, 1907), 56–58.

Vecoli, Rudolph J. "Contadini in Chicago: A Critique of the Uprooted," *Journal of American History*, Vol. LI (December, 1964), 404–17.

Victor, Frances Fuller. "Flotsom and Jetsom of the Pacific," *Oregon Historical Quarterly*, Vol. II (March, 1901), 36–54.

Vollmer, E. R. "Donato Gasparri, New Mexico–Colorado Mission Founder," *Mid-America*, Vol. XX (April, 1938), 96–106.

"The Waldensians in America," *Mennonite Life* (April, 1950), 23.

Wallace, William H. "Journal of the Great Voyage from the Philippines to America," *Journal of American History*, Vol. II (4th Quarter, 1908), 585–86.

Wright, Doris M. "The Making of Cosmopolitan California," *California Historical Society Quarterly*, Vol. XIX (December, 1940), 323–43, and Vol. XX (March, 1941), 65–79.

Wright, Frederick H. "The Italian in America," *Missionary Review*, Vol. XXX (March, 1907), 196–98.

Index

373

The text for *The Immigrant Upraised* has been set on the Linotype in 11-point Electra, an original face designed by the late W. A. Dwiggins, eminent American artist and illustrator. The paper on which the book is printed bears the watermark of the University of Oklahoma Press and has an effective life of at least three hundred years.

ANDREW F. ROLLE is professor of American history at Occidental College in Los Angeles. He holds M.A. and Ph.D. degrees from the University of California at Los Angeles. Among his many books are *The Lost Cause: Confederate Exiles in Mexico* (1965) and *The Road to Virginia City* (1960), by James Knox Polk Miller, which he edited, both published by the University of Oklahoma Press. He is an annual contributor to the *Encyclopedia Americana* and the *Encyclopaedia Britannica*.